I Do Not Regret

I Do Not Regret

Şen Sahir Sılan

VANTAGE PRESS
New York

Published by Vantage Press, Inc.
419 Park Ave. South, New York, NY 10016

This edition is translated from the original Turkish version,
copyright © 2002 by İletişim Yayınları, Klodfarer Cad.,
İletişim Han No. 7, Cağaloğlu, 34122 İstanbul

Manufactured in the United States of America
ISBN: 0-533-15046-9

Library of Congress Catalog Card No.: 2004096821

0 9 8 7 6 5 4 3 2 1

Contents

Foreword		vii
The Language in General		ix

I.	First Recollections	1
II.	Kindergarten	7
III.	Primary School	28
IV.	Dreams of College and Moving to Ankara	50
V.	Cairo and Port Said	71
VI.	Liberty Ship and America	81
VII.	Simmons College	91
VIII.	The Return Trip Home	106
IX.	Autumn in İstanbul	111
X.	Life in Ankara and the Faculty of Languages	116
XI.	Graduation and My Trip to Europe	131
XII.	Who Can Tell What the Future Holds for Us?	136
XIII.	When Is the Engagement?	140
XIV.	The Rights and the Wrongs	147
XV.	The Wedding Ceremony and the Reception	162
XVI.	Our First Home	168
XVII.	Is It Motherhood?	173
XVIII.	A New Home and a New Baby	181
XIX.	What if I Have a Son?	189
XX.	The Summer at Viranbağ	194
XXI.	The Ankara Golf Club	203
XXII.	Güniz Sokak No. 31	210
XXIII.	Tarabya	221
XXIV.	A New House, Again	225
XXV.	What Is Going On?	229
XXVI.	Aliağa	233
XXVII.	Difficult Days	238
XXVIII.	Starting to Work	241

XXIX.	Whatever Is Happening to Ayşe?	248
XXX.	A Sad Marriage Ceremony	258
XXXI.	Someone Is Running Away	266
XXXII.	Disaster Strikes	281
XXXIII.	Zeyneb Puts on Her Wings	290
XXXIV.	Return to Father's Home	297
XXXV.	Migration	302
XXXVI.	Vaniköy on the Bosphorus	306
XXXVII.	England, Here We Come	311
XXXVIII.	Back in İstanbul to Find a Surprise	321
XXXIX.	Rebellion and Escape	324
XL.	My First Grandchild and a New Kind of Life	329
XLI.	A Ray of Hope	338
XLII.	A New Abode—A New Beginning	342
XLIII.	New Friends	358
XLIV.	Happiness of Welcoming Zeyneb and Her Family and Then Ömer	363
XLV.	The Year 1976	372
XLVI.	With Ömer in Boston	379
XLVII.	Is It a New Horizon?	382
XLVIII.	And Finally, New York	391
XLIX.	Many Things Can Happen Before Daybreak	397
L.	Looking for a Roof over My Family	401
LI.	What the Devil Is This?	404
LII.	Unexpected Happenings	413
LIII.	Father Again	422
LIV.	Şen, the Saleswoman	428
LV.	Ömer Goes to Turkey	439
LVI.	Can I Survive in İstanbul?	447
LVII.	A Great Shock	456
LVIII.	The Last Stop	461
Acknowledgments		471

Foreword

Some friends who knew about my past had encouraged me to write my memoirs. Even the thought of undertaking such a task had frightened me. That would be to write everything and also be truthful. But truth is not always welcome, especially for some people who might be involved. And yet it might also cause them to think.

Everybody has a story to tell, some are short while others may be long. Mine is a long story.

One day my granddaughter Seze asked me to tell her about the house I was brought up in. She was five years old at the time. I started telling her about the sumptuous house in İstanbul, Turkey. I went on describing the oil painted ceilings, the winding stairway going up four floors. She must have been bored. She said, "Now I will tell you about my house. You enter from the door and there is the kitchen. You take two steps, it is our living room. After four steps you come to the bedrooms. And there is also the bathroom." She was living in a studio apartment in Manhattan, New York.

I felt ashamed of myself. It was then that I decided to write my autobiography in the future. That way, I would be able to tell my grandchildren and even my great-grandchildren about myself. And if they are faced with a problem they will remember that Grandma never gave up. I dedicate my memoirs to my precious children, Ayşe, Zeyneb, and Ömer, whose existence gave me the courage to stay alive, and to my beloved grandchildren Seze, Murat, and Lara, who proved that the greatest thing in life is love.

Şen Sahir Sılan
Antalya
December

The Language in General

The Turkish Alphabet

Letters	Name	Pronunciation
A a	a	sun, cut, come
B b	be	bed, buy, bill
C c	ce	jar, jelly, jam
Ç ç	çe	church, chapel, child
D d	de	dear, doll, did
E e	e	red, bed, net
F f	fe	fine, fair, foul
G g	ge	gale, good, guy
Ğ ğ	yumuşak ge	(prolongs the preceding vowel) weight, neighbor
H h	he	hard, hill, hell
İ i	i	sit, thin, pin
I ı	ı	Cyril, wanted, syllable
J j	je	pleasure, measure, French: juste, jeune
K k	ke, ka	kite, cold, cat
L l	le	lilac, lull, lily
M n	me	me, mine, mime
N n	ne	nine, no, name
O o	o	poet, author
Ö ö	ö	French: deux, seul, German: Köln, König
P p	pe	pebble, pie, pipe
R r	re	rhyme, red, ready
S s	se	sister, similar, send
Ş ş	şe	shoe, sharp, short
T t	te	tell, truth, time
U u	u	put, foot, bull
Ü ü	ü	French: tu, sur, German: Glück, über
V v	ve	away, vizor, vital
Y y	ye	year, young, youth
Z z	ze	zebra, zero, zeal

ix

Vowel Harmony

The Turkish language is sweet and melodious, mainly due to the laws of vowel harmony, whereby words beginning with front or back vowels preserve the same quality throughout. It is spoken by more than eighty million people from Macedonia to Siberia. Turkish is an easy logical language. There is no gender, no *he, she* or *it*, but one word for all three. The *der, die, das* of German, the nightmare of the learner, are not found in Turkish.

There are eight vowels in the Turkish language, which are divided into two groups. The first group is (e, i, ö, ü) forming the front vowels and the second group (a, ı, o, u) forming the back vowels. In Turkish, adjectives are obtained from nouns, and from adjectives and nouns, verbs are created. The language is in conformity with the modern science of phonetic-spelling and pronunciation is regular. It is formed of sounds which are the natural result of the laws of position and inflection of the tongue, and the movements of the lips and jaws, and every word is pronounced as it is written. The only exception is the soft (g), which is written as (ğ) and serves to lengthen the sound of the vowel it follows.

The language is based on the principle of vowel harmony. In other words, if the vowel of the first syllable of a word is a front vowel, the vowels of the subsequent syllables have to be front vowels. While, if the vowel of the first syllable of a word is a back vowel, so are the vowels of subsequent syllables. Suffixes have, as a rule, two forms: one with a front vowel and used with front-vowelled words; another with a back vowel, used with back-vowelled words.

—Landon Thomas

I Do Not Regret

I

First Recollections

My cheeks were getting wet. I was trying to dry them with my palms and with the back of my small hands. I was sitting on someone's lap. I looked up. Tears were flowing down from the eyes of that beautiful woman. What wetted my cheeks were those tears. She was my mother. I tried to snuggle my face further into her bosom. Mother had sat me on her lap and was putting on my nice patent leather shoes with barrettes. It was strange. We apparently were going out and Mommy was crying? And yet, if we were going to do nice things, why should she be crying?

Then we were on a steam boat, together with my two elder brothers, Cenan and Nur, and also my nanny. We must have reached the boat with a horse ridden carriage, which was called a "chek-chek." In those days in Kadıköy, which is on the Anatolian side of İstanbul, these were the only vehicles for transportation. Contrary to the ones used in Principo and the other islands of the Marmara Sea, called "phaetons," which were drawn by two horses. The chek-cheks were drawn by a single horse, had a covered wagon and one entered them from the back. Passengers sat face to face, side wise. These carriages had tarpaulin curtains which, in bad weather, would be lowered to keep the rain, snow and wind out.

We were living in Kadıköy. Later on I learned that our address was No. 102 on Bahariye Avenue.

When we disembarked in Principo, we got into a phaeton drawn by two horses. In these carriages the main seat looked directly ahead. We were driven to a house at that section of Büyükada (Principo) that was called the Maden. The house (kiosk) was surrounded by a big garden with lots of pine trees.

1

There was also an orchard of fruit trees. Our cook and the two keepers were at the door to welcome us. They must have come there before us. But where was my father and where was Grandfather? Huge rooms. From one of these rooms, suddenly Grandfather appeared with his flowing white and long moustache. I ran to his arms. Still Father was nowhere to be seen!

As I learned in later years, this house had been rented on the insistence of my mother for the summer. My mother wanted her children to take advantage of the pure air of Büyükada and be able to swim everyday. Father meanwhile, giving different excuses, mainly that he did not like the island, had informed mother at the last moment that he would not join us. That was what had caused Mother to shed those tears. I think that Mother must have believed that the main reason behind Father's refusal to join us, was the existence of another woman in his life. Mother was madly in love with Father. Naturally this made her very jealous of him. Father hardly comes up in my memories of Büyükada. Apparently he would join us only for short periods. Was that why mother felt so sad all that summer?

In due course I learned that I was only four years old at the time. Therefore I remember very few things. A man servant used to do the shopping. I liked him very much because he used to take Nur and me with him on his daily trip to the market to buy the day's provisions, and on our return let us ride on donkeys. This was a usual custom on Principo. People would ride donkeys as well as phaetons. The poor man would be severely scolded by Mother because of this but come the next day, he could not resist our incessant pleas and once again would allow us to ride on donkeys.

One day, my brother Nur, who was always a very unruly boy, had taken me by the hand and the two of us had wandered into the big pine forest behind the house. When we failed to appear, Mother was very worried. She had the terrible idea that we must have fallen into a derelict water well. She had everyone searching for us the whole afternoon. Our return to the house was as frightful. So many scoldings and punishments. Both my brothers were older than I. With Nur though, since our ages were not too far apart, we were generally treated as twins and were allowed to play together and were treated equally.

2

At the end of the summer we came back to our house in Kadıköy. So Father also lived continually with us. Mother used to call our house at No. 102 a "traveler's food box." The house had four floors. It was narrow at the front but long towards the back. On the entrance floor there were the living and dining rooms and a toilet-bathroom. Two stairways, one going up and another going down, were located on the hallway. On the second floor the master bedroom, a toilet-bathroom, as well as Cenan's bedroom and father's study were placed. On the third floor Grandfather, Nur and I had our separate bedrooms plus my nanny's bedroom and another toilet-bathroom.

Grandfather has very distinct images in my memory. He had lost his hearing but he was able to lip read. With his very acute intelligence he was able to understand what people were saying to him. He had lost his hearing during a war in which he was involved when a bomb exploded nearby. Probably since he had difficulty carrying a conversation with others he used to read a lot and I would see him with a book in his hands most of the time. He was an easygoing man who had had a lot of experiences. Although he was my father's Father, he was also a great admirer of my mother. He always had a cigarette going, always attached to a jasmine-wood carved cigarette holder. During our years in Kadıköy grandfather did the shopping for the house. Every shopkeeper in the market knew him and they all enjoyed his company. He was much liked and respected. The butcher, the grocer, the cooperative, the barber were the places he would visit in that order. I remember that white cheese would be purchased in big tin cans as well as olive oil and butter for cooking. Soaps came in big sacks. At the British Cooperative salamis (sucuks) would be purchased in great numbers, the cheese called "kaskaval" would come in big rounds, eggs would be bought in big straw baskets plus big boxes of chocolate manufactured in England (everyone in the house used to call these "shokola" whereas on the boxes it was written "chocolate"). Then all these things would be entrusted to a porter who would deliver them to the house by carrying them in a big basket on his back. At the butcher's either a whole lamb or a sizeable part of a cow would be purchased and then the meat would be sliced and/or minced in accordance with Grandfather's instructions, each part being packed separately and on each parcel there would be a label showing what it contained. As soon as the meat packs were received in the house they would be the first to be placed on ice for preservation. Before I started school, Grandfather sometimes took me by the hand to go along on this shopping trip. During our long walk to the market he would recount endless tales of his exploits to me. Once Grandfather had gone into the barber shop for a shave and had taken me with him. I must have been bored and in order to put a stop to my whining, one of the barbers had me sit on a plank placed on the armchair like a seat and had trimmed my hair. He had cut my hair in a fashionable style called at the time "a la garcon." I remember crying all the way on the trip back and that Mother had complained bitterly to her father-in-law.

I would like to recount a different story concerning Grandfather. All the members of my family were rather high strung people and there was almost always a lot of shouting in our house. However, I was frightened when voices were raised. In such instances Grandfather would take me into his lap and whisper gently into my ear, "It is all your fault." Then I would cry and say, "That is not true, I did nothing grandfather." Then he would explain that he was teasing and say, "Would you like some cherry sticks or some cherry preserves." As soon as I heard the word "preserve" I would forget my fright and ask for some preserves and hug the old gentleman. At the end of this episode he was sure to produce a piece of chocolate or some candy from the depths of his deep pockets. This way I would calm down and forget about the shouting that had frightened me.

The kitchen was in the basement. From the street outside one could take a few steps down to get to the kitchen without going to the entrance door. It had a separate entrance. Next to the kitchen was the pantry and a storeroom plus two bedrooms assigned to the cook and to the parlor maid. In this section there were also a Turkish Bath and laundry room.

A stone stairway led from the dining room to the garden. When the weather allowed, Mother would use this garden as her private living room. Mother always had hydrangeas with their enormous flowers beneath the trees. Near the walls there were climbers like roses, jasmine and honeysuckle. There was

4

always a bed of violets. As it was customary in those days, the garden was paved by stone mosaics. Mother loved all flowers. When in season, she would pick white jasmines one by one, stick them into nursery pins and attach this rosette on her dress. I used to enjoy the sweet smell of lovely jasmine on her lapel all day long.

Adjacent to ours was the garden of a general and his family. The general had placed colored statues of the seven dwarfs among the flower beds. For this reason his house was called "the house of the seven dwarfs." Their garden was always very trim and full of flowers. However, the general did not resemble his garden in the least bit. He was a very tall gentleman with a bald head (his nickname in the army was the Bald General). He was always very trim and neat but he also was a very stern person. They had a big plum tree in their garden and one of its branches extended over the wall into our garden. One day I had picked one or two plums from this branch and the general had scolded me for it so severely that I had cried my eyes out. On the other hand, his wife was a very sweet person. They had one son. He was a rather chubby young man, very well brought up and I was amazed to see him doing embroidery. Although we were neighbors, our families rarely visited one another.

After the general's house and a little further on the street was the old Greek Orthodox Church. I still cannot remember who it was that took me to that church but I remember enjoying the chanting and all the chandeliers being lit up. The walls were covered up with paintings. I remember very clearly that during all the religious Orthodox celebrations I enjoyed visiting this church.

When I decided to write my memoirs, I thought I should refresh my memories and for that purpose I went to the Bahariye Avenue. Our house, numbered 102, was long gone and so were the seven dwarfs of the general next door. It really made me feel sad to watch the ugly reinforced concrete apartment buildings that suffocated the whole area. The only reminder of the old days was the Greek Orthodox Church, which stood where it was, looking sad and deserted.

A little further away, along the same side street, there used to be two places that I had adored. The first one was the building where both the first president and the prime minster of Hatay and their families resided. My friendship with the children of the prime minster, which started in those early years, has lasted all my life. Despite the fact that we may not have been together often, somehow our friendship never faded. We also played with the children of the president, but somehow with so many changes of abodes, we have lost contact. The second very important place was the kindergarten, a little further, where my education started.

II

Kindergarten

On our return from the island in the autumn of 1931, Mother registered me at the kindergarten managed by Mrs. S. Sertel. My mother had great admiration for this well-educated lady. As I later learned from Mother, the school started at 9:00 A.M. and ended at 4:00 P.M. I remember that in the mornings I used to carry my school bag in one hand and the triple food box in the other. I even remembered how angry I would be with my nanny who would insist on carrying one of these so that she could hold my free hand. I was certainly a stubborn little girl. At school we painted, played with modeling clay, of which we made little animals or figures, played games and sang songs. We would all sit around small tables on small chairs and eat our food. After lunch we would wash up and lie down to rest on our small chaise longues for a while. We were also punished at a corner, whenever we misbehaved. I believe I can safely declare that apart from my family circle, I appreciated the meaning of discipline in that school. I never forgot some of the relationships I started there. As an example I can mention the friendship I had developed with a boy. I used to enjoy not only his friendship but that of his whole family. Some days, obtaining Mother's permission beforehand, I would go and visit them at their home after school. His two elder sisters, one of which I still reach out, and their red haired mother used to spoil me a lot. Another friend I had acquired there grew up to become a famous medical doctor, and later died in an underwater accident while skin diving. His family were family friends as well. Still a third boy I recall was Memet Fuat, who became a well-known writer of Turkey, whom we lost recently. In one of his recent memoirs he has a few pages on me and my family as well as a picture of our class at the kindergarten. In his books, Memet also recounted some of his contacts with my family members.

While living in Kadıköy both my brothers were enrolled at the St. Joseph High School, as boarders, as was the custom in those days. My father was at the time the General Director of the Tramways Company of the Anatolian section of İstanbul. Mother had developed a schedule for her life that she kept for many years. On Mondays there was general house cleaning. As was the custom in those days, Tuesdays were mother's "at home" days. So she would be receiving her guests in a well-cleaned house. Wednesdays were assigned to her own pleasure. That was the day that she spent for herself. She usually included me in her excursions on that day. After lunch we would get dressed to go out and, taking the steamboat from Kadıköy, we would cross over to Karaköy. On very fine days, since she knew I enjoyed it very much, Mother would not board the ferry at Kadıköy but we would cross the little bay on a small rowing boat to Haydarpaşa, where the train terminal station was, and board the ferry from there. Actually this rowing service had been developed to help people who missed the steamboat at Kadıköy. People could catch the boat they missed by rowing across the bay before it started its journey across the Bosphorus. Other people coming by train would board the same ferry. Many years later I learned that this crossing service had been given as a monopoly to a village called Çankırı in Anatolia by one of the Ottoman sultans (most probably Sultan Abdulhamid, who had a very long tenure on the throne). I also learned that most of those strong men who rowed these boats did not know how to swim. I was a small child in those days and had no idea about such things and no one would tell me. I simply enjoyed riding on those small boats.

Every child loves her mother and finds her beautiful. But my mother was really a very beautiful woman. I could recognize this fact in the eyes of other people. She was slim, tall and had the legs of a model. Her honey-colored hair was naturally wavy and full. She had intriguingly bright hazel eyes, and a very straight Greek nose. With her well-drawn full lips and with her pearl white teeth that flashed each time she smiled, she was certain to attract the attention of everyone around her. Yet more than anything it was her elegance and personality that would attract people's attention.

From her mother's side, Mother was a Bosniac. Her mother's family line went back to the fifteen hundreds, to when the Ottomans captured Bosnia. Her maternal forebears had been assigned as rulers of Bosnia as "mirimiran" or feudal lord. The family name was Resulbegovic (one can look it up in the Encylopedia of the Moslem Rulers of Bosnia Hertzogovinia, Volume 3, page 420, where a full résumé of Osman Pascha is to be found). Two internationally known gentlemen, one a Turkish ambassador and another who became famous due to his help for peace during World War Two, came from the same ancestry.

The second person I just mentioned was one of my favorites when I was a little girl. He would always call before coming to make sure he would be welcomed and on the phone he would call me "my little wife." I would be very happy to learn that he was coming. My joy was not without a reason. Every time he came, Uncle Satvet Lutfu would be sure to bring me the most unbelievable presents. I am not quite certain, but I believe he was related to my mother both from her father's and her mother's side. The late ambassador's son, Dr. Selçuk Gerede, later in my life became a very good friend. My mother's father was a colonel in the Ottoman Army. Mr. Mazhar Tankovic was originally from Croatia and of Christian ancestry who had accepted the Moslem religion later. Unfortunately, no family history exists on that part of the family.

Whether it was her beauty and/or her elegance, I cannot tell, but I certainly remember that whenever she stepped into the special section of the ferry, where one had to pay an additional fee, every gentleman in the place would jump up, racing to offer her his seat. Every Wednesday when we landed on the pier at Karaköy we took a ride (it was a very short ride) in the tunnel up to Beyoglu. This was the best avenue of İstanbul where all the good stores, movie theatres, coffee shops, and restaurants were situated.

Depending on Mother's plan for the day, we would visit various "in-shops" like "the Mayer" and/or "The Japanese Toy Store." After completing our various purchases in the specialty shops we would go to a movie house that was showing a film

Mother thought she would appreciate. After the movie it was a "must" to go and have tea and pastries at the "Lebon Tea House." I was always amazed at and loved to watch the porcelain wall covers depicting the four seasons that were in that place. If I am not mistaken we would take the ferry back at either at 18:50 or at 19:10 o'clock. Once in a while, if their programs would fit, Mother and I would take a much earlier ferry across and meet Father at the well-known "Abdullah Efendi" Restaurant and we would have a most delicious lunch. When Father was not available we would have our lunch early at home and then start our trip.

Thursday was the laundry day at our house. Fridays were the ironing days. Due to the fact we were a rather large family, ironing could easily take a whole day. One must remember that a lot of the linen had to be starched in those days and that took a long time. On the other hand, the washer women had to do all the washing by hand.

On Saturdays my two brothers would be back from their boarding school. Sundays were really special. We used to spend the day with family friends who had children our age. My eldest brother Cenan would do some sport on his own and/or meet with his friends, or perhaps do his home work for the coming week. The rest of the family would either visit or have families with children visit us. We mainly visited a well-known general's family or my father's best friend, Mr. Sedat Simavi, who was the owner of a daily newspaper. The same evening (Sunday) my older brothers, Cenan and Nur, went back to their boarding school. The age difference between me and my eldest brother was eight and a half years, whereas Nur and I were only two and a half years apart. Probably because of this age difference, Cenan has always been a sort of not easily reachable big brother to me. Since our ages were closer, Nur and I would play together most of the time. Usually Mother would allow me to go out with Nur. I certainly loved my brother. However, since he was almost always doing something un-called for, I used to get into trouble along with him. For example, one day we were walking in the street and seeing a black boy pass by, Nur called after him "Nigger, nigger, trouble maker." The boy was furious and picking a big stone from the road threw it toward us. Nur was quick, he stepped aside. I was standing rather stupefied. The stone hit my head and my face was covered with blood. Probably since from childhood on I mostly played with Nur and his fellow friends, I was always at ease with boys and I enjoyed male company. This naturally turned me into a "tomboy."

I always wondered why my brothers had to board at the school, especially since the school was so close to our house. Apparently Father, in his youth, had very much wanted to go to a boarding school, but financially he could not afford to do so. He also believed that a boarding school would give the boys a better education and discipline. So he had insisted that both his sons should be registered as boarders. In those days the St. Joseph (Catholic School for Boys) High School was considered to provide exemplary discipline. Even at my rather young age I too had sensed that strict formality. Sometimes, when she wanted to visit her sons and to provide them with things from home, Mother would take me along to the school. Frère Joseph was the director of the academy that was called "the Premiere Cartier." He would let me sit on a table overlooking the corridor where the boys had to pass when they came out of their classes. Meanwhile, he would offer me a fresh "petit pain" and a bar of "chocolat." Even today, I still remember the delightful taste of those freshly baked rolls. While sitting on the wooden table and enjoying my fresh roll and my chocolate I would watch the boys coming out of their classrooms. They had to form lines walking in the corridors and they had to follow the lines of the square tiles (les carreaux). I later learned that they were disciplined not to miss a step or change the line of the tiles they were following. The priests (or Les Frères as they were called) imposed that kind of discipline on their students.

Now, I would like to mention various family friends with whom I was able to develop direct personal contact, which one way or another effected my first memories. These people, either the same age with my father or older, were all people loved and respected by my parents. They were also well-known people in Turkey. For example there was an ex-General who was also a member of parliament whom I was always very happy to see. Each time he came to our house he would pick me up in his arms and we would waltz around the room. He was a happy, slightly fat man with a blond complexion. I believed I was actually dancing and I loved that feeling. He had a daughter and I liked her a lot also. She had already married when we met.

Another close friend of my father was a very distinguished and elderly gentleman with a pointed beard. He had been minister of interior in 1911 and was later elected president of the Ottoman parliament. However, he was a strong believer of the republic and after the formation of the Republic of Turkey, he was assigned as governor to some districts and was also appointed as a professor, lecturing at the University of İstanbul. He was always very gentle and quite elegant. Probably due to my keen interest on answering phones he used to call me "the telephone operator lady." He would visit us often and he would bring me a new doll. These dolls would close their eyes when laid on their backs and had partly open mouths. Thinking they would be thirsty, I would pour water in their mouths with a spoon. As their arms and legs were attached together with elastic bands the water would make them slack and they would become something of a "Raggedy Ann." Naturally, by that time, I would have lost all interest in them. So the moment this venerable gentleman arrived, he would enquire if I had a doll and then he would produce a new one. Then I would be happy, thank and hug him. His cheeks always smelled of lavender cologne.

Another precious uncle was also the owner of a daily newspaper. He used to talk very slowly and he seemed to be watching the world behind his very thick glasses. One reason why I enjoyed being with him must have been the fact that he always treated me as if I was a grown-up person. He would take his time to explain things to me and was always ready to teach me something I did not know. Now, if someone would ask me today what he had taught me, I probably would not know the answer, but still I am convinced that I must have learned a lot of things from him one way or another.

It is impossible for me not to mention one other important person in my life, who also was amongst our family friends. This person was Süreyya İlmen Pascha (General) who had become my "Pascha Daddy." When I had grown up enough to go to the movies, every time I went to the Sureyya Movie House, which he personally owned, I was always escorted to his special lodge

No. 11 (with my friends, if any) and during the intermission he would be certain to come and bring us handfuls of chocolates, candies and pistachio nuts. He loved to watch us stuffing ourselves with these goodies. He was always good humored and smiling. Years later when I asked him, he kindly agreed to be my witness at my wedding.

People of my generation who lived in Kadıkoy at those times cannot help remember the name "Süreyya Pascha." His movie house was built as a replica of some mid-European Opera House and it was a very imposing building, erected with extreme care for details. I always admired the marble bust of that most beautiful lady which adorned the very grand entrance hall of the movie house. Later on I was to learn that this bust belonged to a famous singer, Suzan Hanım, who was the mother of that well-known actress of our generation, Ms. Gülriz Sururi. Speaking about well-known people, I would like to mention another name whose fame lay in a different world. The man who collected tickets at the entrance was an elegant black man (no African-Americans in Turkey). Almost always, there was another well-dressed gentleman standing by the ticket collector. Hikmet Bey, with a flock of white hair and the mannerism of a by-gone era, apparently was the father of our very famous poet Nazim Hikmet.

Inside, the movie house had three separate floors. After going up a few steps one would reach the "partere" and the lower loges. Climbing up the white marble stairways on the two sides of the large entrance hall, one would reach the first balcony and the middle loges, where No. 11 also took place. From these middle loges one could discern more clearly the flying angels with long horns painted on the ceiling. There was a very big red curtain and I always wondered what would come out, once the curtain was drawn to the two sides. The "Paradis" was on the third floor and they tell me that at the very top of the building there were special halls for parties and where concerts took place. At the time such special arrangements would be made by Vefik Bey, who had been a kind of Diaghilev, and his son, who made a name for himself in football in later years as Can Bartu. I had met Vefik Bey. He was a tall and handsome gentleman, always full of smiles.

As I may have mentioned earlier, we would spend most of our weekends with the whole clan of Süreyya Pascha's family, where their children and their grandchildren would all be present. Actually, the pascha's father was a famous prime minister or the grand vizier during the Ottoman Sultanate. They were also land owners. My pascha daddy was a strong supporter of Atatürk as well as our republic. He was also a man of many accomplishments and a protector of the poor people. As he could afford it, he was most generous in his donations also.

In the summer we would motor in the sea in their large boat or we would all go to their huge farm on the hills of Maltepe and spend the whole day in the beautiful mansion they had built there. His boat was called "Çatana" or I guess in French it was called "mouche," which was a steam powered boat. We sometimes would go for picnics in beautiful meadows. Their grandchildren were our age and we loved playing with them. I remember one time when we were visiting at the farm and we suddenly heard painful shouting and then there was a big commotion. It turned out that one of their grandsons, who was riding his bicycle in the garden, had lost his balance and fell into the great windows of their dining room, which was a separate, very large, one-storied building constructed to accommodate large crowds. Various arteries in his hands and arms were cut and he was bleeding profusely. That day a great tragedy had been experienced in that household. On another occasion when one of the grandchildren had contracted scarlet fever, a couple of the children had moved to our house and spent the next few weeks with us. In those days this was one way of keeping the unaffected youngsters away from the possibility of contracting the same disease.

The Muslims are very keen about circumsizing the boys. This is usually done when the child reaches the age of five, before starting his school. Therefore it usually takes place near the end of the summer. This is a sort of celebration and therefore it is called "Sunnet Düğünü"—"Circumsion Feast." Rich families gave big parties with many entertainments. Everybody brings nice gifts to the young boy, things like wrist watches, nice pens, cameras, etc. Things that the child may need and use in his future years. A sumptious buffet is arranged. The feast lasts

14

many hours. The idea behind it is to have the circumsized child forget his pain and be kept awake to prevent a hemorrhage. Also the proud family is able to share this happy event of having a son turn into a male, with their friends.

I remember also attending a very lavish cirumcision party at the farm. In line with the customs of the day, the pascha, along with his grandsons to be circumcised, had invited a lot of boys of the village, whose parents could not afford such things, to get their circumcision done and enjoy the festivities. Huge tents were set up and maybe thirty boys between the ages of five to thirteen had been circumcised that day and they were placed in beds prepared for them under the tents. All the beds were filled with gifts and the boys all looked happy. I never forget the pageants, the music, the acrobats and a very impressive magician. Everyone was doing his own trade one after the other, keeping the boys "happy."

When spring came Mother would take me with her to the tea garden at "Şifa," which was a section of Kadıköy. This place was within walking distance of our home and on the way to the St. Joseph College. There, Mother would have Turkish coffee and they would bring me a "lokum," that is to say "Turkish Delight," attached to a toothpick. Somehow that lokum in that garden seemed so much better than all the other sweets we had in the house. I have other memories of that district. A little further away from the tea house, walking down toward the sea, one would come across a big mansion that belonged to a famous gynecologist. Both his home and his private clinic were situated in the same garden. This doctor was a person much admired and respected by my mother. It appears that he had saved her life more than once. From what I heard from others, many people thought the doctor was rather eccentric and for that reason disliked him. As I was getting old enough to converse with my elders and still had the innocence of youth, I had one day asked the good doctor point blank why people thought he was crazy. He laughed heartily at my question and his answer explained the situation clearly. He said "Look, I ask my patient how much bread she usually eats at breakfast. She will answer 'Four slices,' then I have to ask again how thick are those slices. After all you can have a large slice or a slim one. Many a patient quits my dispensary rather than answer these simple questions." The doctor again proved what a good diagnostician he was when he examined me. I was a rather small child and had long spells of "tummy aches." A number of doctors had suggested it was appendicitis trouble and offered a surgical intervention. Finally Mother took me to her much trusted doctor. He took a long time examining me and finally he said, "This little girl has extremely long intestines. Let her sit on the toilet seat a long time. Once her bowels are empty she will get over the aches." Soon my aches were gone and there was no need for appendectomy. In my later years I had to go through many checkups and other examinations in many different countries and the good doctor's original diagnosis was proven to be correct, time and time again. The good doctor had a very beautiful wife. With very long and black eyelashes and a curvaceous body she was always the cause of telltale stories. They also had a daughter, since her age was closer to my eldest brother, Cenan, I did not have a chance to play with her. Some years earlier our family had lived in a house near to the doctor's mansion and that was how our families had gotten to know each other.

In 1927 my father had been appointed to a governmental commission related to the "printing of new paper bills" and as it turned out this job would last for almost half a year. As a result Father had decided to move the whole family, including my nanny, to London. I was nine months old and apparently had caused a mild sensation walking on my own at the famous Hyde Park lawns. Upon our return my father had rented the house at Şifa until he had bought the house in Bahariye Caddesi, where the rest of my childhood was spent. During the period in Şifa, and for a while on Bahariye, Father used to take the night train to Ankara at the beginning of the week and would return to İstanbul for the weekends. This went on for some time, that is, until he was appointed as Director General of the Tramways.

As a child I was quite tiny and frail. As a result my nicknames in the house were "tze-tze" or "çiroz," which in Turkish means "dried fish." I was also very choosy and would refuse to eat most of the things offered to me. I remember enjoying some of the things I ate but nobody bothered to ask me what I would like to have for dinner. When Father and Mother went out to dine with friends, Nur and I would be left under the care of our eldest brother, Cenan. Those nights it was certain to be trouble in the house. Cenan would insist that I should finish whatever he had served to my plate. I would refuse and soon would start crying. Then Nur, trying to protect me, would back me up and would try to raise his voice against our eldest brother. Naturally my nanny would try to intervene and I would really start hollering. I guess even then I must have realized that I was a rather independent and headstrong child. I always wanted to do what I liked and not to do what I was ordered to do. On the whole I was a docile person and would comply with whatever I was told to do in order to make my elders happy. On the other hand I always felt that I had my rights and would hate being prohibited from certain things. Quite probably, despite the fact that I was pretty sure that I was loved by everyone in the house, there may have been a hint of jealousy toward my elder brothers.

At this juncture of my story, I believe I should go back and recount my family history. As I may have already mentioned my mother came from a well-known Bosniac family called Resulbegovic, from her mother's side. Mr. Cemal Kutay, who is a popular writer and a historian, in his book titled *The Turc Who Saved Belgrade,* explains in great detail the life and the ancestry of my cousin, who was also a descendant of the Resulbegovic family. The "Bey Konak" (a veritable palace) was where my grandmother had been born and brought up. One of their ancestors, Osman Pascha had built the "Begovska Kuca" (the castle of the Bey) plus a mosque under his name. Apparently when word reached İstanbul that the Pascha's mosque was bigger then the one that was built for the Sultan, the Pascha "lost his head." I was told that the same Pascha had built a fountain in İstanbul, as well as many other things.

Mother's grandfather, Hamdi Pascha Resulbegovic, had moved to İstanbul, taking all his family with him. At the same time his daughter Hasniye Hanım and her husband (his son-in-law) had also moved to İstanbul. Mazhar Bey was appointed as a colonel to the cavalry division and the current Sultan, Abdulhamid, had given them a house in Ortaköy where they had

17

settled. The then minister of the navy, Hasan Pascha, made a gift of some land next to their house. Their first male child died of meningitis at the age of two. Then my mother was born at the same house in Ortaköy. Mazhar Bey, who wished to somehow replace the son he had lost, would always call Mother "Cem Sultan" (after an unfortunate Ottoman Sultan who had died abroad). In his free time Mazhar Bey would take his daughter (Cemile) riding alongside of him as if she was his son. When mother had reached the age of four, she was placed at the French Convent School at Ortaköy called "Seurs de Charite." Whenever she came home, she would be given religious education by reading the Kuran. After some forty years, we were staying in Boston (U.S.A.) by chance Mother met Anahit (Bashian), a girl who had been her bosom friend at the convent school for girls. Amongst her other school friends there were several that I also had the pleasure of meeting. Mother never let go of her old friends. All these were lifelong lasting relationships.

Unfortunately Mother's father, Mazhar Bey, died because of an illness called shingles (Zona in Turkish) when mother was only nine years old. The little girl also lost her mother due to tuberculosis when she was only twelve. It appears that the orphan girl was pretty prosperous by her inheritance and her grandfather Hamdi Pascha took over the custody of the child. As a result, Mother continued her life in the house at Ortaköy with her grandfather, grandmother and two aunts, one with her husband) with all moving in. Her education at French Convent School also continued without change.

In later years Mehmet Resulbegovic, a cousin who resided in Vienna, came to İstanbul to visit his great uncle, Hamdi Pascha. Mother at the time had reached the age of fourteen. When Bosnia-Hertzegovina had been separated from Ottoman rule, Hamdi Pascha, who was a Resulbegovic, had decided not to stay there and had come to İstanbul, whereas Mehmet Bey, who was from another branch of the same family, had chosen to go to Vienna.

There, he had been assigned to the Hussar division of the Austrian emperor. Mehmet Bey was a good-looking gentleman, a good horseman, well-off and of good upbringing, met Mother in İstanbul and promptly fell in love and asked for her hand in marriage. With the approval of Hamdi Pascha, Mother was married to Mehmet Bey and moved to Vienna. Mother always reiterated, "I went to Vienna (as a bride) with my baby doll in my arms." Her rigid upbringing and her knowledge of several languages helped her to mix into the Viennese society without much difficulty. Enchanting happenings like dancing at the Schonbrunn Palace, tea parties with Princess Esterhazi, riding the horses that Mehmet Bey was raising on his stud farm were all very exciting indeed. However, after a while these beautiful things began to lose their importance, and Mother began to feel somehow uneasy. Although she yearned to have a child, she was told that this would not materialize. Coupled with this unease and the nostalgia that had developed for İstanbul plus the news that Handi Pascha was ill, Mother was able to obtain permission from her husband to go to İstanbul. Meanwhile, World War I had started. Following the clashes at the Dardannelles, İstanbul was suddenly flooded with wounded soldiers and officers. Cemile Hanım was able to register as a volunteer nurse at the Red Crescent Hospital in Cağaloğlu. (This fact is registered by a letter Dr. Adnan Adivar had signed and given to Mother when she had to give up her work at the hospital.)

While she was still working, a young newspaper reporter had come to the hospital to interview the wounded soldiers. He was working for the daily paper *Tanin*. There he was introduced to the volunteer nurse Cemile Hanım. He almost instantly fell in love with the young nurse and proposed marriage. Naturally Mother had to explain that she was already married and was due to return to Vienna in the near future. Indeed, as mother started her trip to Vienna, the young reporter Necmeddin Sahir had joined the army and was sent to the southern front in Syria. He had become the press officer for General Cemal (Pacha the Grand) who was the commander of our southern front. It appears that during their brief meeting both had been rather impressed with one another. Cemile never forgot the young journalist she had met in İstanbul and similarly Father always dreamed of the beautiful nurse he had met so briefly. If I am not mistaken, Mother spent the next two years in Vienna. When she found out that they could definitely not have children, she begged her husband for a divorce and when he finally consented

19

she was finally able to return to her grandfather's house in İstanbul, now as a young divorcée.

She naturally knew that it would be impossible to meet that young journalist again. İstanbul was such a crowded, big city. Furthermore, as a young divorcée now, she was very much under control. One day as they were going to their dentist accompanied by her aunt, a young army officer started following them. It turned out that the young journalist, Necmeddin Sahir, had returned to İstanbul as an officer. All of a sudden they both recognized one another but only from a distance. The young officer followed the ladies discreetly all the way to their home and took notice of the mansion in Cağaloğlu. He felt sure that the young nurse had obtained a divorce and had returned to İstanbul. The fact that she was accompanied by an elder relative going to the dentist proved that fact. A few days later the officer called on the Pascha and asked his permission to marry his granddaughter. The old general, after talking to this young and rather daring officer for a while, gently showed him out. After all, how did this young man have the courage to ask for his granddaughter's hand, coming singly, all by himself? Surely he could not belong to a respectable family.

It was the custom in those days, and even now in Turkey, to send some elders of the family to ask a young woman's hand in marriage. So Mr. N. Sahir was turned down. My father's mother, although she belonged to an old family of Nevsehir, had been born in İstanbul. My grandfather Salih Necati Bey was from a family whose forebears had been naval officers under Sultan Mehmet the Conqourer. The sultan assigned Yahya Pascha to stay in Trebizond when he captured the city, and the family name was recognized as Haci Ali Molla Zade. So Grandfather's father was Ibrahim Haci Ali Molla Zade. When Grandfather married father's mother, there was a big difference between their ages. Nevertheless she gave birth to two daughters. Unfortunately both of them died in young age. Following their death, my father was born. However, even this couldn't keep them together and Grandma deserted her husband, as well as her baby boy. So Father was raised by his father and his father's two sisters (his aunts).

20

One reason why father had called on the Pascha on his own must have been due to the fact that he never had much of a family, having been raised without a mother. Also, perhaps his aunts, realizing that he was on an impossible mission, had refused to visit the Pascha on his behalf.

Well, love conquered all and Mother married my father, who at the time was again working as a journalist but he also had a job as a clerk at the Ottoman parliament. In her new home Mother as usual was reading novels most of the time. She soon found out with great happiness that she was to become a mother. At that time she was reading a novel by Pierre Loti. One name in the book caught her eye and hoping for a girl, she decided to call her daughter "Cenan." Some months later she gave birth to a boy but nevertheless they named him Cenan. İstanbul had been occupied by this time and they were expecting their second child. Once again a name for a girl was chosen and again a boy arrived. They went ahead and called their second child Şadan.

Some years earlier, Father, as a journalist, had interviewed Mustafa Kemal, a general who had made a name for himself as a defender at the siege of Dardanelles, when he had returned to İstanbul as a hero. Apparently he had won the general's trust. When the new baby was only ten days old, Mustafa Kemal Pascha sent word to Father from Ankara, that if he wanted to come, he would be welcomed to join the revolutionary forces for the War of Independence in Anatolia. With no regard to the fact that Mother was with a newly born child only ten days of age, Father had responded to this call positively and had left for Ankara immediately. Cemile Hanım was left in İstanbul with her two sons and her father-in-law. Under the very harsh conditions of the day, Mother had to sell most of her jewelry in order to survive. After many months of hardships, she heard from her husband, calling them all to Ankara. They first started their journey by boarding a steamboat to the port of Inebolu on the Black Sea. When they disembarked, they had to wait in that town for over ten days before they could secure a safe passage. There was a single inn where they could stay. Since there was hardly any sanitation, both her sons Cenan and Sadan contracted rather serious illnesses. No doctors, no medication! The trip from Inebolu to Ankara on a horse drawn carriage lasted nine days.

At the time Ankara was a settlement of "nothings," almost like a ghost town in a desert. When Father offered to rent a house at Ulus for the family to settle in, Mother objected and said she would prefer to live in a villager's cottage so as to have a garden to raise her children in. At that time my father was employed as the director of the press in the new parliament. Mother sold some of her family heirlooms and tried to give some sort of a semblance of a home to the very meager cottage they were able to find. Even the last pair of her earrings were sold to purchase some furniture. Mother never wore earrings from that day on, and being afraid that I might find myself in such a predicament later on in life, never had my ears pierced. Mother had brought her heavy velvet curtains from İstanbul. Now she was able to cut them and use them to cover some wooden boxes with pillows, which she was able to transfer into some sort of settees in the cottage. My father's meager paycheck was barely enough for the food expenses. Besides, many things, especially pieces of furniture, were not available even if they had had the money.

This story was repeated many times in our house. One entered the cottage from the outside by wooden stairs. The first floor had been used as a stable in the old days. There was no running water, so Mother had to draw water from the well with a pump in the garden and carry the water into the house. As for doing the laundry, Mother had to join the village women and do the family washing in the meager river called Incesu. Naturally there was no electricity either. So they used gas lamps. Each morning all the gas lamps had to be cleaned and refilled and made ready for the night. They had no table but they were able to purchase a "sini" (a large copper tray) which they set on another wooden box to serve as their dinner table. They would put cushions on the floor since they had no chairs. Father told us all the time "Your mother never served me dinner on that 'sini' without some wild flowers on it."

Mother was also able to purchase a horse. Every morning she would ride around the countryside and pick whatever wildflowers she could find on her way. Then she would put them into a bottle and adorn my father's dinner table with them. During those days Mustafa Kemal Pascha and other dignitaries began to visit and honor this cottage during the very early hours of the morning, like 3:00 or 4:00 A.M. Many a times Mother, just like the peasants did, would swathe her usually sick child to her back and would prepare special dishes for their honored guests. She even made ice cream. Many years later when I used to grumble about electricity cuts in Ankara, Mother would smile gently and somewhat ruefully say, "During the War of Independence all we had were oil burners and when the Greek Army came very near to Ankara, the families were evacuated to Nallihan and there we could not even get any oil to burn."

One of the sad stories of my mother, in this cottage life, concerned her hair. I heard this story several times both from my mother and father, on different occasions. Mother had very long and full hair at those days. So long in fact that when she would let her hair down it would reach almost to her knees. She would braid her hair in two or three rows and then knot the braids on top of her head as a chignon. Father was specially in love with his wife's beautiful hair and when at night she would undo them, Father took a long time brushing them in delight. She had been accustomed to wash every night before going to bed. However, since there was no question of having a hair dryer she had to contend with brushing. As a result she could not dry her hair properly and soon pimples or boils began to appear on her head. Realizing that there was no other way out, one morning, after Father had gone to work, Mother cut her braids leaving her hair short. That night when Father saw his wife with her hair short and the lovely braids lying on the bed he was stunned. He cried all night hugging the cut braids. Years later Mother brought out those braids that she had saved and I was able to use them in various ways, in accordance with the fashion of the day. During those first years in Ankara, Mother could only have a few relations with other ladies. Luckily those elegant ladies were Mrs. Latife Kemal, Mrs. Galibe Okyar and Mrs. Mevhibe İnönü.

In 1921 an Egyptian princess named Kadriye Hüseyin visited Ankara. Upon her return she wrote a book in French about her experiences in Ankara. My father recounted the story: "The National Parliament had just convened. Our Attaché Militaire in Rome had introduced the lady to me since I was acting as the director of the press for the parliament. Later the princess sent us some three hundred copies of her published book. I took a copy to Mustafa Kemal Pascha. He said, "Child (he used to call his subordinates in this manner), these should be distributed amongst members of the parliament, however, since it is written in French, not everyone will be able to read it. As I heard from our mutual friend Ruşen Eşref (Ünaydın) your wife was an officer's daughter and has good command of the French language. Ask her for me to kindly translate this book into Turkish. And when her translation is completed, make sure that our ministry of education has it printed for all to read."

The translation that Mother had done at the time was recently republished by the ministry of culture and the *Cumhuriyet* newspaper distributed copies of the book together with their paper as a gift for its readers.

Meanwhile their second son was suffering of amipien dysenter. Since there were hardly any health service available, the boy could not be saved. This was a terrible blow to the family. Sometime later they realized that Mother was again pregnant. By this time the War of Independence was over and Mother was able to visit her relatives in Izmir. The main reason behind this journey was that better health services would be available there, and moreover, Mother would have the help of her relatives with whom she would be staying. As always Mother wanted a girl and had decided to name her Nur. As it turned out, another son arrived and they still went ahead and called him Nur. During that whole period, Father had stayed in Ankara since his duties would not let him go elsewhere. With her newborn son, Mother recovered somewhat from the shock she had gone through with the loss of her second son.

When it was possible, Mother returned to Ankara together with her first son and the new baby. Finally the family was reunited. Now the Republic had been proclaimed and it was decided that the capital of the new republic would be Ankara. Meanwhile my father had been appointed Chef de Cabinet to the prime minister, first to Mr. Fethi Okyar and then to Mr.

İnönü. As the new capital of the new republic, Ankara was going through a rapid change. New buildings were erected all the time and many people were coming to settle there. In the meantime father was able to attend evening courses and he was able to obtain a university degree in law at the new Ankara Law Faculty. The couple were working all the time and living at the cottage was getting more and more difficult as time went by.

So Father was able to purchase a small plot at what today is İsmet Pascha Caddesi and started building a two-storied house. One Sunday morning when he was overseeing the laborers working at the construction site, Mustafa Kemal was passing by in his car. He recognized Father, had his driver stop the car, called my father and asked whose construction this was and what he was doing there. Father answered, "Sir, by your leave, if all goes well, I am hoping to build a home for my family." The Pascha was quite impressed and said "Cocuk (my son), you are very wise. Soon we shall build a new city here and call it Yenişehir. May you live in peace."

This was the house No. 27 on İsmet Pascha Caddesi, where I was born. As the condition of his health required, Father was in a hospital in Vienna at the time I was born. So both the minister of foreign affairs, Mr. Tevfik Rüştü Aras, and Mother sent him telegrams advising the arrival of his first daughter. Father's cable to Mother said something like, "The joy (Şen) of our family is most welcome." As they had not been able to pick a name for the newcomer, Mother went ahead and called me Şen (joy).

There is a saying in English. They say, "born with a silver spoon." This means a child is born into wealth. That certainly was the way I was born. However, rather than being very rich, I was lucky to have a mother with such a rich heritage and knowledge and she was able to bring me up accordingly. For example, I was born into a house where European-style toilets and bathtubs were used. There was running hot water and showers and the house had central heating, all of which were rarities in Ankara at the time. All through my life, my luck held in this score and even when I was penniless (due to the fact that I was in the States at that time) I was never without the necessary and civilized facilities.

In one of the chapters above, I mentioned that I must have felt a sort of jealousy against my brothers despite the fact that I knew I was very much loved. I therefore do not wish to bring the chapter to a close without further elaboration on this subject. Cenan was the eldest. He was very brilliant and highly industrious. He would be looking over his textbooks even during meals. He always listened to Mother's advice. He was always trying to be successful in whatever he was doing and as a result was always successful. Furthermore, most probably since their ages were nearer to one another, Cenan had become a sort of friend and confidant to Mother. Naturally Cenan was the apple of their eyes. Both Father and Mother adored Cenan. My older brother, Nur, however, was quite a different character. Although intelligent, he was not particularly interested in studying and was a bit high strung and mischievous. Actually, he was a kind boy at heart and was also very sensitive. Sometimes his goodness went together with his irresponsible character and it resulted in disaster. For example, without asking anyone he had taken some paper money from my father's wallet, torn them into small pieces and distributed them to the poor children he had come across in the street. In other words, he was at an age when he could not understand the difference between coins and bills. Naturally this was followed by a good thrashing from Father and all sorts of scolding from everyone. I was too young to understand what was going on at the time but I learned about it some years later. Nur was also not too robust. He would be prone to fall sick most of the time. As a result, Mother (who had lost a son earlier) was most attentive to Nur. Furthermore, Mother claimed that in her dream a dervish had appeared and advised her that her lost son, Şadan had been returned to her in the body of Nur. I guess she must have loved Nur as well for her lost child. On the other hand, knowing his wife's affections for Nur, Father was more alert to his failures and punished him continually. I was the youngest, the baby of the family, and I believe I was a normal child. There was nothing very exciting about me and I did not need to be protected all the time. I was rather easy going and did what I was told to do. Even at that very early stage I must have felt that I was only a plaything in the family and that my brothers were more important than I. That must have been the reason why I had cherished a sort of secret jealousy against my elder brothers.

Mother generally treated Nur and me as if we were twins. This meant that our siesta times, our feeding times and play times would always be shared. At certain dates she would take us together to a very nice pediatrician, for our checkups. In his clinic we would both go through a physical control, as well as being subjected to "ultra-violet rays." It was great fun lying down with dark glasses covering our eyes and with funny colored rays going through our bodies. Almost next to the clinic was the house where an old Greek lady used to bake and market delicious and fresh cakes. So after our checkups we were certain to stop by her house and get those pastries.

III

Primary School

It was time for me to enroll in the primary school, or to be more precise, the director of the primary school No. 8 on Bahariye Caddesi advised my parents that I could start even though I had not reached the prescribed age. As she and her husband were great friends of the family, she thought that even a year younger than the rest of the first class students, I should be able to manage. Mother, it appears, was thinking of enrolling me at the Notre Dame de Sion, the French Convent School for Girls in Kadıköy. However, shortly before a new law had been put into effect, forcing foreign schools to close their primary classes. Primary education was given to the monopoly of the state.

When it was understood that I was to attend school that fall, Cenan suggested to Mother that I should be introduced to other girls my age since until that time I was always playing with Nur and his boy friends. The only girl friend that I played with was Matilde, who was the granddaughter of our washer woman, an Armenian who came to our house once a week. She was older than I.

On a weekend two of Cenan's friends brought their younger sisters with them and we all met in front of our house and went to a movie. One of them was going to be my lifelong friend, Hayriye Neyzi (Menemencioglu). We had liked being with each other and from then on we three girls began to meet regularly. The three elders would take us youngsters along with them wherever they went. We also began to visit one another in our respective homes. As far as I can remember the game we enjoyed most was to imitate the film stars whose pictures we had seen that week. We would be trying to put our mothers' shoes on and apply lipstick to our lips (usually unsuccessfully) and try to wrap table clothes for long skirts. For this reason a number of shoe heels had broken spikes and rouges were manhandled or custom jewelry was broken. Another thing we enjoyed doing was to sneak from the top of the stairs and watch our elders dancing n the hall below. Sometimes they would take us to the well-known pastry shops "Stasuli" to eat cakes and pastries. Our friendship, specially with Hayriye, has continued to this day without any interruption.

Starting at the primary school No. 8 was highly exciting for me. Every morning Mother and my nanny would prepare me for school. Then my nanny would hold my hand and together we would walk to school. I was sorry to realize that Mother was not coming with us. I had thought that she would also come to school with me.

I loved my school. I had new friends and teachers. We were learning and playing all kinds of games, but still, returning home was the best part of going to school. Thus going back and forth I had began to notice things that I had taken for granted in the past. For example, our home had lovely odors. It was wonderful to pass through various smells of soap, of polish and of fresh flowers and finally to find myself in Mother's warm arms. What a beautiful woman was my mother. I would always find her reading or knitting and/or playing some musical instrument. Since my brothers were boarders during the week, I could have Mother all for myself. Generally I was allowed to do my homework beside her. On the second floor of the house in Kadıköy there was a living room with a bay window. Mother usually sat beside the window and watched me coming home from school and I would be so happy to see her silhouette there. Our rooms on the third floor had a small balcony above the bay window.

When I started my second year at the primary school something happened that caused a great change in my life. Nur, probably objecting to the living conditions at the French school, had lain on the snow without his coat and developed pleurisy. So that year he was to stay at home. He had to be very careful for his health and his diet. As a result, a German governess was hired to take care of Nur and I was also entrusted to her care. As my mother later explained I was too young anyway and I could take piano lessons from the same governess and also learn

French. Therefore I was kept at home as well. Mlle. Helene was of German origin but she could speak both French and Turkish fluently. She had spent many years in İstanbul and had educated children of well-to-do families. In other words she had impeccable references. She was a strict disciplinarian and at the same time she was quite a good-looking lady. With her arrival and Nur and I both staying at home, our lives had changed tremendously. Everything was being done according to the clock. We were getting to be perfect mechanical toys. To be sure, Mother was always at home and would oversee whatever was going on in the house but we had to live with Mlle. Helene. In the mornings, after our breakfast, I was forced to sit for my piano practice and in the next room Mlle. Helene would start Nur's French lesson. Whenever she did not hear the sound of my piano, Mlle. Helene would suddenly appear in my room. Actually, there was no getting away from Mlle. Helene or from the piano. We were allowed to talk in Turkish only to the servants in the house (who did not know French anyway), otherwise we had to talk French with Mlle. Helene or the family members. At 10:30 in the morning we had some fruit to eat and would then go out for our morning walk. Once we had been given an orange that was spoilt and Mlle. Helene had squeezed it on the cook's face. When we returned from our constitutional walk we would wash our hands and face and the chore of having lunch would start. I say chore because this was definitely one of the difficult hours of my life. Due to his past illness, Nur had to eat "healthy food." These were bloody things like steaks, kidneys, knuckles, etc. Naturally, I too was offered the same food. However, my appetite had always been rather delicate and when I refused to eat such bloody meats all hell broke. Scoldings and punishments would then start. Many a time I was forced to chew the same piece of meat in my mouth for a very long time and then swallow it down with water. At the end I would fall down weak from crying. On account of this experience I never forced anyone to eat anything against their wish, including my children. So much so that the children's father once admonished me that I was being too lenient and that I was causing my children to go hungry. However, I could never bring myself to force them to eat.

After the trial of having lunch we had to go through the same cleaning and changing process and after changing into sleep attire we were put down for our afternoon siesta. This again was another chore. After a certain time of staying in bed we were told to get up, wash and get dressed again. This time it was my turn to start my French lesson together with my brother. When the lesson was over we would have our afternoon tea. Thank goodness this was much easier than having lunch, for me. After having tea we would again go out. It was either a walk or to meet other governesses and the children entrusted to their care. Upon our return home we were allowed a free period. We could either play some game together or be with Mother. Mother usually made us play word games from the dictionary, such as "Larousse," which we thought was great fun. She would pick a word, say "bijou" and we had to race to find words that had similar endings. Later the whole family would have dinner together, then a period of relaxation and pretty soon came the time to wash up and retire to our beds.

During that time I had started taking ballet lessons from a Russian lady. These lessons took place at the sumptuous residence of a well-known general. His granddaughter was actually our hostess and friend. There were several other girls who joined these ballet lessons. Some of them continue to be my friends to this day. While we were having our lessons, our governesses would sit around and chat with one another. When the class terminated our hosts never failed to offer everyone a very lavish tea with pastries and so on. If I am not mistaken these dancing lessons continued for three or four years. During that time, I remember our friend had a new baby sister. Ayşegül Sarıca was a very beautiful baby with blond hair. We all loved her very much. She has grown up to become a well-known concert pianist and is internationally appreciated these days.

I never learned why but Mlle. Helene suddenly went away and was replaced this time by a real French lady called Mademoiselle Ménard. I used to be cross with Mlle. Helene because I felt she had a soft spot for Nur. Our new governess, Mlle. Ménard, started treating us equally and I loved her for it.

During those years I remember that we went "to the country" for the summer. I recall the first time we had rented a house

31

near Ethem Efendi Caddesi in Erenkoy between Bagdat Caddesi and the seashore. The house we rented belonged to a gentleman whose wife was also called Cemile Hanım. It was a veritable paradise. There was a private alley that led to the house from Bagdat Caddesi entrance. It was covered with white pebbles and on both sides of the alley there were trees whose branches reached one another turning the alley almost to a tunnel. Near the end of this alley there was a tennis court. The owner's daughter used to play there with her friends. After that one reached the main house, which had two stories. Further along in the garden they had built another one storied house. I believe Father had rented that house for the summer. In the courtyard one always found a profusion of colored flowers. A little further on one reached the seaside with a small beach. The house next door was known as the "house of chains" because they had hung chains to complete their wall. The owners's children must have enjoyed having their friends in. On account of this many youngsters who lived in the vicinity used to congregate in their garden. I learned how to swim at this beach. I probably had not started school yet, but I seem to remember my red shorts with two thin suspenders. Within the whole crowd (of both the houses) I must have been the youngest and tiniest. Another house that we constantly visited around the area during those years was the house that belonged to a radiologist doctor's house. Their mansion was in the middle of a very big garden that reached the seashore. The lady of the house was the daughter of a literate man who had made a name for himself with the dictionary he had written. His son, a respected sportsman and his wife, lived in another house in the same garden. The doctor and his wife had a daughter. She was slightly older than I but we enjoyed playing together. There were two distinct things in that garden that I still remember. One was a very aged and lonely oak tree, planted on some sort of a platform and its branches were always full of attachments like ribbons. Some people had the superstitious belief that this was a sacred shrine and they would tie pieces of cloth with inscriptions on them. Those people would secretly get into the garden, pray under the tree, tie their slip of cloth, make a wish and quickly go out of the garden. The big oak tree was quite far from the house and I guess the owners had decided to ignore what was going on and look the other way. The second thing I can never forget was a small painted wooden carriage that was driven by a pony. Since my friend was a lonely child this contraption must have been built for her pleasure. She would make me sit beside her and we would go round and round in the garden, laughing all the time. The family had some friends who had two able-bodied boys, who were my friend's age. Once, for whatever reason, the pony was unavailable and my friend begged these boys to pull the carriage for her. One of the boys was easygoing and complied with this request. The other one was quite nasty though. It is sad that neither the beautiful mansion nor the wonderful garden exist anymore.

The place Father rented the next summer was a single story house called "the pavillion" due to its circular shape. It was situated in the large land owned by an old Ottoman general. Father rented this house for two consecutive summers. I remember enjoying that house very much. I was getting older and there were a lot of children to play with in the big garden where several houses were built. The general, who was the grandfather of a known writer in Turkey, was a venerable gentleman. In those years his grandson, who was about my age, used to live with his grandfather. I remember him riding his bicycle all around the garden and making huts out of cut reeds. He had once pushed me into the fish pond that was in the garden. Near the wall that overlooked the avenue there was a place slightly heightened, which was usually referred to as the "set," on which they had placed a wooden bench. We girls would sit there and watch everyone that went by, without being seen. Two granddaughters of the general and some other girls living in the other houses built in the garden were all close to my age, although I was the youngest. One of these girls was an Ottoman sultan's granddaughter. There were also a number of boys who would saunter along the road and secretly watch us.

Within the same garden there was another small one-storied house and a White Russian couple called M. and Mme. Goumilin used to live there. After our first summer there Mother and Mme. Goumilin became great friends. Although she met many people, Mother used to keep her distance all the time. As she told me once, she had only three bosom friends throughout her life. Her first great friend was apparently a girl she had met during her childhood in Bosnia-Hertzegovina. That lady had later married a well-known Bosniac writer called Hifzi Byelevatz. I never met her, however, I did meet her husband, Hifzi Byelevatz, during his visit to İstanbul. It appears that they were very close friends and that Hifzi Bey had written a biographical novel covering Mother's life from the stories he had heard from his wife. It is a novel in two volumes and only Mother's name was changed. Cemile was renamed Melilha. I still cherish those two volumes in my library. Unfortunately, I could find no one to translate them as I cannot read Bosniac.

Following her Bosniac friend, and many years later, Mother met a German lady, whom we used to call (Auntie Emma) or "Tante Emma." Her full name was Emma Krueger. Tante Emma was the daughter of a German engineer who had come to Turkey during the construction of the Bagdat Railroad and had fallen in love with the country and never returned to his native land. Even after her mother and father had passed away she stayed in Turkey. Emma never married. She used to read a lot and played the piano very well. She was a blond, tall woman, but not really pretty. She wore rings on almost all her fingers. She was very serious but very affectionate toward us. She used to come as a house guest and stay for a few days. I believe her friendship with Mother was really based on a rather high level. We always saw them both either sitting down comfortably, each reading her book, or they would be making music, Tante Emma at the piano and Mother with her violin. They were very good friends but they would keep their distance at all times. I used to admire Tante Emma. She returned to Germany when the Second World War started and we lost track of her completely.

My mother's third friend turned out to be Mme. Goumilin. The general's grandson, in his autobiographical novel *Years in the Shadows* also mentions the Goumilin family. In the same book Memet Fuat also mentions our family. I was very interested to find that he recounted an incident that involved Mother and his grandfather. I enjoyed the story so much that I could not help take that incident from his book (frankly without obtaining his permission) since I am sure he would not mind my doing so. This is the incident in his words:

One day, in the garden, in front of the dining room, Grandfather was chatting with our neighbour Cemile Hanım. She was an elegant lady with three children. She was middle aged, always very elegant and well-groomed, attractive lady. So-called a woman of the world. She did not mind saying her word freely. Her husband was a well-placed government executive who had been elected to a Parlimentary seat. They had been renting the pavilion for the last couple of summers.

As they were sipping their coffee, Grandfather spied a figure that passed through the laurel plants and walked towards the pine wood. Due to his failing eyesight he could not quite figure out who it was.

He asked me who was it that had walked by. I did not reply. Cemile Hanım, who must have thought that I had not recognized the man who walked away, answered in my place, "It was Nazim Hikmet Bey."

When grandfather heard the name at first started to confirm his admiration of the man by muttering things like "what a brilliant man, so intelligent and exceptionally good looking." Then came his apologies, "Unfortunately he has himself involved in a most undesirable kind of politics, it is a pity . . ."

In the beginning Cemile Hanım had remained silent. A well-dressed attractive lady of the 'salons,' I was expecting her to join Grandfather in his regrets—but something very unexpected took place: Cemile Hanım suddenly straighted up in her seat and in order to make herself heard by my grandfather raised her voice and gave a vehement lecture on parasites and profiteers who were sucking the blood of the nation and the country and she ended her speech by saying, "Let us have some honest men in this country, my dear General."

Grandfather was quite perplexed, he had not expected this well-groomed lady to defend Nazim Hikmet in such complementary terms. What can one do when confronted with such a vehement speech, the only solace he could muster was to smile ruefully and that was what Grandfather did. In order to hide his astonishment he used me, by cuddling my head and getting involved with other subjects.

The Goumilins were very elegant and refined people. I believe Mr. Goumilin was an engineer. That year, 1935, my eldest brother Cenan had graduated from the St. Joseph Lycee and had been sent to Germany to study engineering. Mother had taken him there. My mother had given birth to Cenan when she was 19 years old, and since he had grown up to be a very mature young man, very industrious and well-mannered, the two had become good friends as well. Whilst in Germany people thought they were sister and brother, instead of mother and son!

This trip took place during the summer vacation and Nur and I were entrusted to the care of Father and to our common governess, Mlle. Ménard, during Mother's absence. Mlle. Ménard was a well-read and wise woman. She was also very patriotic and realizing that another world war was about to erupt, she wanted very much to return to her country. Therefore as soon as mother returned from her trip Mlle. Ménard left for France. Our parting was full of huggings and tears. We never heard of her again.

Our third governess was of Austrian origin of very good upbringing and a very agreeable person. She had spent many years in İstanbul. She had been a governess for the Sultan's daughters at the Ottoman Palace. Later on she had taken care of the children of many well-to-do families in İstanbul. As the children under her care grew up, Mme. Lesyak would change her charges and find employment in another mansion. I believe she must have been in her fifties when she arrived into our lives. It was pure luck that Mother had found her. She had also been the governess of one of my friends at the ballet lessons. Now, with the arrival of Mme. Lesyak a real friendship developed between us and this girl and her brother. Mme. Lesyak once told us that in her youth she had been engaged to marry the well-known writer Stephan Zweig but at the last minute she had refused to marry him. She had found out that "his feet smelled."

It was sometime during these days that Father had decided that rather than renting houses for the summer we should have a permanent summer residence. So one day he told Mother, "Cemile Sultan, I have bought a very nice piece of land by the sea for you. I believe we could build a house there as a permanent summer residence." The whole family went to see the land Father had bought. It was situated close to the first summer house that we had rented. Nur and I were both elated. We would be able to simply walk into the sea from our garden. Suddenly

Mother said, "I do not like this plot of land, it is barren and there are no trees." Years later I saw the plot and it was full of trees. So Father sold that land to a friend of his. Many years later I was due for an unbelievable surprise. The then mayor of İstanbul was able to build a highway filling in the sea and the mansions that had access to the sea were left behind this huge double highway.

Finally Mother, who liked the sea but would prefer not to live nearby, was able to find a place to her heart's desire. This great mansion with its huge garden was a great place for us also. At present all busses and jitneys go back and forth incessantly beside our old land. What Father had bought was a mansion built for the household of a prominent Pascha of the Ottoman period. During that period well-to-do families used to build two houses, one would be called the "Selamlik," which was intended for the male part of the family and also a sort of working place for the master, and the other one was called "the harem," which was intended for the ladies of the household. People with lesser means arranged this separation under the same roof. What Father had bought was the "Selamlik of Zihni Pascha," who owned the surrounding houses and gardens. Our house was placed in a garden covering 24 acres. The mansion had 27 rooms and 3 kitchens. We had moved in when the renovation, with three modern bathrooms and Turkish Baths plus a central heating system, etc., was completed. In the garden, partly in front of the house, there were pine trees reputedly 200 years old and rising up to the top of the four-storied building. On the land covering the back of the house, which we called the "back garden," there were many fruit trees and a windmill and further a vegetable garden. On the front, after the pine trees, the garden reached down to the avenue. One could enter the land either from the main door on the avenue or from another door that opened to the side street. Close to this entrance there was a one-floor octagonal pavilion with a huge room, bathroom and kitchen surrounded by a large terrace where my parents entertained large groups of friends on warm summer nights. It was an ideal place for big occasions.

By the side of the main garden door there was another single-floored house that had rooms for the cook and the gardner plus a laundry room and a bedroom for the washer woman who also stayed in. Further down from the pavillion there was a vineyard that reached all the way to the front garden wall. I remember that many different kinds of grapes were grown there. There were grapes that smelled heavenly and there were black grapes as well as white ones with very thin skins. There were also small pitless grapes, good for drying, and there were grapes almost as large as prunes! I can never forget the various smells and the different tastes that we were able to enjoy in this vineyard. All around the land a high wall was built. By the vineyard, right beside the wall, fig trees had been planted. There were many different kinds and the fresh fig with its honey dripping was such a delight for me that even today I get excited when the fig season arrives. The fig is still one of my favorite fruits. Although the branches of the fig trees may look sturdy, we were told they can break easily, so we used to climb on the wall and pick the figs from the nearby trees.

Now it would be good to talk about the garden in front of the mansion. Almost each huge pine tree had huge and colored "hydrangeia hortensia" circling it. Under these trees dining tables, tea tables, hammocks, lounging chairs, and garden chairs were spread. Thus almost all family members would entertain their guests individually and separately under different groups of trees. Small flowers were planted around each group of pines.

To reach the main entrance door of the mansion one had to climb a few marble steps. When the huge wooden door opened, one came into a large hallway. There was a flight of steps going up to the first floor. From there on there were double staircases, one on the left and the other on the right going opposite ways and these would reach all the floors above. Toward the north side of the house the stairs were single and toward the south, double. On each floor, first there was a big hall and then there were four rooms on each side of the sofa plus one more room in the middle. On the first floor there was a large salon that covered the space allotted to three rooms of the second floor, plus a smaller room with a toilet beside it. On the other side of the large hall was the dining room, covering the space of three rooms, plus an extra room with an adjoining W.C. (There were further rooms in the attic.) In the middle of the large hall was my father's study. Below the first floor my parents had installed a newly designed kitchen with various modern contraptions plus the old kitchen with its coal burning stove. There were also a number of rooms, together with hammams (old fashion baths) for the servants, in this basement. There was a separate service stairway that started from the basement and reached the other floors above, so that the servants could reach any floor above without going through the main staircase. These stairs first reached a small kitchen alcove next to the dining room so that food brought up from the kitchen was controlled for the last time and if necessary redecorated before being served. This small kitchen alcove would also be used to prepare tea or coffee, pastries and cakes and these could be served from there. It was also a place where meals could be kept warm prior to serving. The personnel were admonished to use this service staircase for all purposes.

One of the most exciting parts of the mansion was the fact that all the ceilings of the first floor rooms had beautiful, hand-drawn oil paintings depicting moonlight, sea sides, sunsets, etc. in the large salon. The ceiling of the dining room was covered with pictures of various fruits, fish in beautiful dishes and a gold decorated soup ladle. Right beside the dining room there was a smoking room (fumoir) and going toward this smoking room on each side of the dining room was a marble fountain. Before or after meals we could use these beautifully carved fountains to wash our hands. The dining room had a long table with the capacity of sitting 24 persons at the same time and it was made from a single piece of wood. Naturally there were proper dining chairs around the table plus a number of other armchairs and some small service tables. On the side of the dining room, beside the terrace, looking towards East. Father had added a small stairway that reached directly into the garden. This was to make sure that Mother's after breakfast (or after lunch) coffee could reach the garden where she enjoyed sitting, without getting cold on the way out. Mother spent almost all of her days in her beloved mansion, in or out, in the garden most of the time, weather permitting. She had taffeta dresses made for the summer and velvet dresses for the winter, all with long skirts, almost reaching to the floor. She always did something with her hands. This could be a book in her hand and something she was knitting or some embroidery she was working on. Her motto was "A lady should never have idle hands." Mother spoke seven languages, even "Elenika" (Classical Greek). She could play five different kinds of musical instruments. She was certainly a very intellectual lady. I never saw her slovenly or with her hair undone or sitting in an improper way. She never raised her voice or said anything improper. Her education and her upbringing had almost become a second nature.

When the family settled in the mansion in Erenköy, Mother had developed two new modes of living. First she prepared separate bedrooms for Father and herself and she arranged a sort of personal "boudoir" for her own use. She could stay all by herself in this room. She decorated this room with her favorite books plus her musical instruments. There were some paintings and she also had a small writing table for herself. We had to obtain a special permit and/or get invited in order to get into this very private room. Among the paintings that she had hung on the wall of this room there was one that used to frighten me. On this painting there was a large, leather bound book, opened in the middle, with a human skull standing on the pages. On one side of this book there was a candlestick with its candle almost burnt out and nearby stood a black bird (an owl). Mother had explained this picture to me in the following manner: "The owl is the messenger. The burnt candle means the end of life is never far away. The book represents knowledge and the skull signifies death. So it means that a person can never complete her knowledge even when death is near. Knowledge is endless." After this explanation I was no longer afraid of that picture and I was filled with an insatiable hunger for knowledge. I started reading and tried to learn constantly. However, even to this day, when I am writing these memoirs, it saddens me to realize how little I know.

The year the mansion was bought we were still living in Kadıköy, as the renovations were still not completed in the place. One day we received the sad news that Father's mother had passed away. I had seen very little of my grandmother and I was very sad to learn that we had lost her.

I was quite young when I first met Melek Hanım (Father's mother, my paternal grandmother). One day, an elderly lady whom I had never seen before had called on our house. While she was sitting in the receiving room, Father and Mother had been talking for a long time in another room. Finally Mother came out and holding me by my hand, took me to the receiving room where the elderly lady was waiting. Mother introduced me and said "This lady is your father's mother, she traveled a long way to come to visit us, you must kiss her hand." The old lady held me in her arms and sitting me on her lap, kissed my cheeks. Meanwhile, Father, who was angry with his mother because she had deserted him as an infant, had refused to see my grand-mother. But Mother did not give up and brought them together and they made up. From that day on, Grandmother began to call on us every once in a while. She would take me in her lap, kiss my cheeks and recount fairy tales. Then she failed to show up and we heard that her health was failing. It appears that she never recovered from that illness and passed away.

Father had long before been appointed the general manager (director) of the Tramway Company on the Anatolian section of İstanbul. He was working almost continuously. He was very insistent on extending the lines further and was so busy that we started seeing him rarely at home. He had made a very tough schedule for himself and worked even to late hours of the night. He was intent to make his dream come true. Finally, when all these lines became operative, he decided he should take a vaca-tion and to give his family more of his time. Although I did not realize it at the time, he was also trying to show his young daughter a bit of the world and introduce me to some people. One day I had a surprise. I was to go on a trip with Father. We travelled on a passenger boat and landed in İzmir after spending the night on the boat. It appeared that Father had taken both Cenan and Nur on separate occasions on the same trip. So this was now my turn. Once in Izmir, I was introduced to my moth-er's uncles and aunts. Apparently I had been to Izmir when I was only at the age of three when mother wanted to visit her family. As Father had gone to a place called the Polish Village, near İstanbul, with male friends for a vacation, Mother on her side had taken all her three children and my nanny on a trip to İzmir. We had traveled on a luxurious steamer. We had reached the port of İzmir on July 2, 1929. Mother's family met us in the building where we had to wait for the luggage to arrive. While the excitement of meeting was going on and my nanny was busy with the luggage, it seems I was able to get away by myself out of the building. By the time they had realized I was nowhere around, loud brakes of a lorry were heard followed by people's shrieks. Mother, who had sensed something had gone wrong, had rushed outside the building and found me in the arms of a policeman. I was covered in blood and had passed out. They rushed me in an ambulance to the best private clinic of the city. The story, as it turned out to be, was that when I had gone out of the building the traffic police had stopped a passing truck and I had gone around and leaned on one of the truck's mudguards. A while later, when the policeman signaled the driver to continue, no one noticed the little girl and so I was run over.

The first diagnosis at the clinic was that it would not be possible for me to live. A number of my ribs, my collar bone, my skull and my hip were all broken and I had serious injuries. There were internal hemorrages both in my abdomen and in my brain. While they were trying to tend to me, Mother cabled the governor of İstanbul, who was together with Father, to give him the news. I still have my tiny blood-covered dress that my mother kept.

I was hospitalized in the recovery room for three months and had several surgeries, there appeared some hope for my survival. The doctors still expected that I would grow up into a cripple. I was lucky enough not only to survive but also to be able to develop into a healthy woman. However, the shock this accident created in my mother lasted for many years.

My trip to İzmir with Father, on the contrary, was full of enjoyable memories. I had liked my mother's aunts very much. One of them had married a lovable man of Albanian extraction. The other aunt, who had never married, had always lived with them. Although each had her own personality, the two sisters were full of love. As they were born and raised for some time in Bosnia, they talked Turkish with an accent. Mother's uncles were living in the center of the town. The elder uncle was an extremely tall and affectionate man. His wife, their three sons, their wives and the grandchildren were all living under one roof. Theirs was certainly a very cheerful house. I have always loved every member of that family. I still keep my friendship with one of my cousins. The younger uncle was a lawyer. He too was a charming man but somehow we lost contact as life went on. I think of them always with love. From İzmir we took the night train to Ankara. This was my first visit since my birth there. As soon as we were settled in the hotel, my father took me to the house I was born in. It was a nice-looking two-storied house with a garden in front. Big apartment buildings have now replaced these nice houses.

Our second visit, which was very important for me, was made to the house of Mr. İsmet İnönü. The house was called "Pembe Kiosk" on account of its outside paint, which was pink. I was to meet the whole family for the first time. Mr. İnönü's respectable mother, as well as his wife who for me has always been a most cherished and revered person, two sons and daughter received me with much affection. We were also asked to stay over for lunch. During lunch İsmet Pascha asked me, "Your father and mother, do they fight with each other?" In my innocence I hurriedly answered, "Yes, they do." It was a great happiness for me to have met this honorable family. Next to Mother, the person Father revered most was certainly İsmet Pascha.

Upon our return Father was happy and relieved to see that all the tramlines were working well. He had with great zeal done his best to extend the lines. He had also gone to Germany to order new tram cars. Among these the most popular ones were the open-air wagons that had curtains that were put into use during the summer. While naming the tram stops on the line Kadıköy-Bostançi, there was a stop that had no name and Father went along and named that stop after me as "Şen Durak." (the Joyful Stop). Father had worked as the general director of the Tram Company between the years 1929–1938. During that period Father had become a member of the "Moda Yacht Club." The club had some sort of a houseboat that was used as the members' swimming facility. One had to go on a rowing boat to reach what they called "the raft." This had two stories. The changing rooms were on the first floor and on the second floor there was the sun deck plus the trampolines for diving into the sea. Many families living in Kadıköy and Moda were members of the club and we had made many friends there. We also owned a private car, with the license plate number 1007. Since there were very few private cars in that part of the town, we had become quite known because of our no. 1007. Some of the friends we had at the club lasted for life. Şeyda Demiren (Mrs. Versan now) is one of them.

Our friendship with Şeyda led to our meeting other youngsters. We used to attend parties mostly at the Sertel family home, where mostly Robert College students would congregate. I believe I used to be the youngest at most of these meetings. Even so, I used to enjoy listening to their endless arguments on various subjects. The American way of education had made them more ready to speak openly in public. This was somewhat different from the kind of education received in the Turkish public schools. However, thanks to Mother and my various governesses I also had a European education at least. The reconstruction work at the mansion in Erenköy having been completed and the central heating system installed, Mother decided to move there and leave our winter house for good. By this time both Nur and I had returned to our old schools. Then the question of our commuting to our schools had to be solved. Mother thought she could solve this by registering me to a school in Erenköy. My brother Nur was to return to the French Lycee as a boarder. After some further consideration Mother decided that I should graduate from my original primary school and hired our coachman to take me in his one-horse-drawn coach to my school in Moda every morning and take me back every afternoon. On the way to school we would stop and pick up one of my friends and we would do this long journey together. Despite the cold winter we used to have lots of fun on these horse buggy rides. When it was really cold and there was snow on the roads our driver would drive us in father's car, Ford no. 1007.

We had really settled in Erenköy. I can never forget the beauty of the big pine trees bent with snow. Such a big mansion naturally required a lot of help. Therefore the number of people working for us had grown. Let me recount the list of the people working at the mansion. There was a male cook and his assistant, a waiter to serve at the table, our old retainer lady plus two Greek girls for housework, the gardener and his two sidekicks, father's driver and a washerwoman who also lived in, plus the governess. Their numbers would vary between ten and thirteen. During the summer months, when the number of visitors increased, there would be a lot of work for all of them.

Although I had started school again, Mother had kept Mme. Lesyak for my benefit. Our beloved old Greek retainer worked almost exclusively for Father. Father had ulcers and had to stick to a restrictive diet. Mme. Eleni would oversee his food and served it to him. The waiter would serve the rest of the people at the table.

Our first winter in the new home was very pleasant. On weekends Nur and I would meet friends and go in a group to a movie, always under the supervision of Mme. Lesyak. Otherwise we would have parties at home and play games or go to the yacht club. When summer came our days began to be more enjoyable. In the mornings there would be a big breakfast table in the garden, where eggs, butter, fruit, toasted bread slices and various cheeses and preserves, plus olives would be served. Following breakfast there was an intermission either for reading or learning some handcraft or for doing some embroidery. Then came the time for our trip to the sea, which was always a big event. At ten o'clock the coach would arrive. Mother, Nur and I would take all our swimming gear and take a ride in the carriage. Our destination would be one of the several beaches on the Marmara Sea. In those days the Marmara Sea was not polluted and was always bright blue. Our swimming would last at least until 13:00 P.M. and then we would take the coach back. The distance, on a horse-drawn carriage would take half an hour each way. One day the sea was so good that we had delayed our return and Mother was worried that by delaying our trip back we had let our coachman go hungry for a very long time. Mother was very cross with both Nur and me for the delay we had caused. So as a punishment she had invited the coachman to join our lunch table and admonished us that we should eat just like him without using knives and forks, just a spoon. We even had to use our fingers at times, it was difficult and I guess we did not enjoy this at all. I had grown out of the sickly child who was very picky and choosy. I still had my reservations toward certain foods but the discipline I had been receiving had taught me not to refuse things all the time.

Mother had very definite ideas about my upbringing. For example, as she wanted me to have a good posture, she would draw a line on the floor with chalk, put a book on my head and ask me to walk on this line without dropping the book. It took a lot of practice but I remember I finally managed to walk on the line and not drop the book. During my piano lessons she would pass a cane between my elbows and back so as to force me to sit very erect as I was playing the piano.

That summer at the beach we were introduced to another sister and brother with whom we became very good friends. Their father was a well-known medical doctor who also owned a famous laboratory. He was quite a disciplinarian as well. They had a very modern new house close by the beach and on the main avenue with the tramway passing right in front of their house. They were allowed to stroll on the avenue and have ice cream in the fashionable ice cream parlor until their father's arrival home, which was always on the same tramway. Then they had to be home to welcome their father. That ice cream parlor was the "in place" where all the young people congregated every afternoon. Naturally Nur and I also wanted to be part of the crowd. Our home was quite a ways from Bagdat Caddesi. Nur had a bicycle and was allowed to go out on his own. My position was quite different. Although I also had a bike, my possibilities were rather limited. I had to have my governess with me wherever I went. This made me feel awful. Finally, after long arguments we struck a deal with Mother. Mme. Lesyak would still come but she would follow us from a discreet distance and at the ice cream parlor she would sit at another table by herself. This way we were able to develop a long lasting friendship, especially me and this girl friend, Cemile.

It would be about 1:30 P.M. by the time we reached home, returning from our morning swim. As usual we would have a "siesta" after lunch. Naturally my brother and I disliked this ordeal since we would be daydreaming of what we would be doing at the ice cream parlor in the afternoon. We could not sleep a wink. Nevertheless, we would lie down quietly, sometimes also in the hammocks with a book in hand. Some days we would simply visit our new friends at their modern house and listen to jazz records, or sometimes they would come to our place.

Since we had settled in the mansion, both us children and our parents had been meeting new people and forming new relationships. For my parents the first couple they met were the great granddaughter of the general, whose second house father had bought, and her husband, who was a very successful cartoonist. They were both very good looking and interesting. As we had to walk from our garden through a gate door, the families visited each other often. Their house was for me a dream house. This nice lady's mother was an elderly and very elegant but sad-looking lady who played the piano all the time. Since I had been having piano lessons for some time, that romantic looking lady playing Chopin in a wonderful manner had impressed me very much. The beautiful sound of Chopin's music coming through her wisteria-filled balcony would be a delight to my ears in the garden. It must have been also that I was somewhat coming out of childhood and was involved in music as well. Anyway, for me she was some romantic creature who had stepped out of a novel.

Inside the house I was doubly impressed. They had antique furniture in almost every room. I saw a "love seat" for the first time in that mansion. This is a funny contraption where two people can sit side by side but opposite each other. There were all sorts of crystal vases and boxes of Bohemian cut glass containing sweets on the tables. All the walls were covered with oil paintings in gold plated frames. The ceilings were also oil painted. The curtains and upholstery were of heavy silk or velour. All these were quite different than what we had in our house. Also there were all sorts of servants who had been trained at the royal palace and these fairy-like women would be fleeting in and out of the rooms so inconspicuously. These women had come from all kinds of extractions, some were black, some Caucasian, and they all had old-fashioned names. I had been told some of the very old retainees were living in the basement and the younger servants were supposed to care for them. Amidst all the crowd the grandfather always came to the fore. Although very old, he was still very good-looking with his white goatee. His long hair was also white. He resembled a lion with a mane. He was someone I admired watching. He was the father of the romantic lady. He always dressed beautifully and impeccably and he was definitely the head of the family. Sometimes they would ask us to stay for lunch.

There would invariably be at least fifteen people sitting at the table. He would be sitting at the head of the table. A full course of meals that started with a soup followed by some meat dish, then some vegetables followed by a rice dish and then dessert and fruit would be served. For him this would never be enough! He would then signal an old woman attendant who carried a chain full of keys on her belt, and she would start serving some special cheeses from the pantry. After the cheese very possibly another round of dishes would follow. Since the kitchen was in a separate building all dishes would be carried in covered copper containers, reheated in the house kitchen and served by several helpers. One of the things that had attracted me very much was the golden ring this elderly gentleman wore around his very large necktie. Another special thing he did was to give to the lady, whose company he enjoyed, a small blue bead. This could be for luck as well as to connote his preference. I had seen him giving these beads to many different ladies on different occasions. He must have had a pocket full of them.

Another family that both our elders and ourselves got together with, used to live in a Palace opposite our garden, on the other side of the avenue. The palace was known as the "Cemile Sultan's Palace." Two sisters, who were both married, and their children used to share this large palace. The older sister's daughter was a few years older than I but we used to enjoy each other's company and thus we met quite often. Their great grandmother was one of the Ottoman Sultan's sister and he had given her this Palace when she got married. Quite a glorious life had been lived there once. The second great-granddaughter was a most charming lady who was married to a very handsome man that I used to like to watch. He was a horseback rider and he owned beautiful hunting dogs. These two families still lived elaborately but nothing to be compared with their ancestors. My first experience with death was when this lovely couple lost their beautiful little girl. This event had made us very sad. It took years for this charming woman to get over it, if ever she did!

One of our esteemed family friends visiting us often, whom I remember from my earliest days, was the famous Ottoman admiral who was also a close friend of Atatürk, Mr. Rauf Orbay. Although already in an advanced age, he was very attractive. One could find in him an English gentleman's allure mixed with the Ottoman refinement. Later in his life he was also the Turkish ambassador to England. For some reason or another Uncle Rauf used to address my mother as "Kadin Efendi" which carried the connotation that she was the Sultan's favorite wife who had given the Sultan his first son. As to myself, who adored him, he used to call me "Mebus Abla," which meant a "Parliamentarian Sister." He and another close and important political man (both unmarried) used to visit our house together. My parents did not like alcohol but for these gentleman they always had a "meze" table prepared. This was naturally accompanied by the national drink, "Rakı." I used to have my share of the delicacies on the table as Uncle Rauf would hold my hand tightly in his and say, "Let Mebus Abla listen to what I have to say, one day when she will be in politics she will know what happened in our history." Another thing that we never had at home was playing cards. Our parents would play only backgammon. I never was interested in this game but both my brothers would play with Father or Mother once in a while. No gambling was involved, it was only for the challenge the game involved.

Another couple that was always welcomed in our house were Princess Ziba and her revered husband. The princess was said to be from Egypt and I believe she was an aunt of the late king of Egypt, Farouk. She was a very soft spoken and well-dressed lady. Her husband, Mr. Tugay, was a jolly man, tall and slightly blustering and always ready for a joke. People usually called on the phone before coming to the mansion. Mother liked to keep her distance but enjoyed receiving people she liked. One day, Mr. Tugay appeared at our dining room unannounced and recognizing that there were a bunch of pears decorating the center of the table made a blustering joke saying, "Madame, how come you knew of my arrival?" Mother was rather perturbed since his joke was making a reference to a Turkish adage that "bears get the best of pears." She was very apologetic and had difficulty in finding words to cover her discomfort.

IV

Dreams of College and
Moving to Ankara

At the end of our third winter in Erenköy I graduated from my primary school, No. 8. My greatest wish was to go to the American College for Girls at Arnavutköy, İstanbul. However, Mother would not allow me to attend a boarding school! After much persuasion and a lot of begging on my part, she agreed that I could attend the American College for Girls at Scutari, since I could commute there and be driven back and forth in our private car. All formalities were completed in no time. Even my uniforms were purchased. I was delighted. I was going to be a "college girl" like my friends. On top of this I would no longer have a governess! Sometimes dreams do not come true. The previous year father had been elected to the parliament. He was taking the night train from Ankara on Fridays, to come to İstanbul and on Sunday evenings was taking the train to return to Ankara. Since we did not have a house there, he was staying at the Bellevue Palace Hotel. Father had some sort of a protracted illness that spring and summer and the doctors advised that he should have better care and be subjected to a particular diet. As a result, Mother decided to move the whole family to Ankara. This new move had delighted my elder brother Nur since it meant that he would be relieved from attending the St. Joseph High School. On the other hand, for me this news was almost like death. Even my uniforms were purchased! My skirt, my shirt, my necktie and my sweater. On top of it all, I was going to a city where there was no sea! How dreadful! My friends and Erenköy, my heaven, would be left behind. This was a disaster! Where was Ankara? I had been there once. It was such a small place.

While this decision was reached, Mother was already quite worried. The Second World War was about to start! My eldest brother had moved to France a few years ago as he had found the education offered in Germany not up to his expectations. After having completed the necessary classes at the "Jançon de Sailly," and after he had gone through some rigorous examinations, he was accepted to the famed "Ecole Centrale de Paris." My parents were very worried for the pains the war would bring as well as for my brother's future.

During the first days of September before the school year started, we moved to Ankara. Mother was in a turmoil. She had never really wanted to move to Ankara. She knew that the cemetery of her late son had been bulldozed while new highways were being built. She kept saying, "I could well be walking over my son's grave." She dreaded the idea. On the other hand she wanted to take care of her husband, suffering from ulcers. In short she was very sad.

Father had not been able to find a suitable house for the family and instead had bought some land and had started building a new homestead. For about a month we all stayed at the Bellevue Palace Hotel. After a month of Hotel life, father rented a flat at Maltepe, somewhat in the middle of the new city. It was the top floor of a two storied building and father knew the owners. All the members of the Barlas family were composed of rather interesting people. Dr. Gürbüz Barlas, who was their youngest son, was a high school student in those days. He was always very industrious and would not join any of our games. Cemil Sait Bey, who later became a minister of the cabinet, was just about to start his political career. He used to visit father very frequently.

For a while there was no news from my elder brother in Paris. Then one day he suddenly arrived to the house in Ankara. It appeared that a group of Turkish students had cycled from Paris to Vichy! From there, they had managed to return to Turkey after suffering many hardships. Among his friends were many who later became famous in politics. Friendships hammered out during hard times lasted a lifetime among them.

Nur and I were both registered at a Turkish school called Ankara College. Being registered to a "college" had softened the

51

shock for me. From where we lived we could walk to school, which was at a reasonable distance. Father had sold the family car when we had moved to Ankara.

A chance meeting had cheered me up to no end, during my first days at school. I came across one of my first girl friends, who was Cenan's friend's sister. I had not seen Hayriye Menemencioglu (Neyzi) for some years, following our Kadıköy days. Finding her again was great.

The school consisted of two buildings, one for girls, the other for boys. They had installed a barbed wire in the middle of the garden, which separated the two groups from one another. Consequently, I could not get in touch with my brother and felt lonely among all those girls I did not know. That is until I came across my old girl friend. We were enrolled in different sections, but that was not too bad, since we could get together during every recess. During lunch hours we would also meet at the dining hall, share our meals and talk. Hayriye introduced me to another girl and she too became a lifelong friend. She also had a brother Nur's age. So during weekends we three girls and two older brothers started sharing our days. I especially enjoyed visiting Semra's house. Apart from the fact that her mother was a very attractive and elegant lady, her father always gave me copies of the classics he had translated. I always had an incessant need for knowledge and in those days this desire for learning was beginning to emerge.

Although I was gradually getting to enjoy Ankara, my homesickness for the sea and for my friends left behind were not easy to overcome. During winter, almost every time we had a break at school, mother made sure to take us back to Erenköy. On those occasions the return trip to Ankara gradually started looking nice. On weekends "us five" were sure to be together. We would either go to the movies or we would meet in our houses. As long as my brother was with me Mother would not object to my going around. During the week we would pick up Hayriye from her home, which was on our way, and walk to school together. Hayriye's mother was a very likable person who always had a smile for us. Her father was a tall and thin and most elegant gentleman who always had a book in his hands.

Walking to school took time and was becoming wearisome. In the year 1939 there was hardly any automobile traffic in Ankara. So Mother did not object to have our bicycles brought in from Erenköy. We would thus cycle to and from school and also around the city on weekends. Hayriye, Semra and her brother all had bicycles as well. I guess many youngsters used to ride bicycles during those days. On Saturdays and Sundays we would start cycling from the center of the city, on the main boulevard, all the way up to the city, called Çankaya. Since it was rather a steep climb, when we reached half way we would get off our bicycles and walk, carrying our bikes. Then down that hill, we would place our feet on the handles, cross our arms over our chests and almost fly all the way down to where we started. This used to be a very giddying experience. In time Mother learned that there was a school in the middle of the city where both modern dancing and gymnastics were being taught. The school was owned and managed by a German lady. Mother lost no time to have me enrolled at this school. Hayriye was already registered there. So, I started attending classes there two afternoons a week. Who would have thought that the dance school Mme. Marga was running in that basement would one day be turned into that very successful restaurant and night club called "Club Serge" (Süreyya Kulup & Restaurant).

During those dancing lessons we met and became very close friends (until her very unfortunate early death) with Leyla. Her parents were divorced and she lived mostly with her father, visiting her mother once in a while. Her father was a diplomat. Their home was very nicely furnished with furniture brought in from Europe. They had spent many years in Germany and Leyla spoke German fluently. The flat they lived in was in the middle of the city, the address was 10 İzmir Boulevard, where we girls spent a lot of time. We also shared many experiences in that place. Therefore that flat has been for all, including myself, filled with memories. With the inclusion of Jale, we had formed a group of five girls. We had a lot of "firsts" at Leyla's apartment. Namely we had smoked our first cigarettes and we had discussed the boys around us for the first time in that house. By a strange coincidence, many years later, that flat had become "our home" during some of my married years. In fact, I gave birth to my

53

second daughter in that flat and I was able to raise all my children, including my son, in this flat until the end of 1960.

Including Jale into our group was my enterprise. We used to come across her very often. We admired her from afar and knew that she was our age. So one day I had accosted her and suggested that she should join our group. Her elder sister Nilüfer was a person I had been looking up to in the image of an older sister I did not have. I used to come across her now and again and always admired her serious attitude as well as her beauty. Finally we also became friends with her as well and many years later, as they had both settled in Manhattan, she became a good friend of my daughter, Zeyneb. As a result, us five girls, namely Hayriye, Semra, Leyla, Jale and I, were able to forge a friendship that lasted all our lives. For some years two of our brothers escorted us as well.

My parents, together with their happiness on my elder brother's arrival, started being concerned about his future. The question of where he would complete his studies came to be a problem. After making many enquires, they decided that he should go to the United States of America. However, Europe was involved in a bloody war. So Cenan first had to go to Cairo. Then came the news of a long and protracted voyage aboard a ship. After having to cross the equator twice, we received a cable advising us that he had reached the West Coast of the U.S.A. Then, after some long time, we received another cable informing us that he had crossed to the East Coast and had been enrolled at M.I.T. in Cambridge, Mass. Following these cables, his letters, due to restrictions and controls on account of the war, had began to arrive to Ankara, one after another.

Mother, who was very attached to her children, was having a bad time, with her favorite son so far away. What made matters worse was the fact that letters took a very long to arrive and she kept worrying. Somehow this condition had resulted in her becoming over caring for me. Although as a child I had hoped and wished to have this show of affection, now that I was becoming a young girl, it was getting to be a bit too much. Mother was, in a way, trying to share her worries with me but now I am not at all sure that I gave her the necessary support at that time.

54

I guess I must have been somewhat scatterbrained during those days. I no longer had a governess in Ankara but the fact that I could not go out without being properly chaperoned bothered me. For many years, I could go nowhere, not even to the movies, unless my brother or mother chaperoned me. On the other hand, probably due to her European kind of education, all my friends, be it girls or boys, were welcomed to our house. As a matter of fact, Mother encouraged these visits.

Both Nur and I could take our friends to our rooms, have tea, play music or games. On such days I would notice that Mother always contrived to stay at home! Another mannerism that our parents had and which at the time we could not understand, was the kind of enquiries they directed to us. Whenever we mentioned a new friend, they would immediately ask, "Whose son is he?" or "Where do they live?" and/or 'Do you know their phone number?" The trouble for us was that we hated asking such probing questions to people we had just met. Our salvation lay in the fact that the population of Ankara was still very small and that most of the youngsters we would meet at school would be the children of families our parents either knew of or were acquainted with. Several of their parents were in the government or high officials, anyway.

After spending a year at the flat belonging to the Barlas family, the apartment building on Sümer Sokak No. 42 was completed and we were able to move in. The place had three floors and six apartments. The two top flats were combined to fit our family. This way we had ample room to settle. Although Cenan was far away, father had prepared a separate bedroom for each of his three children. It was almost like Erenköy. We had the "sütne" dating back to our Kadikoy years and a stay-in chambermaid and the two women shared a bedroom. The male cook and the man taking care of the central heating had been given rooms in the basement of the building. Apart from the bedrooms, there were two bathrooms including toilets, a separate pantry and a large kitchen. Father had his study and there were two separate reception rooms and a large dining room. A charwoman used to come three times a week and her duties included cleaning the windows, doing the laundry and cleaning the carpets with soap. Despite her army of helpers Mother was always busy, mostly controlling the work done in the house. She also made me do some of the chores. When I objected to these things, she would say, "One chief for a thousand helpers." Every corner of the house was always kept clean, the vases always contained freshly cut flowers. Mother loved her house and enjoyed being surrounded with beautiful objects. To have her freshly cut flowers last longer, Mother had developed various applications. Each time I came home from school I would ask, "Is Mother home?" and she would call "Here I am Ninişka!" Mother used to call me Ninişka. Father would say Şenim; (which in Turkish meant Myşen) and Cenan would call me Şenkom." Somehow in later years Nur had started calling me "Little Mother."

I would like to return to the person who had been hired to take care of the central heating system of the building. I cannot recall the exact date but it must have been in the early '40s. It was lunchtime when the door bell rang. Since I happened to be nearby (I rarely answered the door) I opened the front door. There stood a young man of about 16 years old, tall and dark but speaking in a strange dialect. He said he was coming from one of the cities of eastern Turkey where father was the representative at the National Assembly. He said he wanted to see my father. I took him in and informed my father of the young man's arrival. It turned out that Father had met him during a political rally and seeing that he was a brilliant young man asking for Father's help to find a job, Father had given him his calling card with his Ankara address. After having a chat with him in his office, Father announced that 'Haşim' was to work for us, taking care of the central heating system of the building. This young man was both brilliant and industrious. He used to come up for meals. One day when he did not show up for dinner, Mother was worried. She said, "The boy could be sick" and went down to the basement. She was shocked to find Haşim in his room, crying with a book in his hand. The young man had a Turkish translation of Dale Carnegie's famous book in his hand. When he noticed Mother's caring attitude, he started begging, "Please help me to study for a diploma." Mother was utterly touched. It turned out that he had only had primary school education in his remote village. At once all sorts of books and pen and paper were purchased for him. And of course we all gave him

56

a hand. Thus, while working for us the young man completed his secondary schooling, as well as high school. Sometime after his graduation from the Lycee, he found a job in the bus company managed by the municipality of Ankara. He was always loyal to the family. The last we heard from him was an invitation to his son's wedding.

When the family moved to Ankara Grandfather declined to come with us and preferred to stay in Erenköy. Mme. Eleni, a cook's help, and a chambermaid were left back for his care. During all holidays we used to go there as well. The garden looked beautiful in winter. Since we had central heating, watching the falling snow over the huge pine trees, without being cold, was delightful. Naturally we also played snow balls and loved hiking with Mother.

Meanwhile I had gotten used to living in Ankara. Although I still missed my friends in İstanbul, I enjoyed my friends and my life in Ankara. I also had a new piano teacher in Ankara. The wife of the well-known violin player, Mrs. Leylâ Atak was an excellent teacher. It was fun being with this lady who was of German origin and I enjoyed piano playing even better on account of her.

Although Turkey was never in actual war, as a very harsh war was taking place all around us, we too had begun to experience some hardships, however minor! Both in Erenköy (namely İstanbul) and in Ankara there was curfew at nights. All windows were covered with dark blue papers so as to prevent light from showing. Many foods were rationed. Even so, the bread we used to buy was full of funny materials and the flour was almost black. This kind of dark bread was very bad for my father's ulcers and he developed horrid pains. The governor of Ankara was a very close friend of the family. One day Mother told me to visit the governor's family, explain Father's plight and ask if he could find us some white flour. I did as I was told. The governor was at home. He listened to my tale and was very sorry for my father. However, he took me by the hand and took me to his kitchen and showed that they also had the same flour. I guess he wanted to convince me. I felt thoroughly ashamed as a result.

In the meantime I was making more friends as time went on. The Karl Ebert family used to reside opposite our apartment.

So I had met Karl Ebert's daughter, Renata, and through her, her very good friend Uta. Both of them were very intelligent and well-educated young girls. I always remember the tea table Mrs. Ebert brought out for us with delicious cakes she would bake. At home, Maestro Ebert was a jovial and kind gentleman. Our friendship with these young girls was mostly based on art. We would listen to classical music, analyze books we had read or exchange ideas on painting, etc.

I had a most pleasant life during those years. In spring, when the weather was agreeable, we would cycle to the tennis club and play tennis. During the week we sometimes did the same before school hours. On the weekends we would spend the whole day at the club. On those days Mother would also come to the club. Naturally she would join her acquaintances in conversations but this would also give her a chance to supervise me. I will never forget the advice she once gave me. She told me never to confide my innermost feelings to my friends, however close they might be, instead share these feelings with the stars at night! She would be quick to notice if I was interested in someone. By giving me this advice she was, I believe, trying to protect me from useless gossip. Thus, I also learned to keep other people's secrets. I never repeated things confided to me. Gossiping was never tolerated in our house. Father, who shunned any kind of gossip, had even sold his car when the family had moved to Ankara. After all, Ankara was still a small town and very few people had private cars. We, the young ones, could walk everywhere and/or use our bicycles almost everywhere, and when it was inevitable we used the public busses. Mother had never used public transportation, and would take a taxi wherever she went. She would walk than go on a crowded bus. She had developed a peculiar philosophy about this. She used to say, "I love my home anyway. If I can't afford to get a taxi, I can happily stay at home." She kept her way, until her last day. Actually she was very free with her money and tipped every driver profusely. Many a time taxi drivers whose cars she used would ring the bell in the morning and asked Mother for a start-up tip. They would say her money brought them luck! Father, on the other hand, would mostly walk and only in bad weather use the busses.

Mother had separated her bedroom from Father's for two reasons. Well, maybe the reasons were three. First of all, Mother smoked cigarettes. Father on the contrary had never touched tobacco, let alone smoke. The second reason was that Mother loved to read in bed whereas father did not. The third reason was Mother loved to linger in bed in the mornings. She would ring for her coffee when she woke up and would read the morning papers in bed. Father was an early riser. As soon he woke up, he would shave, clean up and dress. As a matter of fact, I never saw him unshaved or in his pajamas or the robe de chambre, except perhaps when he was sick and in bed. Nevertheless, Mother, even if still be in bed, always combed and braided my hair and kissed us good-bye before we went to school. This ritual went on for many years. We were a family full of love. Years later I was to sadly realize that this was something that my mother had kept alive.

The Halkevi (People's House) in those days was a very important center for culture. The Halkevi under the direction of Mr. F. C. Güven had become for me a window through which I was able to view the world. My first experience at the Halkevi was a performance called Kervan (Caravan), which was staged by a professor of theatre and wherein I was given a small part to play. On that stage, several famous or famous-to-be people had taken place, among us students.

Apart from such local activities I was able to attend the performances of actors like Jean Marais and Jean Cocteau on the same stage. I was even able to obtain their autographed pictures. One of my most valuable memories of the Halkevi was the piano recital the famous Mr. Paderewski gave us. That was quite an experience. I was sick with smallpox at a rather late age. My parents had bought tickets for the concert months earlier, naturally. When the time came for the recital date I was still not quite well. So Mother was very much against my going. However, I made such a fuss and cried so much that she had to give in and I was able to attend the concert even if still not fully recovered. Gradually my friends and I were on the way of becoming young girls. Our personalities were getting into shape and our interests were developing, as well as our tastes in dressing up. We were going to concerts and theatre shows and also

59

being invited to parties. One of the things I liked to do on Sunday mornings was to go hiking with Jale's father. I also loved to be invited to Jale's house for lunch. Her mother was an ideal wife and mother, who loved having her family around the table. It was a meal full of laughter and fun with her four kids.

Our group of five girls had become very close. This was a time when we had become aware of the young men around us and had begun to enjoy showing ourselves off. Sometimes we would dress up and go to a movie, and at other times, we would be cycling as a group. In that part of the city, there were several pastry shops and some university clubs where handsome young men would congregate. So we liked to parade in front of these places on our bikes.

One day a uniformed policeman stopped me and told me it was illegal to cycle in that part of the street. I was quite annoyed and surprised. Sometime later I learned that Mother had noticed our parades and asked the family friend, the governor, to put a stop to this. That was his way of putting a stop, at least, to my parading. When summer came we moved back to Erenköy. Before our tours with other youngsters and ice cream parlor days started, Mother made sure to get Mme. Lesyak, my old governess! Thus I was forced to have a governess until I was sixteen.

World War II was still raging in the year 1942-43. A young diplomat who the family knew well had just gotten married and the newlyweds were planning a honeymoon in Vienna. Taking this as an opportunity, Father said to Mother, "Why don't you take Şen to Europe before war obliterates everything." Naturally, he wanted me to see the places mother had lived in as a very young woman. So we joined this couple on their trip. The four of us boarded the famous Orient Express from İstanbul.

Our first stop was Sofia. A friend of Cenan's and a councellor at the Turkish Embassy in Bulgaria had been informed of our arrival. He kindly came to meet us at the station and invited us all to his home. Mother knew this young man since he was a boy at St. Joseph, together with my brother, and he used to visit our house frequently. We all liked him very much and while my brother was away he had acted as an elder brother to me. That evening he took Mother and I to a restaurant-night club called the "Arizona Bar." It was quite an "in" place in Sofia. After dinner they elevated the dancing floor, which was quite a surprise for me. I had previously danced at some open-air casinos during the summer months but had never danced in a nightclub and more than that never on an elevated and turning dancing floor. This was quite an experience for me. Our trip had a good start. However, the next day, while strolling in the city, where the young diplomat had taken us. I was shocked to see many people with yellow stars attached to their lapels. They all walked quickly and obviously were under great stress. To my question the answer simply was, "They are Jewish people." This was the first time I had come face to face with the barbarism that Hitler was applying in Europe.

On the evening of our second day, we went onboard our train once more. Our next stop was Bucharest. However, we did not leave the train at that stop and many soldiers boarded the Orient Express. They were a motley crowd. The German officers were very well dressed and polite but very serious looking. The Rumanian soldiers were very badly dressed; with their long hair and beards they were somehow frightening. The Italians, carrying musical instruments like guitars, mandolins, etc., looked frightened, sad, and some had tears in their eyes. During passport control the officers were so rude that I got scared while Mother and the married couple were aghast! The train had been filled over its capacity with only the German officers being given seats. Of course this soured our trip to no end. After a while the train started and then suddenly would stop in the middle of nowhere. Then we would start again in jolts. It was pitch dark outside. All of a sudden, from the noises going on, we realized that our wagon had been taken over the rails aboard a boat.

We could not understand what was going on. We later learned that we had crossed the river on a boat during the night. The same procedure was repeated in the morning and finally we had arrived to Budapest from "Curcia." We had to go through another unbelievable and detailed custom's inspection. At long last we were allowed to go to the city. Since we made many previous reservations, we took a taxi directly to the Hotel Gellert. There were very few cars on the streets. We saw many people walking with those horrible yellow stars on their lapels, like the ones in Sofia. However, our hotel was comfortable and the weather outside was brilliant. The diplomat traveling with us made a few phone calls and in a short while we were delighted to meet a lovely couple. The Reisners were Hungarian. Mr. Reisner was an elderly but elegant gentleman, while his wife was young and beautiful. He had a position at the Turkish Embassy. At the time, our ambassador in Bucharest had introduced Mr. Reisner to the Turkish Embassy in Budapest and through his advice they had given him a post. In this manner they were being protected since they were of Jewish extraction and would have to wear the dreaded yellow stars otherwise. This lovely couple were also staying in a very large suite at the Gellert Hotel. They helped us a lot during our sightseeing tours in the city. Sometimes both of them, but mostly Eva Reisner, became our guide. They were both very well educated and spoke several languages. It was quite obvious that they were very well off.

In one such trip in the city, Eva took us to a jewelry shop that sold semi-precious jewelry. When we were introduced to the owner, we learned that he was the father of the well-known movie star Zsa Zsa Gabor. He was of fair skin, rather fat, his hair thinning but nevertheless quite a handsome man The elderly man complained bitterly about his wife and daughters, who had deserted him and gone to the United States. Mother, who had known Zsa Zsa, while she lived in Ankara as a Turkish diplomat's wife, tried to pacify the old and bitter gentleman.

On another day, Eva invited us to her suite. I was quite surprised! One piece of the suite was assigned to be her dressing room. There was a closet containing only her fur coats. I mean there were all kinds—astrakhan, chinchilla, mink, leopard, ocelot, fox, etc. In another closet were hanging all sorts of evening dresses, all made by well-known fashion designers. Yet in another closet there were dresses and suits for day wear. Boxes full of hats, many pairs of shoes, many kinds of handbags, purses, gloves, etc. in various closets. An unbelievable richness! But the original wealth of this couple was in their personalities. They both were modest, generous, helpful, warm-hearted people. Of course they never said a word, but one could discern in their sad eyes their fright of being Jewish during this horrible wartime. We had heard later on, after our return to Turkey, that they had lost everything they owned and took shelter at the Turkish Embassy. Many years later, it was by luck that we met this couple again in İstanbul and I had all my trousseau done at her house.

We were in Budapest in 1943, during the months of March and April. Spring was lovely there. Our efforts were to no avail and we could not travel to Vienna under the circumstances. So Mother tried to show me the places she had enjoyed in Budapest during her youth. She had the shock of her life at the first place she took me. She had told me that there was a most lovely hotel situated on Margaret Island. However, when our taxi arrived on the island we were most disagreably surprised. The hotel had been turned into some sort of a hospital and was full of crippled people. Those were soldiers who had been wounded during the war. Men who had only one leg, another without any, a man with no hands, patients whose eyes were tied. We were in deep sadness and depression looking at those poor young men. The lovely place she liked so much had been turned into a recuperation center for crippled soldiers. So Mother had to give up and tried to show me the beautiful parks and other natural phenomena. Not only nature was beautiful but it also had effected the ladies living there. I have never again encountered so many beautiful women as I encountered in Budapest.

Despite all the ravages of the war, the people in the city were still very kind, smiling and polite. All food was rationed, the Jewish people wore the yellow stars but it did not matter. They were still alive, they were trying to survive and enjoy what they had. And they were wearing this inside beauty with the world around them. They did not care anymore, just tried to survive.

Many years later, in 1963 to be exact, I went to Budapest again. This time they had soldiers with guns in their hands and frightening faces. They searched us all over. We found out that the hotel on Margaret Island was once again a hotel but the guests were mostly Russian officers. These people did not even know how to eat properly. They were all drunk and actually we saw some acting improperly with the poor, odd looking women without the need to reach their rooms. They were quite away from being anything refined. We could hardly spend one night in that beautiful place. The restaurants were another misery. Hungry people with sad eyes were looking through the windows while people were eating inside. I could hardly bring myself to have a bite.

In the old days our "Republic Holiday" was celebrated with an official ball at the Ankara Palace Hotel. It was also sort of a "Coming Out" party for the young girls of Ankara Society who had reached their eighteenth birthday. As I was going to be that age next year, Mother thought she should get me my evening gown while we were in Budapest. Through the kind intervention of Eva we obtained a rendezvous with the well-known fashion designer "Firstner" and had my dress made. There was also a very famous pastry shop on "Vaci Utsa" called "Zserbo." Who is who in Budapest was said to have tea there in the afternoons. We loved going there also.

Although we could not make it to Vienna, we were at least able to have a taste of Europe. After a whole month we had come to the end of our travel. Using the same route back we reached our peaceful country. This trip had been most instructive for me. I had learned a lot and my sense of values as well as my outlook toward the world had changed.

One of the places my family visited often in Ankara was the "Gazi Farm," which was built under the supervision of Atatürk. This was a large farm where we could take long walks and relax at the tea house or have lunch at the restaurant. Another place the family enjoyed going was the restaurant called "Karpich." It was actually the best restaurant in Ankara. Aside from the delicious food served there, and the atmosphere of the place, the elegant style of Mr. Karpich welcoming his guests was legendary. It was said that the owner, Mr. Karpich, was a White Russian immigrant who previously had been a high ranking officer of the Russian Army. He had escaped to Turkey during the revolution in Russia and had ended up in Ankara. He was a large and fat man, with a completely bald, round head. His eyes, under the heavy half-closed eyelids, twinkled when he looked at a guest. Invariably he would be wearing a White Russian tunic made of silk and despite his weight he would swiftly welcome and take his customers to their tables. His maitre d'hotel was also a White Russian called Serge. After receiving the customers' orders he would quickly disappear. While people were waiting for their orders to be served, Mr. Karpich would suddenly approach the table with a cup of caviar and/or some thinly sliced fish eggs or some other delicacy, which was on the house, and thus show his respect and appreciation for his customers. Whenever we went there with my parents, knowing that I adored it, Mr. Karpich would offer us caviar. He had shown the same delicate attention, many years later, when I was a grown up young girl.

Once, during her stay in Ankara, we had gone to Karpich Restaurant with my childhood friend Şeyda. We were waiting for our order when suddenly the waiter placed a large bowl of caviar on our table. Şeyda and I had agreed to split the cost of our lunch. We were delighted to see the caviar but we were aware that we could not afford the cost of black caviar. As we were looking at the bowl rather hungrily and at each other skeptically, "Baba" (as he was usually called) Karpich suddenly appeared at our table and with a large smile said, "Eat it, it is on the house"—and discreetly disappeared. Naturally, we gleefully devoured the bowl of caviar.

In later years, when we went to his locale night club-restaurant, "Serge's," Mr. Süreyya (Serge) continued this tradition of offering us special treats. He was a very extraordinary restaurateur. He knew how to treat people in accordance to their time of arrival and to their various tastes. He would always offer something one could not refuse. Mr. Serge's taste and choices hardly ever failed.

At long last the day had arrived for me to wear the evening gown that had been specially tailored for me in Budapest. The colour of the material used was green. The dress had a square décolleté, short sleeves and a full-length skirt. Handmade pink roses with green leaves were sewn irregularly all over the dress. Two young men, whose parents were loved and respected friends of my parents, were living in Ankara during that year. Both of them were well-educated and refined people and they had been allowed, separately, to accompany me at various occasions. They were regular guests at our house. One would take me to the horse races and the other would take me, say to a movie, a concert or play tennis with me. On certain occasions, like my birthdays, they were allowed to make me a gift of a book or a decorative article to put in my room.

Knowing that I would be attending the ball with my parents, both of these young men had offered to be my dancing partner. I had to make a choice between these two nice people, who had never met each other and that was a most difficult task. I liked them both very much and I enjoyed and valued their friendship. On the other hand, my feelings toward them were not sentimental. I was lucky. One of them was forced to go on a trip that week. My other friend had arranged to have "tails" to be made in order to wear on that occasion. Naturally, several lovely young girls would be attending the ball and all of us were to be "introduced" to the society of the day. We were all very excited (all wondering in anticipation what would happen that night). Finally dancing started and contrary to all my expectations, I found myself dancing with an important, retired general instead of my escort. I also was pleasantly surprised to notice that this, to my mind elderly, general was a better dancer than most of the young men around. I felt honored that he had chosen me and always relished the occasion. All of us girls danced so much that night that finally we were all sitting on the stairs of the hotel from sheer exhaustion.

Following this, so to speak, "coming out" ball my life began to change. For example, I was expected to accompany my mother on her visits to our president's wife. Mrs. İnönü on her "at home days" was the perfect hostess. Despite the crowd, she would take especial care to talk with every guest, enquire about their health, their personal concerns, children, etc. She would also make sure, supervising the personnel, that the service of tea was made properly. Her elegant posture and modest but elegant attire always impressed me.

Religious holidays were very special days for me. Our house would be flooded with guests. As the young daughter of the family, it was my duty to make the guests comfortable and offer them candy or the traditional Turkish delights and Turkish coffee. Years later I was to learn that a large part of the horde of visitors were due not to personal relations, but rather to the position one held in society. When Father resigned from his position in the parliament and also from his beloved political party,

66

those numbers dwindled most dramatically. There is an adage in Turkish that can be interpreted as, "The offerings are for the outer garments (the fur coat) and not for the real person inside the garment."

It is very sad that I never had the chance of meeting Atatürk in person. I always felt his presence and was thankful for all that he had done for my country and for all of us. Especially for us, the Turkish women. I regret that I never had the chance to thank him personally. My only satisfaction is that I have always tried, as a Turkish woman and as a mother, to be worthy of this great person, Mustafa Kemal Atatürk.

On the other hand I had the chance of meeting Mrs. Latife Uşşakizade, who for some years had been the wife of Ataürk, personally and close enough to be allowed to call her "Aunt Latife." Her father, Mr. Uşşakizade was a close friend of my father. Moreover, since father had been the press attaché to Atatürk for some years, he had had the chance of meeting her personally during their married years. This close relationship continued for a lifetime. Whenever we went visiting to her mansion in İstanbul with my parents, we always made sure to bring her favourite "eau de cologne," 4711. Her sisters, Mrs. İlmen and Mrs. Açıkalın, were also close family friends. For me, especially Mr. Uşşakizade's visits to our house, were delightful days. I would jump into his arms. I guess children can understand quickly when they are being loved and by whom. Therefore I felt his love and affection toward me. I also thought that he was most handsome.

Each time we went to İstanbul, Mother made a point of visiting Aunt Latife. She was living in a beautiful mansion overlooking the Marmara Sea. Her garden was always full of flowers and tall trees. Although she was a tiny woman, her personality always projected and her femininity came forward. She was very much beyond the reach of those around her and I very much appreciated her innate grandeur. She was highly educated, very modest in her attire and was very lonely in her own world. She had accepted her destiny with equanimity and she never complained. However, I always felt that she was sad. Despite the fact that I was almost a child when we first met, she always greeted me as a grown-up person. Sometimes her adorable mother would also join us during our visit. I remember reading somewhere an anecdote concerning Shakespeare and his mother. It appears that Shakespeare once had said, "My mother was a big woman." Some elderly person who had met the lady when she was alive, objected to his words, saying, "But your mother was tiny." So Shakespeare simply answered, "She may have been tiny in size, but nevertheless she was big." Just the same way, for me, Latife Hanım was a great lady." It was impossible not to be filled with respect and excitement when she entered a room.

I believe I have already mentioned that one of her sisters, who was Gen. İlmen's daughter-in-law, the young Mrs. İlmen, although younger in years, she was the protecting angel of everyone within her sphere. Very well educated, always elegant and very warmhearted, she was loved by everybody. The youngest sister, Mrs. Açıkalın, was very tiny, beautiful and like her beautiful elder sisters, intelligent and well educated. Her husband was the secretary general of the foreign office. They had a son and a daughter. Their daughter was too young to be playing with us but their son was about our age so we used to play with him, my brother and I. They had a house on the top of the hill in Ankara. We were already young girls when one of Mrs. Açıkalın's nieces was visiting her aunt, we were both invited to a reception to be given by the Açıkalıns. The party was for the diplomatic corps of foreign countries. Naturally, Turkish diplomats would also attend this reception. Mr. Secretary General jokingly said to us, "You two young girls must also come and look over the young men in the foreign office." We were delighted to have this chance of meeting young and upcoming diplomats. However, events turned out to be quite different. The young blades of the foreign office were much more interested in the elderly wives of the ambassadors, as they were hoping to get promoted. Those young diplomats were good-looking and nice but they preferred to dance with those ladies that we unsparingly called "the old bags." How mean one is when young!

Since I am recalling various incidents that took place in Ankara during those years, I would like to mention a rather remarkable occasion. A family friend, who was also the publisher of a daily newspaper whom I liked very much when I was a little girl, was visiting us in Ankara as well. This certain day he came together with a colleague, who also had made a name for himself in the media of the day. Mother was rather depressed those days since she had not received any letters lately from her eldest son, who was a student at M.I.T. They were discussing with their guests, predetermination and predestination. Somehow the conversation went on to trances and séances where spirits from the other world could be called in to join. My favorite writer mentioned that he was arranging such séances in his home. Mother showed a keen interest and they said they would invite her the next time they arranged such a séance. Of course I would not miss such a chance and begged to be included. So a date was decided. We were to meet at one of the gentleman's house. The day finally arrived. I cannot recall now what they were, but there were some conditions to be met. The four of us sat around a flat wooden table. Our arms were extended on the surface of the table, with our fingers touching one another. The lights were lowered and we were waiting in anticipation. Presumably Mother was hoping to obtain information about her beloved son in the United States of America. Then suddenly the gentleman I called uncle, started intoning with a very low and baritone voice. He was saying something like, "Oh! Spirit! Please stay away if you are from the devil but approach if you are peaceful." I could no longer stand this and I could not help myself doing what I did. It sounded so ludicrous that I burst out laughing. Suddenly the low voice changed and I heard him shouting, "Get out, get out of this room at once." Naturally I was already running out and laughing at the same time. That was the end of the séance and as far as I know Mother never attended another such meeting.

Nur had graduated from the Lycée. He had been registered to the law school of Ankara University. He felt very miserable since he had no say in this choice. Father had made the decision. Sometime later Father realized that his son was not happy with what he was doing, so he decided to send him the United States and alongside of his brother. His point was that the two brothers would back each other in their studies and Nur would study in the field of his choice. On the other hand, this posed a big problem for Mother. Aside from her weakness for her younger son, she was still treating and protecting him as a little boy. It was bad enough to have one son away from home, now it would be that both of her sons would be so far away! At the end she had no choice but to accept this situation. So Nur left for America.

Finally, despite the travel difficulties caused by the ongoing war, the two brothers were able to meet in Boston. In the meantime the atmosphere in our house started to become unbearable. Now Mother was awaiting news from both her sons. Cenan had found a place for Nur to live and had helped him register at the Graduate School of Architecture at Harvard University. So Nur who had always wanted to become an architect, had finally found the school he wished to attend. On the other hand, their situation was not satisfactorily settled. Cenan was of the opinion that Nur should be left on his own, so that his personality should develop properly. He was giving his little brother a hand when needed. Cenan had studied mechanical engineering at M.I.T., getting his M.S. in air conditioning. Now he had started his doctorate thesis, so he had a very tight schedule and little time to spare. It was also true that he was some years older than Nur and had been on his own abroad for a long time. He had naturally developed his own circle of friends. On the other hand, Nur was brought up with a lot of attention and was very much attached to Mother. Being left on his own was not something he could enjoy, much less handle. He felt lonely and discarded. So Nur started to develop a yearning for home. He was homesick and wanted to go back.

V

Cairo and Port Said

Now it was Mother crying her eyes out each time she had a letter from Nur. She kept insisting and pleading that Nur should return home. Since the war was still going on, it had been quite a problem sending him there. He had been forced to go to Cairo and spent a lot of time there before he was able to find passage for the U.S. Finally, he was able to reach Boston and was able to register at the Harvard School of Architecture. This would give him the possibility to become an architect as he always yearned for. Father wanted Nur to stay in America and not return until he had his degree. He believed Nur would get accustomed to his surroundings, given some more time.

As these discussions were going on in the house, it appears that Father had asked Mr. Abdülhalik Renda for his advice and opinion. Mr. Renda was a portly gentleman who always talked very slowly with a deep voice. He was an ideal father figure and loveable man in every respect. He always influenced people with his magnanimity and I always felt very close to him. After listening to my father's tale of woe, apparently Mr. Renda asked, "What does Şen say to all this?" Not expecting such a question, Father was rather taken aback. However, Mr. Renda continued by adding, "Şen has a good mind on her shoulders, bring her to me and let us get her opinion." So the next day Father took me to his house in Çankaya.

I just realized that in many instances I have been mentioning visits to "so and so's house" most of the time. In those days, people lived in houses. The modern apartment building had not conquered all, as yet. Today, even in the resort town of Antalya we are surprised to see people living in private homes.

Everybody has a flat. I really regret this. I find modern civilization and people's ambitions are depriving them from many fine things of the old days.

Mr. Renda, an important figure in the government, had me sit by his side and simply asked, "What is your opinion regarding the problem of your elder brother Nur?" I was not expecting this but on the other hand I knew what the problem was. I said it would be a great pity for Nur not to complete his studies but it was too much to ask his elder brother Cenan, who was doing his own doctorate thesis, to take care of Nur and forgo his own studies. So one good solution would be for Mother to go to the States and live with her sons for some time. At the same time, I felt sure that I could be of help to my father and run our house while Mother was away. I never forgot that scene. Uncle Renda got up, came and kissed me on both cheeks and turned to my father. "I told you, Şen would find the right solution, try your best to send Cemile Hanımefendı to the States."

Father was really taken aback. Mother's going to Boston would of course be good for Nur, however, the war was still on and such a trip could be very difficult. On the other hand, he had the greatest confidence in Mr. Renda and would like to do as he suggested. At first he almost scolded me by saying, "Where did you get this idea of sending your mother away?" However, by the time we reached home he must have thought things over and his first words to Mother were, "Congratulations, Cemile Sultan, it was decided that you should go to your son." Suddenly tears started running from Mother's eyes. But her happiness was short lived. Mother asked, "What happens to Şen?" and she added, "How can I leave my young daughter by herself and go away for such a long period of time? You are spending most of your time at the parliament with your fellow parliamentarians. We have a male cook and Saadet Hanım (Sütne, a woman who had been with us many years) running the house. Who would take care of my Şen when I am gone?" Father and Mother were both facing a dilemma. I did not know what to say anymore. Then Father started making plans to send both of us to America. Questions of finding passage, of financing such a difficult trip and staying bereft of his family in Ankara all by himself were some of the questions bothering Father. Soon he told us that he had solved the financial side of the problem. He had been able to raise the amount necessary for such a trip. He had gotten in touch with a family in the States who wanted to make financial aid to their relations in Turkey. So they would pay us the dollars that they would be sending to Turkey and Father would pay the equivalent of this aid in Turkish liras in Turkey to the recipients. He would be willing to stay by himself in Ankara, hoping that Mother's arrival in the States would solve Nur's problems and that Mother and I should return to Turkey as soon as possible. Father then started looking for a safe passage for us to travel. Finally he was able to arrange for us to board a British military plane flying to Cairo. Some sort of a similar financial arrangement with some people in Cairo was made so that Mother and I would not face difficulties during our stay there. Naturally, the news of our arrival had reached Cenan and Nur and had pacified them somewhat. After a rather hectic flight across the Mediterranean we found ourselves in Cairo. It was a small plane and we were the only passengers. Furthermore, this was the first time both Mother and I had flown in a plane in all our lives. Naturally, we were both very uneasy and quite scared during the flight.

We had been booked to stay at a good hotel called the Continental Savoy in Cairo. My good friend Cemile (Garan), who had just been married, was also in Cairo for her honeymoon. Mother and I first called on our ambassador. This was defined as a courtesy visit. Numan Tahir Bey had already received news of our arrival. He promised to help us find a passage to America and was good enough to invite us to dinner a couple of times during our stay in Cairo. In the meantime, I was able to get hold of Cemile. Now she was a married lady and it felt odd to see her with her husband. But even so, it felt good to find a friend. We tried to get together as much as we could. During our stay in Cairo we met the well-known singer Münir Nurettin Selcuk and his wife, as well as some other famous couples. Apart from them there was the manager of the Anatolian Press Agency, resident in Cairo and his family. Another young man we met in Cairo was İlhan Unat, who was trying to find passage to Europe. Later he became a professor at Ankara University and married Professor Nermin (Abadan) Unat, with whom I have been able to develop a long-lasting relationship. We all were trying to find ways to get out of Egypt to different destinations.

We were also lucky to find Princess Ziba and her husband Esat Fuat Tugay in Cairo. Leyla Mardin Hanımefendi was a resident of Cairo. She had a magnificent townhouse in the Maadi Quarter of Cairo called "Villa Flora." Another good friend of Father's was Mr. Selahattin Refik, who owned the best antique store in Cairo. I was really amazed when we entered his shop called "Dar Sırmalı." I had never seen such a magnificent store before. One entered a huge salon through a very ornate wooden door. There were valuable rugs spread on the floor in the building and over some marble steps. At the foot of the stairs, on two sides, there were huge Ming vases that were as tall as I was. In both vases there were very tall stemmed roses. I had never seen such tall stemmed roses before and they smelled divinely. There were two luxurious salons on each side of the large entrance hall and again in the huge salon that covered the whole building on the second floor one came across a most unbelievable collection of all kinds of antiques. There were Lalique vases, special plates, all sorts of gadgets and valuable gold and silver candle bars. It certainly was a paradise for an antique lover. Uncle Refik, remembering that I liked Lalique best, years later gave me a beautiful Lalique service plate as a wedding gift, which I still use.

As I have already mentioned, Mr. Sirmali was a friend of my father's from way back, when they were young. He was a thick set man, rather short but heftily built, his head was completely bald, his eyes resembled a fish and he was always smiling. He was a very elegant, well-dressed and a highly educated gentleman. He was also a very generous man who never cared for money, so much so that he had been bankrupt more than once, only to start all over again with the backing of his many friends. Being with him in Cairo had actually effected my taste in things and had changed my attitude toward life. He had furthermore influenced my taste in food and I had my first whisky with him. He introduced me to asparagus, a vegetable that I still cherish more than any other. No doubt one of the best things

74

that happened to me was to be able to meet the people that I mentioned before and the ones that have escaped my memory.

Mrs. Leyla Mardin was one of those persons that I had the good fortune to meet. She was very generous and always very elegant. I remember that I had the wish to grow up and become someone like her. I cherish her memory with great respect and admiration. Naturally I do not think that I grew up to be someone like her at all. Personalities differ so much. One day she had sent her driver to pick us up from the hotel where we were staying and had us driven to her sumptuous house in the Maadi Quarter. The big door was opened by a black African footman dressed all in white, who took us in almost ceremoniously. A little further in the house, seated in her wheelchair with a most engaging smile on her face, was our hostess greeting us. I was instantly smitten. She deftly moved her wheelchair and took her place in the corner of the big salon. I was interested to note two things. On one side she had a number of books, all within her reach, in various languages and on the other side was her knitting, she had half finished a woolen scarf for her grandchild. She was exemplary in her speech, her courtesy, and the way she received guests. When she took us in for lunch, the table had been laid in a most lovely manner. The table cloth and the napkins were all what they call "dantelle anglais," the plates were very thin porcelain painted with scattered flowers on them. All the cutlery was very heavy silver. The food served was especially chosen for lunch and everything we ate was very tasty. The table was served by black footmen, all dressed in white, including white gloves, who almost glided around the table from guest to guest. Conversation at that lunch table as is directed by protocol, excluded politics, religion and sickness, but covered all other subjects of the day.

During our stay in Cairo we were lucky to be with her many times. Each time we met, my appreciation of her heightened. She learned my date of birth and asked us to celebrate my birthday as her guests. During that party she gave me a very ornate and heavy silver bracelet and also a leather bound old copy of the *Complete Works of William Shakespeare*. The bracelet was stolen later on but I still cherish the book, it has a special place in my library. I hope that after me, my children or grandchildren will enjoy that book. I have always been a lover of books. Both Mother and my various tutors had helped me to develop an appreciation for books. I had first started reading books like *Zig et Puce* or *Becacine* in French. They were followed by books like *Le Petit Prince* or *Alice in Wonderland*. I remember reading *The Little Prince* as a married woman as well, on and off or reading it aloud to my children. Then followed the classics, as I was growing up. Russian, English, French classics in various languages always adorned my library. Since Father, assuming that reading at night was bad for the eyes, had forbidden my reading at night, I remember reading my books under the blankets with the help of a small flashlight. Music and books have always been my best companions.

Cairo was a very cosmopolitan city full of all kinds of people. On one side were the king and the very rich people, on the other side were the down-and-out (street beggars) who did not have even the energy to chase off the flies that kept getting in and out of their eyes. Again I was amazed to see the English and American officers in their impeccable uniforms sauntering along the boulevards. It certainly was an amazing crowd. There were a number of luxury clubs in the Maadi Quarter. We were invited to some of them a couple of times. There was even an Ottoman Prince, called Farouk Efendi, who always appeared at the best places. He was an unbelievably good-looking gentleman. Egypt at the time was governed by King Farouk. Whenever he left his palace a long cavalcade of limousines followed him. We had seen him from the sidewalk as his cars whisked him away. Every day he would be riding limousines in different colors. One day all the limousines would be white and the next day they would all be black and on the third day they would all be blue.

One evening Princess Ziba and her husband Esat Fuat Tugay Beyefendi had taken us to a restaurant called "Oberge des Piramids." As our dinner was coming to its end there was a commotion and a crowd of people came into the restaurant. When they were seated we understood that King Farouk and his entourage had come in for a late dinner. The king was a grossly fat fellow with very small spectacles with dark lenses. Years ago, when he was installed as the King of Egypt, I remember seeing his pictures in magazines. He was a dashing young man in a splendid white uniform. I was wondering how such a slim young man had turned into this obese fellow, when the princess said to us in an urgent manner, "Quickly, you must disappear through the back door." Esat Tugay was instantly up and he guided me toward the back door of the restaurant and I was quickly bundled into their private limousine. I was too astonished to understand what was going on. The car went around to the main entrance and there were Princess Ziba and Mother! It appears that the king was interested in young girls and especially in young Turkish girls. The princess was quick to realize that behind his dark glasses his attention had been diverted to our table. He had said something to one of his aides and that person had begun walking toward our table. The king had also displayed his respects to Princess Ziba, who was his aunt, by bowing his head to her. The princess had realized that I was about to be invited to the king's table and that it would be almost impossible to refuse such an invitation. So she had quickly sent me off through the back door together with her husband, to where the restrooms also were situated. The envoy the king had sent came casually to our table and asked about me and where I had gone. Mother was of course frightened out of her wits. The princess, who had been prepared for this, calmly told the gentleman that I had suddenly been taken sick and that her husband had taken me to the ladies' room. When we failed to show up some time later, the princess told the gentleman that my sickness must have been worse than what they had expected and that her husband must have taken me to a doctor's office. Since Mother was worried about my condition, the two ladies had quickly left the restaurant. In a way, the bird had flown away. So this is my small story of the ugly king who was dethroned after the war. Many years later, when I was walking on Via Venetto in Rome, I had seen the man again. The dethroned King Farouk was drunk and had an ugly street walker with him. It certainly was a pitiful sight. Why do people destroy themselves with debauchery when they could be high and mighty.

We were forced to stay in Cairo for three months. Every morning we used to get up wondering if we would be lucky to find passage that day. When we knew there was no hope for that day, then we would start making arrangements to see some friends or do something else. After seeing the Mosque of Mehmet Ali Pascha had built, we visited all the pyramids of Giza, Cheops and the Sphinx. Each one was more interesting than the other. Especially the Pyramid of Cheops, which is considered one of the wonders of the world. It was impossible for us to understand how people with almost no mechanical tools could have cut all those stones and built those great edifices by sheer manpower. We also tried riding on a camel. It was quite an experience. You get on top of the animal when he is sitting. Then it begins to get up. It first goes on its hind legs so you begin sliding toward the front of the animal's neck, until it gets fully up. Not only was I frightened but I also hated the ugly and smelly beasts. Thus my camel riding did not last long. After the short-lived camel ride, I remember that we visited the hotel called Mena House. From its terrace one could see the Sphinx in all its grandeur. We had lunch there. It was quite a popular place since it had a magnificent view of the pyramid and the Sphinx. We were invited there for lunch or tea several times. Many years later I was back in Cairo and stayed at the same hotel. The newly installed "Sight and Sound" show among the pyramids was certainly a reminder of my early visit. By that time the Mena House had been enlarged to a five-star hotel but Cairo was now dirtier than ever.

In the afternoons we would have cocktails at the bar of the hotel and or visit the bar of the Shepard's Hotel where most of the society of Cairo could be observed daily. Among them I remember an Egyptian whose name was Lamlum Pascha, who had married several famous Turkish women. Also the world famous Egyptian singer Abdulvehap would be seen mingling in that crowd. One of the things we enjoyed most was going to the movies. The better houses had air-conditioning and there was no restriction against smoking. That possibility was something Mother enjoyed especially as she liked to smoke. I also enjoyed the films we saw since there was no dubbing and films could be enjoyed in their original versions.

Although we always found something to do, as time went by our patience was getting thinner day by day. We had arrived in Cairo in February and we had been forced to stay there already three months. Also this was costing us too much. We had read in the papers some time earlier that the Allies had landed in Normandy, which was called D-Day. Everyone was saying that the war would soon be over.

One day the Turkish Ambassador called and invited us to lunch with him at his residence. After receiving us graciously and having us seated, he gave Mother a telegram he had received from Turkey. The news touched us both, very deeply. Grandfather, who used to reside at our Erenköy mansion, had passed away following a long bout of flu. He had reached the age of 96 but seemed always so spruce and fit that everyone thought he would last forever. The ambassador was kind enough to leave us by ourselves for a while. Later when we were invited to lunch he gave us the good news. A passage had been arranged for us and our seats had been booked on the train for Port Said for the next morning. The ship we were to board would leave Port Said in a few days, so we should be on hand and ready to sail. Hotel reservations at Port Said had also been arranged. Our delight on receiving this good news had almost dispelled our grievance for having lost someone so dear to our hearts. Mother never lost her sorrow for the kind old man who had given so much support to his only daughter-in-law for so many years. We started packing as soon as we were back at our hotel. Naturally we called all our friends and gave them the good news. Princess Ziba offered to take us to the train station personally. Next morning she actually came to our hotel in her huge limousine, all our luggage was packed into the trunk of the car and off we went. What was more surprising for us was the fact that the car did not stop when we had reached the station. There was red carpeting laid out all the way to the train cars and our car was driving on this carpet. Apparently the king and other members of royal family had this privilege and naturally Princess Ziba also enjoyed this right. As we boarded the train the princess refused to go back and waited until our train had started puffing, to wave us good-bye with her small gloved hand. It was certainly a touching tableaux.

After a few hours of train ride we found ourselves in Port Said, at a small hotel where our room had been booked. Life in Port Said was totally different from Cairo. All we could do in this small port town was to take long walks and go to the movies.

Naturally, every morning our first task was to call on the shipping agent and enquire about our departure. Each time the answer we got was a blank "no news yet." There were a few Turkish students who were also trying to find passage to the States. Since their bookings were made for a later ship, they too were praying for us to go so that their turn would come. I do not recall the number of books I must have read during this prolonged period of waiting. We had spent almost three weeks in Port Said when one morning the shipping agent told us that we would be sailing the next morning. A Liberty ship named S.S. *Arthur Dobbs* would be taking us to America. It was the first ship of its kind travelling without a convoy. We were at the agent's office early in the morning. There we learned that two other ladies of Greek origin would be sailing with us on this ship. They turned out to be young and fine-looking ladies.

VI

Liberty Ship and America

The date was June 5, 1945. There was a gray-looking boat an-
chored in the port. There were hundreds of American soldiers
running about and we were the only (four) ladies. Two officers
met us at the landing and took us directly to the captain's deck.
After climbing many steps we reached the deck and were facing
the captain. He was a man whose hair had gone completely
white. His face was full of wrinkles, being exposed to the wind
for so many years. He seemed to be colorless. His first question
to us all was whether we were ready to start a trip that would
last many days and that there would be no stopping between
Port Said and New York. When we all confirmed our desire to
go he said, "Then follow me." He took us out of his office to a
tiny platform that was supposed to be the promenade deck. On
one side were planks placed on large tin cans. Looking down we
could see a lot of soldiers running around and arguing. When
they saw us above some started waving and others were shouting things we could not understand. Then the captain started
his lecture.

"There are four hundred soldiers on board this ship who had
been fighting all the time since four years. It is not allowed for
you to go around in skirts. You have to do with slacks and decent
tops. You will be allowed to converse with only a couple of officers
that I shall assign and no talking to strangers is allowed. Furthermore, this is the only place where you will be allowed to
have fresh air."

After this curt speech the Captain turned around and
walked back to his command post. The officer who was already
with him took us to our cabin. It was a very small room with
two double-deck beds (one bed on top of the other). He showed

one to us (Mother and me) and said the others would be occupied by the Greek ladies. He left us in this claustrophobic room and left saying that he would come and fetch us at lunch time. There was also a toilet/shower next to our cabin. Mother must have been warned before, since we both had on slacks that morning. The beds looked reasonably clean. We tried to accommodate ourselves as well as we could. The Greek ladies had put on dresses good for hot weather. They had to go through most of their baggage before they could find some slacks. We all sat down on the lower beds (since there was no place else to sit) and wondered about our coming trip. Every one of us had been surprised with the kind of reception we had had. How long would this suffocating trip last? Mother was willing to take any hardship in her stride, so long as she could reach her sons. However, she now regretted the fact that she had decided to take me along on such a difficult and dangerous trip.

A little while later the same officer who had taken us to our cabin came back and took us out to the deck that had been allocated to us. The ship was leaving Port Said. The air was balmy. A warm sun was shining on the glittering and very clean blue sea. We could listen to some soldiers singing below us. All this took place almost a half century ago and it is difficult for me to remember everything. However, there are some vivid memories left and I will try to recount them.

We were having our meals at the captain's mess with the rest of the officers. Everything was being offered to us. I was tasting some of the things offered us for the first time. As an example, I had never eaten scrambled eggs, although we had all sorts of egg meals, this was a novelty for me. Much of the normal American food was new for me also. For example: bacon, ketchup, filter coffee, pasteurized milk, Coca-Cola. It was also the first time I was eating American ice cream, this was quite different from the handmade "kaymakli-vişne" sort of ice cream we used to have at home. I had no difficulty with these new kinds of foods, in fact I enjoyed all of them. Our days were spent peacefully, if not boringly. If we had not had so many books with us, we would probably all have gone mad. There were three officers on board who had declared themselves as our guardian angels. One of them was the ship's doctor. The second one was the ship's engineer and the last one was the engine officer. The Greek ladies seemed to enjoy forming relationships with the soldiers. In our case, every time we went out of our cabin, one of the officers mentioned above, would make sure to accompany us wherever we went, which actually meant most of the time to the small deck allowed us. All of them were Freemasons. I can never forget their decency and the respect they showed us.

The passage through Gibraltar was truly spectacular. I had no idea that the way through was so narrow. The two sides of the Straits were almost closing in. This would be the last piece of land for some time. After a few days at sea, we heard a commotion among the sailors. Everyone was rushing to the port side, all quite excited. Finally they pointed it out to us. It looked like a big metal ball with many protruding metal pieces. It turned out to be a stray mine and if our boat had hit that thing we would surely have sunk. We were lucky to have missed it. This was repeated once again and we began to understand why the captain was sailing so slowly and so cautiously.

Following a few days of calm weather in the Atlantic Ocean we were caught in a serious storm. Huge waves were playing with the military transport vessel as if it was a toy ship. The soldiers had to tie themselves in order to walk on the deck. Almost everyone was sick and even the captain's table was deserted. Mother and the Greek ladies refused to get out of their beds. Being a great lover of the sea I was up and about all the time. I could eat and drink without any difficulty and I preferred not to stay in the cabin with three ailing ladies. We were lucky this terrible storm did not last long.

After twenty-two days of sailing, the shores of America came into our sight. It was very exciting to see the Manhattan skyline, a sight I had only seen in movies or books until that day. I must admit that the sight of the Statue of Liberty was quite breathtaking.

Our guardian officers had told us from the start that they would help us on land as well. After such a long passage they had learned almost everything about us. When I first set foot on land, I thought I was still swinging a little, after being on sea for such a long time. The officers helped us to get a taxi. We went through a very long tunnel and finally reached our predetermined hotel near Penn Station. As soon as we got settled at the bar we tried to reach my brothers on the phone. After talking to Cenan on the phone, Mother was naturally in tears. The officers told us that they would wait with us until Cenan arrived. These men had not seen their families for many years but still they felt bound to keep us out of harm. Cenan had told them that he was starting to drive right away and that the trip would not take more than four hours. So the officers sat with us in the hotel bar until they saw my brothers arrive and our family was united. Only then they would take their leave and go their various ways. Of course names and addresses were exchanged with these great people before they left.

We talked excitedly well into the night with my two brothers. By the time Mother and I went to our room the sun was almost up. I believe our room was on the twenty-fourth floor and we could almost touch the full moon just as it was going down. The windows were sealed. It was a funny feeling. It was as if I could lean out and touch the moon, that is, if the window would open. At last we had reached New York and Mother had finally found her sons. Now, what would happen after this? What were we going to do? Mother and Cenan decided that we should spend one more day in Manhattan and talk over our situation. There was also the question of getting in touch with two family friends residing in New York. One of these was the Manyas and the other was the Çakuş family.

Father and Mother had made some arrangements to ease our lives before we had reached the States to facilitate our life in the U.S.A. However, when we had a family discussion the next morning it was clear that what was planned for in Ankara did not fit the situation in America. Father had suggested that we share a flat with either Cenan or Nur. We soon found out that this was not possible. Cenan had what they call a studio apartment. In short, this was a single room with a small kitchen and bath and it would be impossible for us to move in with him. Nur's situation turned out to be a most unexpected and completely unwanted surprise. He had changed his quarters and had moved to another rooming house and had fallen in love with

84

a girl living in the same house. He had lost all interest in returning home and was not at all interested in sharing a flat with us. Any consideration that he may have had for Mother and me was now completely taken over by this new love of his. To make matters worse Nur declared that he had decided to marry this girl. This was a terrible blow to Mother. That her son should marry a "foreigner" was quite a shock. How would she be able to explain this situation to her husband (even if she found the arrangement acceptable for herself). Looking over our settlement in America, a third problem of financing our stay there loomed very much on the horizon. We were not at all sure if we could afford to take up a third residence for Mother and me, separate from the boys. We had suffered so much and had spent so much money trying to reach America and now it turned out that we had done the whole trip for no reason at all. We were faced with a dilemma. At the same time there was no way we could return home immediately. Mother almost had a nervous breakdown. She had long spells of crying. We had been together with Nur in Ankara only a short while ago. But we had not seen Cenan for over six years. He had received his master's degree in engineering and I believe he had started doing his Ph.D. work on something like central heating systems. We spent hours and hours talking over our situation and looking for solutions.

Finally, Cenan decided that it would be best for Mother and me to take up residence in a separate apartment. He had already found a furnished two-room apartment in the same building where he had his studio. Once we were installed in our own place then we could discuss the situation further and make our plans for the future. It was finally decided that we would start early in the morning and drive to Boston. Once this decision was reached we called up the two families we wanted to meet before leaving New York. Only then could Mother and I retire to our room in the hotel. Mother kept crying all through the night. The most disagreeable situation for her was the fact that her son had decided to marry a foreign girl. She did not know how to communicate this information to her husband. She was certain that his reaction would be wildly contradictory. Well, she almost cried out her eyes that night and I guess this was the beginning of her crying spells every night that never ceased during all the time we were in America. She must have been only forty-eight years old at the time. She seemed to be so old to me. Young people have difficulty understanding their elders. I had no way of imagining what would happen to me when I got to that age.

In the morning Mother insisted that we visit the Çakuş family first. She was also hoping to consult her predicament with them. We went directly to their home. They had arrived to New York some time ago and had settled down. Their reception was certainly very warm. They showed us their house and insisted that we should spend the night with them. They had been informed about our arrival from Father's communication. So they had made some arrangements to receive us. This had given Mother some sort of encouragement. As we the youngsters were playing with Ali, the youngest of the family, Mother had already started her tale of woe. When it was decided that we would spend the night with the Çakuş family, Cenan offered to take me out for a walk. This was going to be the first time that I would be alone with my eldest brother, whom I had not seen for over six years. Since now I was in my teens, the age difference between us seemed to have dwindled. We should be able to reach one another as grown-ups. This seemed to be rather gratifying. We walked for a while on Riverside Drive. One can think better when one is walking, but it is not easy to talk to one another. Cenan must have felt the same thing, so he held my arm and suggested that we sit on a bench. I have great difficulty in talking with someone if I do not see his face or eyes. We talked and talked. Unfortunately we could not find a solution to the predicament we were in. By the time we had returned, everyone in the house had gone to bed. The next morning, since Mother had talked to the Manyas family on the phone during the day, we got up very early, packed everything into the sports model Studebaker that Cenan was driving and started our journey toward Boston. In those days one used the Merritt Parkway to reach Boston from New York. That highway went through some very lovely forests. Mother enjoyed the scenery very much and wanted to stop and have a cup of coffee somewhere. Cenan explained that there was no way of doing such a thing and that there was no place to park once one was on the highway. Mother was taken aback. I guess the shopping malls and the motels had not become popular in those days and Cenan did not want to get off the highway.

Finally we reached Boston. We first went to the apartment Cenan was staying in in Cambridge. He talked with the manager and sure enough he came back with a set of keys in his hand. He was ready to take us to our future apartment and if Mother approved we would rent the flat.

The building we had gone into had only six floors but it was a sprawling building containing many apartments. A highway went by the front of the building, then there was a stretch of trees and lawn and some flower beds. Then one could reach the Charles River rolling on as ever. There were all sorts of canoes or small sailing boats where people were enjoying the water. We went up in the elevator to the fourth floor. First we went through a miniscule entrance into a rather wide living room. It was very sunny and there was a large bay window overlooking the river. There was a very small kitchen that had a separate entrance to the corridor outside and on the opposite side there was a bedroom and a bathroom. From couches to pillows and sheets, everything was provided. It was a fully furnished flat. Mother found the rent acceptable for what was offered. It was at least a clean and comfortable place to gather her clan around her. In a way she could develop a "home" from this cozy place. Our address was 420 Memorial Drive, Cambridge, Massachusetts. The poor woman could feel a little relieved. After settling and making arrangements in her new home to her satisfaction, Mother wanted to see where her sons were living. It was easy to reach Cenan's since he had a studio in the same building. We simply went two floors down and entered a tiny apartment that consisted of one room with a kitchenette and a small bathroom. The one table he had could be used both as a dining table as well as writing table. There were a few chairs and a sofa that could be turned into a bed at night. The room was quite disorderly since Cenan had left Boston in a hurry. He had started for his doctorate after receiving his master's degree. He was also trying his best to help Nur. Now we had been added to his worries. He hardly had time to tidy up his flat and could not afford a charwoman. He was receiving the allowance the Turkish government allotted to students in America and he could barely exist on that income.

Next on the agenda was a visit to Nur's place. He was living at a rooming house on Beacon Street. The Charles River separates Boston from Cambridge. Boston is the main city and there are many bridges that connect the two towns. Cambridge is more of a university town where well-known institutions like Harvard, Radcliff and M.I.T. are situated. Cambridge is a smaller city compared to Boston and is naturally more quiet.

Nur had a room on the third floor of an old mansion. His room was much tidier. This stemmed from the fact of his personality and the kind of life he was leading. After showing us his room Nur wanted us to meet his girlfriend. Mother, naturally being curious and since she inwardly hoped to change his mind, agreed to meet her. The girl was called Patricia and she was from Maine. She had come to Boston and in order to earn her living had found a position as a waitress in a restaurant chain called Howard Johnson's. She had found a room where Nur was staying and they had met there, coming in and going out. When Nur was in bed with a bad cold she had nursed him a while. So Nur had grown accustomed to her presence and eventually love had flourished.

We went to meet Patricia as a group. Actually all of us were feeling rather awkward. The poor girl was also taken quite aback. There was nothing wrong with her, well behaved and so forth, so we had something to eat at the restaurant and then we returned home. Mother was beside herself. She simply could not stop crying. Cenan had his own problems and I did not know what to do. What could I possibly do in such a complicated situation?

The question of "I" was an eternal problem for me, all my life. There was one "me" who was the dutiful daughter of my parents, very obedient and always condescending. Then there was another "me" who wanted to find out who she really was and who wanted to be a person-woman of her own. To be honest and good were traits both part of me had developed. I was growing up to become a girl/woman who wished to be free and develop my own individuality. As I was growing up I was getting to be more decisive and more selective. For example, I was beginning to criticize myself for being jealous of my elder brothers while growing up, as a child. The second "me" had already began to evaluate my relationship with my family. I had begun to question the validity of my father's severe relationship with his children as well as my mother's gushing protectiveness. However, the other "I" would never allow these sentiments to surface and be heard. When I look back I realize that the unseen "I" was almost always right and was able to reach the best decisions for me.

Frankly, all along this trip, I had no idea what I would be doing once we got to where we were going. I had just joined Mother on a trip to meet my brothers who had gone away and was in anticipation of our reunion.

After a few days in our new apartment our life began to take some shape. We had even rented a piano so that I could continue my piano studies. Mother and I were sharing the single big room as a mutual bedroom and Nur, to save expenses, had moved in with us and was sleeping in the original bedroom of the apartment. In the evenings Cenan would also join us and we would have a family dinner together. For the first time in many years Mother once more was cooking and we were enjoying her delicious meals. In the morning Cenan and Nur would go to their various classes and Mother and I would do the housework. For many years in Turkey, since we had a multitude of servants, Mother would only go into the kitchen to make special desserts like "Palachinka" and/or cook cabbage in the Bosniac manner. Now, however, she had started cooking daily for her children. I was amazed to observe how much Mother could do (and sacrifice herself) for the sake of her children.

Whenever the daily chores were over I would start playing the piano. Mother would probably mend things or do some ironing, but secretly she would keep crying incessantly. Whenever I suggested that the best thing for us was to return home, she would refuse to listen and she would shut me up. She was convinced that by prolonging our stay she probably could change Nur's mind about getting married. There were many problems to be solved. One of the most important problems was the question of our finances. Since I could do nothing on the first, I decided to concentrate on the second question, namely finances. Finally, one day I declared that I would start looking at the "help wanted" ads in the paper and would like to find a suitable job to help the family finances. I said, "Maybe I cannot earn much, but anything would be better then nothing." Both Cenan and Nur said this was a very good idea. On the other hand, Mother was beside herself and almost went out of her mind. How could she agree to let her only daughter to become a "slave!" Finally, when she grudgingly gave her consent, I was able to get an offer from a department store to become a salesperson in their hat department. When I had an interview with the people who would hire me, I had cold feet. Then I asked Cenan if I could not be registered at a college. It seemed that if I was enrolled at an institution of learning, then father would be able to secure a student's allowance for me from Turkey. Cenan made some enquiries on the subject and brought me the information. I was first to go through "State Examinations" and if I was successful then I would have to take an entrance test to get enrolled to a college. When my status would turn into a regular foreign student enrolled at a recognized college then father would be able to send me a regular student's allowance from Turkey. This information had come in mid-summer, so I started studying feverishly for the State exams. I was sleeping four or five hours at night and spending all my time for my studies. I used to get up early and prepare Nur's breakfast so that Mother could sleep a little longer. It was years later that I learned that Nur in fact would just smear his plate without touching any of the things I had prepared for him and would go and have breakfast with his girl friend.

VII

Simmons College

Since I had been a good student in Ankara, and since I had had a lot of courses in English, I was able to pass both the required exams and was able to enroll at Simmons College. This was a festive occasion for all members of the family. I had accomplished something. My father had also been surprised and was very glad. Thus the student's stipend of 151 dollars per month began to come from Turkey regularly.

I had the possibility of choosing other colleges. Frankly, Wellesley would have been my favorite. I had seen the campus and had liked it very much. The abundance of beautiful trees and the buildings looked inviting. However, Mother refused to let me attend a boarding school. Simmons College was my second choice. I had learned of its perfect curriculum and of its accomplished and serious students. Cenan was all for it. Simmons was situated in wonderful grounds with the beautiful Fenway Park close by.

On my first day of school Cenan was forced to drive me. As I had mentioned before, the campus was in Boston and one had to cross a bridge to get there. So after dropping me off, he would recross the bridge to go to his school.

Simmons was a girls college with a four-year B.A. program. For my freshman year I was required to take eight courses. I decided to specialize in sociology and journalism. For my first semester I had courses in American history, sociology, French and American literature. On our first morning all four hundred students were assembled together and the regulations of the school, or what was allowed and what was not allowed, was discussed in detail. Being serious about our work was the most important point that was raised. Then everyone had to meet

91

their advisor or tutors. We would be scheduled for various classes but we would each have an outside advisor with whom we would be consulting about our studies. This would be a professor in the school who would be meeting us once a week and check how our studies were developing. The same teacher would also guide our extra-curricular activities and would also advise what shows and lectures we should be attending in town, as well as what books we should read. My advisor for the first semester was Mr. Ross Lockridge, Jr. In my second semester the same Prof. Lockridge became my professor in French. This gentleman had obtained his doctorate at the Sorbonne in Paris and later on wrote a best selling novel called *The Raintree County*. This novel was later turned into a movie with Elizabeth Taylor in the lead role. The book was first published in 1947 and a second edition appeared in 1948. I was very sorry to learn later that Prof. Lockridge had died in an unpleasant manner. Who can tell what will happen to people in life? Another well-known teacher was my history professor, John Larkin. It was certainly an honor and pleasure to be in his class.

The school had some strict regulations. No one would be allowed to come to school in slacks. No one was allowed to smoke on the campus except in an assigned room in the basement called the "butt room." No chewing of gum was allowed anywhere and class attendance was obligatory. Another restriction was not to be out in Fenway Park after 17:00 hours since the administration believed it could be dangerous for us to wander around the park after dark. There were many soldiers who had returned from active duty and many had psychological problems. Muggings and killings had happened in the past and they had to be careful.

Many years ago I had yearned to attend an American school in İstanbul but had not been able to do so since we had moved to Ankara. Finally, now that I was able to enroll at a proper American college in America, I was very happy. Gradually I began making friends. This was a totally new adventure for me. Everything about me, the way I dressed, the way I reacted to new people, in short many things, were changing. I enjoyed my classes and I liked my instructors.

Almost next door to Simmons was the Isabella Stewart Gardner Museum. The lady who had the building erected and given her name to it was a very distinguished person. She had collected many paintings, sculptures and other valuable pieces of furniture. There was a courtyard with very beautiful flowers and rare plants. They used to have concerts there twice a week. As soon as I learned about this wonderful place I began to spend all my free time there. One could listen to music and wonder around in beautiful surroundings for hours. Some days I would be just thinking or day dreaming, fantasizing, etc. It had become my sanctuary. A lot of people visited the museum for many different reasons. Apart from their regular tourists, art students would come with their teachers. One would see many people sitting and copying various works of art. There were probably others who had come there to find solace—like me. It was certainly a sort of heaven for the likes of me.

As the courses progressed I realized that I had to learn how to type. My elder brother Cenan quickly came to my rescue. He introduced me to a friend of his, a girl called Lynn, who was teaching at the well-known secretarial school called Katherine Gibbs. Thus my days became more full with my regular program plus these lessons in typing. Every day after school I would attend to my typing lesson and then come home to help Mother with house chores. Later I would play the piano. After the family dinner Mother would retire and I would start my homework for the next day's classes. I was becoming almost automated and there was hardly anything else in my life. Mother's life was no better. During the day she was taking care of the house, cooking, cleaning, etc. She was writing letters to Father, crying and sometimes she would be reading or listening to the radio. Mostly she was trying to solve Nur's problem. Letters were coming and going between her and Father constantly.

Bülent Çambel and Ekmel Moran were friends of Cenan, who also lived in the same building as we. Bülent was the son of a member of the parliament like my father. He too was a student at M.I.T. and I guess he must have been studying engineering. Ekmel was the son of a well-known translator, Mr. Moran, and he was doing graduate work at Harvard. Both belonged to families we knew and both were struggling to get along

93

on their student stipends. I seem to remember Turkish students in the States were allowed 151 dollars a month in those days. Since we were paying rent of 125 dollars a month for our one-bedroom apartment, one can visualize this stipend was not much. When one considers the costs of transportation, et al, this was certainly not excessive and the poor boys were really struggling to survive. Mother, as soon as she realized the difficulties they were having, started inviting them to dinner, especially near the end of each month.

Mr. Moran, Ekmel's father, was a favored friend of our family. When we were living in Kadiköy, we were neighbours and we used to visit each other regularly. Many times when Mother and Father were going there for a visit, they would take me along. The Morans had three young children. At a later date, Nermin, also a daughter of Mr. Moran (from a previous marriage), became a very close friend of my brother Cenan. Nermin had been my ideal of a young lady in those days. Her poise, her good looks and her manners were all things that I would look up to. I used to watch her with admiration. Since I liked the rest of the family I also enjoyed Ekmel's company. He used to tell funny jokes and knew how to get along with everyone. It was fun to be in his company. Years later Nermin married Ambassador Menemencioğlu and spent many years in New York while her husband was the Permanent Representative of Turkey at the U.N.

I had some interesting experiences at Simmons, especially at the beginning. I believe it was my first month at college. One day they told me that some reporters from the *Herald* would come to interview me. When I asked why I was chosen for this, they told me that I was the first Turkish girl ever to have registered at Simmons. It sounded interesting. After a while two somewhat elderly persons came to see me. One was a woman. After getting introduced to one another, their first question was "How did you get accustomed to these dresses?" When they saw that I was taken somewhat aback by this question they tried to explain what they meant by adding, "Were you not wearing the veil before you came to this country?" I really got vehemently angry and told them since the reforms Atatürk had realized in my country the veil was no longer being used and that I had never used a veil all my life. The next question was, "How many wives does your father have?" followed by a question like, "Do you live in houses?" I was certainly turned off. Instead of answering their strange questions I started asking them, "Can you find where Turkey is on a map?" "Have you ever heard of the name Atatürk?" "Have you any idea about the reforms the Turkish government had put into practice?" So we bantered a bit further and they began to enjoy talking with me. The next day there was a rather nice article in the paper, together with my picture.

Many years later, I was living in Ankara (I was a housewife with children by that time) I met the wife of the U.S. Ambassador to Turkey. Mrs. Phyllis Macomber, who turned out to be a Simmons graduate and we became great friends. She even remembered the *Boston Herald* article about the Turkish girl at Simmons. This college for girls had been founded in 1899 and has been operational to date. Their forte was in social studies, sociology, history and journalism. It is still a girl's college with the goal of educating successful women.

Boston had basically a Christian population and consequently on Sundays liquor would not be sold and amusement places would be closed. This meant that people could have fun only on Saturdays. So at times I would go out with Mother or sometimes Cenan would take me out. Depending first on the weather and secondly on our finances we would go to a movie, a show or listen to a concert. On Sundays we would either visit museums or go to various parks. Cenan and his friends would sometimes take me along with them to a "jam session" on Saturday nights. On some occasions we were able to drive down to New York, spend the night with friends and go to some night club where Benny Goodman or Duke Ellington were playing. This way I was able to listen to Count Basie, Billie Holiday and Artie Shaw, all in person. Our school would also arrange for groups to attend theatres in town. I was lucky to watch Jose Ferrer in his memorable performance of Cyrano de Bergerac.

This was a wholly new world that had engulfed me. Until that time or rather since I had come to the States, we had a rather nice relationship with my younger brother Nur. Yes, we used to bicker incessantly between ourselves but deep down we loved one another. For years, since our ages were not too far apart, we had enjoyed the same group of friends and had been together a lot. On the other hand Cenan had always been the "big brother." One could appreciate him but it was difficult to reach out to him. Furthermore, he had been away for such a long time. However, after his American experience Nur had changed very much and I could hardly understand his reactions anymore. I sincerely could not approve of what he was doing most of the time. On the other hand Cenan and I had been able to develop a much healthier relationship in America. He was both helping and guiding me around. We were getting to be great friends and the difference between our ages had visibly dwindled. He had become a sort of a "guru" for me.

I had began to really enjoy Boston to the full. My ardent backer in this achievement was Cenan. He had been away from home for many years, he had been successful at M.I.T. and he was being asked to lecture on Turkey at many clubs. All this had given him the chance of meeting well-known people. Among them I can mention the famous anthropologist Margaret Mead and the historian and explorer Colonel Furlong (the man who had first met the pygmies). We had visited Sister Mary Theresa at her home on 110 Glenallen Road, West Roxbury, several times. We had Margaret Mead for dinner at our apartment more than once. The relationship that developed between Colonel and Mrs. Furlong actually lasted much longer. The colonel used to recount with much pride that he had been in Turkey during our independence war and had met Kemal Atatürk in person. Some years later, through the intercession of my father, he was able to visit Turkey once again and meet İsmet İnönü, our president at the time. We were invited to their country home very often, usually on Sundays. We would play badminton in the garden, take walks and have picnics in the groves beyond. I was introduced to peanut butter in one such occasion and I must admit I had not enjoyed it one bit. They had all sorts of odd things in their house. For example, there was an unusual sort of a table. They later explained what it was. Apparently the colonel had shot an elephant. Then one leg of the beast was used as the base and one ear of the elephant was stretched to form the top of the table. Many animal heads were hanging on the walls, all preserved. I never went into that room again. I was somewhat revolted and was surprised that this amiable gentleman would be capable of doing such things. I later read in the *Who's Who in America* that the colonel was also a famous hunter.

Among the new people we were meeting we also developed good friendships. One such pair was Noobar and Anahit Bashian. They really became bosom friends of the family. Our meeting them was a total surprise for both parties. As I have already explained, our finances were rather restricted. My student stipend brought in 151 dollars a month. Nur was chipping in 75 dollars (half his student stipend) for his room and board and Cenan was paying 50 dollars for the food he was getting at the family table. So, in order to provide additional financial support to his family Father had made an arrangement with a family living in the States who wanted to send financial aid to some relatives in Turkey. Father would pay the equivalent amount to the party in Turkey and the people in the States would pay the same sum to us in Boston. One Sunday morning the phone rang. A Mr. Bashian was asking if he and his wife would call on us. So Mother asked if they could come around eleven and have some coffee. When the doorbell rang, I opened the door. A tiny lady in a fur coat with a matching fur hat walked in followed by her husband. Mother was standing a few steps behind me. Suddenly I heard Mother shouting "Anahit." She ran toward the lady and they were in each other's arms instantly. The woman was also shouting "Cemile, Cemile." Mr. Bashian, Cenan, Nur and I were watching this scene in utter amazement. Both women were crying and hugging one another with no end. Finally we all sat down and the story was told.

I am sure I have mentioned earlier that my mother had been a student at a Catholic French school when she was very young, at the age of four to be exact, in Ortaköy, İstanbul. The nuns had appointed this calm and warmhearted young Armenian girl (Anahit) as a sort of elder sister to Mother and so the two girls had become great friends. This friendship lasted some years until their paths had parted. So it was almost half a century later that Mother recognized her dear friend of early years. It was pure chance that the two would meet after so many years. From that day on we had all become bosom friends. After we had lost Mother in 1963, Aunt Anahit had written a very long letter to Father, recounting their meeting and all childhood stories. I still keep and cherish her letter. Uncle Noobar was a dealer in furs and had a nice store in Boston. The Bashians had one son and one daughter and we, the young ones, had developed friendly relations with them as well.

We also met and fell in love with a Greek family, Alex Costi and his sister Marianti. They were living in a nice house in Wellesley, together with their mother. Cenan had met this family before we had arrived. Alex was an accomplished photographer and if I am not mistaken Marianti did some sewing. Their family had come to the States from Turkey when the children were very young and they had kept their Turkish by continuing to speak the language in their home. In a way this had given us a chance to speak Turkish with others in the midst of Wellesley, Massachusetts. Although they were not by any means well off, they still kept inviting us to lunches and dinners all the time. Their mother was an excellent cook and we spent many good hours with them. In those days we rarely encountered such warm friendships from others. Those two families, one of Armenian origin and the other of Greek descent, turned out to be real friends.

Now that I think of it, isn't it a pity that in half a century politics has changed this atmosphere of friendship into unpleasant feelings. In the last twenty years Armenian terrorists have assassinated many of our well-educated diplomats in foreign lands. Greek governments have also been displaying unending animosity against the Turks. All my life I never had such feelings toward what we used to call minorities and I had many friends of different origins. We never differentiated people according to their religion or nationality.

Apart from these, we also had the chance of meeting some nice Turkish families living in Massachusetts. One couple that we kept up our relationships with for many years were Dr. İhsan Doğramacı and his charming wife Ayser. Our relationship has always been cordial. They were living in a suburb of Boston with their two children, Şermin and Ali. I believe Dr. Doğramacı was an intern. Ayser Hanım was a dedicated mother taking care of Şermin and their son Ali (who now happens to be the rector of Bilkent University in Ankara). We used to meet regularly and enjoyed each other's company. I had learned at that date that Ayser Hanım's father had known Father from way back.

Another family whose friendship we valued very much was Dr. Ethem Vassaf and his wife Belkis Hanım. I believe Dr. Vassaf was a neurologist and his wife was a psychologist. They had a young son called Gündüz. I guess our families lost contact since I do not recall meeting them after our return to Turkey. There was one occasion I remember vividly. We had been invited to the Vassaf home for dinner. We had spent several hours with them. Since they were living in the suburbs it had taken Cenan half an hour driving back to our flat. On our arrival, as we were getting ready to go to bed, Mother suddenly and rather agitatedly asked Cenan to ring Dr. Vassaf on the phone. It was almost midnight and Cenan objected due to the lateness of the hour. Mother, however, was very insistent. She kept saying that unwillingly she had taken a box of matches on which was written Dr. Vassaf. She was sure the doctor would think she was a kleptomaniac. We were all laughing and saying he would do no such thing and that to wake them up in the middle of the night would sound even worse.

We were finally able to convince Mother not to make such a call and settled down for the night. However, Mother could not sleep one wink that night and was up bright and early and she was on the phone to the doctor. He apparently was laughing and said, "My good lady those matches are especially ordered to be distributed as they contain our address and I purposefully give them to our friends." Well, Mother was always very attentive to such details. The reader may wonder why I keep mentioning Mother all the time, but there is no question that she had a very great place in my life.

We also made friends with an American family. I do not remember how this relationship had materialized but meeting Mr. and Mrs. Williams was a godsend to mother. Their daughter Marie was my age. They were a very attractive couple and well-to-do family. Since I had started to attend college Mother had begun to find herself very lonely during the day. Mrs. Williams started to take Mother around. She was able to show Mother most of the better shops of Boston and pointed out to her what to buy and where. Since Mr. Williams was quite a hard working businessman, the two ladies found lots of time to go around. Marie was a boarder at Wheaton College in Norton, a little out of Boston. On weekends, Marie had started joining me and Cenan in whatever we were doing. Wheaton College was a school where well-to-do families sent their children and through Marie we had begun to meet some of her college friends. Soon we had developed quite a circle of friends. I never forget an experience I had through that connection. For some special occasion the principal of Wheaton College had given permission to the students to invite their friends to spend a weekend at the college. Marie had invited me. Cenan drove me over to the college Friday evening. I only had a small overnight bag with me. Marie took me up to her room. I had thought we would be sleeping in a dormitory with many girls. It turned out that this rather posh college was more like a luxury hotel. Marie had a wonderful bedroom which had a connecting door to a similar big bedroom assigned to her friend Virginia. They had installed an additional bed for me in Marie's bedroom for the weekend. On the same floor there were more than ten girls enjoying the same kind of luxury. There was also a section allocated to showers and toilets. The toilet doors were half size, in other words one could see the occupant's legs or if they were standing up one could see the girl's head and shoulders from outside. In the showers they had no curtain. I later learned that there were more than a hundred girls at Wheaton enjoying this kind of accommodation.

That evening we had dinner at the large dining hall with all the students and teachers. All the tables had linen table cloths and napkins. The food served was as good as what is served at a very good restaurant. After dinner we joined other students in the huge hall where there was a log fire in a very big fireplace. Songs were sung and we even went out to play snowball for a while.

When the time had come for us to go to bed Marie, Virginia and I went to our shared bedrooms. The connecting door was almost always open. The girls started undressing. Since until that night I had been accustomed to undress only when I was by myself, I was standing by and trying to decide how to act. One of them told me to get undressed since we were going to the showers. Rather shyly I took off my dress but remained in my underwear. They kept saying, "Take everything off" and they themselves were already stark naked. I did not know where to look, since I was too ashamed to look at them, naked as they were. Suddenly one of them said, "Why do you refuse to undress, do you have some sort of a blemish on your body?" Finally I was forced to go naked (at least to show them that I had nothing to be ashamed of) and we all went to the showers. I was very perturbed. I had never felt so odd. The girls kept trying to convince me that it was quite all right to go naked among friends. After shower we all put on our pajamas and went to bed. Before going to sleep, I had to ask, "Who will close the window?" The girls were again aghast. It was snowing outside. The building was centrally heated but I could still watch the snow flakes falling. They said they always slept with the window open and that was the healthy way. I was afraid I would catch cold but soon I had fallen asleep. The next morning I found that I had slept wonderfully and that it really was healthy to sleep exposed to fresh air. We again had showers, got dressed and went down to have a delicious breakfast.

The real fun began after breakfast. The girls' families and boy friends all had crowded in the college grounds. Everyone was walking on the snow covered fields and then converged into the school's auditorium. I learned that it was customary for girls to arrange some shows before the midyear break. There were also displays of art work produced by the students during the semester—paintings, sculptures and other handcrafts. Some showed their dexterity by playing musical instruments like violin and flute, others had arranged a ballet show. Finally, they had a Shakespeare play, produced by the students. At last, the time came for the big reception. All guests were invited to the buffet tables especially arranged for the occasion by the students. The students were acting as hostesses and were showing interest to all the guests. I was quite taken aback with what I was witnessing and thought about the conditions in my country. Who had ever heard that the principals in our schools would involve themselves in such social events, let alone back their students to show their art work. Back home our teachers used to be like goblins and would not even bother to learn the names of the students in their classes. Students were referred to by the numbers assigned to each. That was the reason many children in my country hated school and showed their disregard by copying in exams and doing things contrary to regulations. I am not saying that all teachers in my country are bad. As a matter of fact I had enjoyed some very valuable teachers that I still cherish. What I am trying to say is that somehow, something was going wrong in the education system of my country.

Boston had given me a new impetus for learning and for bettering myself. There was so much culture and art displayed for almost free that I could not help absorbing these things and trying to learn more and more. The possibilities for knowledge were so very conducive at the same time that I believe I would never leave my college if conditions had been different.

One of the first things I learned at Simmons was the fact that the girls passing by would say "Hi" or something like "How are you doing?" and by the time I had started giving a proper answer, they would be gone. I had to learn that this was more a manner of greeting and that they were not really interested in what you were actually doing. In any case, no one had time for such details. It took me some time to realize this.

Another problem I had on the campus that caused me concern was the way of dressing. At the beginning the way I was dressed almost made me an outcast. Most girls would wear a "twin set" and a pleated skirt plus a pair of saddle shoes and socks. Whereas I had silk stockings and shoes with low heels as well as a blouse and a tight skirt. I felt so awkward that I went shopping as soon as I could, so as to be able to dress like my fellow college students.

Another thing that surprised me at first was their outlook on life. At the cafeteria I used to take my food over the counter and carry my tray to an empty table to eat. Once I saw a girl working behind the counter in the cafeteria. I knew she came from a well-to-do family and that her father was a senator. So I was surprised to see her working in this manner. In Turkey, we would be more prone to ask our servants to fetch a glass of water, let alone work for others. One day, between classes, I was able to get a hold of this senator's daughter and enquired why she was doing the chores that she had been doing. She said, "My family is paying for my education. I dislike asking for more money to meet some of my extra expenses. This way I am earning an additional income to cover my personal needs and I do not have to ask my parents for money." I thought about what she had said and soon I found myself working at the cafeteria and I felt proud of this act.

Christmas time was around the corner. Mother asked Cenan to take us to church to attend a Christmas sermon. Cenan disliked the idea and countered it with the suggestion that he would be willing to take the family to church, if we all agreed to attend a burlesque show afterwards. Mother accepted this challenge. We first attended midnight mass and following that we went on to watch the famous g-string girl or the striptease artist Gypsy Rose Lee. In a town so full of religious people it was a wonder that the striptease was so densely attended. It was certainly quite exciting to watch these two activities one after another. Even Mother enjoyed Gypsy Rose Lee.

Massachusetts is a state full of universities. As a result Boston, the capital of the state, is full of museums, theatres and galleries. The Boston Museum of Fine Arts is well known all over America. One can visit these stately halls any number of times and still find new things to admire. The Boston Symphony Orchestra is one that is recognized all around the world. Well-known conductors and artists take turns with this orchestra. The Boston Symphony also has what they call "pops" concerts that are carried out in the open air by the side of the Charles River. These are called Esplanade Concerts. In this very refined city one can always find an interesting lecture to listen to, almost every day of the year. Many plays have their "try out" shows in Boston before opening on Broadway. This way they can estimate the quality of their show. If their show is well received in Boston then they feel more confident to carry their show to Broadway. There are also many libraries (all kinds of special collections will be on display). Once, when I was trying to write a paper, I had found at the Boston Public Library books written by the Turkish writer Ahmet Emin Yalman, who was also a friend of my father.

I was fully involved with my classes and enjoying my life in Boston very much. By the time my third semester was coming to an end, our quiet family life had began to get unsettled. After

103

a prolonged correspondence between Father and Mother, things had began to turn sour. Mother had started to say that no matter what was to happen to us, she felt she was duty bound to return to her husband. Cenan, whose quiet life had been ruffled with his whole family converging on him, had also lost his taste for his doctorate work. He had began to say that he had had enough of living the student's life and that he would rather return to Turkey and see what life would offer him in his fatherland. Nur was quite ready to go back and show his new bride the wonders of İstanbul. I was the only one left in a quandary. I would love to graduate from the college I was attending. I had sent my credentials to Father. It turned out that without consulting us, Father had shown my credentials to the minister of social works, Dr. Sadi Irmak, and that venerable gentleman had offered to give me a scholarship that would finance the rest of my college education, with the provision that I should be willing to work for the ministry on my return. This looked like a wonderful chance for me. On the other hand, staying by myself, all alone in this foreign land, especially away from my mother, seemed somewhat daunting to me. It was a very difficult choice to make. By this date I had completed my third semester classes.

During that time something very unexpected took place. A male voice, on the phone, started calling the apartment. He would not give his name but would cite incidents that showed he was following me everywhere in the city. This affair scared me. I even wondered that if I had accepted his invitation and met him somewhere, then I might fall in love with him and settle in the States. No matter how much I loved it, could I accept to spend the rest of my life in America? How would I survive in Boston, all by myself? There were so many attractions and dis-tractions in the town. Would a man who might love me, agree to come to live in Turkey? If I decided to stay all by myself, with the rest of the family gone, would that be a mistake? All the members of my family were getting ready to return to Turkey. Poor Mother was totally spent and quite depressed. She no longer had any strength to help me reach a decision. I even believed that she no longer cared one way or the other. She had come to the States and had gone through so many difficult phases for a certain purpose. However, that mission had now backfired. She just wanted to go back to her husband and home.

With all these difficult decisions to make and still carrying on living there, we had not properly prepared ourselves for our return trip either. For example, we had thought of purchasing an automobile. This ideal was not to be realized. All I had for myself was a portable typewriter, a portable sewing machine and a lot of books. Father wanted us to return by air. However, the only international airline that touched Turkey was Pan American and their flights were always full. Furthermore, getting plane tickets for five people turned out to be prohibitively expensive. Cenan had already suggested that we return by boat. Nur had been married and was living in a dream world, not bothering about anything. There was no one I could ask for council and sound advice. My fourth semester was about to start. If I was going to stay, I should be making arrangements. Since no one was willing to help and since I could not do much on my own, I saw no other way out but to return to Turkey with the family.

VIII

The Return Trip Home

Finally, our family of four, who began to come to the United States starting in 1939 (Cenan's arrival to Boston) and kept on coming till 1945, was now returning home in 1946 with one additional member (Nur's new wife). Again Cenan had been instrumental in finding a boat suitable to take us back. Actually, S. S. *Marine Corps* was a cargo ship that could accommodate some passengers. It was to travel from New York harbor to Haifa. We would be leaving New York on August 30. It took a long time for us to get Father's agreement to this arrangement.

Father was to come to Haifa on the Turkish passenger vessel *Güneysu* and we would all return by that boat to İstanbul. We were returning just as we had come, with very few things! All of us were very excited. I must confess that neither Cenan nor I was very comfortable with what had happened. We both felt we were leaving many things behind. I was especially sad for not having finished the education that I had enjoyed so much. Furthermore, I had no idea what the future held in store for me. One of the things I had learned in the States was that it was "no use crying over spilt milk."

In New York, the Çakuş family, who had so generously hosted us in the past, were again ready to receive us. So we decided to take the train to New York three days before our ship was due to sail and stay with them. Cenan finally sold his beloved and long suffering Studebaker and Mother almost gave away most of our household utensils we had bought during our stay to our neighbours.

Now that I mentioned Cenan selling his car, some connected stories came to my mind. The previous winter we had a lot of snow. One day cooped up in the apartment Mother had been almost suffocating and Cenan offered to take her for a drive. This was a much welcomed diversion. We all put on our coats and piled out. We found that the car was covered with snow. This meant that we had to shovel and scrape ten inches of snow. Once that chore was done, Cenan saw that he had a busted tire and had to change it. When he opened the trunk, however, he saw that he had no jack. Without a jack he could do nothing. In Turkey we use the French term for this contraption, namely "kriko." So I asked Cenan to confirm if what we wanted was a "jack." Mother who had been standing by all this while thought we were talking about a person and said, "Do not bother calling him Jack, just call him 'Sir'." We all burst out with laughter.

The date of our departure had come. We packed all our baggage into the train that was to take us to New York. Mother was finally glad, knowing that she would be united with her husband and return to her proper way of life as she was accustomed before. Nur and Pat were quite content, knowing that they had finally married and that they were going to Turkey where life would be much easier. Only Cenan and I were still wondering if we had made the correct choice and if what was waiting for us was better than what we were leaving behind. The train ride took four hours. We had to be careful with our finances. Mother, hearing a man call out "Are you hungry? Are you famished?" suddenly jumped and asked, "Yes, yes, where is the dining car?" She had thought the man was a waiter. In actual fact he was trying to sell a few buns he had on a tray. We were all dying with laughter. Finally Cenan got the man to come along and show us his stuff. There was no dining car on this train. So we had to do with what we found. We had all realized that in our morning rush we had had no breakfast.

While in Boston we had experienced another funny incident concerning Mother. I believe it will be nice to write about it. This took place during the time when Mother had started feeling lonesome in the house. She decided to get a dog to keep her company. After prolonged debates on the subject, she finally convinced us. During one of our outings, when Cenan and I had stopped in front of an elegant store on Newbury Street to admire the window display, Mother also came out of the car to join us. Then she said, "The personnel here should know of a place where dogs are sold." She entered the shop. A while later she joined us with a piece of paper in her hand and said, "Cenan, it seems we can purchase a dog at this address." So we ventured toward that destination. Cenan was a bit dubious about the address. Finally we found ourselves in front of a store where they sold ducks! It was then that we all burst out laughing while mother looked rather puzzled. Apparently the man who wrote the address down had confused Mother's pronunciation of "a dog" with "a duck."

Our good friend Kemal Çakuş was waiting for us at the station. We were to spend the following two nights at their apartment on Riverside Drive. It was a tiny apartment but we all piled in. Cenan went out to make last minute arrangements regarding our sailing and in the evening he took me out. We were able to go to a night club where Billie Holiday was singing. There was also a small dancing area and young people were dancing like crazy, while that wonderful singer was singing her famous songs. The dancers were packed and rather than dancing they were more like rolling with the crowd. I was very excited and impressed. Most people in the club were African-Americans and they simply were born to dance and one could feel this. The next day, after handling other chores, Cenan was able to take me to the Museum of Modern Art to see Georgia O'Keeffe's paintings. I could never forget my fascination and all my life I have been an admirer of that remarkable painter.

We finally left New York Harbor on August 30, 1946. Our ship belonged to a shipping firm called H. E. Snow Master Marine Corp. It was a big ship and had lots of passengers but since it was basically a cargo ship it had no extra comforts like an ocean liner. However, the passengers on the boat were nice people, our cabins were clean and the food served was really good. While reading most of the time and talking to some of the passengers and occasionally sun tanning, we were able to pass the time. We reached Haifa on September 13.

As he had informed us earlier, Father was at the pier to meet us. It was quite an exciting get-together after such a long parting. Father looked somewhat thinner and slightly aged. Mother was in his arms crying, Father was also tearful when he hugged each of us separately. We could see he had suffered and he mentioned that he had longed for Mother most. At the same time he was kind to Patricia but one could feel that he was somewhat heartbroken with Nur. He welcomed Cenan most willingly and somehow I felt he was questioning me why I had not stayed in America as he had suggested and when he had found financing for it. How could I explain my reactions and feelings to him?

Once landed in Haifa, we went on board the *Güneysu*. It was a small but very comfortable passenger vessel. There were not too many passengers on board. We had a very courteous captain and we enjoyed his company. Our boat spent a few hours in Beirut. There we met the Gandour family together with their children. Mr. Gandour was also the representative of the Turkish passenger ships in Beirut. Our boat stopped in Antakya, Antalya and then went into the Aegean Sea to stop at Izmir and finally we reached our destination, which was İstanbul. This trip took ten days. After having watched the Atlantic's bareness for a long time, this trip in home waters seemed so much more likeable to us. We were all enjoying the beauties of our coastline. Our country was certainly very beautiful in many respects. Both Cenan and I were getting to appreciate our country and glad to have reached the decision we had reached. Now it was my time to find some sort of an outlet and obtain my financial independence and not be a burden to my parents anymore. I had realized that financial independence was a very important thing.

During this long voyage I also had the occasion of actually watching Turkey through the eyes of an American girl. I cannot forget the remarks Pat made when we were strolling on the pier of İzmir harbor. We were passing by a coffee house and there were lots of young males, mostly playing backgammon and sipping tea. Some were also enjoying the local water pipes. Pat was surprised because there were no women among them and she was wondering how come so many men could be loitering about with nothing to do. It was rather difficult to answer both questions properly. After a while we saw a man carrying a big load on his back. Pat immediately asked, "Don't they have machines for such big loads?" I could not give her an answer because I was asking similar questions to myself. Then we saw a donkey and a young man was running after the animal with a big stick in his hand. This time Pat asked what kind of an animal this was. Being a city child she had not seen a donkey all her life. After a few months in Ankara I would witness the difficulties this young American girl had, lacking some of the simplest materials she was used to having. Looking back now, I laugh about the discomforts I had those days and how I used to get angry with her for some of her reactions. Nowadays, thanks to Atatürk, my country has all material things as well as the beauty of nature.

IX
Autumn in İstanbul

The port of İstanbul was the final destination of our colorful boat trip. How can one not fall in love with this beautifully situated city? All our worries, lost dreams and our disappointments had been left behind. At least this was the case, as far as I was concerned. A new life was about to begin for me.

Passing through a crowd of people we had to take three taxis. The first one took Mother and Father. The second one had Nur and his wife Pat. Finally Cenan and I took the third taxi. Our luggage was distributed as well. We were going to our mansion in Erenköy, which meant we had to cross to the Anatolian side. In those years there were no bridges across the Bosphorus and we had to take the car ferry. We were all very excited. Especially Cenan must have felt the strain, since he had been away from home in his most formative seven years.

Our taxis, one after another, turned the corner on the boulevard near our garden to the small alleyway to enter our garden through the big wrought iron doors. The help, who were waiting for our arrival, had heard the cars coming and all hurried to the entrance. Sure enough, Mme. Eleni, the gardner, the cook and other hired help had all gotten together to receive us. Everyone was excited and everyone was hugging one another. We were all in tears. It was a very sentimental reunion.

My heart almost broke when I realized that Grandfather was not there to greet us. How I would love to kiss his gnarled hands, stroke his pure white and very long mustaches, look up into his always happy eyes. He was no longer there to give me his blessing and his love. I think I saw the same sorrow in my mother's eyes as well.

Father had instructed everyone to have the house ready for the arrival of his beloved wife. Even the dogs in the garden and

Mother's cat were all trimmed and ready for us. Mother loved all kinds of animals and for that reason we always had all sorts of animals in the house; love birds, canaries, cats and dogs and there was even an aquarium with Japanese fish in it. Of course we also had some geese, hens and cocks in the back garden. All the animals had been trained to live together and not harm one another. I have had my own dogs and my squirrel at one time.

It was natural for members of the family to get excited about coming home. I had an occasion to look and observe how all this had effected Pat, our American bride! She was certainly amazed and could not believe what she was watching. This really meant an absolutely new kind of life for her. I tried to help this young woman who really loved Nur dearly. I went and hugged her (since no one else had bothered to do so) and she said, "I feel like Alice in Wonderland."

Slowly we all went to our own rooms and started unpacking. By breakfast time the next morning we were finally and really at home. That year autumn had been lenient, we could have breakfast in the garden and even swim in the sea. We spent some time in Erenköy and enjoyed the remnants of a beautiful summer. Gradually everyone had settled and we got back to our old ways. So it meant that the family would now be moving to Ankara. When Grandfather had passed away, Father had purchased a plot at the nearby cemetery and had made it into a family preserve. There were six places with only Grandfather being placed in one of the plots. We visited his grave a couple of times. However, I always felt as if he was somewhere in the big house, ready to come out and surprise me.

We took the night train called the "wagon-lits" from Haydar-paşa to Ankara. I had always enjoyed that ride. We had three double bedded compartments, one for me and Mother, another for Cenan and Father and third for Nur and Pat. We got together at the "wagon restaurant" for dinner. White, well-ironed table-cloths, linen napkins, beautiful cutlery and plates carrying the emblem of the old French company that used to run this line were all set. Everything was like the old times.

I had started a new habit while I was in the States. I was having a cigarette after lunch and dinner. This had come about through my surroundings and somewhat due to my wish to be singular. However, I was still a little squeamish about smoking in my father's presence. Naturally, such a restriction was not to be practiced in America, during those days. But we were now in Turkey and old habits do not die easily. Funny, by the time these lines were written, conditions have totally reversed and it is now difficult to smoke in the United States. Especially in public places.

At the big mansion in Erenköy, my smoking habit had not bothered anyone, since I could duck into the garden or run up to my room and have my cigarette in peace. However, there was no place that I could duck into on the train. So, that night as everyone was having coffee, I took my leave and withdraw to our compartment. A little later Cenan knocked on my door and said that Father had asked me to come back to the table. On my return to the table, Father asked me to sit where I was sitting, took Mother's pack and offered me a cigarette and he said, "Dear girl, there is no reason why you should not join your Mother for a puff, however, please try not to over do it." And he went on to light my cigarette. I had missed Father all the time, this gesture of his made me appreciate him all the more. Well, were they not the same father and mother who had given me a key to the house. I never forgot that gesture. On my eighteenth birthday they had offered me a small box and opening it I had found a key to the front door, attached to a silver key chain and they said, "You are now eighteen, it is up to you to decide when to come in and when to go out. Please try and use your own discretion." I believe this was the first time that I had to reflect seriously about my own responsibilities.

This after-the-meal cigarette story brings back to my mind another occasion that I feel I should now recount. Soon after we had settled in Ankara, we had the occasion to make two rather important calls. The first of these calls was made to the house whose master was always an idol for me. The president of Turkey, Mr. İsmet İnönü. My father had been the private secretary to the prime minister when İnönü had been elected to that post. Their relationship had developed over the years, so much so that Father had been allowed to call the prime minister's mother, Cevriye Hanımefendi "mother." Father and Mother took me along with them to the house and we were asked to stay over for lunch. The Pascha, as it was his custom to do, asked me to sit by his side and all through the meal asked in his whimsical manner about my reflections on America. At the end of the meal I asked if I would be allowed to light a cigarette. İsmet Pascha's answer was very positive. "Yes, you may smoke, but only with the condition that you must blow the smoke towards me." He also very graciously lit my cigarette. My appreciation of him had instantly quadrupled. At this juncture, I would like to relate another episode in my family life related to İsmet İnönü. When they had promulgated a law making it compulsory for everyone to have a surname, Father felt he was in a quandary. His family's surname in the past was "Haci Ali Molla Zade." However, the new law also prohibited the use of old or non-Turkish names. So apart from "Ali" the rest of the names he had were contrary to law. In fact, one evening Father said to Mother, "Cemile Sultan, I am afraid the only part of my old family name is a simple 'Ali'." Later on he was able to register his father's name "Sahir" as his surname. Some time later, during a visit to Mr. İnönü, that venerable gentleman had asked what surname Father had taken. When he heard that Father had taken his father's name as a surname he objected and said, "I would like to give you a surname. Your surname should be "SILAN." Father asked what that meant and İnönü said, "tall and loyal." Father countered this by saying that he was hardly a tall man and İnönü said, "You are a very loyal person and you have two tall sons." Then he wrote on his personal paper in his own hand "The surname of Necmeddin Sahir should be 'SILAN.' May it bring fortune to his family." He gave this note to my father. So our family surname became Sılan and I still cherish the original handwritten note İnönü gave Father. The note is also dated, 27-12-1942. I still enjoy having this note in a silver frame and it still has a place of honor in my drawing room.

Getting out of the train the next morning in Ankara was also rather nostalgic. We had done so many trips from that station, to and fro, during all the past years we had lived there. After all, we had many friends and acquaintances in Ankara whom we had missed for such a long period. Now a new life for each of us was about to start.

At Sumer Sokak No. 42 there were again servants waiting for our arrival. Only the cook had traveled with us. There were two new ladies to do the housework. Our family had also become larger, by the addition of a new bride. My room had stayed as it always was. A new bedroom had been prepared for the newly-weds. The next morning as usual I found my allowance in an envelope, on top of my piano. My parents had never given me money outright but chose to place my allowance in an envelope placed on my piano. The amount included in the envelope would be increased from year to year. If I needed something extra, I could always consult Mother.

X

Life in Ankara and the Faculty of Languages

We were slowly getting to settle down in Ankara. Our second important visit was to that very honorable gentleman, Abdülhalik Renda. After all, he was the cause of our journey to America. Without his insistence and backing of my point of view, Mother would never have been allowed to go. I was somewhat apprehensive on this visit because our journey had not achieved its goal. Nevertheless, that mature gentleman was appreciative of my unfinished education. By this time the parliament had convened and Father was engulfed in his political life. Mother was delighted at being once more with her beloved husband and at the same was able to divert her attention to her children plus an American bride.

Cenan had a scholarship from a state institution, namely Sümerbank, and since it was obligatory for him, he had accepted a position in that institution. He was immediately appointed as a control engineer in the new parliament building about to be built. Nur on the other hand wanted to do his compulsory military service.

I was the only one who had nothing to do. So I started to seek my old friends. I found that Semra (Soysal) had married a businessman and had a son while I was in the States. I found her as a beautiful housewife and mother, happily settled in Ankara. Hayriye (Neyzi) had returned from Afghanistan, where her father had accepted a post some years ago, and was now engaged to a young engineer. They really looked charming, together. Jale (Eralp) was still a student at Ankara University. Leyla Şaman (Pekdeğer) had already gotten married before we had left for Boston. Poor Leyla had had a rather funny sort of a wedding.

Her father had been appointed ambassador to some South American country. Leyla had thought that she would be going there together with her father, however, suddenly her father announced that he was going to get married (again) and travel with his new wife. That meant Leyla would no longer be needed in the embassy. So suddenly Leyla decided to accept the wedding offer that a young doctor had made and had repeated his offer a number of times and to stay in Ankara. However, the situation was somewhat unfortunate. Dr. Pekdeğer was doing his military service at a distant town. Her father insisted that his daughter be properly married before he left the country. So all formalities were done in a hurry. The wedding was to take place in their home at No. 10 İzmir Caddesi. At the last minute the groom's leave was cancelled or he was snowbound where he was stationed or something, so Leyla became a bride without the groom being present at the wedding. She was certainly a beautiful bride. On my return she was already a mother. They had their first son. In a way I was able to contact all my old friends and with the inclusion of Cenan we began to develop a cohesive and enjoyable group.

One night we had a guest for dinner. Mr. Sedat Simavi, a person I had the privilege of calling "Uncle" and who was a well-known newspaper magnate. During dinner I said, "Uncle Sedat, I have had three semesters in journalism in the States. I also spent some weeks as a trainee at the paper called *The Christian Science Monitor,* would you consider giving me a job?" He laughed heartily and countered, "You do not need a college degree for journalism. Come to my office and I will assign you to a job. You will learn as you work." Before I could open my mouth, both Mother and Father had loudly voiced their opposition to such an offer and no one would listen to me. I was heartbroken. His offer had meant for me to be stationed in İstanbul. That was something inconceivable for my parents.

Some time later the chief of staff, General Erdelhün, and his wife, came to our house for a visit. This had given me another opportunity to enquire about a job. The general said, "Come and see me, we can use your talents at JUSMAT." He also gave me a date. I prepared my C.V. and visited him at the date he gave.

117

I was assigned to work immediately. The building where JUS-MAT was quartered was a small house at İzmir Street. There were two or three military personnel in one room and they sat me at a table with a typewriter. I was told that my salary would be a considerable amount. One officer would come in and give me a piece of paper and say "Please type this immediately" and go out. I started typing and went on typing (without a lunch break) till 18:00 hours. I was home dead beat. I rushed to have a shower. The family was against my working. However, they could not very well refuse the chief of staff when he had shown such interest and willingness. After taking my shower, I dressed and called the general on the phone and explained that I was not interested in working as a typist and would like to be excused. The general was very kind. He said he understood my problem and would try to find me another position, however, I had had enough and I excused myself from working for the military. So that was that.

Next morning I got together all the documents connected with the education I had received in the past and without telling anyone what I was going to do, left the house saying, "I am going out to take a walk." When I left home I went directly to the Ankara University's faculty of history, geography and languages. I was aiming to obtain a diploma that would lead me to a career. My papers were in order and by noon I had been registered to the school for English language and literature. I chose sociology as an elective, since I had some classes on the subject when I was at Simmons. In those years a classical language, either Latin or Greek, was a requirement, so I had chosen Latin. When they studied my educational record and tested my command of English, I was told that I would join the fourth semester's classes. That meant skipping three semesters.

For quite a while I had told no one in the family what I was doing, even when the classes had started and I had to go to school more regularly. I was always creating various excuses for my absence. After classes I would go to the National Library to carry out my homework in peace and quiet.

There was a reason why I had to keep this a secret. Mother had always opposed my having a university degree. She was forced to give in when we were in America, since when I was enrolled as a student we were able to get my student's stipend from Turkey and we sorely needed the money at the time. Mother believed that women who had obtained higher education would tend to develop a high opinion of themselves and would be prone to look down on their husbands. She had enjoyed private education. She had learned several languages but had no university education. Nevertheless, her educational status as well as her general knowledge had made her somewhat superior to Father so that she had come to believe that Father resented his being less knowledgeable. On the other hand, father had made no bones about it. He always declared to all and sundry that his wife was a wonderful person and that he had learned everything from "Cem Sultan." Mother was called Cemile and Father always called her "Sultanim" (my Sultan) or Cem Sultan. Only when he had to deal with her in a serious question would he start calling her "Cemil," which is the masculine term for Cemile.

I was enjoying my classes at the university. Among my professors were many well-known figures, namely Orhan Burian, İrfan Şahinbaş, Prof. Gatenby and Hamit Dereli. At the same time my sociology teachers were Niyazi Berkes and Behice Boran. I am proud of having the chance to have attended their classes for more than two semesters. I had admired these highly educated people. They were actually scientists and they were being subject to some sort of a witch hunt by being accused of being Communists. During that year I had witnessed a number of occasions when other teachers would slam their doors when they saw Prof. Berkes or Boran coming! It really hurt me to be a witness to such unfair actions. Finally they both had to leave the institution and the real losers were us, the students. For Latin language I was following the course Prof. Samim Sinanoglu was conducting and for Latin literature, our teacher was his brother, Suat Sinanoglu. Like most of the students I admired Suat Bey, who was very attractive as well as romantic.

We were also getting to know a lot of people in Ankara. Since Cenan was still a bachelor we tended to go out together. I do not remember where or how we met, but I remember we had made friends with a young girl called Meral. She was a tall and good-looking girl with a light complexion who wore very simple but chic dresses. We learned that her surname was Ataç,

119

and she invited us to her house to meet her father and mother. That was how I was introduced to Mr. Nurallah Ataç who had made a name for himself as an essayist and critic. Somehow he took an instant delight in me and was very cordial. I felt rather proud. I was reading his articles and admiring his prose. Maybe that was one of the reasons why he liked me. He naturally knew my father. After a few visits to their house, Mr. Ataç had developed a habit of asking me to sit by his side. He said he admired my emancipation and open mindedness. I on the other hand believed I was learning something new each time he opened his mouth. In one such visit I was introduced to Oktay Rifat, the young poet who had become famous, and who was there for a visit.

Once they asked me to stay for lunch. Then Nurullah Bey forced the issue and said that I should set a date and also tell them my favorite dishes. I was at a loss and ashamedly I mumbled that I liked "Circassian Chicken" and "Aşure" best. I must have been really confused and did not realize what I was getting into. Both dishes I mentioned are famous local dishes and both took a very long time to prepare. That beautiful, motherly lady not only prepared both of them exquisitely but also kept insisting that I should have second and third helpings. That evening I developed a severe tummy ache!

Being in company with such people one could not help getting to learn about what was going on in Turkish literary circles. I had a chance to read some of the new Turkish poetry, reported published in a book called *Garip*. When I enquired where I could purchase a copy, Uncle Ataç instantly had a copy for me. I enjoyed the book so much that I wanted to meet the poet, Orhan Veli. I was told that he had some sort of a bureaucratic duty at a bank near Ulus Square. So, one day I decided to dare myself and went into his workplace. I asked where Orhan Veli was and found myself facing a very thin and tall young man whose face was full of pimples. I had the book with me. I pushed the book toward him and asked for his autograph. He was quite surprised but gently signed the book for me. His eyes were so melancholy that I was filled with compassion for this much misunderstood genius.

Since I had become a regular at the National Library, the manager of that institution, Mr. Ötügen, also developed an interest in me. He was a very well-read person. Since I had become accustomed to speak with my professors at Simmons, it was not difficult for me to develop personal relations with my elders. I was quite happy with what I was doing. At the university I had been reunited with my former school friend from high school.

My University venture could not be kept secret for long. At the time Father was bitter about Nur not obtaining his diploma from Harvard. So I said, "Father, what is the difference. In a few years I will make a gift of my university diploma to you. Why don't you let go of Nur." I doubt if Father appreciated what I had told him.

Just as everything looked like settling down new problems erupted in the house. Nur wanted to do his military service as quickly as possible. However, he had learned that the regulations at the time were such that if a man was married to a foreign woman, then the army would only take him as a common soldier and his term of duty would be three years. Whereas in other conditions his term would be much shorter and he would be a cadet officer. Under these conditions the best thing Nur could do would be to officially divorce Pat before getting into uniform. It was very difficult to explain this situation to Pat. I guess she must have been frightened and thought that she was being duped. Our bride was having all sorts of troubles in the meantime. Pat was accustomed to paper tissues but they were unavailable in Turkey. The milk we were getting locally had a different taste for her since it was not pasteurized. Of course she could not get the kind of lipstick she used to find in the States. Neither could she find on the newsstands the kinds of magazines she was accustomed to find back home. Gradually Pat began to turn into a woman who hardly left her room and sulked all day in the house. Mother was terribly worried. She liked her daughter-in-law and would like to make life more enjoyable for her. Naturally the duty was falling on me. I was supposed to be able to help her. Luckily there were other "foreign brides" in town. Pat was introduced to a few such people we knew. For example, there was Ata Berker's wife from Sweden and another wife from America. All these ladies had found jobs.

121

So Pat followed their example and applied and got a job in the American Embassy. This calmed her down somewhat. During this time Nur had started his service somewhere away from Ankara. He was, however, back after a few months and registered at the Cadet School in Ankara. He was boarding at the school and came home only for the weekends. When the school term ended Nur was transferred as an aide and interpreter to an American general in Ankara.

Cenan and I had become good friends in the meantime. We had gradually mixed our friends together and formed a sort of group that got together almost every weekend. Most of Cenan's friends that I met were brilliant young men who had had a good education in their background. Among them were several people whose friendship I still enjoy.

I was always forward in social affairs. So I asked Mother if I could arrange "open house" parties on Sundays. Anyone in our group could come to our house from 3:00 P.M. on. These parties got to be so popular that many people started coming so we had to use pillows to sit on the floor due to the crowd. Some of the younger set from the Department of Foreign Affairs had started to join our parties as well. Sometimes people would get into fierce arguments about politics or we would listen to the latest jazz music, all having fun one way or another. About 5:00 P.M. tea and cakes and or pastries would be offered and usually a program would be arranged for the evening. We would all go to a movie or a restaurant, etc.

In those days the Süreyya (Serge's Night Club was the "in" place in Ankara. As I have already mentioned, this night club was opened in the basement at which Mme. Marga used to run her studio, to which I also had been enrolled as a student for dancing lessons. The owner of the new night club was the previous maitre d' of the Karpiç Restaurant called Süreyya Bey (his original name was Sergei, a White Russian). His was the sort of night club where well-known people and diplomats would frequent. We, especially as unmarried young girls, could only go there with our parents up to that date. However, most of our friends were already working and they enjoyed going there on their own. For me Mother drew the line. I could only go there in the company of my brother Cenan and I should be back by midnight at the latest. Süreyya's was rather an expensive place and unless our parents would agree to take us there we could only go there after having our meals at home and have just a drink and dance to our hearts' desire. There would always be a good orchestra and all kinds of dance music would be played. Since we were all young and gay, we enjoyed dancing and having fun. This sort of a thing took place only once a week or twice in a month. My open house parties had began to help grow our circle of friends, since our friends were encouraged to bring their friends as well! We were all single and enjoyed having a good time. We enjoyed dancing, jabbering and discussing things. The nucleus of the group, as far as I was concerned, were my earliest childhood friends. In short, we were a happy group.

My only problem, especially whenever I was going to Süreyya's Night Club, turned out to be Mother. Our house was situated on the corner of an avenue and a street. Just as I was returning to the house I would be sure to find the silhouette of my mother in the corner window watching the street. I knew she was waiting to see what time I came home and who had brought me in. She just would not go to sleep until she had made sure that I had returned home safely and on time. I was always very punctual. After all they had entrusted me with the key to the house. I could be a few minutes late and Cenan always took me home. Sometimes he would walk with me to the house and return to join the ongoing party. He was a grown up person, working as an engineer. On the other hand I was a young girl living in a community where social rules were still considered very important and I was living under strict regulations developed by the society around us.

I guess we must have gone to dance somewhat too often that month and Mother mumbled something like "You cannot find a husband at a night club." I was terribly cross, especially since I was not at all looking forward to getting married yet. I had seen a number of my friends as married women and did not relish the thought of becoming like them. I was interested in education and wanted to be able to obtain my economic independence. Of course many of the girls around were dying to find a suitable man and to get married. In fact, I knew that matchmakers had been calling on my mother. Such an approach to marriage seemed frightful to me. It sounded like buying a horse. You buy because it has a good pedigree. I would never agree to come out of my room, whenever I felt there was a matchmaker visiting mother. Mother would keep telling me about such and such a gentleman who was very well educated, had personal means, had finished his military service and I would leave the room immediately. Once we were arguing the point and I asked Mother, since the gentleman in question had all these qualities, why did he not find a wife for himself among the girls he must have met but instead agreed to send his "aunt" to observe someone he had never laid his eyes on? I wondered how such people existed, having no choice of their own but doing things someone else told them to do, even if this was their mother. Marriage should be consummated between equals or at least between persons with similar backgrounds or similar education. Otherwise how could diverse personalities suddenly get married and try to live together? All of this was quite unimaginable for me.

There were some young men that I found attractive. However, such feelings would not always be reciprocal. On the other hand, I enjoyed some very dear friendships. I was getting a proper education, I had a good life and a happy family. On top of all that I was a healthy human being. What more could one wish for?

The summer of 1947 the family was back in Erenkiöy. Our old cabby was once more taking us to the beach every morning. There we found our other local friends. Apart from the usual beaches there was a new club called the Marmara. We started going to this club also. Since I did not like sandy beaches too much, I began to prefer the club where one could plunge into deep water from the wide marble terraces. This club was housed in one of the old mansions, which had huge ballrooms and contained some of the luxurious furniture left over from old times. There were two different restaurants, one inside the building and the other in the garden. On balmy summer nights it was heavenly to dance under the big pine trees and the gorgeous moonlight. The mansion was more like a seraglio. Despite its size it had very few bedrooms but a huge ballroom with wall-to-wall marquetry. There were many full-sized mirrors with gold plated frames. It certainly carried all the Ottoman grandeur.

In daytime we would all pile into a friend's very small automobile and wander all over town. We had done so many trips so many times that we decided to call the little car "why travel always." I can never forget the fun we had that summer.

Our life was divided between İstanbul (in the summer) and Ankara (for the rest of the year) Nur was still doing his military service when Pat realized she was expecting. So they decided to go back to the States as soon as Nur's service ended. Pat wanted to give birth to her baby in her native land and her mother had invited them to stay with her. This was a normal desire for an American girl. However, it was very hard for Mother to accept this arrangement. As Cenan used to describe her, Mother was like a hen who wanted to oversee all her chicks all of the time. This was going to be her first grandchild and she would not be able to attend him or her. So it was a prolonged period of secret cries and long letters being read over and over. Finally the good news came. Can (John) was born in Boston. This was especially cause for jubilation for Mother. It was a sort of sour and sweet occasion since she had had no chance to cuddle, let alone to see and hug her first grandson! So Mother now was spending most of her daily life looking for suitable gifts for her first grandson and writing and waiting for letters (also for photos of the newborn).

As Nur was going to the States, Cenan had registered for his military service. He wished to do his service before settling down. Mother was again in a tizzy. What would her eldest son do, would he survive army life? Cenan was very straightlaced where his duties were concerned. He did not skip a single day from duty and graduated from the Cadet School with high honors and he was given a golden watch! Once out of the Cadet School, Cenan was assigned as an aide to an American general stationed in Ankara and that meant he began to have regular office hours. Thus Mother was once more her calm self. During his military service Cenan came across some of his old friends. One of them was a classmate of his at the St. Joseph Lycée. He had been a very good friend of Cenan's. Since his family lived in İstanbul, he was allowed to declare himself as our household guest, thereby being able to spend his weekends in our house. He was always the fun maker of the party. His mother was a well-known painter, who had a very elegant salon in Moda. When we were also living in Moda, the families used to visit one another.

I was happy the way my life was developing. I enjoyed studying at the university and my grades were always good. I was especially proud of the fact that Prof. Gatenby and his wife enjoyed my company so much that I was constantly being invited to their home. Prof. Gatenby was instrumental in my getting an introduction to the worldwide recognized author, Agatha Christie, who had come for a visit to Ankara. I was proud to have met this brilliant woman.

I used to cover my extra hours by playing the piano or be reading. Mother had rather tired of attending official receptions and would ask Father to take me along on such occasions. So I began to attend cocktail parties and receptions as a partner to Father, mostly at the embassies in Ankara. Mother had another peculiar system. Especially if we were to attend a reception where there would be a buffet, she would insist that I eat a proper meal before going so that I would not demean myself by trying to get my plate filled. At first I was resentful but gradually I began to realize why she was so insistent. In a way neither of us had foreseen, I had began to get the chance of talking to important people of the day, while everyone else was rushing for food. Some of the leading diplomats of that time would not go to the buffet either and then I would have a chance to talk to them to my heart's content. Their conversation was always stimulating and very instructive. There were also some foreign diplomats with whom I was delighted to have a chat. Probably because of the fact that I had grown up with two elder brothers, I had grown accustomed to be with men. I usually avoided women's groups. Listening to men one could always learn things, whereas women's gossip never interested me. Naturally there were especial ladies that I admired but as they say, exceptions do not change the rules.

I liked indulging in sports and in Ankara the best period for that was the spring. I used to cycle and play tennis. When summer came, in Erenköy, besides cycling we were swimming and rowing. Mother, however, never allowed me to ski or to ride horses. Her declaration on horseback riding sounded to me almost ludicrous, but she stuck to what she believed in. According to Mother, one should only ride a horse one owned. Since we could not afford to have one of our own, I should not consider riding someone else's horse. On the other hand, she was deadly afraid that I would get involved in an accident if I skied. All my life I only had one occasion to ride on a horse. We had gone to Yalova, to visit a cousin of my father. He was an officer of the navy and had been assigned to a village near Yalova. He had let me ride his horse. I was delighted and was not afraid of falling off the animal.

Quite a while had passed since our return from America. A number of my friends had gotten married during this period and I was happy for them. On the other hand the idea of getting married was not in my mind at all. I wanted to first graduate from the university that I was attending. Possibly I would do some graduate work after that. All my life I had been interested in creating things with my hands. Maybe I could also study painting or sculpture in the future.

For the first time in my life I fell in love. It was the summer of 1948. This did not happen suddenly. I had met a friend of Cenan, who was about his age. He was not only very good-looking but he was also well educated, sensitive and a colorful person. Our families had known one another for many years. He already had his own business and was considered quite well off. He had been married before and had just divorced his wife when we met. Our friendship had started through Cenan and was blossoming under his supervision. Our meetings by the sea sometimes continued in our houses, where he would recite sonnets from Shakespeare to me. Or else we would be talking, going around with mutual friends. We had quite a group of friends that we both enjoyed. Meanwhile, feeling his interest in me, I had began to fall in love with him. Since he knew that Mother would not allow me to go places with him on our own, he would always invite my brother, as well as some of our friends along. For example, if I wanted to go to a place on the European side of İstanbul, he would ask my whole entourage to come in the motor boats or several cars he would hire. He would invite the

whole bunch of friends again, if he wanted to take me out dancing, offering them all caviar and champagne dinners, etc. Meanwhile, I was the important one and I was in love. This platonic
love started developing into a mutual attachment. Its being platonic was entirely his desire. He had been quite a womanizer
beforehand. Now what attracted him was my innocence and he
wanted this to last.

He knew we were about to return to Ankara. One evening
he told me that he would like to marry me. I was delighted. That
night when I told the family about his offer, all hell broke. Giving
utterly different reasons, all the members of my family violently
disapproved of such a match. As if this was not enough, I was
forced to leave for Ankara the next day without even having a
chance to talk to him again.

Today, I still cannot understand how I could have been so
docile and what kind of subservience I had toward my family. I
was over the age of consent, namely I was over eighteen. I could
have opposed them. Somehow I had not resisted in the slightest
degree. They could be right in one point, the man I loved was
drinking too much but I could have changed him. All I did was
cry my eyes out, but that changed nothing. No marriage could
be consummated. They just would not budge. Turgut would
phone from İstanbul at least twice every day and would plead
with me to marry him. He thought I did not want him. Lovely
bouquets of fresh flowers were sure to follow each phone call.
This made me feel more miserable. I hated all members of my
family. On the other hand I did nothing but cry and stay at
home. It was a hopeless situation. I was very unhappy. Mother
and Father started making alternative suggestions. "We'll take
you to Switzerland" or "Since you want to further your education, we'll send you to Paris for your Ph.D. program" were some
of the offers. Whenever I said I wanted to marry Turgut they
were adamant. I would not give up easily. My logic kept re-
minding me that my parents were probably in the right, however, my heart would not stop beating for my love. We had been
going around for a long time but apparently my parents had not
been aware that we were getting interested in one another. Now,
it was too late.

After some time, gradually I began to go back to my usual routine. I was attending my classes at the university and I was playing the piano. During those days I had become a student of the well-known pianist, Mr. Fenmen. He was a remarkable piano teacher. With his encouragement, I can say that almost all of my free time was spent at the piano. I was still against all prohibitions. I believed that when something is prohibited, one cannot help develop a quest for the thing that was prohibited. At least that seemed to be true for me. At the same time, for the first time, I was beginning to realize under what sort of protection and custody I was brought up!

It seemed that if I was ever going to think about marriage, it would probably be subject to the conditions laid out by my mother. What were these? First, the man I was to marry should be at least five years older than me. He should have a university degree. He must have finished his military service. He must have obtained his economic independence. He should belong to a family that resembled ours or our background anyway. He should be able to provide for me a life in comfort and should not be prone to things like alcohol or gambling. As is, this sounded like a man to be produced in a factory! Mother was a thoroughly well educated and experienced woman, however, she was over protective where I was concerned. And probably I was brought up to be overly docile.

It took me a long time to go out again. One evening, as usual together with Cenan, we went to a recently established restaurant, "The Three Horseshoes." The brother of one of our friends was also present. After my shattering experience, for the first time I felt a surge of tinge inside me for this good-looking young man. However, as the evening was over, according to the information I obtained about him, I told myself to avoid that young person since my family would never agree to him either. He was about my age. He did not have a university degree and he was just doing his military service. His family was good enough but he was not economically independent. This meant on almost every count he did not fit Mother's recipe and therefore I should forget him as soon as possible and try not to meet him again! In those years it was not possible for a young girl to go around with a male companion unless it was accepted that the liaison was to end in marriage. Only after they were officially engaged would the couple be allowed to go out on their own. How social conditions have changed in the nearly half a century that has just passed. It is difficult to comprehend the degree of change that has taken place. I believe the change had already begun when I had finally married, but still there were a number of occasions when people tried to "matchmake" for me. I would not even agree to meet the women who came "visiting" for such a purpose and create a big fuss, proclaiming that "I was not for sale and would not agree to be displayed for such a purpose." Mother had began to be worried about my future. She was looking forward to my delivering her the ever wanted grandchildren. I should get married, make babies and she would enjoy her grandchildren to no end. This was a subject that came up on almost every possible occasion.

XI

Graduation and My Trip to Europe

One spring day Father came home rather thoughtful and exhausted. He was highly strained and nervous. It turned out that afternoon in the cession of the parliament he had made some declarations and they were received rather badly by the man he adored most, namely the president, İsmet İnönü! Father was a man of convictions and probably his insistence on what he believed in had caused him to go against his leader. Since he could not accept this defeat, on May 22, 1950 Necmeddin Sahir resigned from his seat in the parliament. He also resigned from his much loved party and would never accept to join another political organization. Only after a year was he again being accepted to İnönü's circle of friends and could visit the president, even after that venerable gentleman had lost in the elections. What I find very unfortunate is that although he frequently mentioned it, he never wrote his memoirs and we could not find any notes after he passed away.

That same year, in 1950, I graduated from the university in June. After getting my diploma I asked Mother if I could go to Paris to continue my studies. Possibly painting. The first objection came from Cenan. He said, "You'll become a vagabond, you are too pure to be able to survive in a megapolis like Paris." After prolonged research and discussions we were able to agree on Florence. In the fall I would be sent to Florence. First we found a school for languages. I had to learn Italian. Then a search was started for a suitable boarding house that would be in the vicinity of the Institute of Arts and the necessary applications were made. My preference for Paris had really stemmed from the fact that I would not have any trouble with the language. However, learning Italian was also a gain for me and I was sure to enjoy it.

During the summer, one of our professors from the Department of Geography had started to form a group with the idea of a tour in Europe. I thought I would enjoy joining such a group. A number of students from my department had already joined. We heard that there were some actors and actresses from the National Theatre joining the group of students also. The trip was to start from İstanbul on the National Maritime Company's vessel also called *İstanbul*. Then they would ride the train to Paris and then cross over to London. There would also be arranged bus tours along the south of France and the group would board another boat, this time called *Ankara,* from Marseille for the return trip to İstanbul. We would probably be staying at student hostels in Europe or even camp out as the case may be. So we were advised to obtain backpacks, blankets and sleeping bags. All these precautions were deemed necessary to make the cost of the voyage cheaper for the students.

I had to beg for a long time and finally I was able to get my parents' approval to join the trip. The real reason why I was able to obtain their approval, I knew, was due to the fact that Mr. İnönü's family had approved their daughter's joining this trip. Anyway, after long preparations and sermons on what to do and what not to do and being given some foreign currency for possible extra expenses, I found myself on the boat. Since the family had already moved to İstanbul for the summer, all the members of my family were on the pier to see me off! I waved to them from the top deck in glee. İstanbul was like a picture postcard as the boat was leaving the port. We, a group of girls, were to sleep in a common cabin below deck. After settling down and washing up, I went up on deck to meet the rest of the group. The only people I knew in the group were Özden İnönü and another young girl who was a cousin of a general, once again a close friend of Father's. There were also a number of actors from the National Theatre whom I enjoyed meeting.

As I mentioned, that shower and the cool breeze on the deck was to cause my downfall. When I woke up in my bunk the next morning I was running a very high fever. They took me to the ship's infirmary and I spent some days there. Finally, a few days later, as we were reaching Marseille, I was allowed to get dressed provided that I promised to take care of myself. So I went into the ship's main restaurant and sat at the bar and ordered some coffee. There were a lot of people sitting at the tables but I recognized no one. After a while a portly gentleman approached, indicating to another portly man sitting at one of the tables and said something like, "My friend would like to invite you to our table, would you please oblige and accept his invitation." When I looked over I saw the person involved and I immediately recognized who he was. I was under the impression that he too had recognized me and was being polite. He was indeed very polite, he even got up when I reached their table and held my chair. He said, "My dear young lady, where were you all this while, you never appeared at the bar or at the restaurant until today?" I explained that I had fallen sick and that I had spent the time in the ship's infirmary. He continued by asking with whom I was traveling. When I explained about our student group and our plans, he said, "Please, you should not go and sleep in tents, you have already been sick once, we are going to stay at the George V Hotel in Paris. Please come and stay with us, won't you?" I was very surprised and also angry. I could not help myself and encountered his dubious invitation by referring to something that happened in the past. I said, "My dear sir, you may recall that some years ago in Ankara a certain lady had called on your house in the early hours of the morning and had told you that she was planning to go to the National Assembly that morning and enquire 'Who are the gentleman who declared prohibition in the country and then turn around and get people's husbands drunk like a horse?' " He had turned absolutely white. I calmly added, "I happen to be the daughter of Necmeddin Sılan and I thank you for your kind invitation. Now, I am afraid I have to go." I left their table in a huff. Life always plays funny tricks on people!

This was a true story that had been repeated many times in our family. Father was working as an aide to Mustafa Kemal. He never drank and asked Gazi Pascha to allow him not to take alcohol since this would interfere with his work and he was not accustomed to it. The Pascha had agreed and Father joined his table but did not drink. Many nights the Pascha's dinner table lasted into the wee hours of the morning. One early morning when Father arrived home he was totally drunk. Mother was

133

very surprised. Then she heard a motorcar going away. So she asked Father who had driven him home. He told her the name of the person. Mother was very angry. So immediately she put some warm clothes on and not caring the time of the night she started her trek to town. It was almost dawn. When she reached the gentleman's house, naturally his bodyguards met her. The man had already gone to bed. However, when the bodyguards realized who Mother was, they had to wake him up. When Mother was able to confront the gentleman she explained to him of her decision to appear at the National Assembly that Saturday morning and raise a fuss. In those days the assembly recessed on Fridays, and Saturdays were a working day. Anyway, the gentleman was very apologetic, and promised Mother that he would not let Father drink again and most probably woke up his driver and sent Mother back home in his car.

By the time we disembarked at Marseille the group had become more cohesive. Everyone was enjoying the trip and I was able to meet them all in the train. I am sorry that I cannot remember the names of all the people who had joined the group. However, I remember enjoying all of them. Once in Paris, they took us to a boarding house of a Lycée in Vincennes, quite in the outskirts of the town. It had a huge garden which reminded me of Erenköy and I already had started missing home. After our beds had been assigned and we had settled down, they took us in a bus into Paris proper.

While I was sick in the infirmary, our group had met a couple called M. and Mme. Poupaert. He happened to be the Chief Inspector of the Police in a quarter of Paris. His wife was born in İstanbul. She was of Armenian descent and loved İstanbul. We had met them again on the boat before disembarking and our relationship had been very cordial. With his help we were able to see many parts of Paris that we probably would never find on our own. One evening he invited some of us to a restaurant. Years later I was delighted to be able to introduce these people to my friends who had settled in Paris. Ahmet and Hayriye Neyzi were delighted to meet this kind couple who loved Turkey and the Turks.

I could never learn why but the visit to London was cancelled. We boarded busses and our return trip started. We went through Menton and reached Nice. I remember some of the richer people in the group going in for some gambling in Monte Carlo. We had visited a large aquarium as well, and had seen many kinds of fish. Finally, on a rainy day, we reached a field and they told us that tents would be raised for us. It had rained heavily the night before our arrival. We were told that we would be sleeping on sheets filled with straw but the straw offered to us was also soaking wet. I refused to sleep there under those conditions. I still had some money on me and I decided to find myself a boarding house. Suddenly I saw Özden İnönü. Not caring about her long hair already wet, she was getting ready to bunk on those wet straw beds. No wonder. Her upbringing was such that she would willingly suffer whenever the conditions warranted it. I do not recall how long the trip lasted but I always cherish the memory.

XII

Who Can Tell What the Future Holds for Us?

While I was traveling in Europe, Cenan had met a young man whose company he had enjoyed. This young man had been educated in America and had obtained a master's degree in architecture from Cornell University. After he had succeeded in getting his A.I.A. and was given permission to practice architecture in the United States. As a result he had worked for four years at a very reputable firm of architecture in Manhattan. His family owned Viranbağ, a sprawling pine forest in Büyükada. Their introduction to one another had occurred through our mutual friend Cemile. A rather funny story was told about this budding relationship. It appears that Cemile had told him that her friend "Cenan" was coming to visit her and that he should also come. He had expected that the visitor would be a girl. At another time Cemile had told the architect that "Nur, another friend, would be coming this afternoon" and again he was surprised to meet my younger brother. Finally Cemile had mentioned that I was coming and the young architect, expecting to meet another man, had asked, "Don't they have any girls in this family?"

When I had returned to Ankara, the same architect was also in Ankara to do his military service. The family had met him and everyone was telling me that I was sure to like him. I, on the other hand, was thinking about nothing but to go to Florence, as it was arranged. The way they kept describing him was very much like my mother's description of an eligible young man in the past. Were they playing a game behind my back?

One evening our mutual friend Feyyaz Söker phoned. He said he was celebrating his birthday at Sureyya's and would I and Cenan agree to join his party. At first I was a little cross.

136

He could have called us a few days earlier, I thought. I was in the mood to refuse his invitation. Furthermore, we had tickets to view Orson Welles in his much acclaimed film called the *The Third Man*. Finally Mother said, "You two cannot refuse such an invitation, he is a dear friend after all. However, you can say that you are booked for the movie but would join them after the film. That way you can congratulate Feyyaz for his birthday and leave the party early."

So we did as Mother had suggested. As usual the night club was swinging. Feyyaz had gathered quite a group of friends. They were all very happy to see Cenan and me and said "better late than never." I was still trying to keep somewhat aloof. We said hello to everyone. Someone I had not yet met offered me his seat. I was a bit taken aback. He looked a lot like the actor that I admired so much and whose film I had just seen. It was as if Orson Welles had walked into the room. He presented himself as "Togrul Devres" and managed to sit next to me. So, this was the man all the family kept talking about! The famous architect who owned Viranbağ! Drinks were served and people had started dancing. I had told Cenan beforehand that I would not be dancing that evening and when the architect asked me to dance, I refused. However, the man was already up. He would not take "no" for an answer. He said, "I will wait here until you make up your mind." Everyone at the table was watching us. I was creating a scene. So I was forced to get up and walk with him to the dance floor. We circled on the dance floor once and I said that this was enough and that I was tired, however, he would not let me go. He was dancing superbly. I was still trying to show that I was cross with Feyyaz because he had forgotten to invite us till the last moment. At last we sat down. I persuaded Cenan to take me home. All my efforts had been to no avail. No one had realized how turned off I was for not being invited earlier and Cenan simply took me home and went back to the party.

After that party we met Togrul Bey a couple of times at various places. Mostly we would be in a group and our conversation would be cordial. He did mention that he had heard I was going abroad to study painting. At another time he suggested that he could give me some preliminary lessons in painting before I went aboard. I had heard from friends that the architect

137

was also quite a good painter. At the time Feyyaz and Togrul were sharing a bachelor's flat in Kavaklıdere. Since both were bachelors, I knew I could not go to his flat for painting lessons. When I mentioned this objection he offered to come to our house for the lessons. That was, if I liked the idea and if my parents would approve. When I consulted Mother, her answer was simple. She said, "Why not?" So the painting lessons started. He brought all the paints and the brushes, etc. During lessons we both were very serious and never gave way to loqacious familiarity.

We went to celebrate the New Year, namely 1951, at a friend's house. Both Feyyaz and Togrul were attending the same party. I had had a bit too much to drink and I was actually enjoying the party that night. Togrul Devres meant nothing to me for all I cared. As a matter of fact he must have been bored at the party and he left early. Later, while the party was still going on, he called me on the phone and he said something like, "I came home and painted you on the canvas while you were having a good time at the party." It sounded like he was cross at something and frankly I could not help wondering what kind of a portrait he had done of me.

Toward the end of January, Feyyaz and Togrul arranged to have a party at the apartment they were sharing. I agreed to attend, especially to be able to see my portrait and went with Cenan as usual. That night Togrul not only showed me the portrait he had made but sat and talked with me for a long time. Toward the end of the party, just as I was asking his leave to join the others, he suddenly said, "Tell Cenan I am going to be his brother-in-law." As far as I could make out this was his way of proposing marriage. Out of the blue! I was quite surprised. He added, "Yes, I would like to marry you." I answered back with a few questions like, "Are you sure you are not drunk?" and "Did you actually think about this?" At the same time many things were twirling in my mind. This young man fitted everything Mother had described. He sounded like he was seriously in love with me and he made me feel this. I knew I was to be wedded one day. I also realized that I was certainly enjoying the attention he was showering on me. This would be a good match for all concerned. Cenan was passing by at that moment, I called out to him and repeated what the young architect had just said. Cenan must have thought that our relationship had developed along a serious line, he was delighted and he congratulated both of us most heartily. This was my first step into marriage.

XIII

When Is the Engagement?

Eight months after that night we were married. The period in between was rather peculiar and therefore it is rather difficult for me to remember details after so many years. Marcel Proust has written in his book *In Search of Lost Time* that "trying to live our past life is a futile endeavor." I shall, however, try to recount what took place during those eight months.

That night Cenan invited all the people to the party at Süreyya's for champagne to celebrate our coming marriage. I was still somewhat perturbed. What would be Mother's reaction to all this? Was I making a terrible mistake? That night when it was time for me to go home Togrul took me instead of Cenan. Mother as usual was up and waiting for me. As soon as I entered home Mother asked, "Where is Cenan, who took you home tonight?" In a frivolous mood I answered, "Dear Mother, I found myself a husband at Süreyya's" Mother dropped the cigarette she was about to light. Questions followed one another like an avalanche. Finally I got her to sit down and lit her cigarette and got her to calm down a bit. Then I told her the whole story. At the very end I told her that I had accepted the offer Togrul had made. The smile that had appeared on her face was instantly gone. She was curiously angry. She said, "Why did you have to accept his offer so quickly, did you think that you were going to be an old maid? You should have waited until all enquiries had been finalized." At the end she also asked when the young man would come and ask for my hand from Father in a formal way. I just answered that I had no idea!

In the morning Togrul was on the phone. He suggested we should meet and take a walk in the afternoon. He was doing his military service and as a cadet officer he was attached to an

American general as interpreter. So he could take time out in the afternoon. I agreed. I knew nothing about him except what Cenan had told me. I did not know him. Yes, I did like his looks and I was attracted to him, still who was this man? This person I had agreed to marry?

There was snow on the ground and it was freezing cold. We took a long walk regardless. I told him what Mother had said about asking for my hand. He said he would phone and get an appointment. When we were walking he began to mumble a song I had never heard before. Something that went like "When summer comes I love camellias" or something of the sort. I asked him how come he knew such a song, he calmly answered to the effect that he had been working in the theatre in the past and had been trained as an actor. Oh, my God! I was shocked! There is a Turkish saying "If you let a girl on her own, she will find a gypsy to get married to." Mother would now say, "Where did you pick up this actor?" Why had I accepted this man's offer so quickly? Was this a quirk of fate? As we were parting he gave me a small cardboard and said, "This portrait was drawn by a painter who did it by just listening to my description of you. I will tell the rest of the story later." Of course it was the first thing I looked at as soon as I was safely alone in my room. On the back of a cigarette box (I believe we had Yeni Harman cardboard packs those days) was an ink drawn portrait that actually did resemble me! I placed it next to my books in my library on the book shelf.

Togrul phoned that evening and asked for an appointment for 18:00 hours the next day. He came a little early and waited in my room for his appointment and during that time he told me the story about the portrait. He had an architect friend and one evening they were drinking rakı together and Togrul had started talking about me. Cihat Burak had asked if he could describe me to him and started drawing the portrait as Togrul was describing me. Funny, I never lost that small portrait and many years later one afternoon I went to Cihat Burak's vernissage (by that time he had become a well-known artist) at a gallery in Bebek, in İstanbul and displayed the cardboard painting. He was delighted. He agreed that it was his drawing but he had no idea when and where he had drawn it! So I told him the story.

141

He was very happy and he said, "This then needs more than one signature." So he signed both the cardboard and the passe-partout in which I had placed it. As Togrul's tale of the portrait was coming to an end, we realized it was time for him to meet my parents. Togrul suddenly said, "I do not think I can go through with this!" And he quickly left the room. I was left all by myself! I did not know what to do! Why had he left so suddenly? What should I say to my parents? I was so ashamed that I did not know where to turn or what to do. There was a knock on my door and one of the servants told me that Mother was asking for me. I was not at all sure that I could face Mother under these conditions, having been jilted a few minutes before! I had to drag my feet toward the drawing room. And what do I find! The future groom and my parents were chatting very amicably. Father started by saying that as long as my approval for this marriage had been obtained, they, as my parents would also approve. He was quite satisfied that we should make a perfect couple. So we were going to have a toast on it and since there were no alcoholic beverages in our house we all had a glass of white wine.

That day I had realized that the man I was getting married to had a peculiar sense of humor and that he enjoyed surprising me! I was not too sure but I did not mind this. I always enjoyed people who knew how to laugh and enjoy a joke.

After this small ceremony with my family, Togrul had to go to İstanbul and advise his family about his decision. On his return he informed us that he had obtained their approval. So the question of when we could have our engagement party came up. He wanted to have that ceremony to be carried out right away. I had different feelings about the affair. I wanted to make sure that all the traditional formalities be carried out. The first step should be for his parents to come to our house and ask my parents' consent for the marriage. Togrul said that his mother was afflicted with Parkinson's disease and it would be very difficult for her to travel to Ankara. However, I was young and adamant. They simply had to come and ask for my hand! So we delayed the date of our engagement to April 12, 1951. This way it would be easier for her to travel after winter. Furthermore, Togrul would have completed his military service and started working.

As planned, on April 11, the Devres couple (his mother and father) arrived by train to Ankara and after checking into their hotel, came calling to our house. They were accompanied by Togrul's elder brother Nezih and his wife. My parents already knew this couple. My mother-in-law to be was rather a fat and very jolly lady who laughed a lot. She had a dark complexion. I was told that her father was the late Hüseyin Haki Efendi. The information about this gentleman contained in various history books was quite interesting.

It appeared that he was born on Kandiya (on the island of Crete) and his father was a trustee of a certain foundation. The young child had lost his father at the age of nine and his uncle had sent him to Cairo, Egypt. There the young boy learned Arabic and French and grew up to be a very able and astute young man. He was able to attract the attention of the governor of Egypt, Kavalali Mehmet Ali Pascha and was appointed as the French teacher of the governor's son. He was later appointed as the trustee of a trust the Pascha had bestowed for his daughter. He had translated the classical French tragedy *Telemaque* and had obtained some sort of a recognition from the Ottoman Sultan Abdulhamid. After many exploits Hüseyin Haki had become very rich and married four times. His last wife had given birth to my mother-in-law, at the time Hüseyin Haki had reached the age of 80! That was why she was named "Gayet" since that word meant "the last." She was the last of sixteen children that Huseyin Haki had.

My father-in-law was also from Crete. He was a good-looking and serious man. His father owned a big farm and he had lost his farm and his life in a raging fire. After this calamity Mustafa Nuri had moved to İstanbul with his widowed mother together with his brother and sister. His perfect knowledge of Greek and French helped him to develop in his profession. He had studied law and had become a well-known lawyer. Later on in his career he had been elected chairman of the Legal Board in İzmir. He had now retired. They spent the winter in their sumptuous apartment in İstanbul and for the summer they would go to their big summer place on the Prinkipo Island. Their land on the island was said to cover some forty acres, including some woods.

Gayet and Mustafa Nuri Devres came to our house with their hands full of gifts. Everyone met one another, and we all chatted together. I enjoyed their company. I was marrying into a family just as mother had hoped for. They had four sons. The eldest resided in İzmir. The second son was living in Ankara and the third was in İstanbul. Togrul was the youngest son of the family.

After some more discussion and planning about the coming engagement party they asked to be excused since they were rather tired from the train ride. My future mother-in-law was really having trouble with her health. She had Parkinson's disease. Apparently something called dopamine was getting low in her brain causing these disturbances. I was somewhat sorry that I had insisted on their coming to Ankara when I saw the condition she was in, but it was too late to be sorry.

They came back again in the evening and we had a family dinner at our house. Knowing that I fancied a smoke after the meals, Togrul had told me that even his elder brothers refrained from smoking in their father's presence and could I please refrain myself, for once. I had not enjoyed this suggestion in the least bit. I was about to get married and I should not be told what I was to do or not to do. I also refused to hide my reactions and did not want to start a new relationship with lies. So, at the end of the meal I asked Mother for a cigarette and my father lit it for me. There was a moment of silence among the Devres family but it was for a moment only and the conversation went on as if nothing had happened. This show of courage on my part actually caused a bond between me and my in-laws and till the day he died my father-in-law (whom I used to call Mustafa Nuri Daddy) was always ready to light my cigarette. My understanding of showing respect was somewhat different.

My engagement gown also caused a stir. Together with Mother we had studied various alternatives and finally had a well-recognized dressmaker in Ankara make a strapless short dress (a style very much in the vogue those days) of green tafetta. Just a few days before the ceremony, Togrul saw the dress and reacted negatively. I was taken aback. Here was a man, who supposedly had been educated in America and had worked as an architect in Manhattan and now he was behaving in quite an unexpected manner! Seeing his displeasure I consulted my dressmaker, and she was able to find the same material of the same kind and she tailored a little bolero, covering my otherwise naked shoulders.

Our engagement was realized at the ballroom of the Anadolu Club. Our great benefactor and family friend Mr. Renda gave a beautiful speech and among well-wishers he put on our engagement rings. The general practice is to put the wedding ring on the ring finger of the right hand at the engagement ceremony and then change it to the left hand when the wedding takes place. I do not know what made me do it, but I asked to have the ring put on my left hand ring finger from the start. This meant I would not change it at the wedding also. I was trying to show that this was forever.

A few days after our engagement my fiancée went to İstanbul together with his parents, who were returning to their home. He had applied for various positions for work and he wanted to follow those leads. At that time we had not decided where we would want to settle down. Under the circumstances we could settle either in İzmir, İstanbul or Ankara. However, there was the possibility of our going to America, as Togrul had previously worked in New York. I had refused vehemently this possibility from the very start, since I did not wish to be too far from my family and my mother. On the other hand, returning to America could have an important effect on Togrul's career as an architect. However, he felt that my happiness and contentment was to be considered before everything else. My preference was to settle in Ankara. Although I loved İstanbul above every other city, being away from my family and developing a new milieu in İstanbul had somewhat frightened me. Togrul was to reside in his parent's apartment in the city during his stay in İstanbul. Therefore during the following days we were constantly on the phone. During the summer the Devres family would move to their summer place in Büyükada.

With Togrul's departure to İstanbul, Mother suggested I spend my free time to prepare for my future family life. At her suggestion I started taking sewing lessons. She consulted with an Italian lady dressmaker and for a certain amount of compensation she started giving me sewing lessons. My Spanish friend,

Nita Fernandez, luckily joined me during those lessons. I believe her father was later assigned to İstanbul as the council general of his country. Their youngest son had been enrolled at Robert College in İstanbul. Nita and I had started to devote our mornings to our sewing lessons. This practice did indeed turn out to be very useful for me in my future life. By the time my family had decided to move to Erenköy for the summer, I had developed quite a skill in sewing.

XIV

The Rights and the Wrongs

Erenköy was heavenly, as usual. Our wedding was to take place in September. The exact date could not yet be fixed for two reasons. Togrul Devres had just finished his military service and did not have the means to support his family and since he had made his decision to get married he wanted to start working and earn his living. His family had all the means in the world but Togrul refused to accept any help from his family. Actually, he was somewhat on a leave of absence from the architectural firm he had been working for in New York. He had returned to Turkey to visit his mother whose health was deteriorating and once in the country had decided to do his military service and get it over with. I still remember many of his friends enquiring (even in my presence sometimes), "Had you not planned to return to the U.S., what changed your plans?" Since he had returned from the States Togrul had been living on the savings he had accumulated and would refuse any financial help from his father. On the other hand, his savings was not much, at least not enough to set up a new home. I did offer to work at least until he was able to earn enough for both of us but he would not hear of such a thing. Getting married meant that he should be renting a flat. Mother, who was always ready to help, had kept one flat empty in case we would agree to move there. I was in no mood to be living in the same building with my family. It would also be degrading for my husband to be accepting charity from my family. Now that I was starting a family I should be flying my own wings. Mother and Father were always ready to help, but I turned down all their offers.

Since the day we had decided to get married, Togrul had been looking for opportunities to earn money. He had been engaged to design a couple of showrooms at the İzmir International

Fair. This meant that he would get paid when the fair started. A second cause for the difficulty for fixing a date for our wedding was getting my trousseau prepared. Mother was adamant that her "only precious" daughter should have a wonderful trousseau. After all, this was the first real wedding in the family.

On our arrival for the summer to Erenköy, work had started with this object in mind. First of all, the private dressmaker that used to come to our house for a few days in the past, was this time engaged for the whole summer on an everyday basis. So a room in the attic was assigned to Madame Maria and she was installed there with her son. She would be ready to sew and repair things as they would be needed. It was a time when we could not find or purchase everything to our heart's desire. Many things had to be done at home. For example, clothes-hangers were available only in wood. On Mother's orders these wooden hangers were covered first with a cotton cloth and then silk covers were sewn so that they would look better! If I am not mistaken, Mother had some fifty of those hangers prepared. Each hanger's iron parts were also covered with colored silk strips. As for the bridegroom, these wooden hangers were nicely polished. Of course there were many wash cloths, kitchen wraps, special glass cleaning napkins, silk covers for drawers and lockers of various sizes were cut and sewn and prepared. Some of the inside covers were "capittonee." There were also silk bags sewn for dried lavender leaves. These would be placed between our underwear, giving them a fresh odor while waiting in the drawers for future use. So there was a lot of sewing to be done.

Regarding my trousseau, I could mention a few items. Silver cutlery, including all sorts of knives and forks, et al. Silver cigarette ashtrays and boxes. Silver or painted serving trays and plates. On the other hand, items like brushes with silver handles, silver mirrors, other holders or boxes for cotton or other materials, most of them silver. Some other items would be crystal.

Then comes the bed covers, sheets and other linen for the bedroom. In the year 1951 finding good textiles in Turkey was quite impossible. Turkish textiles available on the market were rather tough and coarse. So Mother made some arrangements and so some importers especially brought bales of special materials of various sizes and of various colors, like pink or white, etc. Since I wanted a rather large single bed to sleep in, bed covers and pillows were all especially designed, cut and sewed. Then these were delivered to a couple of Armenian girls who specialized in embroidery. In the end, I had four colored pairs and six white pairs of sheets and several bed covers, all with matching embroideries. There were two dozens pillow sets to go with them.

Mother, who had spent most of her youth in Europe, did not like the local system of having previously sewn bedcovers or sheets with buttons to which the cover would be buttonholed. So in our house, like they do in most modern hotels all over the world, two sheets were utilized with the bedcover in between. You place the first sheet over the mattress (or the bed), the second sheet is laid on top of the first, then the blanket is spread with the top of the second sheet being turned down over, where the sleeper's head will be. I did not like to have too much embroidery, so each sheet had only my new initials (STD) embroidered. For pillow cases the same pattern was followed and my new initials (STD) were embroidered on one corner.

For tea and coffee services, the same girls prepared quite a number of table covers, napkins, mostly with flowers embroidered on them. The list also included goose feather pillows, blankets, bed covers and for the kitchen all kinds of spreads, covers, cleaning cloths, etc., all specially lined, monogrammed and sewn according to its purpose, as well as kitchenware.

A few years prior to my wedding, a family of foreigners who had to leave the country in a hurry had to sell their complete dinner set of blue and white Meissen porcelain and Mother had bought the whole thing with my eventual betrothal in mind. This was a complete set to serve twenty-four people. They were adorned with blue and white small flowers and looked very beautiful. She did not forget to get a set of white porcelain for our everyday use. Also there were full sets of water, wine and champagne glasses plus cut glass decanters, bottles, et al.

Bedroom sets had also been ordered. Besides the big double bed there would be two lockers to hang our clothes in, two separate half closets (chiffonier) a make-up table with mirrors on the two sides. This was to enable a lady to see the back of her hair

149

as well as the front. This table also had its own small settee. There had to be two side tables on each side of the bed (table de nuit). For the dining room a table and eight chairs were planned. There had to be a main buffet plus some side lockers for various cups and saucers. While purchasing the Meissen service set, Mother had purchased an elaborate bedroom set. However, that had two separate beds and the bed stands were "capittone." Since the man I wanted to marry and myself both preferred a big single bed, we decided not to use this bedroom and ordered a new set to our taste. I was able to use some of the chairs that had come with the previous set in my living room.

Since I did not like lights hanging from the ceiling, various standing lamps and table lamps had to be purchased. Curtains were the last to be considered. These had to be prepared according to the house we would be occupying. A number of bookshelves, plus various wooden closets for the bathroom utensils were ordered.

Now, we had to consider dresses, shoes, bags and the like. Apart from my wedding gown, two suits, two evening gowns, two cocktail dresses, two dresses for daily wear, two sets of sports clothes, two overcoats—one for special occasions and the other for daily use would be needed. Apart from these, other items like scarves, gloves, belts, hats, stockings of various kinds plus all kinds of lingerie, bathrobes, morning robes, etc. had to be ready. Some of these would have to be specially tailored and some could be purchased ready-made.

Then we had to prepare things for the bridegroom, as well. The bride's family was supposed to prepare some sort of a dowry for the groom. This included a bath robe, a robe de chambre, three pairs of silk pajamas, underwear, slippers, half a dozen silk shirts and ties, a golden wristwatch, cuff links and a tiepin and a number of handkerchiefs made up the list. When the list was concluded, we started discussing how and where these things could be obtained. Those that were to be ordered for the groom turned out to be the easiest. There was a well-known Greek shop on Beyoglu that specialized in such things (probably called Zara) from whom my father and my brothers were buying and ordering their shirts and ties. So they were assigned to complete the groom's list. My mother's favorite jeweler was an Armenian gentleman (actually they called him Saran) so he was entrusted to design and develop the jewelry for the bride and also some gold items for the groom. I have a nice story to tell about this Mr. Saran. I must have reached the age of thirty and I had gone to his store. At first Mr. Saran was not quite sure who I was and had difficulty recognizing me. When I explained to him who I was, he was very happy to see me. The old man critically surveyed me from top to bottom, and finally he said, "My dear young lady, you certainly have grown up to become a very chic young woman, but, please excuse my age, I still cannot forget the allure and the poise your mother possessed. The way she would almost glide into my store, sling her furs to one side and taking a seat, light up her cigarette, her perfume suddenly filling up the store. I used to get really excited. She had a different kind of charisma!" So, that was how Mother was seen from her jeweler's viewpoint. I was rather proud to listen to his tale.

Those days a family friend, Mrs. Cemal, had started a specialty shop on the second floor of an apartment building in Beyoglu. She had been entrusted with devising and tailoring all my personal underwear. I never forget. A dear friend of mine had also ordered her trousseau from the same lady and we were able to develop even stronger ties when our orders had been mixed up and we had to get together and separate each item. All items, like night gowns, etc. had been done to measure and all had been embroidered, so much so that they were good enough to be worn to a ball. Those days women used to wear a slip under their dresses. Later on this custom was discarded. One day Mother saw me put on my dress without a slip and she said, "My dear daughter, in this manner both your body and your dress can be soiled, a slip in between is actually a protection for both."

Mother knew many well-recognized fashion designers of İstanbul. So she and I started calling on each and looking over their various collections. I was listening to all their suggestions and painstakingly going over the materials they offered. Some I found to be too forward, then again some I found to be too conservative. I had liked some of the things a male designer had done, but I still had reservations. Anyway, I was having difficulty in choosing one among the many.

151

After a long day of visits to various designers, Mother and I were about to take the ferry back to Kadıköy from the boat landing at Karaköy. Suddenly a very well-dressed lady called out "Şen." At first I was not sure who she was, but as she warmly hugged me, I realized she was Eva Reisner. Sure enough Josi was also standing behind her. Since our boat was about to depart, we quickly exchanged calling cards, getting each other's phone numbers and promising to call one another. It had been eight years since we had met in Budapest. As soon as we reached home we told Father about this chance meeting and we called them on the phone. While talking with Eva I learned that they were now settled in İstanbul and that she had developed a "maison de haute couture" in partnership with Mrs. Tanrıöver. When she heard that I was searching ways to develop my trousseau she suggested that I take a look at her work also. The next day we went to the address she had given us. I was delighted. To cut a long story short, it was Eva who prepared all my dresses. All were very modern and very chic. Both Eva and Mrs. Cemal had flats overlooking the famous avenue called Beyoglu. We had started going to that quarter almost daily. After the wearisome sessions of trying on and checking the details of the new dresses, one thing that I enjoyed very much was to go to a pastry shop called "Muhallebici" and consume some "su muhallebisi" (a Turkish dessert). By luck this shop was just across from where Eva had her atelier, so we only had to cross the street. One day when we were crossing the street to go there, someone pinched my bottom. It really hurt and I could not help crying out loudly. Mother, when she realized what the man had done, was suddenly galvanized and caught the man by his lapels. However, that ruffian, instead of apologizing, started shouting back at her, and Mother lost her control, got frightened and fell on the pavement. Many people had gathered around us. A gentleman ran and brought a glass of water to revive Mother. By that time the culprit had already disappeared in the crowd. I guess the incident was an early warning how the people sauntering on this famed street would change character in the years to come. Poor me, I could do nothing but grieve for my mother and try and forget the soreness at my bottom!

Most of the dresses were black. In those days young girls hardly wore black. Marriage was an excuse for them to wear black. However, my situation was somewhat different. During the time I spent in Boston, I had began to wear black and had enjoyed it. Perhaps due to this experience, all my life I have enjoyed wearing either black or white. After getting married and settling in Ankara, my mother-in-law had come to visit us and as a natural womanly curiosity she asked me to show her my dresses. When she saw that most were black, she could not help saying, "My dear girl, why don't you have some lively colors, like red or yellow?"

At this juncture, I would like to repeat something that I told my mother-in-law. During our stay in Boston we had met an American lady who used to stay in a flat on the same floor. She used to visit us occasionally and join us for tea and cakes. Every time she would be wearing very bright colored dresses. One day, with the boldness of youth, I had asked her why she preferred such bright colors. She took my rather daring question in her stride and gave a very simple answer. "When I was young I had a body that attracted attention anyway, since I am getting older I found out that I have to have colorful dresses to attract attention."

As I was getting ready for my wedding, there was a visit that I had wanted to do. I had to pay my respects to Latife Teyze (aunt) and give her the good news of my coming betrothal. That beautiful lady received Mother and me with her usual elegance. After tea was served and we were settled, I gave her the news. Her first question was, "Do you really love him?" My answer was "I do not know that, I like him but I am certain that he loves me." Her answer was "That is much better, let him admire you, this way you may save yourself from future disappointment." She also asked Mother her opinion and we took our permission and left the house.

Apart from working on my trousseau, that summer of 1951 was rather different from my past vacations. Togrul was at Viranbağ working on his projects. There was neither electricity nor telephones in their house far out on the island! So there was no way for me to reach him. He had to go somewhere on the island

and call me from there. One day, on the phone, he said getting to a phone each day was taking too much of his working time and could I not visit him on the island. Mother on the other hand would not let me go on my own. After a few calls back and forth on the subject, Gayet Hanım finally asked Mother and me for an overnight visit. This time Mother insisted that Cenan should join us on such a visit. We all got ready to visit them on a weekend. It turned out to be a rainy day and Mother refused to go. However, there was no way for us to let them know we had changed our plans on account of the weather and were not coming. I wanted to go since we had not seen each other for quite some time. Mother was grumbling and Cenan was being sour since he did not wish to accompany us anyway. We started our excursion in a bad mood. I knew why Mother had insisted on bringing Cenan along, this way she was making sure that I would not be left alone with my fiancée.

Togrul was waiting for us at the ferryboat landing. Although our meeting was most pleasant, I had an unexplainable foreboding. Rain was falling slowly but continuously. Four of us took a phaeton, the usual horse-drawn carriage used on the island. Since the road was wet the horses kept losing their balance. The sun had started going down. We passed first the Luna Park and started going down the slope that would take us to Viranbağ. I was feeling very low indeed. Very near their house, one of the horses slipped and our carriage was upset. We were all shouting and crying. I was the one who was worst off. Since I was sitting on the side toward which the carriage had upturned, I was in a predicament. My leg was badly squeezed between the side of the wheel. Since we had almost reached the house, people heard our cries and all rushed out with lanterns and other lamps. Everyone was covered in mud. They were finally able to pull the carriage on to the road and we were all thankful that my leg had not been broken. Of course Mother was beyond herself and Cenan was very cross, Togrul and I were both too shocked to be able to say anything to one another. Thank God my father-in-law, Mustafa Nuri Bey, was quite a man of the world. With aplomb he was able to quiet our nerves and carry on a conversation, while his wife helped him with her short guffaws. Soon we all had cleaned up and changed our clothes and had started to

154

feel normal again. Under the shadowy lights of the gas lamps we had as good a meal as we could under the circumstances. Everyone soon retired to bed. Naturally they had put Mother and me in the same bedroom. As a result my fiancée and I had not even had a minute of solitude nor being able to exchange a few words between ourselves.

The next morning when I woke up the sun was shining and a strong, the delightful smell of pine trees was everywhere. I found Togrul already working on his projects. Just as we began to talk about the possibilities of our being able to see one another more, other members of the family had started their day. After breakfast, Cenan, Togrul and I went down the slope to the seaside. The sea was shining, one could count the stones beneath the water. For the first time Togrul and I were seeing each other in bathing suits, namely half naked. I think we enjoyed this and would enjoy getting closer. However, as Mother had forseen the possibility, Cenan was with us and we had to behave ourselves. So we swam for a while and returned to the house.

In the past I had come to the island and also to Viranbağ with my friends for picnics. It was one of the places that I adored. Sometimes I have wondered whether Viranbağ was one of the reasons that had attracted me to Togrul. What could I have expected? Surely one could not settle on such a remote spot. Or was it the evergreen pine trees, or the exquisite smell of all the wild flowers that had turned my head?

Our weekend was soon over and the return trip had started without our getting a chance to talk to one another and especially make plans for our future. We were back in Erenköy and the usual work for my trousseau had started to take up all of our time. I guess Mother had understood the difficult position I was in. There was no way for me to even talk to the man I was about to marry. So one morning she said, "Let's have a chat." I was rather surprised. Why could Mother wish to have a "private" chat with me! Finally, she said, "Togrul is very busy with his drawings and it is difficult for you to see him. I have already consulted with your father. We could remove some of the furniture from the large receiving room and arrange a workroom for him. Since Nur is away, his bedroom is free. Togrul could sleep there. He could also invite his assistants during the day. It could even be easier for them rather than going to the island everyday. This way we could all have lunches and dinners together and you two would get a better chance of meeting one another, while he can continue with his work for the İzmir Fair. During the days while he is working with his assistants you and I can continue our work with the sewing and so forth. What do you think about this arrangement?" How could I refuse such an offer! Of course I was not at all sure how Togrul would react to such an invitation. Mother said, "Invite him to lunch the next time he calls and we can talk over this plan with him." Both Father and Cenan had approved this plan. We were in June. The wedding was due to take place in September. If this idea could be put into practice we two would get a better chance to be together more often. We had already been engaged to marry but we had never been alone together!

When Togrul called I asked him to come to Erenköy to talk over something important. He said he would take the first boat available. He was delighted with Mother's suggestion and invitation. In a few days he was able to transfer his studio to our house without much trouble. Drafting tables were easily installed.

During those days, although this had looked like a brilliant idea, a few unwanted or unexpected things did also take place. The first concerned what we now call a T-shirt. No one in Turkey knew about such sporting shirts that are so popular in the States. So one day, while we were having breakfast under the big pine tree, Togrul joined the family in a T-shirt. Well, it was summer and hot, but I still could not help making a remark like "Now, you look like an Italian sailor." I had said this in a mild and what I thought was an endearing manner. However, he was almost instantly frozen. He made no return remark and not only so, he would not talk to me for two consecutive days! I had already forgotten that I had made such a remark and did not know how to break the ice that had come between us. Finally in exasperation I forced the issue. The answer I got was somewhat like this: "If we start by calling each other names, we may end up breaking our hearts." I was aghast. I had always thought that he was good for a joke. On top of that he had a cruel streak in him. He could stand living under the same roof and not say a word to me for forty-eight hours! He certainly was a tough nut to crack!

The second problem that developed was of a more important nature. Togrul was supposed to make the formal application for our wedding to the municipality. However, being much involved with his project he had completely forgotten to do this and had come to realize what he had done, or rather what he had not done, at a very late date. This had really affected me. He had to go through another channel called in legal circles "the lightning registration," which was a system that was rarely used. Furthermore, it made no sense to have an engagement period of eight months and then apply for a lightning wedding. This was a procedure that also carried the taint of being forced to get married in a hurry! I was certainly going to be a virgin bride and I did not want tongues wagging about my marriage. On top of this the only time we had a meal together (without the family) was to munch a sandwich at a cafeteria near the registration office.

These two occasions and a few other minor happenings had forced me to think over the whole arrangement. I had to confess to myself that I knew nothing about this man except that he had asked me to marry him. The few times we have had alone with each other were the evenings when we were able to leave the dining table after dinner and take a walk under the trees. Even that was usually cut short by Mme. Eleni, who would call out saying that the coffee was being served. Which meant we had to get back and sit with the family members.

Our wedding date had finally been fixed as September 21, 1951 and the invitations had been printed and mailed in good time. Mother and I had gone to visit Latife Hanımefendı and I took my wedding invitation in person, rather than sending it by mail. That wonderful lady opened the envelope I had given her, read the invitation, then excused herself for a minute and got up to open a marqueterie locker and took out some packages wrapped in fancy papers. She brought three such packs and gave them to me. She said, "I could not bring myself to buy some wedding gift for you, my dear Şen, so I chose these for you. If you like you can open them and I will tell you where they came from." I opened the first package. It was a thin but heavy package. It was a silver tray for two coffee cups. The Sultan's monogram was encrusted on it. She explained, "This tray was a gift from the Sultan, when my father (who was so very fond of you) was getting married to my mother. You should serve coffee to your husband when you are married. You must remember how much my father loved you." The second was an oblong package. When I opened it I found a silver cocktail shaker. She explained that it belonged to her father and was rarely used in the house. She said, "I hope you can make martinis and remember to raise your glass to your late uncle." By this time tears were really flowing down my cheeks. I was so excited. I remembered the previous occasions, especially in my childhood days, when that venerable gentleman would take me on his lap and holding me lovingly would sing songs to me. There was yet another package which she took the trouble to open herself. This was an antique, large, square Sevres porcelain bonbonnière. It was blue and white, covered with small flowers. Its cover and the lower piece were circled with a gold metal piece. She said, "This was sent to me as a wedding gift from the president of France. I hope you will be able to enjoy the sweets you will eat from it, without tear drops." Her eyes were far away in her memories. I did not know what to say. I hugged her and kissed her hands and cried and cried.

My wedding gown had finally been finished, it was wrapped for protection and hung outside Mother's large garderobes. Only twenty days to my wedding day! That day I got up with a terrible feeling. I was perspiring all the time and my head was aching. I had decided to cancel the wedding. At last I got hold of Mother alone and I simply told her that I had changed my mind and that I would not go ahead with the wedding. I did not want to get married. Mother was dumbfounded. She could hardly muster a few words like "But your gown is already finished," or "But the invitations have already been mailed." Apart from these she had not asked me "Why?" So I told her all my worries. I had finally realized that I still knew nothing about the man I was about to marry. That one day when we were rowing at sea, he had forced me to put on a bathrobe because he did not want other people to see me in my bathing suit! His reaction to the dress we had prepared for our engagement party and how we had to have alterations to suit his desire. He had told me that he would not allow me to dance with anyone else once we were

158

married—just him! During this long period of engagement we had hardly been alone together. I also told Mother how he had refused to talk to me for two days when I had made an innocent remark about his T-shirt. My question was "How can I marry someone I hardly know?" We had not even gone to a restaurant, just the two of us. What I meant of course was that I had had very little chance to learn what kind of a man he was. He was staying in our house but I had no chance of being with him. Mother lamely said, "But he is working terribly hard and it is for your future." Finally, when she saw that I was adamant, she said, "Well, if that is the way you feel, then I suppose we can send cables to everyone and cancel the event." Then she posed the crucial question, "Have you told Togrul your decision?"

That evening I told Mme. Eleni that we did not want coffee that evening and I took Togrul out for a stroll under the pines. We walked slowly away from the house, all the way up to the derelict windmill in the back. We were both quiet. There was a small settee near the windmill. I sat on it and Togrul was standing by. I told him that I had decided not to go through with this wedding. For a moment he stood as if he was frozen. He barely could say "What do you mean?" I repeated everything I had told Mother and ended by saying that I felt I could not go through with the wedding. Suddenly he was on his knees, he had clasped my legs and he was crying profusely. He was crying and between sobs he was talking. He told me that he had never loved anyone like he loved me, that he was doing all that he was doing just to be able to marry me, that he had given up a beautiful career in the States just because I did not want to go there. He was also kissing my hands and his tears had wetted my hands and my knees. This was such a profound display of love and affection that pretty soon I too had started to cry. A little later, with tears flowing from my eyes, I was able to say that I wanted him to let me alone and not to curtail my freedom once we were married, and he promised to do everything I would ask of him. I was gradually calming down. It was over. There was no turning back anymore. I still do not understand how I, Şen Sahir Sılan, had agreed to marry a total stranger in the first place. Now I was gradually becoming fond of him. Love was something else, I suppose.

159

As we returned Mother had quickly understood that my fight was over and was overjoyed. A few days afterwards Togrul had to go to İzmir and start to build the fair stands he had designed. He was constantly on the phone and wrote a number of letters. When his work at the fair was over he had gone to Ankara to search for our new residence. He was on the phone. He said his work was over in İzmir and that he was able to rent a flat at the Okşan apartment building, which was on Sümer Sokak (street) where my parents' house was located. Our future home would be within walking distance to Mother. He wanted also to talk to Mother. It turned out that he had asked her to arrange sending all our household goods to Ankara and also would she kindly go there as well to help him arrange the new flat. Mother was delighted to oblige. In this manner, Mother and my husband would together prepare the house wherein I would be living!

All the arrangements for the wedding were finalized. Our marriage ceremony (registration) would be carried out at the Beyoglu Registration Office. This office was very near the tunnel's entrance, near the Hachette Library in Beyoglu. After this ceremony there would be a reception for our guests at the "Circle D'Orient," presently called Büyük Kulüp in Turkish. After the reception we would change into our travel suits and catch the overnight train (the Ankara Express) to Ankara. We would reach our home the next day.

In accordance with Togrul's request, Mother had sent everything to Ankara and had gone there herself. Their phone call from Ankara had made me very happy. Mother had liked the apartment and had seen to it that everything had been placed where it belonged, including the kitchen utensils in their proper closets. She had used her usual servants for this work. The new refrigerator and the oven were also installed properly. This way we would be travelling from İstanbul with only one or two suitcases. The material that was purchased earlier was made into curtains and were hung in their places. Mother had kept the servants at her home (No. 42 Sümer Sokak) and I would be able to call on them whenever I felt like it. A few days before the wedding Mother was back in İstanbul, radiantly happy and satisfied with the work she had done. Togrul would be coming to

İstanbul only the day before the wedding. This meant that there would be some more days when we would be apart from one another.

During this time something rather unexpected had taken place. Somehow his father, Mustafa Nuri Bey, had been angered by something Togrul had said and declared that he would not meet the expenses of the wedding. Togrul was a proud man and also very sure of himself and had refused to beg for the money from his father. When I heard what had happened I was a bit taken aback. However, when I realized that there was nothing he would not be willing to do to make me happy, I was gratified.

According to the instructions Mother had given the servants, they were to cook for us daily and the meals would be delivered to my house. Later, one of the servants would come and do the dishes and prepare the table for the next meal. This way during the two weeks, when Mother and Father would be in İstanbul, I would have no chores to do and this would be some sort of a honeymoon for us. Mother had an old wives tale that she would repeat often—"Three days of being a bride, ten days of being a Sultan and for the rest of life, one is bound to be a housewife." When she told me about the arrangements she had made, I could not help remembering this old saying.

XV

The Wedding Ceremony
and the Reception

Togrul was on the phone as soon as he arrived to İstanbul on September 20. We were both rather excited. He in love and I frightened to death. He told me he would send a car and my bouquet for me the next day and that he had missed me a lot and that our home was a delight. He also added that he had made an appointment at his barber for his bridegroom's shave early next morning and inquired about my arrangements.

I told him I would not go to a hairdresser. I would like to be as I was, clean and pure for him. That my only ornament would be my veil. How times have changed! I had not given any thought to bridal decorations. However, these days women enjoy bridal gowns even for their second or third marriages! So many things have changed with time.

My bridal gown turned out to be just what I wanted. With Eva's help we had selected a design of Givenchy. It had long sleeves and the skirt was almost touching my shoes on the front and in the back it had a sort of tail about half a meter long (two feet). The dress was made from off-white satin, the front had a triangular opening and drapes started on one side which were buttoned up with very small buttons. My veil was very long and it was gathered at the top of my head and on each side of the veil, long and heavy silver threads, almost as thick as my wrist, were reaching the floor. These silver threads were so beautiful that I did not want any other jewelry, neither on my neck nor in my hair. I wanted to be a real Turkish bride! And on my fingers I wanted to have only my engagement ring. The only extravagance was to be my veil. My shoes were also made from the same material as my dress. On my sleeve I was going to carry my handkerchief decorated with Belgian lace.

I had had no sleep the previous night. We had carried on a long conversation with Mother and we had discussed many things. She had told me the duties a married woman should have toward her husband and I had asked her a thousand questions.

My brother Nur was in America. That morning at breakfast in the garden everyone was rather tense. Cenan at first tried to be jocular and make small talk, but he could not keep it up for long. He looked too sad. Suddenly he said, "What will life be without you Şenko?" That started everyone to cry. Since we had been back from the States, I had been the one who made plans and developed trips, etc. I used to do this mostly at breakfast time as we were about to start the day. It was I who would declare "Let's go there" or "Let's do this today." What was to happen to me? Why did I have to go and get married! What sort of a life would I be leading with a man I hardly knew? What would I be doing all day long when he was at work? Luckily my piano had been installed in my new home! However, I had done nothing to make that house mine. I still did not know what my home looked like! Why had I not asked all my wedded friends about what married life was like. How two people with completely different backgrounds and different life experiences could suddenly get together and share their lives? I was lost in such thoughts when a car appeared on the driveway and Eva and Josi started walking toward us. Then everyone was suddenly galvanized. The time had come. I had to get ready. While Mother and Father were having coffee with them I went to my bathroom, had a hot shower and as I was drying my hair in the sunlight I was also trying to view the garden for one last time. The pine trees that I used to so much enjoy climbing, the flower beds and the lawn, the settee on which I had read so many novels, the fruit trees in full bloom. Somehow I was thinking that this was my last look! Someone called us, "The car is here." This time the arriving car was for the bride. A little later Mother was on my side, she had a lovely bouquet of tuberose. It smelled to high heaven. Eva also said it was lovely. She also said, "Time to get dressed." Mother and Eva were both helping me to get ready. First I put on my white lace underwear that Kamuran

Cemal had made for me. Then my silk stockings and then the high heeled shoes. Someone combed my hair. I was not using any make-up anyway. I put on some very light lipstick. The day before I had had both manicure and pedicure at home. I was as pure and clean as my bouquet. I used my usual perfume, Arpege, and it was time for me to put on my gown. Mother had already dressed while I was taking my shower. Father was getting into his "jaquette a taille," a sort of ceremonial attire, in his bedroom. Eva helped me to put on my gown. Mother arranged my hair and my veil. I was watching myself in the mirror as if it was a stranger! Everything seemed to be in perfect order. There was a knock on the door and Aunt Vedia, who was my cousin Feridun Sevil's wife, together with their two children, a little girl called Tülin and her younger brother Ümit, came into the room. They all admired me and said nice things. It was time to go. As I was going out of the door, I had to turn and look back to my now old room, for the last time! I could see the big pine tree through the window. As I started toward the stairway, Father also appeared from his room, fully dressed. Just as we had started going down the steps, I suddenly turned back and ran to my room for one last look at everything I was leaving behind. Then I came round and joined Father, who had kindly waited for me on the steps.

At the main entrance door all the help in the house had made a line, waiting to see me go. First I had to hug Mme. Eleni with tears in my eyes, then everyone else in the line was hugged one by one. The cook and the gardener kissed my hand in the old-fashioned way. Soon I had left all of them behind and had gone into the black limousine that Togrul had sent for me. My father and mother were sharing this ride with me. My brother Cenan had joined the Reisners. The Sevil family had their own car. So three vehicles started following one another. I was watching the flower beds and the big pines that I had enjoyed so much. The household help had álso run to the main gate to wave the procession of cars one last good-bye. I was trying not to cry. I must have forced my hands into such knots that my nails hurt.

The bright sunshine of the morning was no more, the weather had turned sultry and dark clouds had began to gather. We crossed the Bosphorus in a ferry and it had already started raining. Father said rain was always a good omen. I was afraid

164

we would all get wet. However, luck was with us. By the time we had reached the Registration Office the rain had stopped.

As our car was reaching the sidewalk I could see people who had been invited climbing up the steps of the Registry Office. Father stepped out first and helped me to get off the car. At the same time Tülin and Ümit ran to hold and carry my trail. Togrul was waiting for us, among the guests. We had not seen one another for almost two weeks. Suddenly I felt I liked the fact that I was to marry him. In his bridegroom outfit he was extremely good-looking. Beside him were his father, Mustafa Nuri Devres, and his two brothers, Nezih and Dündar.

As everyone was going into the big reception room, Father, I and the two children stayed a bit behind. A small veil covered part of my face. Father gave me his arm. I was very tense. I felt I was trembling. He was saying things I could not understand. I guess he must have been trying to make me relax. Or perhaps he was giving me some last minute advice. Under the veil, I noticed a few drops going down his cheeks. We passed through rows of guests and as we got near the big table where the ceremony would be carried out, Father passed me on to Togrul. The two of us were seated next to one another, opposite the Registration Officer, who was sitting on the other side of the table. My witness was Süreyya Pascha (İlmen) and Katipzade Sabri Bey, who was a mutual friend of both of our families, was the witness for Togrul.

As the officer was saying his usual words I felt Togrul was watching me. As I was wondering if he liked my looks, his hand had already found mine. Suddenly a pen was pushed toward me and I heard someone say, "Sign here please." How was I supposed to sign. Someone whispered, "Sign as Devres." This was news to me. Everyone had signed the same document. Togrul lifted my veil and kissed me and said some nice things. I was now married and had become Şen T. Devres.

It is impossible for me to remember all the details but among the jokes, congratulations and laughter we were finally able to get into a car, this time just by ourselves. It was a short drive to the club but we were alone, talking and saying nice things to one another. As we got out of the car, he was holding me from my waist very strongly and since I had no bridesmaids anymore I had to hold my veil up with both hands and the elevator took us to the second floor. Some of the guests who were at the registration ceremony had already arrived. Members of our families were receiving them as they arrived. Lots of pictures were taken and the wedding cake had to be cut. Since I had insisted on the traditional "zerde and pilav" (rice and a certain dessert), those were also offered to the guests. I heard Mother say, "It is time to go" and Togrul, Mother and I went into the rooms on the third floor that were especially reserved for us to change in. Mother and I were alone in the room as she helped me get out of my bridal gown and put on my travel suit. She was kissing me, saying nice things and crying at the same time. By that time my husband knocked on the door. I was ready to go. We went down to say good-bye to all the family members and again rode in the black limousine, this time going to the train station, Haydarpascha, to start our trip toward Ankara.

I had asked to travel in two compartments. After all we were going to our home in Ankara. I did not want to be squeezed into an uncomfortable train bunk with my husband to be. Togrul had agreed to my wish. When we went into a single compartment to place our bags I was a little taken aback! Togrul quickly sensed my reaction and opened the doors in between. He had actually booked two compartments that opened into one another. He hung my overcoat there and also helped me to take my jacket off. I felt relieved. As we were talking and joking the train had already started. A little later there was a knock on the door. It appeared that Togrul had made all the arrangements beforehand. A waiter appeared with our dinner on a very large silver tray, served in our compartment! I felt all the more comfortable, we did not have to go out and meet a lot of people in the wagon restaurant of the Ankara Express. We must have talked for hours. Then he quietly took his overnight bag, went into the other compartment and closed the door behind him. A little later he opened the connecting door and came back. As I had changed into my nightgown, he too had changed into his pajamas and his robe de chambre. He gently asked me if I would like him to stay. When I made a negative notion with my head, he sat on my side and we talked for a short while. I was beginning to know the man. Finally, he wished me a good night's sleep and went back to his compartment. He was now my husband, however, I had not agreed to become his wife on that train ride and he had respected my girlish desire and I appreciated his understanding and felt closer to him.

XVI

Our First Home

That night on the train was uncomfortable. I could hardly sleep. When I opened my eyes in the morning, he was in my compartment watching me. He had already shaved and gotten dressed, our breakfast tray had been brought into his compartment and was waiting for us. I was rather ashamed. He understood my frame of mind and told me to get dressed so our tea would not get cold and went back to his compartment. When I joined him a little later, he began to feed me from the tray, joking and kidding all the while. He really was trying to get me to relax!

Finally our train reached the Ankara station. This was the first time I was coming to Ankara without the members of my family and with a man I hardly knew! However, it appeared that now we were the family! I was confused. I really did not know what to think.

The taxi stopped in front of an apartment building on Sümer Street. On the entrance of the building was written "OKŞAN Apt. No. 10." We climbed three flights of stairs. Togrul left the bags he had in his hands, took out a key from his pocket, opened the door, turned around and suddenly picked me up in his arms and carried me in. I had found myself in my home and in his arms. This was our house. It looked like heaven! On the left from the entrance, I could see my piano. In the room there were book racks now containing our joint books. The windows were looking over Sümer Street. I started touring our apartment with excitement. On the right, as one entered the apartment and again overlooking the same street, the furniture that made up our salon was placed. Through the salon one could enter another room that had no windows and there, our dining table and chairs were placed. On the right side of the dining room there was a door that opened into the kitchen. On the other side there was a small hall through which one could reach the bedroom and the bathroom. The bedroom had windows that looked over to buildings behind our apartment. My husband, holding my hand, was now taking me around our home. All lockers and drawers had been arranged with whatever we owned. He told that he had arranged the furniture and that the rest was done by Mother. I could not have been happier. My drawer was filled with my underwear and was placed on special covers all done by Mme. Maria. Dainty little dried lavender sachets were put in between so that one could smell their lovely odor as one opened the drawers. My dresses were neatly hung in their proper places. In every room there were cut glass containers filled with chocolates, Turkish delights and other sweets. The whole house smelled beautifully. In the evening I had seen Togrul taking out some parcels from a bag, it turned out that he had brought with him some edibles from İstanbul and now I saw that he had placed them in the icebox.

We had been married and now were at home! I was being loved and I was very happy. This was the beginning of a new life for me. Before leaving İstanbul Mother had told me that our sheets were made of Indian linen and they would easily wrinkle, so I should make sure to change them every day. I followed mother's advice and started calling her servants for supplies that we might be needing. I would ask for our food, decide on what they would cook for us, bring in the food and take away the dirty dishes. My husband would go out and buy things to our taste. On the other hand, I had been refusing to go out and was somewhat frightened that I should come across someone I knew! I did not go out for ten days. Mother called from İstanbul and told me they were coming a week later and asked if I needed anything from İstanbul. She later told me that if my voice on the phone had sounded bitter or sour, she would have come immediately!

We went to meet the family at the station. We were all very happy to get together again. Mother had brought along our wedding gifts with her. I immediately placed the gifts Aunt Latife had given me to the places I had planned for them. We had received so many gifts! I had not realized there were so many people who loved me so much. General Sureyya had put a huge amethyst ring on my finger at the wedding. Now as we opened the boxes of gifts, I found that he and his wife had also given me a very heavy silver tea set, including an ornate tray and I was taken aback! Atif İlmen and Auntie Fatis had sent a huge antique table clock. Hayri İlmen and Aunt Vecihe had sent a set of Baccarat glasses, twelve each for champagne, wine and water. Dear family friend and a former ambassador, Behiç Erkin, had sent a very heavy silver frame, into which he had placed his portrait. So many gifts that I could not (not just now but even then) count down all at one go! I was at a loss how to display or where to place all these beautiful items.

Days were passing by. Our daily life was getting to become normal. Togrul was looking for a job. He had many offers but he was hesitant and choosy. By this time I had began to get bored, the princess of the house! When my husband left the house, looking for work, I would call Mother on the phone. We would chat a while and I would take recipes from her. Then the doorman would bring in the things that I had ordered and I would start cooking. I had never done any cooking in my mother's house. We had a male cook who did not enjoy competition in his kitchen. That meant that I could only go into the kitchen when the cook was on leave and that usually was to make some special cake that I was interested in. However, now, since I was the lady of my own house, cooking had become a joy for me.

One day my husband told me that our finances were getting very low. So we quickly cut our expenses accordingly. Since he had not accepted any offers of work, we had been spending whatever he had saved in the past. I remember our being satisfied by having bread and fresh onions a number of times. I guess we must have been spending too much in our early days. On the other hand, I was adamant about talking about these things with my mother or father. I could not bear the thought of having him belittled by them for no reason. We had a lot of furniture but we had no paintings to adorn our walls. We had wondered what could be done on the subject. One day Togrul brought in the necessary materials and he started painting on his free time. At such times I would sit by him, read some book or go to play my piano and sometimes I would just sit by him and chat. I have a fun sort of memory of those days. We had decided to go to the Atatürk Model Farm for lunch one sunny day. We emptied our pockets and counted the money we had in the house. There was very little. So we had to buy third class tickets on the train. When we reached the gardens we first took a stroll enjoying the weather and the scenery. Then we were hungry. We could afford only a bottle of Coke to share and one toast also to be shared among us. We were wildly happy and enjoying every minute of it. So at the end we said "why not" and walked all the way home. By the time we had reached home our feet were almost swollen and were both dead beat. My legs hurt for days but it was still a memorable day for us.

Finally, one day Togrul came home, all happiness, and told me that we had to celebrate! He had finally found work. Skidmore, Owings, Merrill (an architectural firm of some reknown) had given him a job. He was going to be paid a salary of 2,000 dollars a month. This was a marvellous salary in those days. We were both elated. However, this salary would become payable only at the end of the month and we were really broke for the time being.

Nevertheless, Togrul was able to draw some plans for someone else and earned enough to keep us going. In the meantime, we would visit and have dinner with the family. Mother, while helping me with my laundry and ironing chores, to be done in her house, would also send some of the food she knew I enjoyed that the cook had prepared for them. So we were able to make ends meet that month. Not once did I mention to Mother that we were living on the border line. I had recognised that Togrul was an architect with exceptional talents. In everything he designed, his ability to draw and his creativity was manifest. That was why he was offered such a lucrative salary by such an international firm.

Mother and I met often. She would visit me or I would go to my old home. I was not used to sitting at home all by myself all day. When I was a young girl I had always attended some school or another. We also had a pretty active social life. I had grown out of my old home and Mother said she missed me a lot, just as I did miss her and Cenan's company. I guess just playing the piano and doing some cooking at home was no longer satisfactory for me. I had always felt that learning things and becoming a better person was ever more important for me then just doing house chores. Cooking sounded like a boring repetition to me most of the time.

XVII

Is It Motherhood?

A short while after we were married I realized that I was pregnant. This gave me an unbelievable kind of happiness. One morning I realized that my stomach was upset for no reason at all. I had thought I must have some sort of a cold or something and had not consider it serious. However, when this condition began to be repeated every day, I informed my husband. At first he could not understand the situation either and said that I must have eaten something that upset my stomach. When I mentioned this to Mother, being an experienced woman, she quickly understood the situation and immediately called and obtained an appointment from Dr. Zekai Tahir Burak, a gynecologist. Yes, I was pregnant! Togrul received the news with infinite happiness and joy. He kept saying, "I wish we can have a daughter as beautiful as you!" He was all around me, caressing and kissing my hands. As far as Mother was concerned, this was her greatest wish come true! She had been waiting for a grandchild ever since she had given birth to her last child. Actually, Nur had had a son some time ago, however, Mother had no chance of meeting or hugging that boy. Both father and Cenan were very happy with the news. I was beside myself with happiness, but at the same time, I was truly frightened deep down. Apart from the joy of becoming a mother, this daily repetition of stomach troubles was making me apprehensive. Despite everything I was developing a real and deep love toward my baby, which was growing inside me from day to day.

Mother was instantly on the go for preparations. She quickly went on a buying spree. Knitting needles, wools, baby clothes, special bed for the baby, et al. After it was established that I was pregnant, Mother's interest and attention over me greatly increased. She was constantly on the phone and had began to decide on what I should or should not do! It was getting somewhat awkward. It was as if I was being patronized both by my husband and my mother. Togrul had also been a little easy going in the beginning and Mother had become an overseer for all of our actions. There was no question that this reaction was due to her utmost devotion to her only daughter but at times she seemed to overlook the fact that I also had a husband. On the other hand, I was so happy in my new condition of being pregnant, I did not mind doing anything that anyone told me to do. Anyway, no one was asking for my opinion and in a way I had given up all my personality. Mother would say that I should not over exercise. My husband would suggest that we should go out for a walk. So I would start walking with him, but soon realizing what Mother had said, pretend to be tired and we would return home after a few steps. Unfortunately, I was under the false impression that in this manner I was being acceptable to all around me. Mother would be on the phone at all hours of the day and Togrul had began to feel annoyed by this over indulgence.

It must have been the fourth month of my pregnancy. As we often did, that night also we had dined at Mother's. It was about ten o'clock when we returned. As we entered our house we heard the phone ringing. It was Mother. She was enquiring if we had returned home safely. It was a two minutes' walk between the houses both on the same street! I had put the phone down and was about to walk toward the bedroom, my husband suddenly said, "Please come and sit here" in a voice that I was not at all accustomed to. He had already sat on one of our dining room chairs. I took another chair opposite him. I was waiting to listen to what he was going to say. He got up, walked to the bar, fixed himself a drink, came back and had a sip. I was rather surprised at what was going on. After having his first sip I noticed that the muscles of his cheekbones were almost contracted. In a deep voice he said, "We shall have to put an end to this affair. You have to choose between your mother and your husband." And before I could open my mouth to remonstrate to this outburst, he added, "Morning, noon, night—all the time it is your mother! That is enough. You have to make a choice. It is either her or me." My answer was naturally something like "How can this be? How do you expect me to make a choice between you and Mother?" He suddenly jumped from his chair. To this date I cannot remember, had he struck me or had we both gotten up and collided. But I knew that I had fainted. When I came to again, I was lying on the floor and he was now sitting on the sofa, finishing his drink, completely composed and unruffled. I looked at my watch. I must have been lying there quite some time, unconscious. He had done nothing but continued to drink his whisky the whole time. I got up, walked into the bathroom. Washed my face and went to bed. My hands were clasped over my belly. I was deadly frightened whether anything had happened to my baby. I must have fallen asleep after a while.

The next morning when I woke up my husband had already left the house. The phone rang. I would not answer. I got up and got dressed. Then I went to Mother's house. I told her that I had decided to have a divorce. I hugged her and started crying. Then I recounted what had happened the night before. Mother listened to me for a long time. At the end she said, "You cannot divorce now, you are four months pregnant and your baby should not be born fatherless. It is now too late to have an abortion either." I was totally heartbroken. What was I to do now? Just at that moment there was a sort of movement within my body. My baby had moved inside me! I cannot explain the feeling of complacency that swept all over my body at that moment! I was both crying and laughing at the same time. I could not help caressing my belly. My baby was alive and was telling me that she was there. Mother had joined me in this happiness. She was both drying my tear drops and caressing and following the movements of the baby inside me with excitement. We heard the door bell and right after that my husband appeared in the room. He came and sat on the floor in front of me and clasped my legs. He was crying! He had not shaved and he was wearing the shirt he had on the previous night. He must have slept in it, if he had slept at all! Mother said, "The baby has just moved" and discreetly left the room, leaving us alone. We both had already forgotten the events of the evening before and were both immersed in what the baby was doing inside me.

175

I still do not know the answer. How should I have reacted on that occasion? There is, however, one thing that I am sure of! I do not regret what I did that day or rather what I did not do! I now believe that there is something that is called destiny! We always remembered the day when Togrul brought home his first pay check. When I saw the cluster of paper money he was waving, I had shouted happily and had started to count the things I would be able to buy for my baby. Togrul gently led me to an armchair, made me sit, then slowly started counting our main expenses. So much for the rent, so much for groceries, so much for utilities like electricity and water. By the time he had finished there was not much left for indulgences. Still, we were happy and enjoyed our togetherness. That was the most important thing for both of us.

Yes, I believe my love for him had begun to grow. This was a normal reaction. He was my husband. He was always caring for me and doing everything possible to please me. On top of all this I was carrying his child inside me. The baby had made us quite inseparable. The only thing that troubled me now was his uncontrollable jealousy! Just as I was considering that the events of that night had blown over, I began to realize that he was not just jealous of my mother but also of my friends. He was trying to arrange things so that it would be impossible for me to go out on my own. One day I had realized that my last pair of silk stockings that had come with my trousseau had a run! I disliked the idea of showing it to him and asking for money to buy some new pairs. I was ashamed of asking money for my personal things. That evening Togrul saw the run on my stocking and I immediately covered up saying that I would buy some new pairs in the morning. He came home toward noon, despite the fact that he rarely came home for lunch. He had bought for me a dozen stockings and said that the weather was bad and that I should not go out. For shopping also. Either we would be going out together or he would order things to be brought home. I was either not caring or had become oblivious to everything except my baby. All I cared about was the baby inside me and it was growing day by day. We were preparing small jackets, small stockings, embroidering special sheets for the baby, together with Mother.

Mother had some strange beliefs or convictions. For example, many mothers began to prepare for their daughter's dowry early in their lives. Whereas Mother thought otherwise. She explained that she had experienced a situation when her aunt, who had never married, displayed her dowry chest. Aunt Behiye apparently was a very beautiful young girl and her family had prepared for her a very rich dowry. However, for some reason, she had never married. I was under the impression that she had been jilted and that the man she had fallen in love with had married someone else. Many years later when Mother had gone to İzmir for a visit, Auntie had decided to give Mother some of the things she had in her dowry chest. The situation had turned out to be awful. Everything in the chest had either decayed or had lost its color! Mother was so dismayed that she promised herself that if she ever had a daughter, she would not start her dowry until she was engaged to be married. So that was what she had done for her only daughter! She was to influence me to act as she had done, when I had my own daughters. My morning sickness lasted for almost four months. Every month I visited Dr. Burak and had a checkup. For some reason known only to himself, the doctor kept advising me not to walk too much and not to exercise. His advice was "Sit whenever you feel like it and do not exert yourself." My pregnancy was developing very normally. In my seventh month, when I was going to my doctor, Mother accompanied me. When my measurements were taken we saw that I had gained twenty-seven kilos! Both mother and I were quite surprised. Mother then asked the doctor if he was quite sure that he himself would be there to deliver the baby. When we realized that he was giving rather evasive answers we left his office in a hurry. The famous doctor had taken no notice of my condition all this time. Mother was furious. I had been rather frightened. How could a doctor be so careless. Mother kept saying, "How could a doctor allow a pregnant woman to gain twenty-seven kilos and still be vague about delivering the baby under those conditions!" She immediately started searching and among father's friends found another doctor. We went to a very clean and spacey private clinic which Dr. Saip Özer owned and carried on his practice. It was a much nicer place than that of my old doctor. After examining me thoroughly, my new doctor advised me to walk at least four hours a day, to eat nothing but vegetables and fruits and to stop gaining anymore weight. So I followed his advice during the last two months of my pregnancy.

June was over and the weather in Ankara had gotten pretty hot. We had almost finished our preparations for the coming child. From an American family who were returning to America Mother had purchased a cradle on wheels, had it repainted and then covered all the wooden parts with a yellow material that she herself had embroidered. Her choice of yellow was to ensure that it would not prove contrary to the baby's gender. Those days the doctors were unable to tell the gender of the baby before it was born. From the moment that he had heard that I was pregnant my husband had declared that he wanted a daughter, a baby girl. I was praying for a baby that was healthy all around. Mother, by using the color yellow, had at least solved the problem of gender.

It was in the morning of July 5, after long hours of enormous pain our baby girl, Ayşe, was born at 13:50 hours. As I was entering the delivery room I had asked my doctor not to put me under anesthesia and that I was willing to endure the pain. I was hoping to feel everything while my baby was coming out of my body. It was not an easy birth, a number of things had gone wrong, but at last my baby was born! And it was a girl. Although I was very tired, I asked my doctor two questions. Was everything about her normal? When I was told that everything was normal, came my second question. Can I have another child later? Dr. Saip Özer suddenly started laughing. He said, "I have heard many complaints, even I heard women cursing, but not until today did I hear such a beautiful question! Yes, my dear lady, you can have many more babies in the future." His answer had given me the world.

When they gave me my baby, I hugged her firmly and cried. She smelled divinely. She was a big baby. She weighed three kilos, seven hundred and fifty grams and her height was fifty-two centimeters. She had a nice oval face and dark-colored eyes. However, the forceps that the doctor was forced to use had given her a small scar. Her father was also delighted. Mother had at last her wish and had become a grandmother. All three of us had difficulty in sharing our Ayşe! My father-in-law, who wanted a grandson, had asked us to name the child Muzaffer. In those days, it was customary for elders of the family to give a name to a newcomer. However, I had always been against such codes or customs and wanted to name my child myself. In deference to the old gentleman's wish we agreed to give that name to our daughter also and called her Muzaffer Ayşe. Granddaddy Mustafa Nuri had also written a small poem for his granddaughter, later on.

For a long time I was only for Ayşe! I had no other interest in life. That summer we had been unable to move to Erenköy. Cenan had decided to spend his summer in Büyükada, Nur had returned to America. So Mother and Father cut their summer season in Erenköy short and returned early to Ankara. That summer Cenan had met a girl called Ayşe Ander and had began to think of getting settled rather seriously. I felt that he had been quite serious about marrying Ayşe Ander. With the birth of my baby, my life had taken a completely different turn. My husband was still under contract with the American firm. His working hours were rather ardous and long. This gave me more of a chance of spending all my time with Ayşe. My days were spent nursing, caressing and dressing her, then I would take her out in her pram, sing her songs, etc. I used to take care of the house chores when she fell asleep. Financially, our position was much better. We were able to engage a proper woman to help me with the house work. Togrul enjoyed going out at nights. We would go to a movie or to Sergei's nightclub once or twice a week. On such occasions Mother would be a delighted baby-sitter for us and would stay with Ayşe till we returned home.

During the day I was always at home. Once in a while I would entertain guests at home. Ayşe was alert to sounds around her. From her babyhood on she would be awakened if a dog barked in the garden or if a car slammed its brakes. Even the whistle of a distant train would be enough to wake her up. On such nights I would have very little sleep. However, I was very happy. I had a husband who adored me. I had a lovely house and above everything else I had the loveliest daughter to make my life a heaven. My daughter was a bit over one year old when Ayşe Ander and Cenan got married. Their wedding ceremony was held at the Ankara Palace Hotel. The bride's family, including her grandfather, her aunts, her cousins, Ayşe Ander's (Bibi) girlfriends and close family friends had all come from İstanbul to Ankara for the wedding. Nur had divorced his first wife, Patricia, in America and returning to Turkey had married another American girl named Myra. Ayşe, my husband and I were all present at the wedding. Our family had once again come together for this happy occasion. Now we had two Ayşe's in the family but this caused no trouble since most of her friends and Cenan also was calling her "Bibi." We all adored Bibi! She was not only very pretty but also was a very polite person. From the first day of their marriage she had become a member of the family and had won the love and respect of all family members. Although we had our differences later on in life, we became lifelong friends, Bibi and I.

XVIII

A New Home and a New Baby

A short while after Cenan's wedding, Nur and Myra went to America. A few months later I realized that I was once more pregnant. The flat that we had enjoyed until that time seemed too small for a family with two kids. We started looking for a place where we could be more comfortable. Finally we found a flat on İzmir Street. By a funny coincidence this was a place that held many memories for me! This was the flat, where many years ago, my good friend Leyla and her father, Ambassador Şaman, had lived. He was a bachelor at the time and Leyla had the house for herself during the days. We had smoked our first cigarettes there and we had tried our first gossip, etc. On top of it all, Leyla's wedding had taken place in this very flat. Furthermore, the flat below belonged to Mr. Birgi and his wife, he was the son of a friend of Togrul's mother and was also living there. The apartment had three floors and on the top floor lived another good friend of my mother-in-law. She was living together with her son-in-law, Dr. Alatas, and his family. I used to know all these people since my teenage years. So, in a way, two very good friends of my mother-in-law had become sort of double mothers-in-law for me, one living above and the other below my flat. I was always somewhat reserved toward the one below, but Aunt Kadriye became almost like a second mother to me.

Our new flat was much larger and we arranged it to our taste. From the entrance hall, toward the left, there were two rooms both overlooking İzmir Street. They were interconnected and we turned one into a dining room and the other into a living room. The connecting doors could be closed when required. Following the entrance hall there was a large room that also had a connecting door to the dining room and we turned it into a

181

general sitting room where we could enjoy our children and our daily life. Our library and some comfortable sofas were placed in this room. My piano was there also. I may have mentioned these bergère armchairs Mother had bought for me, but my husband had considered them too old-fashioned and we had not taken them into our first apartment. Then with Ayşe's arrival I had taken one of them. Now that I had ample space, I took the second armchair. They were spacious and I could nurse my baby while sitting in them most comfortably. Through a door to the right hand side of this general living room, one passed into a space where there were two bedrooms and a bath. There was a big window that almost covered one whole side of the living room, which in a slanted manner looked over İzmir Caddesi. The bedroom windows on the other hand looked over to the street in the back and we could see Menekşe Sokak from there. One could turn to the service quarters from the entrance hall. There was an office, a kitchen and further on there was a bedroom for the help plus a toilet and a shower. The flat was full of light most of the day. We moved in toward spring. My daughter Ayşe, just like me, had started walking rather early and we had gone around the flat with her. My new baby was also to be born in July. We decided that with two children, I would have difficulty running the house with a daily woman only. My husband's business had also grown. He was still employed by the American architectural firm, but he had entered architectural competitions and had won the architectural design for the new Etibank Building. This meant that our social life was also growing together with his work. We had begun to entertain at home or go out to receptions. On the other hand, I was a meticulous mother and wanted to make sure that I would be taking care of my children personally. I loved nursing my children. I did not wish to neglect Ayşe when I had the new baby. After a lot of discussions and survey of the possibilities, we decided to get a governess from abroad. In those days most families would get local nurses, most of them coming to Ankara from the village of Kızılcahaman. So it meant that although they could be well-meaning and good people, they were sure to be uneducated peasants. Furthermore, most of these women would insist on spending the summer in their villages to help their families in raising the seasonal crop. A proper nanny would at least know how to administer the required medicines and the like. Furthermore, such a nanny would be instrumental in getting my children to acquire a foreign language at an early age.

With all these ideas in mind, we were finally able to engage Schwester Lotte. This was a German nanny with a diploma for raising babies and she had been employed by a family we knew and had very good references. However, Ayşe was having difficulty warming up to this Schwester. Since I was always at home during the day, I had hoped I could bring them together. Unfortunately, Frau Lotte was a typical German nanny, all discipline and no fun!

Of course discipline was very important. However, there was another source for trouble. My mother was always at our house to visit her granddaughter. She could not bear to hear Ayşe cry and she would advise me to carry her in my arms until she had fallen asleep. No doubt I was lucky to have the help of her experiences. Nevertheless, carrying the baby was getting more and more difficult. One night we had invited some new acquaintances for dinner. Actually my husband was building their new house. I had planned an elaborate menu for them. We would start with cheese soufflé. By now, I had become an established cook. Ayşe usually went to sleep at about 19:00 hours. So we had decided to serve dinner at 20:30. Somehow that evening, Ayşe had refused to go to sleep and kept crying every time I put her into her bed. My soufflé was burnt and my dinner was in a shambles. Even just before I went to the hospital to give birth to my second child, I was forced to carry Ayşe in my arms to put her to sleep. I just could not refuse Mother's requests. Even when we had the Schwester, Mother had been adamant. Some sort of discipline had indeed become a necessity.

In those days doctors could not figure out the gender of the baby before it was born. I was thinking that if I had a son now, I could stop having children. Togrul on the other hand kept praying that we should get another daughter. He came from a family of four sons, him being the youngest, so he had a liking for girls. On July 25, 1954 at 9:40 A.M. Fatma Zeyneb, a baby girl, was born. My gynecologist was Dr. Pekdeğer, who was the husband of my very good friend Leyla. It was rather an easy birth and I was able to enjoy every minute of it, pain and all. Mansur also liked girls, so when the baby was born both he and Togrul kept shouting, "Thank God it is a girl." Zeyneb was really a beautiful baby. She too was quite developed like Ayşe. She weighed three kilos seven hundred grams and her height was fifty centimeters. I was so much in love with my new baby that every time they took her away from me I would turn around in my bed and watch her. Ayşe had been left at home, under the care of the Schwester and Mother had come to the hospital with me. I was worried about Ayşe. Thank goodness their father brought Ayşe to the hospital and we let her hold the new baby and I could see that Ayşe's eyes were full of love for her baby sister. They did not look like one another. Zeyneb also had an oval face, but with her tilted nose, slanted eyes and thicker lips she looked very much like a baby doll. Her hair was fair and her father had started loving her and saying, "My blonde beautiful little girl."

Whenever my children came into my view I became tremendously happy. I think I had then realized that my reason for being was to have children. Despite all the worries, the headaches and the enormous responsibilities they brought with them, motherhood also had developed in me a kind of love that nothing could surpass. That morning, having my two girls by my side, I could not have been happier. They were giving me the greatest strength in my life.

As soon as we were back home, I realized that Ayşe had been frightened by the nanny. She was clinging to my skirt all the time. Unfortunately, I was not well, healthwise. I had developed what they called the childbirth fever. Despite the fact that I was running a high fever I did not give up nursing my new baby, Zeyneb. However, I found that the baby quickly fell asleep after a few sucks! The maid saw that I was getting worried and said, "It may be that she is given the pacifier." I had expressly told the nanny that we were not going to use pacifiers. When the nanny took both the girls out, I went in and searched in her closet. I found a bottle that looked somewhat suspicious and I took a sample and sent it to be analyzed. Then, although I was still running a high fever, I could not restrain myself any longer. I got dressed and went out after them. I could hardly see straight but I was running. I was running to Güven Park, where most nannies took the children under their care. The nanny was actually spanking Ayşe in the park. When I got a little closer, I saw a pacifier in Zeyneb's mouth. I told the nanny to return to the house immediately and took the children under my care. By the time we had returned home, the lab had sent in their report. It turned out that the bottle contained some sort of a sedative. Apparently not only was she using the pacifier but she was also wetting it with this liquid before putting it in my baby's mouth. I immediately sent her out of my house. This had made me realize that our belief in getting a foreign nanny and giving our children some sort of European education was wrong. As a result I decided to take care of both my babies myself, even if it meant curtailing some of my social activities that I enjoyed with my husband. However, that job I had taken over was not at all easy. I was not getting much sleep and I was always tired. Mother, of course, came to my help on many occasions but nevertheless I was almost exhausted.

Father had bought some land in Çankaya many years ago, below the British Embassy. There were big poplars and other trees in the big garden. There was also an almost derelict house. Mother enjoyed the big garden and the trees. She used to go there whenever the weather allowed. One entered the house climbing some ten or twelve steps, as the basement, in the old days was used as a stable to keep the farm animals in. Since none of the family members were interested in going to the big mansion at Erenköy, Father had sold it. Mother came up with a suggestion. She said, "Since none of us can afford to go to İstanbul during the summer, why don't we use this house for the summer." This "we" meant all three families, Father's, Cenan's and Togrul's! Actually the house had one floor above the stable and had lots of rooms. However, I did not want to live together with others. Togrul Devres, the architect, studied the situation and came up with a project. The floor above could be occupied by my parents, plus Cenan and Bibi. He would renovate the old stable into a studio apartment and a bath with a toilet. There would be a small kitchenette, a bedroom for us and a dining area plus a large sleeping space for the two girls. In the front, a terrace would be constructed where we would have some more space in the hot summer months of 1955. Not only was he able to carry out all these renovations in less than a month, but he was also able to change a small derelict chicken coop into a big room with toilet so that Mother's servants would have a sleeping facility in the same garden at least for the summer. As soon as the house (or should I say the flats) were ready, the garden was taken up. Flower beds, lawns, etc. were arranged among the poplars and the ancient farm house was turned into a lovely summer residence! There was an old pool in the garden. Thinking that our children could fall in by accident, Togrul had covered it with an attractive iron rail. So that summer, with the Sılan living on the top floor and the Devres family in the basement, we all moved into this heavenly farm house in Çankaya.

Butterfly chairs were not known in Turkey at the time. Togrul got someone to make the steel parts according to his design and I worked on the cloth covers. So we had eight butterfly chairs placed on our terrace and on the front lawn. These sort of together, but yet separate, living conditions were enjoyed by all members of the family. Beside the pool in the garden we had gotten an inflatable plastic pool which we used to fill with fresh water from the well. Toward noontime the water in this plastic pool would get warm enough for me to put both my girls in. They would be very happy to splash in the pool. Sometimes I too would join them. At other times I would hose myself and sometimes my daughters in the same manner. In the midday sun this proved to be very enjoyable for all.

Ayşe's toy doll carriage and Zeyneb's play pen (since she was hardly one year old at the time) were also placed on the terrace. Since they had said that it would help her teeth to grow stronger, I would give Zeyneb the bony part of a lamb chop. She would chew it as if it was a sort of game. One day I saw that a small kitten had gotten near Zeyneb and my daughter would let the kitten chew on her bone and had fun as the kitten struggled with the bone. When autumn was getting near and it was time for all of us to return to our flats in the city, this little kitten looked so forlorn that Mother was forced to adopt her (naming her Tekir) and took her to her apartment. Tekir lived with Mother for many years and after she passed away Tekir stayed with Father.

To reach our garden in Çankaya we had to pass in front of an apartment building that belonged to Ambassador Açıkalın. One of the tenants there were the Karaosmanoğlu family. They had a small son called Selim. We had enjoyed their company very much. That little boy is now a respected ambassador of our country, how time flies!

After winning the architectural competition for the design of the Etibank Building, Togrul had left the American firm he was working with and formed his own company, by getting two of his assistants as partners. They were both very young and had just graduated from the School of Architecture. Both were both energetic and hard working men. At first, they were working in our house. Togrul was in love with his profession and he certainly was a brilliant architect. When he got started on his work, he would forget everything else, even having food! So the family schedule would be all upset. In a way, his having an office away from the family turned out to be better. We had returned to our flat at İzmir Caddesi when the Etibank project had been completed. That project had become a sort of a child for me as well. Many problems had arisen, many sacrifices had to be made and many sleepless nights had to be passed during this construction. I could not help getting involved with every project my husband took on, this seemed natural for an architect's wife.

I have always believed in the equality between men's and women's rights. However, one should always keep in mind that these creatures are built differently. For example, one cannot expect to find the same kind of devotion a mother has for her offspring in a father! With considerations such as these the equality between a husband and a wife quickly gets lost. Consequently, most of the time it is the woman who has to give way. The saying that there is a woman behind every successful man is a proverb that should not be discarded. A woman can provide peace and tranquility which is so necessary for a capable man to go ahead in his profession. I guess in any marriage, each side has to give in some, but it is never granted that such concessions would be equally divided between a man and his wife.

As winter was approaching I again found myself expecting and I was very happy. The calculation that my doctor did showed that this child was also due to come in July! Despite the great joy we felt about this addition to our family, other considerations started to worry us. During the summer the women who worked in the house had quit to go and work in their villages and I had a rather hard time. If Mother was not always there to help, it would have been almost impossible for me to accomplish everything. What would I be doing next summer with three children to attend to, one newborn, one two years old and the eldest only four years old! Just their washing would probably take many hours, plus drying and ironing of the same! As I was having qualms about my future, by chance a middle-aged, very nice woman entered our life. She was called Nariye and the children began to call her "Nani." She was always cheerful, full of love for the children and was certainly a godsend for me.

XIX
What if I Have a Son?

As time was getting closer for the birth, we started to think of a name. Both of us had thought we would have a third daughter and we had decided to call her "Elif Nazli." One day when I ventured to say, "What should we call him, if he turns out to be a boy?" My husband calmly answered, "Lefter Küçükandoniadis." Togrul loved fancy jokes, but this was too much. However, I went along with his joke and suggested that he should recite the names of other famous football players of the day (since Lefter was a world-famous football player in Turkey). So he started counting and at one point I said "That one." He had pronounced the name "Ömer." I said if we have a son this time we shall call him Ömer.

We had again moved to Çankaya for the summer. Two days before giving birth, I had a dream. In my dream my daughter Zeyneb had turned into a boy and I was trying to find a boy's name for him. An old man with white beard appeared and told me gently, "You shall call him Ali, my dear girl." When I woke up, I had made up my mind. My son's name would be Ali Ömer!

On July 28, 1956 at sometime like 02:10 A.M., following a rather difficult delivery, I gave birth to my son. I was very happy. I knew my husband wanted a string of daughters, but I was happy thinking that some change in the family would be welcome and a brother could be of some help to my girls. I must confess that my husband was taken somewhat aback. He had so much prepared himself for his third daughter that having his first son was a bit of a surprise for him.

Ömer was a huge baby. He weighed four kilos and five hundred grams and his height was fifty-five centimeters. He was a dark-eyed boy with well developed black lashes and brows.

Sometimes I used to wonder how I was able to carry such a big baby in me? Miracles do take place in this world, almost daily, don't they?

My father-in-law was on a boat trip, traveling around the Black Sea coast line. We had advised him of the arrival of our son by telegram. His answer was rather typical. He said, "Congratulations. Only you could have brought these rival prophets together in your son!" I had gone to give birth to Ömer while we were still living in Çankaya. My gynecologist was once more Dr. Pekdeğer. When I arrived home with their new baby brother, the two girls were delighted with the baby, especially when I had to change his diaper. Seeing him naked Zeyneb suddenly shouted, "Mummy look, Ömer has little balls!" and we all had such a laugh!

I was the happiest mother in the world. Everything was wonderful. Ayşe and Zeyneb were always playing together, displaying nothing but love for each other. Ayşe was very sensitive, shy and sort of withdrawn. Zeyneb, on the other hand, was much more robust, always with a smile and was rather independent. Probably this difference in their temperament was the reason why they enjoyed one another. Rather without thinking about it, I had developed nicknames for my children. Ayşe was my Sultan, Zeyneb was my Doll and Ömer was my Pascha Ömer! I guess Ayşe's difference, Zeyneb's baby face and Ömer's rather serious way of looking at things had made me choose these nicknames.

When Ömer was about two weeks old, Togrul announced that we had to move to İstanbul since he was to work on a new project for the Turkish Pavillion in the International Fair at Brussels together with two other architects. He had to stay there for a long period of time and he wanted me to go with him. I should take baby Ömer with me and leave my daughters with Mother in Ankara. It was rather a difficult decision for me to make! I hated leaving my daughters behind, but I could not very well say no to my husband. He had already engaged a suite for us at the İstanbul Hilton! Getting separated from my girls was quite difficult for me. I had no choice. My mother's advice was that I could not let my husband go away on his own and that it was my duty to be with him. So I had to go, but how I cried secretly!

I had no difficulty in taking care of Ömer at the Hilton. I was breast feeding him anyway and he was a very quiet boy. All day long I was with my son, washing, playing and feeding him. Our suite overlooked the swimming pool of the hotel. I had lots of books to read. When my son was asleep I would be on the phone talking with my daughters or writing long letters to them. I was very worried that such a long period of separation could endanger my relations with my daughters. However, their life in Çankaya under the supervision of my mother seemed to be enjoyable for them. At nights we would engage a baby sitter for our son and I would be able to join my husband at dinner, consumed in one of the various dining rooms of the hotel. Sometimes Leyla and Melih Birsel or Haluk and Neyire Baysal, who were co-partners in the project, would join us for dinner. Whenever I felt that my son was ready to wake up, I would rush up to our quarters, feed him to both our hearts' content and return to my husband's dining table. When Togrul was overworked and tired, we would simply call room service for some soup or sandwiches. My son was getting to become a full grown boy. By the end of September, I think, we returned to Ankara. Getting together with my daughters was the biggest prize for me. Only after our return to Ankara did I realize that in all that time I had not gone out of the hotel even once!

My husband was always loaded with work. He was taking part in competitions, he was getting new offers and was building new houses. Apart from being an accomplished architect, Togrul was also involved in other lines of art. He would do his utmost to incorporate works of other artists into his designs or constructions. Ceramic makers, sculptors and artists naturally tended to show him their works. Especially while the Etibank Building was being constructed we had the opportunity of meeting many well-known artists. Among these I always remember Abidin and Güzin Dino, Selçuk Milar and his bride. I must add to this list Bedri and Eren Eyüboğlu with whom I had been acquainted before my marriage and who had both contributed to the Etibank Building. Meeting with and talking to such exceptional people always enriched my soul as well as my brain. I also had the chance of meeting Füreya Koral during that period. Togrul had also designed a movie house, "Renkli Sinema" and a restaurant, "47 Restaurant" during that period.

We were happily settled in our apartment before the winter came. I was blissfully happy and contented. I always enjoyed being and living with my children. Somehow I began to develop an uncomfortable feeling! I began to wonder if there could be some sort of a feeling of jealousy among my children! I had heard they had recently started a new department of child psychology at the University of Hacettepe. I made an appointment and went to visit the specialist. When she heard that I had three very healthy children, she laughed and said, "You are the first person in Ankara who has called on me, despite having healthy and normal children." When I explained my imaginary troubles, she started asking questions. I recounted the routine I followed daily. During the day I was with them most of the time. They were all equally treated. "I play with them and read to them, etc. They have their meals together. Sometimes I let them play by themselves. By 18:00 hours I give them their baths, one after the other, by 19:00 hours I give them their evening meal and by 20:00 hours I put them all to bed." The advice she gave sounded a bit revolutionary to me! I, who had imagined myself as the "ideal mother" was quite impressed. She said, "Since your children were born two years apart from one another, you should put something like half an hour between say, their bath hours. The elder girl should be instructed to become an elder sister to her younger sister and brother and the young ones should realize that she is older." She also asked to see my children. I took them all to meet with her. After meeting with and talking to each of them, she assured me that everything was normal and that my children had no compulsions that could effect their lives. Gradually I started to put into practice her advice and my days became as blissful as ever. I believe that they also enjoyed these small details.

Taking care of my children and tending to their daily needs constantly was making me very tired. My husband would come usually at a time when my children would be going to bed. We would have our meal after they were settled and chat a little afterward. During the summer months I had only Nani with me.

In the winter we had found a pair of sisters to help with the housework. One was the cook and her sister did the house chores, like cleaning the house, etc. Nani would tend only to the children's laundry, cleaning, etc. At night Ayşe was prone to wake up crying. Her cries would wake up Zeyneb as well. By the time I could get them settled it would be time for me to feed my son. This routine meant that I could get only three or four hours of sleep during the night. Of course I had to be up and around the house during the day! Naturally I was spending time with my husband and we used to go to bed rather late. We also entertained at home or we would be going out. Togrul was also prone to come home for lunch and usually without notice he would bring friends with him. This meant that I had to be ready for all kinds of contingencies. My husband was not easily satisfied. Apart from being a well-dressed man, always careful about his shirts, etc, he also wanted to have his house spick and span and he hated disorder. What I am trying to say is that I had to be so many things all at once. I had to be an attentive mother, a good housewife, an entertaining companion all in one! This was not an easy task to fill. Still I was able to carry on and do all my duties to the best of my abilities. Moreover, I had no complaints.

XX
The Summer at Viranbağ

At the end of May 1957, Bibi and Cenan had their first daughter. Emine, with her blonde hair was a sweet, energetic baby. I remember giving her the basket cradle in which all my children had spent their early days since it was still in very good condition. My children were also very happy since they had accepted Emine as their sister. The whole family had moved into the Çankaya summer house. Although I enjoyed this life with the family, I also wanted to give my children a chance to enjoy the seaside. After discussing this problem several times, we came to the conclusion that I could go and stay with my father-in-law in Viranbağ. My mother-in-law had passed away three years ago. Father Mustafa Nuri used to spend his summers there by himself. Togrul would visit us as frequently as he could. He had constructions going on both in Ankara and İzmir.

At the time we had decided to spend the summer at Viranbağ. I had three people helping me with the housework. I had fallen in love with Viranbağ long before our marriage. We used to have lots of fun going there with friends. However, now we had to be realistic. I had seen the conditions of the house while we were engaged. I realized that conditions at Viranbağ were quite different from what I was accustomed to. There was no electricity. The house was away from all other parts of the island and commuting was quite a problem. Pine needles that covered most roads made them very slippery. To reach the sea below one had to go down a rocky and slippery footpath and the return climb could be hazardous. I had three children aged five, three and one. This meant that I would need a lot of help. Moving there for the summer, apart from the three women I already had, I took also the male servant who was working at my husband's office plus I found a Hungarian lady. Actually Irma was

194

coming to the house to give me massage. When I mentioned this summer's trip to the island, she jumped at the chance. So Irma, Nani and I, we three women, would take care of the children. Sabri, the male help, would do the hard work. The two sisters would tend to cooking and cleaning. It was up to me to organize this ménage!

Togrul came to install us into the house and also made various arrangements for supplies, etc. Meat, vegetables, poultry and ice would be brought in a carriage by land. The fisherman would bring us fresh fish in his boat from the sea. Sabri would carry all provisions into the house. So every morning the first thing I did was to arrange all provisions and organize the day's meals. Only after this was done could I take the children to swim in the sea. We made quite a procession! I would take baby Ömer in my arms, Irma would hold Ayşe by her hand and Nani would hold Zeyneb's hand. Sabri would carry down the big basket into which all towels, toys, fresh water and all other utensils deemed necessary for us on the beach. Although the walk down was pretty slippery, the fresh aroma of the pine trees and the wild pelargoniums made the place heavenly. The children would play with pebbles, run around and splash and all were trying to learn how to swim. Granddaddy would take a position up on the terrace and watch this happy scene with delight. Naturally we saw a few snakes and lots of lizards. Despite everything we were enjoying ourselves tremendously. The return climb up used to be the worst part. The fisherman did not only bring us fish but once or twice he also brought us lobsters. In fact, once the lobster that he had brought was so big and strong that I had placed Ömer on the animal and it was able to carry my son on its back along the terrace! We would use a hose to get rid of the salt water on our bodies. Then the whole family would sit down for lunch. After lunch the children and granddaddy went to have their siestas. The help would take a rest as well. This would give me a chance to write letters to my mother or my husband or sew or repair things that were torn. After these chores, if I had time left, I would take a book and rest my body under the pines. When children woke up in the afternoon, I would create some games for them or take them out for a walk and by the same token give some freedom to the people who were working for us all the time.

I used to give the children their baths and dinner rather early. This was also quite an affair. Since we had no electricity in the house, we had to boil water by burning some logs. So all the children were washed by adding cold water to the boiling water and so on! After putting my children to bed I would join my father-in-law and we would have our dinner together and carry on long discussions on the terrace overlooking the sea. He was a highly literate, accomplished and mature gentleman and listening to him was always a pleasure. He was originally from Crete and had a slight accent, which added to my pleasure. I would learn things from him and we used to laugh a lot. He had written some poetry and he would recite from other poets and had a definite philosophy of life. He used to have a glass of rakı at every meal and preferred eating fish. His Cretean tastes were rather special. He would add some sweetened tomato paste to his pilav and he would eat his börek always with some jam. Eating, for him, was almost a ceremony.

For the first time in my life I was using gas lamps. These dainty receptacles were a great source of worry for me. I was always afraid that they would break and set the house on fire! For this reason I was always the last to go to bed. I would first check if my children were safely tucked in, all the lamps were safely turned off and then I would go to sleep, quite late. Since I had to get up before they did, it meant that I was almost always short on sleep. All this was not easy. Furthermore, it was no joy for a young woman to stay away from her husband for three months under these conditions. I had, however, accepted all this for the sake of my children. Togrul came once or twice, and other members of my family also came for short visits. During that summer Bibi had also been able to come to her family home on the island with her first born, however, it was hardly possible for me to go visiting with my three children in tag. I also felt that getting away from my children did not seem a nice thing to do!

So returning to my home in Ankara at the end of the summer was a great joy for me. My children had developed during this summer sojourn and I was very contented with that. However, something happened and I had my first impression that things were not so rosy all the time. Ayşe was suddenly taken ill. She complained about tummy aches. However, there seemed to be nothing wrong with her bowels and her stomach. She was crying almost continuously. I first called on our family pediatrician, Dr. Demirag. He was a recognized specialist, but he had difficulty in diagnosing and suggested a consultation. So a group of pediatricians, including Dr. Doğramacı, came to our house and looked over Ayşe. They were saying that the cause of the pain she was complaining about was on her left side. They could not agree on a diagnosis and my little daughter was exhausted from all that handling. As they were about to leave the house, Ayşe had started screaming again. This time Dr. Doğramacı said, "We cannot leave this child here, we must take her to a hospital. We must also check her blood, etc." The present Hacettepe Clinic had not even been built yet! So we took my daughter to the University Clinic. After some more checkups, they decided it was appendicitis and took my child in for an apendectomy but by that time her appendicitis had burst and a general peritonitis had developed. She had gone into a deep coma. The doctors were saying that there was nothing they could do any further and that we should all pray to God! I was almost going out of my mind. My very dear friend, Dr. Renda, came to my help. He said, "If you have faith in my knowledge, I believe I can save your daughter." How could I say "No!" I entrusted Ayşe to him completely. By applying a medicine not well known at the time (I believe it was penicillin) he was able to bring my daughter back from that deep coma after a treatment that took seventeen days. I thanked God and him! For seventeen days both I and Mother had not left Ayşe's bedside. I do not think I ever slept. I am not at all sure if I ate anything all that time either. What I always remember were those harrowing moments that never seemed to end. Every moment took a year to pass as far as I was concerned. When Ayşe finally opened her eyes, I was reborn! During those very difficult days, apart from my Doctor Renda, another person that was of invaluable help to me was Aunt Kadriye. This lovely old lady, who was a friend of my late mother-in-law, daily tended my two younger children left behind in my home with the house help available. She was so effective that she was able to convince Zeyneb, who was very choosy with her food, that all that was served should be consumed. When Ayşe recovered fully, we returned home. I was delighted to be with my children again and having Ayşe fully recovered.

Dr. Renda was a childhood friend of my husband from İzmir. I had heard that my mother-in-law enjoyed card games almost to the point of addiction. As Fevzi recounted, boys would go by the seaside and competed in throwing and skipping pebbles on the water. Togrul would pester his mother during a card game and his mother, in order to get rid of the boy, would give him some silver coins to go and play with. Togrul thereby would be skipping silver coins when all the other boys would be throwing pebbles! Dr. Fevzi Renda and his lovely wife Suzan, and their two delightful daughters, were people we enjoyed very much and our relationship has lasted all these years. Of course, by saving my daughter's life, Fevzi had gained a special place in my heart.

That winter a Dutch businessman had called on my husband. His name was Jim G. Drabbe and he was a senior manager in a construction company called Netherlands Harbor Works. They had obtained a number of contracts in Turkey and they were thinking of putting up a building for their company's branch office. One night Togrul invited that gentleman to our home for dinner. Our visitor was a very tall and thin Dutchman who was elderly and rather reserved. However, the dinner went very well. By departure time that night he had become a friend of the family. We had also enjoyed having this very well-educated gentleman in our home. He turned out to be very friendly and warm person toward us. He had relaxed in the family atmosphere we had provided and appeared as if he too had enjoyed the evening. What I had failed to understand that night was that this very tall Dutchman would turn out to be a perennial friend during the years to come.

After a few more evenings at home or outside, Jim Drabbe suggested that Togrul should go to Holland and study Dutch architecture and develop his new designs accordingly. This trip would last three or four weeks. Later on, as this idea was being discussed, I too was invited to join my husband on this fact-finding mission. This was going to be our first trip abroad as a married couple. My first consideration was for my children. Would I be able to stay apart from my children for such a long time! They were more important then anything in my life. As usual Mother volunteered to help. She promised to look over my household during our absence and that she would direct the existing personnel as necessary. She also advised that it was my duty to accompany my husband on such a trip. So I made up my mind to go, despite all my reservations as a loving mother. I had already been in some cities in Europe but had never been in Holland. We were given a suite at the Amstel Hotel in Amsterdam. It was a charming place and the first thing that struck me was the number of cyclists on the streets! There were also many cripples riding on bicycles especially designed according to their deformities. These were the relics of the Second World War. Another thing that surprised me very much was the unbelievable degree of animosity against anything German! Once or twice, on the street, I had tried to ask something in German and people would simply stare at me in astonishment and turn their backs. I was sure they understood the language but they had such an aversion to anything German! It did not take me long to understand the reason for this.

It was a tiny country and we were visiting every city of any importance. At the same time we were being entertained all the time. There were concerts, ballet shows, dinner parties, et al. I was very excited to be able to attend a show by the ballet company managed by Marquis de Cuevas. Mrs. Drabbe turned out to be a middle-aged woman who had traveled extensively and they had raised five children. Her kindness and friendship, especially during the times when my husband was working, had been very comforting for me. The enormous variety of the tulips raised in Keukenhoff had almost taken my breath away. I knew that tulip bulbs had first come to Holland from Turkey, but they had done so much to develop so many varieties of this lovely flower. At times like this, my love for my country would come to the fore and I would complain bitterly to find the reason that we as a nation had been unable to do as they did. Our trips included several cities. In Den Haag we saw the Moderadam. Rotterdam had been totally demolished during the war and was now completely reconstructed! The center of the Dutch cheese manufacturing, a city called Alkmaar, and the purely touristic called

Vollendam were very enjoyable sites. The people carrying the cheeses in Alkmaar, with their many colored hats, looked like flowers. I later learned that the different colored hats actually designated the company the men were working for. These were basically porters but their pure white costumes and their variedly colored hats made them very picturesque. Two men would be carrying a boat-like receptacle full of rounds of Dutch cheeses and they must have been carrying heavy loads. It was hard for me to understand how these men, who obviously were doing a difficult job, could still be so lively and smiling as they toiled all day long.

At Vollendam everyone was wearing their ancient local costumes and visitors could put on similar dresses to have their picture taken. Since I was very tiny, I was forced to put on a dress made for children. My husband was trying to take my picture in costume and some people appeared with a movie camera in their hands and took my picture as well. Unfortunately, they rushed away and we could not get their address or get a chance to obtain a copy of their reels.

I was having a very good time, but I must confess not having my children around me was making me feel bad. Whenever I saw a puppeteer, or if I saw some children playing in a park, tears would start rolling down my cheeks. I was always on the lookout for toys or hats, etc. that I thought they would enjoy. Finally my architect finished whatever he was doing and we were ready to return home. Naturally we had to thank the Drabbe family for all the things they had done for us. At the end of the month I was once again able to hug my children to my heart's content. Finally I was back home with my children. All my life, the idea of my home has been very important for me. Despite the fact that I had people to help, it was very important for me to be with my children. Perhaps this had its roots in the fact that my mother had always been present in my life. I felt that a child who comes home from school or whatever and asks "Is mother home?" should always enjoy the security of getting a positive answer and that a mother should always be there for her children. Similarly, the times I enjoyed most were those when I would be reading a good book, hearing my children's voices or doing something to make my home a better place for my children. Mother once said to me, "You have two more children at home, let me have Ayşe for a while." My reaction was very severe. I was like a mother tiger whose cubs were about to be abducted! I was furious and I answered, "I did not give birth to my children to give them away, no force on earth can take them away from me." Maybe I had broken Mother's heart that day but I could not restrain myself.

This obsession of mine, namely being a homebody, had begun to aggravate my husband, especially when he had nothing else to do. We were quite often out at nights. Theatres, night clubs, parties! We certainly had an active social life. For that reason I felt that during the weekends the whole family should gather together. My children were hardly able to see their father during working days. Togrul was always working very hard and for long hours. This sometimes would extend to weekends also. Somehow he was not pleased with the noise that his children created, as I was! Actually he seemed to be bored with them. Feeling this and trying to amend it, I began to devise occasions that would bring them together in an enjoyable manner.

One of the help had found a husband and had left the house. So I had only Nani and the other woman to help me with the housework. In order to follow my husband's busy social schedule, I had to leave my children under the guidance of this almost illiterate woman or ask Mother for her help. Both were things that bothered me. Despite the fact that we had such bad experience in the past, the idea of getting a nanny from abroad seemed like the best solution for me. So once again we began to write back and forth to Germany. Finally, we were able to find a German girl who had been educated for raising young children. She did not know any other language than German but she had a way with children and quickly got them to like her. We used to call her "Uschi." In order to properly communicate with her, I was enrolled at the Göethe Institute in Ankara to learn German. I must confess that my German never went very far but I could at least talk to our nanny in her language. Thus after I had four semesters of instruction in German, I was able to explain myself quite a bit.

Ursula, "Uschi," was perfect with the children. She would take them out for long walks. They would prepare Christmas

201

trees together. She would paint eggs and hide them and get the children to find the hidden eggs during Easter and have lots of fun in general. She would cook them German dishes, read them tales from Grimm's tales, etc. In short, I had finally found the nanny I had always dreamed about. Uschi was interested in learning things and bettering herself. On top of everything else, she had asked me if she could spend some of her free time, on her day off, at home with me, if I would be willing to instruct her in English. She spent many years with us. Upon returning to Germany she married a nobleman and had two daughters. We still correspond with her and her daughter, Zeyneb and I.

XXI

The Ankara Golf Club

In the year 1947, when we had just returned from America, I had met Mina Özdoğancı. She was the daughter of a diplomat and had spent long years of her life in foreign lands. We enjoyed each other's company and I met many nice people at her home. Mina and I had also developed a close relationship with the daughter of the American ambassador to Turkey, Wendy Wadsworth. Our relationship with Wendy has lasted all our lives. After they left Turkey, Wendy married another diplomat named Walter Harris. Ambassador Wadsworth's interest in golf had triggered the formation of the Ankara Golf Club. Through his guidance and advice, the Ankara Golf Club soon became a very "in place." Apart from an eighteen-hole golf course, there were some tennis courts and a big swimming pool. There were also various dining rooms and rooms for games, etc. On top of all this, they had also arranged special places for children to play. Naturally, most of our friends had become members of the Ankara Golf Club.

Our children had reached the ages of two, four and six. We had a reliable governess. Finally, we too became members of the golf club. This had given us an opportunity to be together as a family, including our children, socialize with our friends and take part in sports, at least during the weekends, at the club. This had added some color to our family life.

My mother-in-law was an ardent card player. Whereas in my family home we did not even own cards! Gayet Hanım (my mother-in-law) had come to visit us in Ankara when I was expecting Zeyneb and naturally she was staying in our house. Once she asked if she could invite her friends for a game of cards. I had politely refused this request, saying that I had an aversion to cards but that I had made prior arrangements for her and had hired a room at the Anadolu Club. The good lady was quite surprised but went along with my fixed idea. My reaction was more to the effect to keep cards out of my home, since I felt that my husband also had a liking for games, or rather gambling, just like his mother.

The golf club had given me another solution. After having some exercises at the club, Togrul started playing bridge with his cronies. In this manner I was able to keep cards out of my house. After a while, in order to spend more time in my husband's company, I also started learning bridge. However, I never enjoyed gambling, either to win money or to get excitement out of it.

The years 1958-59 were full of cultural enjoyment, especially for me. In Ankara, concerts, operas and other theatrical shows were in abundance. Apart from the golf club members, we had developed an enjoyable group of friends and we were socializing freely. Our friends were mostly well-educated and intelligent people. The fact that Müşerref and Kudret were journalists had made me more interested in them. After all I too had some education in that field. At the time, I believe those two were writing for a paper called Öncü. They always wrote what was right and true and that was what we wanted to learn from our journalists. In later years Müş (short for Müserref), apart from her serious journalism, started a gossip column. This was a novelty for Turkey and when our pictures appeared in her column once or twice, my daughters had complained, saying that they were having a difficult time at school since their friends would crack jokes about us! I mentioned my problem to Müş and from that day on Müş was very careful about mentioning our family. I must also add that when I first started writing my memoirs about three years ago, I consulted Müş and she gave me a lot of encouragement. She has been a lifelong friend.

In the year 1958, Ayşe was registered to the kindergarten called "Ayşe Abla." I was hoping this would be a booster for her education. It turned out to be a success. Ayşe enjoyed her school and began to learn a lot of things. The founder of the school Mrs. Hızır was an excellent educationalist. Whenever I had the time and the opportunity, I would visit her and her husband, the well-known professor of philosophy, Dr. Hızır. Sometimes I would see them in the morning, when I brought Ayşe to school, or better still if I went there a little earlier than the time for the classes to end.

I had not lost contact with İstanbul but at the time Ankara had become the center of many things. Since the population of the capital of the country was comprised mainly of state employees, it seemed that many people shared the same things. My life had become so organized that each time I went to İstanbul I had begun as if I was coming from a provincial small town. People in İstanbul were interested in completely different things than I. It reached a point that I began to feel I did not belong there anymore. Apparently I had become an Ankara person!

My children were growing up and they were happy with their governess, Uschi. The summers were being spent in the common summer house in Çankaya. I believe those summers proved to be very happy times for my mother and father as well. Especially after tea in the afternoon Father used to gather all his grandchildren and take them hiking in the grounds up hill. Those gardens going all the way up to Reşit Galip Caddesi have now become the Botanical Garden of Ankara. In those days Father owned all that property. Bibi, Mother and I would chat in the garden, receiving friends for tea and having a generally calm and enjoyable life. Emine had also grown up so that she could join her cousins.

During those years Togrul and I had the chance to visit Rome a couple of times and we had enjoyed those trips very much. The people, the museums, the restaurants, everything about Rome was a delight. Autumn and spring were the best times to visit Rome. During the same period we had developed close relationships with a number of American families who were mostly connected with the American Embassy in Ankara. Among those I could cite, Pat and Tom Metcalf, Jo Ann and George Harris, the Barnes's, the Tanguy's and also Pat and Malia Natirbov. Most had children at about the same age as ours and naturally this would develop into a common interest. By that time Wendy, Ambassador Wadsworth's daughter, had come to Ankara as Mrs. Walter Harris. Being together with

Wendy once again gave me great pleasure. She now had a daughter named Marie.

While we were part of all these nice things, unfortunately our nation's affairs were not going so well. What the Democrat Party was doing or maybe undoing on purpose, was making the population very uneasy. I do not want to get into the politics of those days but there was no question that people on the whole were no longer satisfied with the life they were leading. There was much pressure on the free press. Many people were circulating illegal publications by hand. There had been a meeting, so-called 555 (signifying the fifth of May at 5:00 P.M.) where Prime Minister Adnan Menderes was actually manhandled by the crowd. At about that time Mother's illness had began to upset us. Mother, who had been playing hopscotch with her grandchildren a short while ago, was now always lying down and feeling low. Most of the doctors attending her kept saying things like she probably had a cold and was not taking her case seriously. By this time, Ayşe had started her primary school and Zeyneb was enrolled in the same kindergarten. Both were attending the institution called "Ayşe Abla." At the same time the Izmir Boulevard was also changing rapidly. Some of the small houses facing our block had been torn down and they were replaced by Balin Hotel, a big construction by the standards of the day. Many of our friends were moving from where we were to other parts of the city, to more quieter places like Çankaya or Kavaklıdere. Although my father had offered us land at Çankaya, somehow Togrul (despite the fact that he had the money) kept refusing to build a home for us and we were changing apartments all the time.

Life in Ankara, as well as in all of Turkey, was no longer enjoyable. We all felt the oppression. We kept listening to news broadcasted by foreign radios in order to get information about what was going on in our own country. The social unrest was effecting our daily lives. Furthermore I was getting worried about Mother's condition. Finally, one doctor diagnosed it as gallbladder inflammation and suggested surgery.

One night, on May 26, we had been invited to a friend's home for a party. Togrul was suddenly called away and had left home for İzmir. Since I had nothing to do, I joined the party by myself. After dinner we were playing some kind of a card game and as it was getting near midnight I wanted to quit the game and go home. There was a curfew and it was illegal for people to go out after midnight unless they had a special pass. Among the guests at the party there was a minister of the present government whom I liked and respected very much. He said, "Do not go alone. I have my official car and driver and I can take you home a little later." When he was driving me home at the early hours of the morning, I could not help myself and asked him why they did not resign and go to the polls. He confessed that he was also very perturbed but he said he had nowhere to turn. It must have been 1:00 A.M. by the time he dropped me off at my apartment. I did not go to bed directly, made myself some tea or something, and soon there was a lot of shouting in the streets. When I got up and looked outside the window I saw that there were soldiers running about and the street was crowded with people who did not know what was going on. Immediately I turned on the radio. A deep bass voice was informing us that the military had overtaken the government. The noise was enough to raise the children as well. Actually the country was almost waiting for this to happen. I was also hoping for some change, but a military takeover had frightened me. A little later Mother called. She was in tears. She had witnessed the brutal arrest of Gen. Erdelhün, who was the Chief of the General Staff, only a few hours ago! He was also a long-standing family friend and they were tenants in a nearby apartment. These were certainly disturbing things. On the other hand, the actions of the Democratic Party had become quite insufferable. Still, one could not blame the whole party for what was being done. There certainly were some good people who had been registered to that party. Contrary to Father's inclinations, I had never been interested in politics. There were many people that I liked who had joined the Democratic Party and now they were all being punished indiscriminately. It certainly was a pity and I felt sorry for many of them.

Very soon after the coup d'etat of May 27, 1960, we decided to move to Çankaya, our old summer house, despite the fact that it was still cold. Togrul had planned to rent an apartment whose construction had been delayed due to the political unrest and our present contract was about to expire. So we decided to move into the flat that Mother used to occupy during the summer months. This would give us more time to look for a flat. By the end of summer, when the Sılans had vacated the premises, we moved into the flat vacated by them. We would spend the winter there. In those days Ankara used to be covered by snow for many days during the winter. However, by that time we had a private car, Ömer would be starting kindergarten and I could drive all three children to school and back.

In moving to Mother's flat, we had to put most of our furniture in a depot. The reason we chose to stay on the floor above was due to the fact that our place was rather small but during the summer we were able to make use of the garden when the weather was fine. The building did not have central heating. Mother had an old and beautiful porcelain stove that she had always kept in that building. We had to install a wood-burning stove as well, to make sure that our children would not be cold. Some people are lucky in that respect. From the day that I was born, I had been brought up in houses that had central heating. Sure enough, the house I was born in was one of the very few houses that had central heating. Living in a house that was heated with stoves was a new kind of experience for me. At night, overlooking the snow covered garden while cooking sausages over the stove was such fun for the children. One evening when our car could not go up the driveway due to the snow, I was forced to walk. Since high-heeled shoes were no good in the snow, I had taken them off and had walked all the way to the house with my bare feet. This had become the talk of the town and our dear friend Müşerref had mentioned me in her social column as the "barefoot contessa." So we welcomed the New Year of 1961 in Çankaya.

Despite all its drawbacks, I remember arranging very successful parties in Çankaya. The children also enjoyed the freedom the place had given them. When they returned from school they used to enjoy the liberty our garden gave them. Ayşe and Zeyneb were enjoying their school. However, Ömer was having difficulties of adjustment. For example, there is a rice meal that is called "kuskus" (couscous) and the term in Turkish sounds similar to vomiting. Every time kuskus was offered for lunch,

Ömer would vomit his food. Then I would get a phone from the school and had to go and rescue my choosy son. Ömer never liked kuskus even when he had grown up into a man. Frankly, I always had agreed with my son on this subject.

It was exciting to go into spring in Çankaya. We could follow nature awakening day by day. When summer arrived we moved back to our first floor flat and let the rest of the family move to their usual quarters. Unfortunately, Mother was almost always sick but she refused surgery. Although we had enjoyed our winter in Çankaya, we thought one season was enough and Togrul started looking for a new flat for the winter.

XXII

Güniz Sokak No. 31

We were thinking of finding a flat around Kavaklıdere. We were lucky. We found a flat on Güniz Sokak No. 31. It was a three-storied apartment building and we had the second or the middle floor. Nowadays our ninth President, Mr. Demirel, resides in that building. It was a very comfortable flat. One entered the flat through a rather large vestibule to which two doors opened on the right-hand side. One opened into the kitchen and the pantry and the second opened into a comfortable living room connecting to a very large dining room. From these rooms one could see Güniz Sokak. There was also a connecting passage between the kitchen and the dining room. From the door on the left-hand side of the entrance hall there was a door through which one could reach the quarters reserved for the servants, all from still another door one could enter the master bedroom, and still a fifth door one could enter the part of the apartment reserved for our living quarters. In this last section there were three bedrooms plus two showers and a bath. This way we could provide separate bedrooms for our children. It was a very roomy flat and full of light. This last characteristic has been very important for me all my life. I have never enjoyed dark or stuffy places.

I guess we kept that flat for almost seven years. Some years later we were able to change our bedroom into a dining room and vice-versa. This way I was able to move dining guests into the salon and leave the dirty table as it was behind closed doors.

On July 14, 1960, our family was blessed with a newcomer. Bibi gave birth to her second daughter, Fatoş. She was a lovely baby. This was a special blessing for Mother. Fatoş was her fifth grandchild and she gave Mother a new impetus in her life de-spite the fact that her health was deteriorating all the time. Before summer came to an end our new flat was painted and cleaned and we were able to move in before winter arrived.

In those days the system of hauling students to various schools had not been developed, so I was driving them to their school every morning. On their return, Uschi would pick them up or I would drive them home. There were some American fami-lies working at U.S. Aid to Turkey on the same street. Further along the street lived a young engineer who was appointed gen-eral manager of the State Water Works, called Süleyman De-mirel (who later became the ninth President of the country). Since I knew that he was a friend of my brother Cenan, I used to give him a lift whenever I saw him walking or waiting for the bus. Naturally, we chatted about the daily politics as we rode along.

Togrul liked to get up late in the mornings. So I would be out of bed early to attend to the children's breakfast and have a cup of coffee with them and then we would be off to school. On my return I would assign the daily task to the help, arrange the day's menus, etc. and then have breakfast with my husband when he was ready. Then he would take the car to go to his office. After his departure I would walk to my German classes in midtown, which would take about half an hour. I would later take a cab back home. Sometimes we would have lunch with Togrul at home and sometimes he would bring a friend or friends with him. So I was always prepared to serve more than two at lunch. We had a cook but I was always there to check and direct everything that was being cooked. I had reserved the time be-tween lunch up to the time the children came from school for myself. Either I'd do some chores, read or go to the hairdresser.

The children's return from school was always a delight. I always made sure to be at home for them. The flat would sud-denly be filled with their happy chattering. They would be sure to ask if mother was home and getting a positive answer would run to give me a big hug. After they washed up and changed we would sit for their afternoon tea and I would receive their daily news. Sometimes I would have to give them a hand with their homework, so I would try to make my other appointments at

211

later hours. I would not go visiting or accept visitors at home before 5 P.M. If I had to be out for one reason or another, I would make sure to return home by 6:30 P.M. My children were the meaning of my life. I also was very attached to my mother. She was a woman of exceptional qualities. Naturally, our approaches to life did not always coincide. In any case, she had always given me great support. Every morning at a certain time she would phone me to ask about my day. Whenever possible we would get together. Especially since her health had started to deteriorate, I was trying to make sure to visit with her every day.

Some days Togrul would work till late hours and the children would have gone to sleep by the time he came home. Sometimes he would come home and have dinner with the children. Then we would go to his office after the children had gone to sleep and he would work till the wee hours of the morning. Such incidences occurred when he was working on a new and challenging project. In the office I would prepare him coffee, read a book and generally keep him company. We would return home early in the morning and sometimes we would buy frankfurters on the way home from some street vendor. When he was not tied up with his work, we would either go out or invite friends to our house. This schedule meant that I would go to bed rather late but had to get up every morning before the children and start the day with them. Funny, I was never a night person. Even during my school days, I had never been a late night worker. I always preferred to get up early and do my home work in the morning.

While writing these memoirs, I was surprised to realize that certain things had a sort of repetition in my life. Despite various differences, there was a big mother figure in the home where I grew up. I was then experiencing something similar in my life. The father figure was rather elusive and not quite always there when I was a child. The same thing was recurring in my family life. As a mother I was always interested in everything my children did. However, their father was not always that attentive. Naturally and especially on the material side of the question their father was very involved. However, what was important for him was to see his children well dressed and well behaved, to enjoy their accomplishments, but he would do very little to help them do things and he would hardly give them a chance to talk with him. His questions mostly would consist of questions like "How's school?" or "Did you like the dress I bought for you?" If I had not met other fathers who were different, I would have believed that all fathers were like that. I knew very well that from very early stages children begin to develop their own personalities and preferences. Furthermore, from my personal experience, I knew that questions like "How's school?" usually made children react negatively. Despite all this, I was content to note that our children were happy. I had been brought up to enjoy pets. However, the children's father disliked all pets and would not allow any in the house. One day I saw a little cat milking her newborn kittens in the children's balcony. It turned out that my daughters had found the poor cat and having pity on her had brought the whole brood into their balcony. I knew and told them that their father would never allow pets in the house. However, they pleaded so effectively for the kittens that in the end I had to give in to their keeping the kittens so long as they were able to keep them away from their father's sight. This did not last very long and the kittens had to leave the house.

During the year 1962 we had a lot of snow in Ankara. There were a number of empty lots around our house and the land was on a slope, so children started sliding or sledding down the snow. This led them to meet some American children who lived on the same street. They became good friends and we began to have all sorts of festive days, from the Christmas parties of the Americans to the German feasts through Uschi's services. Apart from German, my children had started picking up bits of English as well. So their outlook to life began to be very colorful. Ayşe and Zeyneb had found out that they were naturally good at drawing. My son Ömer was very intelligent and also had a sense of humor. Zeyneb and Ömer, since their ages were closer, used to play a lot together and approach Ayşe as their older sister. Ayşe on her part was always very protective toward them. As with all mothers, for me, my children were the ideal children.

In the year 1961 in September our country went through a very dark period. Three rather important politicians were executed. They may have made political mistakes but to be hung like common criminals was in itself a crime. And now, only a few years later, they are naming streets and airports after them. When public trials resulted in the hanging of the ex-prime minister and two of his cabinet ministers, Mother was very heartbroken and she declared, "Now, I am ready to sacrifice myself on the operation table, since they hung such fine gentleman." I always suspected that she was clever enough to have understood the real reason for her "illness." She was operated on by a doctor whose name I do not want to mention, in an inappropriate hospital where they had failed to take a biopsy from her and she returned to her home. They said her gall bladder had been removed. After this surgery she was ill once again and Father finally took her to the Lahey Clinic in Boston where they had to operate on her once again.

The findings of the second operation were awful. What they had called a gall bladder infection in Ankara turned out to have been cancer. By the time she had gone to Boston, the disease had extended to all parts of her body. During this second surgery they had removed part of her stomach and also her pancreas. So poor Mother returned in rather bad shape. Unfortunately, her liver had also been infected. It was summer when she returned from America. The family had moved to the mansion in Çankaya. We were all pretending not to know how critical her condition was. I am sure, however, that she had realized what was going on. She had some new dresses made for herself, but when she heard that a girl she liked was getting married, she gave the whole lot to her as a wedding gift. She also distributed whatever jewelry she had among us, saying, "I am getting old and I do not have any use for jewelry anymore." She would lie down on a chaise longe on the lawn and would try to read a book. One day I found her with her book on her lap and looking forlornly around her. She said, "My dear Şen, isn't it a wonder how many kinds of green there are in nature. I never found time to recognize this fact all through my life." When I had unwittingly blurted out, "Mother, dear, had you not really noticed this before?" she smiled and said "I must have been looking after all of you so much that I must have missed nature." I did not know what to do. My beautiful mother who had always supported her children so strongly was now sliding away and we could do nothing but watch her slip away.

There is an incident I could never forget. One day she was going to visit some people. We were both dressed for this visit and waiting for the arrival of the taxi we had requested. Mother noticed a municipal worker sweeping the sidewalk. The man was bent over, we could see he was suffering from some pain. Mother went to him and asked what was wrong. The man looked up and said he was in pain all over. The taxi had arrived by that time. Mother suddenly asked me to go back to the house and telephone the people we were going to visit and explain that something had happened that they should not expect us. She got the sick man into the taxi, making sure that his brush and other utensils were placed in the cab's trunk, and we drove off to a hospital. The good doctor who was in charge of the Numune Hospital at the time, Dr. Çapçı, was a friend of the family. Mother agreed to meet all hospital bills to cure the man's shingles disease. One day during our conversation, she said, "In life people mostly do the things that they have to, instead of the things they would like to do." I never forget her saying that. Three or four days before her death, she asked me to call her hairdresser and her manicurist to the house. She said she wanted to have her hair done and her fingers cleansed prior to saying farewell. After she made sure she had been properly taken care of, she went into a deep coma. Her last request was to have her Kuran, which she held in her hand, pressed to her heart. She waited for Father to come into her room and to her bedside before she gave her last breath. The date of her death was July 11, 1963.

Mother's death had deeply affected me, my daughter Ayşe and my eldest brother Cenan. Mother had been so happy to have been able to attend Ayşe's graduation from her primary school. For two years following her death, every morning I would wait for her morning phone call. Despite the pain I suffered from her loss, I also felt that she had completed her life in a way she liked. Apart from her son Nur, who was in the States at the time, all her children and her grandchildren were around her. Bibi was expecting her third. Unfortunately, little Zeynep arrived after mother had passed away.

Those were bad days for me. My husband respected my sorrow and to divert my sadness he tried to take us away to trips in the country. First he took me and the children to Lake Abant, near Ankara. We had a nice and peaceful time and rowed on the lake. Then we returned to Çankaya. I was still missing Mother terribly. Toward the end of summer we traveled around İzmir and Kuşadası Kismet Hotel was yet to be built and we stayed at the then new Turban Hotel. Our governess, Uschi, had returned to Germany and we were able to engage a new governess at that time. Maria was a plump and happy young German girl. When the schools were about to start we were back in our winter life in Ankara. That year Ayşe was enrolled at the T.E.D. Maarif College (high school with classes in English). Since that junior college had a primary school as well, we were able to register both Zeyneb and Ömer to the same institution. In this manner their trips to and from school could be combined. As it is usual, Ayşe was the first to try things since she was the eldest child. Ayşe had to attend the preparatory class and she lost one year as classes in English started on the fourth year at their school. Consequently, although their age difference was two years, Ayşe and Zeyneb were enrolled in classes one after the other. This was caused by Ayşe's having a year of English prep. On the positive side, all my children were getting English lessons at their new school.

Our life was returning to our winter routine. After the birth of their third child, Cenan and Bibi had moved to İstanbul. A year later Father also decided to move to İstanbul. He had later said, "After the death of Cem Sultan I could not stay there." In the meantime Father had sold the garden and the house at Çankaya to the British Embassy so that they could build their embassy school there. The loss of our summer garden was a loss both to me and to my children. I would not even want to go near that area anymore.

When Mother died, her funeral went by her home on Sümer Sokak, as well as her summer residence in Çankaya, before being driven to the family burial place in Erenköy at İstanbul. Even the street cleaners had shed tears after that "lovely lady." That was the last time I saw the garden in Çankaya. Sometime later I was forced to visit the site to recover some our belongings before the house was sold. I had cried all the time.

One night, when we had returned from a party we had attended, we found Maria very agitated. She said Ömer was having severe stomach pains. She had called our friends at whose house the party was and was told that we had just departed to come home. Since the new Hacettepe Hospital had become operational I had started taking my children to two doctors who were working there. One of them was Burhan Say. He was a young and very able doctor. Despite the lateness of the hour I was forced to call him at his home. When I explained that Ömer, although not vomitting or having an upset stomach, was having great pain in his abdomen, he said that we should take the boy to the hospital right away and that he would soon be arriving there. The good doctor spent almost four hours taking care of Ömer. Apparently he had something wrong with his intestines. After spending a lot of time, that wonderful doctor was able to save my child without operating on him. I could never forget his delicacy and gentle attention. My husband did not mind taking long trips without the children whereas I never wanted to be away from them for a long time. This experience had shown me that I should not be away from my children.

The second doctor at Hacettepe that I appreciated was Dr. Kemal Özkaragöz. His specialty was allergies. Our chance meeting also constitutes a story. At the beginning of the school year, all my children started complaining about a sort of rash in the back of their legs. I took them to Kemal Bey. He first said that I should omit eggs from their diet. After a week of the same complaints he changed their diet drastically but the rash would not go away. Finally, he told me to give each child a pillow and to tell them to sit on those pillows when in class. At first I had thought that this was a silly idea, but I did what I was told to do. The rash was gone in a few days. Then my doctor explained his reasoning. The school had the seats repainted for the new year. A paint that they had used was causing these rashes. Since the pillows did not allow contact with the seats, the rash had disappeared. Doctors had a special place for Mother also. I even remember her holding a doctor's coat for him. I also have great respect for doctors and teachers.

As my children were growing up I gave great importance to their general education and tried to get them to join courses in ballet or take piano lessons. Depending on their ages and sex, different exercises were recommended. I had Ömer play basketball, for example. All of them were capable and creative with their hands. Ayşe had already started sewing dresses for her dolls. None of them showed much interest in piano playing and after a while I gave up their piano lessons. As they were growing up their problems were growing with them. One of the important parts concerned their friends. Following the practice of my mother, I always made a point of inviting their friends to our home. Actually, the parents of most of the children they met were already my friends anyway. However, in many cases they brought home children from very different backgrounds. In such cases I would try to meet the family whose child was getting friendly with my child. I would at least try and develop some contact with their mothers on the phone.

Nowdays, as I go over my memoirs, I wonder if what I had done was worth the effort? On the one hand I believed educationalists who said that children start learning at very young ages. On the other hand, every child has his or her genes or whatever they call their personality. So long as the father and the mother are not doing outlandish things, so long as the children find love, comfort and security in their home, and so long as mutual trust and respect is maintained within the family, one should let it go at that. The most important thing for a child is to know that the parents are there for him or her, all the time. It is also very important that they should be able to bring all their sorrows and their problems to their parents without being afraid of the consequences. However, the parents can never do the right thing for their children. We all do what we think is right, but we never know what is really the right thing.

I believe my husband was a good architect. At least he loved his work. He designed many buildings in Ankara. The Renkli Cinema at Bahçelievler, the restaurant called "The 47" at Kavaklıdere, the home for Hayriye and Ahmet Neyzi, the Pan American Office Building, the headquarters for the State Institute for Statistics, the headquarters for the Directorate of National Security and many others were built according to his designs. He had done a number of pavillions at the International Fair in İzmir. In those days it was not easy for an architect to earn his living by his designs only. A lot of people had gone into the construction business. However, that was not an area for which Togrul had developed himself. Not only was he very free with his money but he also never knew the value of money. As far as he was concerned, money was something to be spent as soon as, or sometimes even before, it was earned. He would always purchase the best and in great quantities. He loved giving gifts of great value, not only to his family members but also to friends and artists as well. One day my friend Adanalı told me that Togrul was a man who was happy only when he was giving away something, but never appreciated what others would give him. In an earlier paragraph I have already mentioned that as a child Togrul enjoyed throwing silver coins into the sea. It was unfortunate that his parents were rich people who liked to spend their money somewhat indiscriminately. If I had known the way he was brought up as a child, I would probably have second thoughts about getting married to him, who knows?

Some of the things I had learned about the Devres family's way of life in İzmir were somewhat disturbing for me. I was told that they lived the life of rich society, spending money and throwing parties night and day. Togrul was the youngest son. He was usually left at home under the tutelage of "adopted" girls who had no families of their own and were refugees from Crete! My mother had always opposed this system of having so called "adopted" girls doing the housework. Rich families would take in poor or orphaned girls, and on the promise of marrying them off with a dowry when their time came, would use them to do the house chores with no compensation except food and lodging. Mother always refused to follow this pattern. She would say, "If I can afford it, I hire servants, if not I can do my own work and not revert to slavery." This was a common practice in the later years of the Ottoman Empire and once in a while one heard stories concerning such "adopted" girls becoming the mistress of the houses they worked for. However, I am sure these were very rare examples.

I must say that I had no complaints. From the day we were married my husband responded to all my material needs in a flamboyant manner. He would never let me worry over family finances or things of that nature. He took care of all the expenses for our home. He would pay even the salaries of the servants we hired or the governesses that came from abroad. All purchases for the house were also arranged by him. Once in a while if I needed anything for the kitchen, all I had to do was to call the shop and things would arrive by messenger. He would leave some pocket money for me on my dresser. This would sometimes be a large sum and sometimes small. He would arrange the importation of materials, cloths, etc., discuss prices with my dress designer, Mr. İbrahim Elmas in İstanbul, and order several dresses for me, so much so that I hardly ever bought any underwear or a pair of hose for myself. All he wanted was that I should be a well-dressed woman waiting at the house for his arrival. As for the children, his only concern was to meet their demands and expenses, for their education, etc. he could not care less. That was my department. As their mother, I was to do whatever was necessary. I was a devoted mother and would spend almost all my time with my children. It was up to me to find a happy medium or balance in the house as their father did not have the spare time for his children. Unfortunately, my upbringing toward financial matters was not much different. Many years later I was to learn how wrong it all was.

XXIII
Tarabya

As matter of fact, I was always an independent person and I
knew that Togrul appreciated and enjoyed me for this trait of
mine. However, as time went by I had somewhat lost this feeling
of independence and I was responsible for that. He wanted to act
like Pygmalion and I had submitted to the idea. Maybe because I
had that feeling growing inside me, for the first time, I told my
husband that I wanted to go to İstanbul during the summer
together with my children even for a short period of time. As
usual he had various contracts to attend to in İzmir. Most families left Ankara during the summer and our staying there bored
the children. They were growing up and they needed a change.
We were wondering how to rent a place and by luck some friends
of ours, Rezan and Azmi Tlabar, came to our rescue. They said
they had a fully furnished summer house on the hills of Tarabya,
which they were not using and they would be glad to rent it
to us. They had another summer place on Sedef Island where
swimming was better. So we rented the place for one month. It
was heavenly. The only catch was that they were not connected
to the Municipal Water Works and we had to get water by tankers. As for drinking water we had to rely on bottled water. Also
there were no phones connected to the house. We were, however,
able use the public phones at the Tarabya Market Place.

That summer Ayşe was 15 and with her tall slender body
she showed the promise of becoming a very good-looking young
lady. Zeyneb was 13 and she loved her food and was a robust
girl. Ömer was 11 and he was a somewhat serious young boy.
We moved to Tarabya in the beginning of August. My good friend
Ülkü (Gürkan) agreed to spend the month with us. After a good
breakfast in the morning we used to go down the hill for swimming. There was a sort of a casino that also had a changing

place arranged for swimmers. Sometimes if I could not drive them for one reason or another, the children could walk down by themselves or climb back home over the hill, as the case may be. I had taken one of the working women with me from Ankara but what with carrying water to the tanks, cleaning the house and cooking, she could not handle everything. So it usually meant that I helped her with the house chores in the morning and would go down to swim with Ülkü in the afternoon. One day Zeyneb had overslept and when she came down I was terribly and happily surprised. Zeyneb had also become slender just like her elder sister. The clean air, the exercise and a better diet had changed my daughter into a very good-looking young girl.

That one month with my children was great. When the time came I sent the charlady by bus back to Ankara and gave her some of our extra luggage to take home. The children, Ülkü and I would be driving back by car. At the time I was driving a Thunderbird. We started early one morning, it was a nice day with a clear sky. Ülkü was sitting by my side in the front seat and the three children were in the back. We were singing songs and enjoying the ride. We reached Bolu and stopped at the motel called Çamyuva. After lunch, as we were back in the car, a small drizzle had started. Ömer made a fuss and I was forced to let him sit between me and Ülkü in the front seat. Since the rain would make the road slippery I would be driving slowly anyway and having Ömer in the front seat would not be too much of a problem. There was a bus coming from the opposite direction and the highway was just wide enough for two cars passing one another. Suddenly a big truck appeared, the truck driver must have thought he could pass the bus by using the other lane. There was no place for me to go. On my right I saw a great chasm, that would be suicidal. The bus and the truck were coming toward me. They would do nothing about my frantic blowing the horn and blinking lights. I realized my only chance was to cross over the other side of the road where the slope looked gentler. So at the last moment I swung my car to the left and went out of the road in front of the oncoming bus. To do this I had pushed my gas pedal all the way down. We went out of the road, by luck without colliding with the bus and started bumping over various rocks, the car hobbled along and at last reached a clearing and stopped. With the tumbling the front windshield had cracked in the middle. I remember that each time the car bumped I was crying, "My children! My God! I am about to kill my children." The moment the car stopped I opened my door and jumped out. Everyone in the car was alive. Ülkü, who was in the front seat with Ömer in between us, had a broken arm. Ömer had hit his head on the back mirror and had a huge swelling on his forehead. Ayşe had her leg slashed and there was blood in her leg. Zeyneb seemed to be all right. My stomach was aching badly, since the driving wheel had hit me as the car jumped up and down. I looked up. The truck who was on the wrong lane was speeding away but the bus had stopped. I forced myself to climb up to reach the highway. The bus driver, as well as all the travellers, were all excited. Some passengers were calling after the truck "Killer do not run away." I asked the bus driver to take my children to a place where they could phone their father and ask for help. The bus driver promised to call my husband from the next phone booth on the road.

Rather miraculously a traffic police car drove up. They took over the enquiry. They found no wrong done on my part. We had not hit the bus and all of us were luckily alive. Apparently they had even asked Ülkü if she had any complaints and she had graciously said no. Togrul had gotten into action as soon as he had heard about the accident. A towing car had come and towed my car to the highway. The motor was still running. For many years I had wondered whether if instead of that American car, I had been using a more flimsy vehicle, would we all be alive today? My husband was both agitated and furious. He blamed me for the accident. Furthermore, that Thunderbird had been imported from the U.S. and we could find no spare parts in the market. The nearest place where a new front windshield could be found turned out to be Beirut! Getting that windshield would take two or three months and we could do nothing about it. Togrul was very angry because our car would be out of action for at least three months. The repair job would also cost a fortune. He was so angry that he almost forgot to say that he was happy to find us alive. During all our married life, I had never seen Togrul so angry. The doctor at the hospital put Ülkü's arm in a cast and we all went home to Ankara. Our doctor advised that both Ömer and I should take a rest in bed for some days. I was very worried about the bump on Ömer's head, therefore I took him into my large bed.

Prior to this accident we had planned a trip with Cenan and his family to the Nemrut Mountain in the east. We had no way of communication with them, since they had already left their home. So they reached Ankara to find Ömer and me in bed. As they say in America, I was in the dog house, I was the driver who was involved in an accident. This guilty feeling lingered on until a new windshield had been imported from Beirut. The traffic police had found me "Not Guilty" but my husband refused to let me drive for almost six months. There is a saying in my country. They say "something hurts inside." That happened to me each time I thought of this accident. Despite the fact that I knew I was absolutely guiltless.

XXIV

A New House, Again

The flat where we were living had been put up for sale and our lease would be ending in a few months. So we had to look around for another apartment. After some extensive research we were able to find a flat that was even nicer and larger then the one we were vacating. Our new apartment was situated on the Governor Reşit Boulevard. On the first floor there was a flower shop. We had rented the second floor and I believe the owners, who were called the Moltay family, were living on the third floor.

Both in this flat and in the old one we had at Güniz Sokak, we really had some fun with Togrul. Some of the things I remember concerned jazz music. I am not sure about the sequence of these events but here is how the story goes.

There was a night club called "Intim" near Meşrutiyet Caddesi where Erol Pekcan's Band used to play. Since we both enjoyed jazz, we used to go there frequently. Some well-known musicians from the States used to come to Ankara for concerts. Once Dave Brubeck was there and at another date Dizzy Gillespie came to Intim for a jam session. We had enjoyed the music so much that we invited both to our house, consecutively. In the wee hours of the morning we had invited these wonderful musicians to our house for a morning coffee and scrambled eggs. They liked us and accepted our invitation. So they gathered around my piano and using pots and pans they got from my kitchen, did a wonderful jam session in our house. It really was great to start a new day with such beautiful music.

When spring was getting near Togrul told me he had had some materials imported from France and that I should go to İstanbul and "get dressed." We had changed our governess and we had a new girl called "Lore" and with Togrul in charge it would be convenient for me to go to İstanbul and stay at the Hilton Hotel for one week. I also thought he was trying to make up and accepted the idea and went and registered at the İstanbul Hilton. On my return he met me at the train station. When our taxi was getting near Kavaklıdere I saw that we did not turn into Güniz Sokak but went on to Dr. Reşit Galip Boulevard. I thought that he wanted to show me something. We climbed the stairs and got into the new apartment. I was dumbfounded. We had moved while I was in İstanbul. Everything was perfect. Walls had been painted, the new curtains arranged, it was a beautiful new home! I was so excited I was crying. Togrul was rather proud of what he had achieved at such short notice. In the meantime I had missed my children tremendously. So I went to pick them up from their school. They were very happy to see me and they were terribly excited about our new home. How many women would get this sort of a treatment. I was very happy to have this remarkable man as my husband.

I loved my new home so much that I did not wish to go out. There was not much chance for me to go out, either. Many friends would drop by. In the mornings a friend would drop in saying, "I was out for a walk and decided to come and see how you are doing." Later on someone would say they had been to the florist and "stopped for some coffee." Of course they would also stay for lunch. In the afternoons it would be tea or cocktails and so forth. Well, we had help in the house so that I was able to manage this continuous traffic. However, we did not seem to be by ourselves anymore! Some friends had become almost permanent. I started to feel uncomfortable with so many guests. Especially I wanted to give more time to my children when they came in from their school. In the same way, having so many guests in the house meant that I never had any time alone with my husband anymore. So I decided to take some precautions. I told the house help to ask people who "dropped by" to please ring before coming, since I was indisposed that morning, etc. Gradually I was able cut down this impossible traffic. I was happy to be with my children as much as I wanted. I guess this must have been the second time since my marriage that I showed my determination.

The women help we hired usually went to their villages for the summer and being fed up with their sudden disappearances, I had engaged a male waiter. The first young man I trained was called Sabri. After learning how to serve at tables and so on, he found a job at a restaurant and left me. After him I got another young boy called Remzi. That year I also had let go of the governess. She was rather an idle woman anyway. However, when she went I had to get rid of Remzi as well. I had two growing girls in the house and I had to be careful. Remzi, when I first hired him, hardly knew how to answer the phone. By the time it was time for him to go, with my references, he had been engaged by the British ambassador. I had really spent time on him. Even for the practice of serving tables. I would make him sit down at the table and show him how meals should be served. He also learned how to set the table. Remzi was an appreciative and loyal young boy and he kept in touch with the family for many years.

By 1968 my relationship with my husband had taken an uncomfortable turn and it was difficult for me to define what was going wrong. On the surface things were going as usual, but somehow we lacked a dialogue. He had started to come home very late. He also began to take rather long trips. I never forget. He used to give me several nicknames. After a prolonged trip to İzmir, he had arrived just as we were having breakfast with the children. Togrul joined us and said, "Tell me what you have been doing, 'Sugar Şen.'" Naturally, I started telling him what had been going on in the house while he was away. I liked to chat, especially with my husband. Suddenly Zeyneb started laughing and when I asked her why she was laughing she answered, "Mother, don't you realize, Father has not been listening to a word you have been saying." Taken somewhat aback, I asked a couple of questions and sure enough I realized that he had not listened to anything I had told him!

Parts of our family had moved to İstanbul but both Cenan and Father used to come to Ankara frequently. On one such visit Father told me that he had bought a small flat in Suadiye and had furnished it with the furniture he had brought from Ankara. Furthermore, there would be enough space for me to stay with my children when they had their holidays. The children were delighted since this meant that they would be able to swim every day. Their father also said that this would be a good idea since he would be traveling to İzmir for his constructions anyway. Giving my children the fun of bathing in the sea made me accept this offer.

XXV
What Is Going On?

I planned to spend the month of August in İstanbul. Togrul
would be coming back and forth between İzmir and Ankara and
I did not want him to be homeless all summer. The new Ankara
Hotel had opened recently and it had a big swimming pool. We
registered as members of their club so that we could swim there
daily. Togrul would come and find us there for lunch whenever
he was in Ankara and go back to his work.

One day I had taken a jitney (dolmuş) rather than a taxi to
go to Kızılay. As we were passing the new hotel someone I did
not know started talking with his friend and he mentioned my
husband's name and mentioned rather disturbing tales happening in this new hotel! I was quite uncomfortable. Of course I
said nothing. I did not know who it was that was telling the tale.
I could not accept what I had heard. On the other hand, one
should not believe in such gossip. Nevertheless, it certainly was
disturbing. I never mentioned this incident to anyone.

Beginning of August I went to İstanbul as planned. I took
one of the help with me. It was just as Father had said. We had
a fully furnished apartment. As my children were grown up I
was always with them. We were going to various beaches, strolling around, etc. I was trying to make them happy. We were
mostly being invited all together. If I would be invited alone, I
made a point of returning home before my children went to bed.
I talked to my husband on the phone every day and gave him
detailed news of the family.

One night my childhood friend Cemile had invited me to a
place on the Bosphorus for an evening dinner. They had a motorboat and they picked me up on the landing in Bostancı. On the
return they again dropped me off at the same landing and a taxi

driver we knew drove me home. Entering the compound I found Togrul waiting in front of the building for my arrival. He said he wanted to surprise me. I was both surprised and very happy that he had come. It turned out that he had spent most of the day and night driving to İstanbul. Since I had told him about the invitation I was going to attend, he had wondered what I was up to and wanted to see at what time and in what condition I would be returning from a boat trip of this sort. This was not at all nice. This showed that he had misgivings about my behavior. I did not show it but I was certainly heartbroken. He spent the weekend with the family. From İstanbul he was going to Ankara and he suggested that he could take Zeyneb with him on the train and they would return the same way. He would leave the car in İstanbul with me. Zeyneb was delighted to travel with her father. We saw them off at the train station. On their return to İstanbul Zeyneb had a big box of chocolates and a bunch of roses in her hand. When I asked how she acquired these, Zeyneb said a lady friend of her father had given them to her as she saw them off at the train station in Ankara. She went on to explain that they were together almost daily and that they had lots of fun. I was really disturbed. I knew that woman. She was a young widow from İzmir. She certainly was not a person I could relate to in anyway. I decided to talk this over with Togrul. That he had involved his daughter in his extra-marital dalliance was not something that I could accept. However, when I confronted him on this subject he was very contrite. He begged me to excuse him and professed that it was not like what I had suggested, and that although he might have been too relaxed, he was true to me as always. So what I had heard by chance on the jitney ride was not just simple gossip. I was terribly upset. Up to that date he had made me think that I was the only woman in the world for him. My pride was hurt. Before he left for İzmir he had promised me many things and we had sort of made up. However, my heart was already broken. I did not complete the whole month in İstanbul after this and returned to my house in Ankara with the children.

This time Togrul was supposed to stay in İzmir for an extended period of time. A number of times he suggested that I should join him in İzmir and that he would send me an airplane ticket. However, something or other came up every time and also I did not wish to leave my children on their own with no mother or father. Ömer was getting to be a teenager and I wanted to be with him especially. I was thinking that age twelve was rather a dangerous and difficult age for a boy. Also there always was some activity with the girls and I wanted to be around.

However, Togrul was very insistent. So I relented. We had three ladies working in the house. My daughters invited some friends to stay overnight and promised to take care of Ömer. I had taken every precaution I could and I went to İzmir. My husband had a suite for me at the Efes Hotel. Although this was just a weekend visit I naturally had brought a few things for myself. Placing them in some of the drawers I found a half-used nail polish in the bathroom. My husband said it must belong to the guest that had vacated the room. He sounded reasonable. Before returning to Ankara I wanted to see if he had any dirty laundry to be washed at home. Looking into some of his drawers I found some papers with translations of Chinese Poetry. It was no use asking him about it. I told him I was worried about the children being on their own and took an earlier plane back to Ankara. I had decided to leave him. How could I explain such a thing to my children. Once at home I explained to the children that I had to go to my father in a hurry and had bought a ticket on the morning bus to İstanbul. I could hardly sleep that night. Very early Togrul appeared in the house. He had realized what I was about to do and had driven all night. He begged and kissed every part of me and confessed that he had spent a few foolish hours unwillingly since his friends had insisted on it and so on and so forth. He was also crying and begging that I should forgive him. I was heartbroken, sad and hopeless. Running away was no problem but what would happen to my children? I had no money of my own, no income. I had never worked before. How could I go to my father with three children in tow when their father was alive?

This extramarital affair had frightened me. I called on my friend Dr. Pekdeğer and asked to have a checkup. He was my obstetrician. He laughed and asked if I had done something I should not have done! I was horrified. I explained that I was

231

afraid that my husband may have had such a relationship and I may have gotten something bad from him. Thank God, the tests gave negative results. However, the threat never left me from that day on.

After this affair my husband had turned into an angel. He was doing everything he could to make me forget this incident. However, the crack in my heart kept extending further and further. I was no longer a happy woman. I could not forget. The woman involved in the affair was not the significant factor. The situation was rather degrading. This was not something a man of dignity, a father of two grown-up daughters and a young son would do. He had forgotten his responsibilities. He had played petty games. Father had come to Ankara for a visit. He sensed that there was something wrong with me and asked me what was wrong. I broke down and told him that our marriage was going through a difficult period and that I was thinking of a divorce. He stopped in his tracks and said, "Forget the idea at once. A divorce is not something I can accept." It was a dead end. There was no one I could turn to. All my life I had lived on the backing of others. I had never earned a penny. I was not independent. I had lived as a parasite. This second affair, would this be the end or would others follow?

XXVI
Aliağa

During the summer of 1969 Togrul had made a contract to build houses for the construction workers at Aliağa. This meant that he would be spending the summer in İzmir, and as there was no place to stay there, he would be staying at the Efes Hotel and commute to the job site. He would be driving for some hours daily and would take the family car for himself. Being the considerate father, he offered us the possibility of a membership at the Ankara Hotel swimming pool or of going to my father's house as we had done the previous summer. He also told me that there was going to be a big reception in the spring where all the bigwigs concerned with the construction of the oil refinery at Aliağa would be attending and that it was a must that I should be there at his side. I did go to this reception in İzmir and there I met a young couple, Mehmet and Deniz Adanalı. They were a beautiful couple.

The following day Togrul took me to the construction site. It turned out that the Adanalı couple we had met at the reception had settled at the site. They asked us over to have tea with them. The beach was full of pebbles and sand. There were a few barracks almost on the beach. They all had large verandahs and from one of these a very good-looking woman waved to us. When we reached what looked like a barrack made for army pesonnel, it turned out they had transformed it into a very nice dwelling place. Deniz had a beautiful dress on, her tea table was laid out immaculately with all sorts of dainty cookies. They had a son who was very cute. Mehmet and Deniz looked like a very happy couple. They told me that while Mehmet was at work at the construction site, Deniz and her son were having a wonderful time on the beach. They could get fresh fish from the local market, etc. Sometimes they would have a barbecue on the beach as the sun went down. Electricity in the compound was available only until 22:00 hours P.M. so they had to wind up whatever was to be done until that time. With their son asleep the young couple could take a midnight dip on summer nights. They were actually enjoying a blissful summer. For shopping they could go to the village bazaar once a week or things could be ordered from İzmir. It looked like a wonderful way to spend the summer, rather than spending so much money at the Efes Hotel, driving for hours and living apart in İzmir and Ankara. I would give up the swimming pool in exchange for the Aegean Sea any time.

After listening to their story, I suggested to Togrul that he should find a barrack like the Adanalıs had and that I would be spending the summer at Aliağa. He was really surprised. I can't say that he was delighted but it was a suggestion he could not very well refuse. A barrack was quickly found. This meant a much cheaper summer holiday for the family. Togrul had no way of refusing. I was able to procure simple things like camp beds, folding tables and chairs, plus some gas lamps for after hours. All these things did not cost anything. Certainly much cheaper than the cost of becoming members of the hotel's swimming pool. When I returned to Ankara I gave the children the good news that we were going to spend the summer camping by the sea. I quickly bought some materials and sewed a few things for our summer barracks. There were some things that would not be available in Izmir but which we would be needing, so I packed some trunks and sent them to Aliağa by a transport company. In this manner my children would be spending the summer in the company of their father and mother and they would have a perfect summer vacation actually living on the beach. Furthermore, our summer expenses would be so much less then if we had stayed in Ankara. With boxed flowers that I had brought from Ankara our barrack home would turn out to be a beautiful place. I was looking forward to have a beautiful summer with all my loved ones around me. As a mother and a wife, I was thinking that the arrangements I had accomplished should make my husband happy. Although I had enjoyed the comforts of civilization all my life, I was never a slave to luxury. Having a decent sort of life was enough for me. The main musts for me were things like running water, light for reading and sanitation as well as healthy food. Music was a must, also. Health and love were the two most important things in my life.

I believe everyone knows the story of the "Blue Bird of Happiness." Anyway, I would like to repeat it. A man consults a dervish about how he could find happiness. The wise man says he should look for the "Blue Bird." The man goes back to his house and wherever he looks he cannot find the said bird. So hoping to find the bird, he starts traveling. He goes almost all around the world always looking for this bird. He grows old and has to lean on a cane and every time he comes across a tree he beats his cane on the leaves and branches of the tree hoping the blue bird of happiness would come out. He grows too old to travel and returns home. As he sits wearily on his old seat and takes a deep breath, raising his head he suddenly sees the blue bird perched at his chair. We are all like this poor man, in a way. We hardly realize that happiness is within us and not hidden somewhere to be found. It seems that we all look but rarely see things in their true perspective. We just look and do not see. Or better still, we do not perceive what is around us and live without seeing anything. We hear others without listening. We never try to understand others and go on our different ways without communicating with others. We never question ourselves or search for our real feelings. For many years, now, every morning when I wake up, I ask myself these simple questions. What do I want to do today? What do I have to do to achieve my wishes? How many of the things I want to achieve today, can I actually achieve? So, I start my day trying to find the answers to these questions. Maybe because I was named "Joy" as I had come into this world and with genes I had inherited from my parents, I generally look at life with love and happiness. I was always trying to develop what the French call "Joie de vivre."

My children were not geniuses but they all had normal periods of education. They always had good enough grades to pass their classes. They had good grades that year also. Now I was going to give them a wonderful summer holiday. I kept one of the working girls and sent the others to their villages for the summer. We were going to İzmir by train. My husband would meet us at the station and he had the car with him. The five of us spent the night on uncomfortable bunks in a crowded train compartment. Togrul met us at the station and after purchasing some necessary items, drove us all to Aliağa. When I put the beds, the table covers on and hung up a few curtains on the windows, hang a few paintings on the walls plus a few flower pots around, our barrack house looked lovely. Later Deniz entertained us with a delightful tea party. We were all very happy. My elder children had quickly adopted the young boy as their own brother. I think I felt that an affinity had quickly developed between the little guy and Zeyneb.

Our first day at Aliağa turned out to be blissful. Full of friendship and love. We knew that electricity would be cut off at a certain hour, however, with all the excitement they had that day the children had already fallen asleep before that time. We had lamps and before turning in, I went in to see how the children were. Suddenly I was very frightened. There were lizards running around the walls. All my life I have been afraid of crawling creatures and insects. Once, at our apartment at Güniz Sokak, Zeyneb had come from school with a grasshopper she had caught. I had immediately started shouting with fright and ran into my bedroom and locked myself in. Zeyneb, in a playful mood, was able to squeeze in the grasshopper under the bedroom door. I had first jumped on the bed and since the creature was flying around the bed, I had rushed out of the room all the way to the street. I spent that night with a flashlight in my hand, shoeing the lizards away from my children. I could not restrain myself and my husband could do nothing to make me go to sleep. The next morning was again a beautiful day. Our barrack was almost next door to Adanalı's. Most of our hours were spent with our children. Togrul came home at about 18:00 hours and said he had to attend to various meetings in town and said he would spend the night in İzmir, jumped into his car and left. That night we had a bonfire on the beach and I asked Mehmet what sort of a meeting there was in town. He did not know of any meeting. I spent that night alone, with my torchlight, still shooing away lizards. Why had I come to Aliağa? What sort of a meeting was it that my husband had to rush out from his home in such a hurry?

On our second fatherless night, our dear friends again invited us to a barbeque on the beach. The moonlight was beautiful and with songs, etc. we had a wonderful evening. Moreover, they explained to me that the lizards were almost a necessity since they killed scorpions who were the really dangerous insects. It was not a complete freedom from fear but still it was a kind of solace for me to know that lizards protected us from worse things. I had been overwrought and for the first time that night I was able to sleep. On Sunday Togrul arrived with his hands full of gifts for everyone and life resumed its normal course. However, there were frequent "meetings" in town and he was "forced" to stay overnight in İzmir. Our three months in Aliağa passed by with these interruptions. I was certainly heartbroken but I still wanted to believe and trust him. My children were having a most wonderful time and I was going along with them. The only thing that I had realized was that by coming to Aliağa I had achieved nothing. My husband was always on the go. I did not believe that our coming to Aliağa had saved anything from my husband's spendings in İzmir. If it had not been for the friendship and protection the Adanalı family had provided for me, I do not think I could spend the whole summer there. Deniz Adanalı who had been a professional model herself, one day told Ayşe that she had the body of a model. Ayşe was very excited about the idea. Deniz would coach her and the next winter she would be a model at a fashion show. The summer over, we packed our belongings and returned to Ankara for the winter. The children were back at their school. My husband returned to his office and I resumed my daily life. The summer vacation was over.

XXVII

Difficult Days

After a short period of calm and quiet in the house, a woman, whose voice I could not recognize started making anonymous calls and disturbing my peace. Among the mean and unmentionable words, I was also hearing things about my husband that I could hardly believe. I had learned to hang up the phone as soon as I recognized her voice but some words would register anyway. I pretended that this was the work of a sick woman and one should not give credence to anything she was saying. At home, there was a disturbing sort of the absence of dialogue between the two of us. Meanwhile, my health was deteriorating. My doctor in Ankara had advised that I should have surgery. I wanted to go and get a second opinion form another doctor in İstanbul. However, I was afraid to be away from home for a long period. Ayşe had become a full-grown young girl. Zeyneb had also changed dramatically. Both girls were beginning to meet young boys at the golf club or at the Kosk Pastry Shop where the youngsters living in our quarter used to congregate. I knew some of the boys they met but there were others about whom I could not get any information. I had to keep them under control. My son Ömer was also getting to be a teenager.

As soon as classes had started in her school, Deniz Adanalı, together with her friend (the owner of a modeling school) had taken Ayşe to a trial show and Ayşe had enjoyed modeling tremendously. Zeyneb was also getting lessons and the two sisters joined one another in a fashion show. Zeyneb did not like modeling at all, despite the fact that Ayşe was enjoying it. After a few trials they both had to give it up. Their classes required much of their time and I wanted to make sure that they had a proper education.

My health was going from bad to worse. Togrul took me to İstanbul for further consultation. A well-known surgeon practicing at the Pakize Tarzi Clinic inspired confidence in me. After various checkups he was perturbed and said I must have surgery right away. When I protested that I would like to see my children first, he reacted and said that the operation had to be done as soon as possible, namely the next morning. I entered the clinic and the next morning he did a "hysterectomy." When I woke up after the operation in the hospital bed I found my husband crying on my bedside. My first reaction was to ask about my children. We talked on the phone and I felt much better. The tender care of the owner of the clinic, Mrs. Tarzi, and the close attention that her daughter Zeyneb (Osmanoğlu) gave to all patients, were things I could never forget. I had to stay in the clinic for a certain period of time. Then my husband took me to a suite at the İstanbul Hilton. He was at my bedside the whole time. Even climbing up stairs was prohibited for some time. I had to rest. Togrul was very contrite and did everything he could so that I could relax and rest. Since he was so caring, I was able to ask him a question I had meant to ask but had never done so. So I said, "Since you display so much tenderness, why did you have to break my heart so badly a few months ago?" He was frank in his answer. He said, "If you keep the children away and I don't have to listen to their chatter everytime I come home, then I will do my best to attend to your every need, we could have a life of our own." I was really dumbfounded. I had never expected such an answer. Our children were the greatest things in our life. They were the fruits of our happiness. The call "Mother" coming from someone you had given birth to was the best thing anyone would love to hear. His request was something impossible. My husband was jealous of my children and did not want to share our life with them. I was under the depression created by the happenings of the past plus the tremendous loss of energy the surgery had caused. When I returned to Ankara, I could hardly get out of the house. However, I had made up my mind. I would do my best to hug and love my children and be with them so much that they would have enough of me before their father came home. Thereby I would reserve the rest of the night to my husband alone. The surgery I had gone through is a difficult one for women. It seems that women who undergo this experience begin to feel that their husbands would no longer enjoy or want them. Well, maybe this was only the way I felt after the hysterectomy.

The first night we were back in Ankara I woke up in the middle of the night and I realized that my husband was no longer in bed. I was perturbed and afraid that he may have an upset stomach or something. I slowly got out of bed and went to our living room. One table lamp was on, our music box was turned on and my husband was sitting there with a drink in his hand and he was crying. Quickly I ran back to bed. So this was it. My husband was no longer interested in me. He did not think I was a woman anymore. I heard that this surgery caused depression in women. I was ashamed of myself, but what could I do? So I was having a full-grown depression. Was there anything I could do? A few days later he said he was again going to İzmir on business. I offered to drive him to the airport as usual, but he refused my offer. This time I was glad that he had gone. I would have more time with my children and could also rest and try to recuperate. Some friends who came visiting mentioned a certain woman and began to ask curious questions. The name was the same that my husband had confessed to have had an illicit relationship with. However, he had confessed that this relation had been very short-lived and he had promised that such things would not recur in the future. Hearing this name again from someone who was not even a close friend of either of us, I was very disturbed. I really could not live with him under these conditions. On his return to Ankara I told him I wanted a divorce. Again he was contrite. He begged my pardon and cried on my shoulder and refused to accept any accusation. I really had no choice. I had to continue my life in this manner.

The worst was to come at about the same time. That was the time when I learned that both my daughters had developed steady relationships with young men I did not know. They had actually fallen in love. I also realized that my son Ömer did not look happy with his life. The main cause of his discontent, I presumed, was the unhappiness that his parents were displaying in their lives. Each one of our family of five was suffering for their own reasons, whereas I was suffering for all of them separately and also for myself.

XXVIII
Starting to Work

On the 22nd of February 1970 we were to celebrate Togrul's birthday. Since we had settled at the apartment on Vali Dr. Reşit Street, he had been very punctual for our lunch hour at home. That day he came home for lunch at a rather late hour. He was rather moody and looked sour. I had bought him a small gift. When I gave it to him, he suddenly exploded. He said that he could not stand this extravagance. I and my children were spending too much money. He could no longer afford such an extravagant life. Since I was always saying that I was an educated woman with a university degree and that I knew foreign languages, then I too should find a job and meet some of the expenses of the house. I was listening to him with awe and I said nothing. Ever since we had been married I had bought him gifts for his birthday. Among them were some money holders but he preferred to carry his money in his pocket and the amount of cash he carried would never fit folders anyway. The previous night he had left a fistful of paper money on my night table and since I had never been interested in money, I had not even counted what he had left. Whatever pocket money he gave me was mostly spent on taxi fares or gifts for the children or for him. He had never before mentioned anything about our economic conditions.

I quickly begged his excuse. Said I would start economizing as requested and I would do my best to find a job. I felt awful and shamed. However, frankly I had no idea what I could do. I had met and quickly married Togrul after graduating from the university and had never done anything to earn money. As a matter of fact, in the early days of our marriage, when he was just beginning to get recognition as an architect, I had suggested to find some job but he had always refused by saying, "I would never allow my wife to work. Your presence in our home is so much more important." Furthermore, he was soon able to earn more then we could spend. What sort of work could I possibly find? Could I give piano lessons or teach English? Unfortunately, I had not obtained a second certificate to be able to teach at state schools. I could have easily gotten such a certificate but I had already been engaged to be married. I was very worried and in a state of shock when my good friend Güngör came for a visit. I knew she had troubles of her own and maybe she could help me. So I told her my dilemma. She was working as the private secretary of the Swedish ambassador. She said "Dear Şen, do not worry so much. It should be possible to find you a job at one of the embassies in Ankara." I hadn't thought of that. I felt a bit relieved.

It took some time but in April of that year Güngör was on the phone one day. She said the Indonesian ambassador was looking for a private secretary and that I should apply for the job. This sounded wonderful. However, I had no idea about what a private secretary should do. Güngör told me a few things. What she was saying did not sound so daunting. I took her advice and rang the embassy and obtained an appointment. I had bought a Chanel suit a few years ago in Paris, so I put it on, took my C.V. and went to meet the ambassador in a taxi. The ambassador, Muhammed Ali Moersid, was a typical Indonesian. A somewhat short man, with almost darkish skin but a very kind and well-educated gentleman. He looked through my C.V. very carefully, asked a few questions, said he would want me to be his personal secretary and told me how much he could afford to pay and finally asked when I could start work. I first thanked him for his kindness and said that it would be an honor for me to work for him. Then I told him that since I had children to take care of, I was thinking of working half a day only. We agreed that I should be working between the hours of 10:00 to 14:00 every day except Sundays and I would be paid TL. 2000 per month. We agreed on these terms and I left the embassy to start work on May 1. I had met a number of men at the embassy and had not encountered any working woman. I was happy to have found a job. I came back and called Gügör to thank her. Now I was ready to contribute to the expenses of the family. So I gave this news to my husband, who came in for lunch. He was rather surprised. He had not thought that I would be able to find a job in such short notice. However, he seemed to be content that I was going to work. I was thanking my good mother and father for the kind of education they had given me so that I was able to get to this point. When the children came in from school, I gave them this information during tea. Of course I neglected to tell them what their father had told me. What I told them was that I had been bored doing nothing at home and at the same time I told them that I had timed my working hours so that they would always find me at home, for them, when they came from school. The children were excited with the news and enjoyed my enterprise.

It was something I could never forget. One day Zeyneb had gone to visit one of her girl friends after school and that evening at home she told me, "You know, Mother, not every family has so many servants at their homes." I felt that although they were enjoying the luxury in which they were living, they were also feeling ashamed for it, especially when they visited friends whose parents were not as comfortable. I also remember that in the days when I used to walk with them to their school, Zeyneb had fallen in love with a tiny wooden shack and had said, "One day I shall be living in such a house." People are funny. They usually aspire for the things they do not have. Zeyneb was always a girl full of love and had never given a thought to material things. She loved to help others and be of service to everyone.

I started work on May 1. I was now the personal secretary of the ambassador. They had given me a nice sunny room overlooking the garden. I had a big desk with two comfortable armchairs facing me, for visitors. I also had a personal phone. I placed pictures of my children on my desk. I had brought in my own agenda and various pens. The room was now mine. Soon the ambassador called and asked me to come to his office. He was very courteous. He asked me to sit down and told me the things he wanted me to do for him and ended the conversation by saying that he was very glad to see me at work. Before I left his office, the ambassador asked his under-secretary to come in. He introduced me to him and asked him to take me around and

243

introduce me to the others working at the embassy. After a very short while I had already started doing what was required of me. The first thing was to read all the papers and find out anything that could be of interest to the ambassador (anything that mentioned Indonesia). Such articles should be cut and be translated into English for him to be able to read. I was to prepare files for his private correspondence and keep them in order. I was to arrange his appointments and keep him informed about the appointments arranged. Naturally, there would be other things to attend to. In a very short while I had developed an affinity for my job. I had realized that an executive secretary had to become an instrument that made things easy for the executive involved. For me, it was a pleasure to be of use to this courteous gentleman. Very soon I had become a part of the family of Ambassador Moersid and his wife. As I had belonged to the Ankara Society since my childhood and since most people in power knew me because of my father's position in the past, getting an appointment for the ambassador was an easy job for me. Friends of my family would mostly help me out in such instances. By coincidence, Ambassador Moersid enjoyed playing the violin and wanted to take lessons. He kept insisting that he should get the famous violinist Ms. Suna Kan to give him private lessons. Well, Suna was already a recognized concert violinist and she had never given any thought to giving lessons. However, I knew her as a friend. Even today I still feel guilty about it, but at the time it had become a question of life and death for me and on my insistent begging. Suna kindly condescended to give violin lessons to my ambassador. He in turn was delighted and felt very happy to have engaged me as his private secretary. The Moersid family had very much taken me under their wings. He always insisted in giving me an honorary place in anything done by the embassy. When the Minister of Foreign Affairs of Indonesia, Mr. Suharto, had come for a visit, I was given a seat next to him in one of the official dinners.

At the end of May I was delighted to receive my salary and proudly offered it to my husband that night. His reaction was, "You can keep it. I do not need it right away." I could not understand what he was doing. Was it not the same man who had

Cemile (my mother) in her uniform of the French school. Beside her is Colonel Mazhar Tankovich, her father, 1900.

The Resulbegovich house at Trebinye, Sarajevo.

The whole family in İstanbul, in 1937. Front row: me, my paternal grandfather. Second row: my oldest brother Cenan, Mother, my older brother Nur, and Father.

General Hamdi Resulbegovich, my mother's grandfather. On account of favoring the group called "the young turks," he was imprisoned for a long time.

Mother photographed in İstanbul in 1916 while she worked with the Red Crescent as a volunteer nurse. It was during this period that she met my father.

Necmeddin Sahir Sılan, my father, while he was Chief of Cabinet for the Prime Minister in Ankara between the years 1924–1927.

On our return from the island of Prinkipo to İstanbul, in 1930.
My brother Nur, sitting on the floor, my oldest brother Cenan
on the side of the armchair, Mother holding me on her knees,
and Father standing.

Massachusetts in 1945, in front of Wheaton College. Left to right: me, Mary, and Virginia.

My photograph published in 1945 by the *Boston Herald* following an interview.

Ankara, 1948. Following my return from the U.S.A. while a student at the Faculty of Letters.

İstanbul, September 21, 1951 at my wedding. General Süreyya İlmen, my witness, is signing. Standing on the left is my father.

Ankara, 1960. A happy moment together with my children. Left to right: Zeyneb, Ömer, the proud mother, and Ayşe.

Ayşe the year she graduated from high school, 1970.

Boston, 1975. At the cocktail party I had arranged for my father. He is standing half turned on the right. Alex Costi, my friend the photographer, is sitting in the armchair wearing eyeglasses.

At the Consulate General of Taiwan in Boston, 1977. Sitting in the middle is Ambassador Shih-ying-woo. On his side, wearing a skirt, is Jaky, the Counselor. I am standing behind Mr. Woo.

1977 in New York by my desk at the Permanent Mission of Turkey to the United Nations.

A reception at the Turkish Mission in New York, 1978. Left to right: Professor Talat S. Halman, me, Ms. Maya Karaca, and the Permanent Representative Ambassador Ilter Turkman.

Another reception at the Turkish Mission in New York, 1979. Left to right: me, Mrs. Zeyneb Osmanaglu with Mr. and Mrs. Kılıç.

One of the rare reunions with my three grandchildren. A happy moment on New Year's Eve in Brussels, 2000–2001. Left to right: Murat, Lara, me, and Seze.

Şen Sahir Sılan in 2000.

Şen Sahir Sılan in 2004 at home in Antalya.

told me to find some work and contribute to household expenses? I just put the cash aside, not knowing what to do.

Sometime afterwards, Togrul one day said that working as an architect was getting to be impossible, one had to get into the construction business but that required a lot of money. So he said he was thinking of migrating to Australia and asked me what I would think about such a move. This time I was more than surprised, I was baffled. I did not know what to say. This was such an unexpected move on his part. However, since I had nothing to say, I told him I was his wife and I would join him in whatever he did. I only asked one question, "Why not the U.S.A.?" After all he had been educated there and had received his A.I.A. and had actually practiced architecture in New York. He said something about it being difficult to get a visa for naturalization. Nevertheless, he took our birth certificates and told me that he would go to the embassy of Australia and ask for citizenship. I had almost forgotten about this conversation when one night he announced that he would be taking all of us to the Australian Embassy for some sort of a health checkup the next day. The children were also very surprised. However, we did go through everything he said. I really did not know whether I should laugh or cry anymore.

That year Ayşe graduated from the Maarif College. That was one of the biggest gifts of my life. Their father had never shown any interest in his children's education. He had not attended any of the school's ceremonies, neither on October 29 (our Republic Day) nor on April 23 (Independence Day). Near her graduation, one of Ayşe's teachers, Mrs. Güneysu, who had been her teacher for the last two years, and was a renowned teacher and a perfect lady, wanted to talk to me. I went to meet her as I was asked to do. After telling me what a wonderful student Ayşe had been at school, she said she had to ask me some personal questions. It turned out that seeing Ayşe so sad and thoughtful, she had asked her what was wrong and my daughter told her beloved teacher that she was very worried about the relationship of her father and mother. What could I tell her? I said something like we had some differences but Ayşe had probably made much more of it than it really warranted. I had tried very hard to keep our differences with my husband away from my children. That afternoon I had a long talk with Ayşe. We had a long heart-to-heart talk. She told me that one day at the Köşk Pastry Shop a boy she did not know had talked about the escapades of a well-known architect in İzmir. Naturally, the young girl had felt very ashamed. I tried to calm her and said that such gossip should not be taken seriously and that people always talked about things they did not really know. I said nothing about this to her father. Our life was getting into an ugly turn day by day. Every day a new disaster seemed to develop. Our life was like a crescendo in a concerto, noises were getting higher and higher.

Much later I was to find a letter Ayşe had written to her father about these affairs. In her letter my daughter was begging her father not to let me know anything about these things and that otherwise my heart would be broken forever. Later I also learned that Ayşe's teacher, Mrs. Güneysu, had also invited Togrul to school and had directed the same questions to him. I was never able to learn what his answer had been.

Since I was working I could not go anywhere for the summer as I used to do in the past. As I was working to help the family finances, going to a summer resort was also out of the question. On the other hand, I did not want my children on their own with nothing to do during the long summer vacation. This worry kept bugging me for weeks. I was thinking about my own experiences. It was true that I had a university diploma. However, when it came to finding a job, it was my upbringing and the fact that I had learned how to type that had secured me my job. So I tried and finally convinced both my daughters to attend a secretarial school during their long summer recess. This would take a few hours a day but they would acquire a skill that could come in handy in the future. I could ask Ömer to work in his father's office at least half a day and be of some use.

I had always made sure to be in close contact with my children. One day Ayşe told me that she had fallen in love with a young man who was a student at Middle East Technical University. His name began with M. After all she had completed high school and she was 18 years old. Since she was so impressed by this person, I thought I would like to meet him and I told Ayşe to invite him to dinner one evening. In this way I would be able to see what kind of a young man he was and at the same time Ayşe would be able to see if M. did fit our family standards. Their father was in İzmir that week. M. came. He was quite good-looking and his father was a well-known government employee. He was quite thin and his black eyes had a cruel streak in them that I did not like at all. He was also very uncommunicative and would not even try to join the table talk. Following certain answers to my questions, I could not help saying, "You must be a nihilist" and he very blandly answered, "How did you know?" I said, "Young man, I have been in this world much longer than you and have met all sorts of persons in my life." I had developed an instinctive dislike for this young man. It was also obvious that by some devious manner, either by his looks or his talk, he had taken Ayşe under his influence.

XXIX

Whatever Is Happening to Ayşe?

It was summer. We were having a drink with Togrul on the balcony. It was a warm late afternoon and it was almost dark. Ömer was with us in the house but the girls were still out, probably with their friends at Köşk Pastry Shop. A day before, when talking with her father, Ayşe had said that one day she might marry M. and Togrul, probably depending on what I had said about the boy, had shouted "I would rather you marry the gardner." Since that encounter Ayşe had been behaving rather queerly toward everyone in the house. I was really worried that the affair had grown into such proportions. That evening, on the balcony we were talking about this problem. A while later Zeyneb came to our side. She was rather agitated. She said, "Ayşe will not come home." I could not quite grasp what she was saying. Zeyneb said, "She went away with M." I thought I was going out of my mind. All sorts of bad things rushed to my brain. They must have abducted her. Ayşe would never do such a thing. I almost jumped and said to my husband, "Come, let us search for our daughter." Togrul did not even move from his seat. He was slowly swallowing his evening whisky. I was near total panic. Where had my beautiful daughter gone? Togrul calmly said, "We can do nothing. Ayşe is over 18 now and she is free to go wherever she wants to. The law is on her side." I took Zeyneb to her room. I begged her to tell me the truth. She explained that Ayşe was very cross with her father and had recounted what her father had said and that M. had taken Ayşe to his father's home. I immediately phoned their house. M. answered the phone and refused to let Ayşe to come to the phone. I said, "Then you must come and talk to me." He said that he would come to our house the next morning and hung up.

I could guess what sort of a discussion we would have in the morning. In any case, I wanted to be prepared. With the help of Zeyneb and Ömer we set up a tape recorded system. I wanted to tape our conversation. That night, while their father was sleeping comfortably, I was prowling in the house till daybreak. Had I lost my daughter? I was blaming myself. Maybe I should have kept things to myself. Why did I have to tell their father about the strange encounter I had with this boy? How could this boy's parents accept to keep a family girl in their house? How could they not call me and let me know what was going on?

In the morning M. appeared at the appointed hour. I asked him questions like, "Do you love Ayşe? Do you intend to marry her?" and so on. He simply said, "No" to all my questions. I then asked why he had taken Ayşe to his parent's house. He said that she had nowhere to go and that she did not want to stay in this house anymore. More or less I had imagined that this would have been his attitude. So I refrained from exploding. As calmly as I could, I said that I realized that Ayşe was of an age when she should be able to chose where she wanted to live, I would suggest that she came home to pick up things that she would be needing. I still wonder how that day I was able to restrain myself and not attack the young man physically! When my children were growing up I had never even once slapped them. I was never one to handle difficult situations by brute force. However, that day I realized that I would do anything to protect my children. All our conversation was on the tape, word by word. About an hour later Ayşe came. I asked her the same questions, doing my best to keep calm. Her reactions were contrary to his. Then Zeyneb turned on the tape we had made. Ayşe listened to everything M. had said. She was very disturbed. She started crying. Soon we were in each other's arms, both crying. She then went on the phone and told M. that she had changed her mind and that she would be staying home. The first thing to do was to get my daughter away from Ankara. This way she would be out of his influence and would have a chance to think over the whole episode by herself. My first thought was to send her to a school in Switzerland. There were so-called finishing schools for

249

girls. However, her father would not even lift a finger. As far as he was concerned his daughter was no longer his.

My good friend Hayriye Neyzi was living in İstanbul and had daughters about the same age and I could trust her implicitly. I called her, explained the situation I was in and asked if she could take in Ayşe as a guest for some time. It was important that she should be on her own and away from Ankara. She said, "Send her over at once." So I helped her pack a bag and I made sure that she took the bus to İstanbul that same day. I also told Zeyneb and Ömer that they should not talk about this affair and that no one should know where Ayşe had gone. Unfortunately, it turned out that Ayşe had told one of her friends where she was going and that foolish girl had been foolish enough to tell M. where Ayşe was. I was on the phone to Hayriye every morning and it seemed that Ayşe was much calmer and saner. Then one morning Hayriye called up. Her voice sounded rather excited. That morning M. had appeared on their doorstep and had almost forced Ayşe to take a walk with him.They had both gone out. Ayşe had taken nothing with her and she had said she would be back shortly. It was over two hours since they had gone and no one had returned. My dear friend was as worried as I was. I did not know what to do. Her father would not even listen to whatever I said about Ayşe. I was about to lose my mind. After a while, I forced my brains and found out the name of a gentleman who was the minister of the interior. After a couple of phone calls I was able to reach this dear and caring person. I said that I was under the impression that my daughter was abducted against her will, that M.'s family had a flat in İstanbul, most probably my daughter could be found there. I begged him for his help. He promised to do what he could. I then called my brother Cenan and his wife Bibi and told them the plight I was in and asked if they could do anything to help. They said they were ready to do anything. So I started waiting impatiently for news.

The next morning I had a call from the ministry of interior. They told me that my daughter and Mr. M. were taken into custody since they had no identification and they were being kept in a police station in Kadıköy. I quickly booked a seat on the first plane and told Cenan where Ayşe was and the plane I was taking. Somehow everything worked out well. The plane was about to take off from Esenboğa as I boarded. The taxi I had taken from the İstanbul Airport had delivered me to the Kadıköy ferry, which had started as soon as I got on. So I was able to reach the police station in less than three hours. Bibi met me at the door of the police station. She warned me that both of the youngsters were very angry for what had happened and that my daughter was also very contradictory, so I should try to take it easy. I could not understand how this man could influence my daughter in such a manner but my lovely daughter was almost frozen and although I was sure that deep in her heart she loved me, at that moment she was hardly there. She would neither look nor talk to me. I was crying all the time and she showed no reaction to my tears. There was nothing I could do. She was of age. The only thing I could do was to give her the birth certificate that I had brought with me. She simply took it without saying anything. She was completely detached from me. Heartbroken, totally deflated, not knowing what I was doing I took the plane back to Ankara. At least I would be with my other two children. This affair seemed to have brought us closer together.

I was still working at the Indonesian embassy. My husband on the other hand, although at first he had said that I should contribute to the house expenses, would not even touch the money I brought home at the end of each month. Since I had started working he was not coming home for lunch. He said he did not like eating alone and by eating a sandwich he could economize. After the affair of Ayşe, our relationship had become more and more formalized. During this time, busy bodies who enjoyed watching the discomfort of others were quick enough to bring me news that my husband was having an affair with a woman in a small hotel in Ankara during lunch hours.

That kind of information no longer interested me. My only worry was my daughter who had run away from home. So I consulted another family friend, who was my childhood friend and was a lawyer. M.'s father was a well-known man. I believe he was involved in gardening or landscaping. The lawyer suggested we contact the father and he obtained an appointment. When we got seated in their apartment, our first question was to enquire how they had allowed an unmarried girl to stay in their house? They countered this question by asking what in our opinion should they have done. I said if these youngsters are in love then the decent thing for the parents to do would be to get them married in a civilized manner. Then the father, whose name I still do not remember said, "All right, what will your contribution be?" I answered, "Naturally, we shall do whatever is customary for the girl's parents to do." He then said I am not talking about your daughter, what are you going to provide for my son?" I said, "The customary gifts will of course be given." He said, "My son does not believe in marriage, therefore before he consents to marry, a large amount of money should be provided for him." I was appalled. I got up and I told my lawyer friend to get up also and I said, "I am not here to trade or sell horses. I was only trying to show some reason but it seems this family has no notion of propriety or decency," and I walked out of their house, hoping never to see them again. My lawyer friend was also aghast. He was saying, "What kind of people are these? Don't they have any shame? Don't they have any respect for the society in which they live in!"

Days were passing by. My sorrow was gradually turning into anger. Ayşe rang up and suggested that we meet together for lunch. She told me she had found a job in a company called Bora Constructions and that she was earning her keep doing translations in English as well as in German and that she loved M. She said, "Under God's providence I consider him my husband. Probably we shall get married one day." She explained that she had sewn curtains for the room they shared. She also said that M. did not allow her to meet anyone. Ayşe had begged so much that he had agreed to let me see her once a week for lunch. My heart was aching for my poor darling, however, there was nothing that I could do. I was glad to even have this chance to meet my daughter, even once a week and for lunch only.

At another luncheon Ayşe recounted an argument she had had with M's mother. It seems she had been helping her in cooking by peeling potatoes. The woman had complained that Ayşe had cut the peels too deep. So my daughter countered this criticism by saying, "In my mother's house I did no such chores." She also had added, "Furthermore, I had paid for those potatoes out of my earnings." This little episode had given me some hope.

At last my daughter was beginning to understand the kind of people she was involved with.

As if my worries about Ayşe were not enough, I received the news that Zeyneb was seeing a young man also. Was this pastry shop next door going to be my undoing? After making some enquiries I realized that this young man was neither someone I nor her father would approve of. I could not understand what was happening. I had always thought that I had tried to give what was best to my children. Where had I gone wrong? What was happening to our family? There was an old saying in Turkish. They say if you do not spank your daughter, you end up spanking your knees. Was this proverb true? Yes, I had never spanked them. However, I was always involved in whatever they were doing. I had always advised them not to lie to me and to tell me the truth no matter how bad it was. It even happened that one morning Ayşe had not wanted to go to school, when she had explained that she had not done her homework and that she was afraid of getting a bad mark at the exam, I had told her that getting a bad mark was better then faking an illness, which would be telling a lie. Finally, I had convinced her to go school even if she was sure to get a bad mark. As a matter of fact, she had gotten a good mark and was very happy afterwards. On another occasion Zeyneb had called me on the phone, she told me she was not going to the afternoon classes and instead would go to a movie with her friends and I had relented and told her to go ahead. It was better than her telling me a lie. Was I now being punished for being a lenient mother?

Zeyneb's friend was called Sertaç Bülbüloğlü. He had dropped out of the Middle East Technical University and he was eight years Zeyneb's senior. He was working as a DJ at some night club. He was not at all suitable for my daughter. I had told my daughter my feelings in no uncertain terms. Then one day a friend of Zeyneb called up and gave us the news that Sertaç had been hospitalized and was about to go through open heart surgery. My heart suddenly gave way. I took Zeyneb and we went together to the hospital where Sertaç was going to have surgery. I did not want to feel sorry afterwards.

As I was battling with myself, with Togrul and between my two daughters, one night Ömer came home rather late. He had received some bad marks in his exams. I asked him what was going on and he explained his situation in no uncertain terms. At first he said he was sorry for me and that he was afraid of his father and finally he broke down and said that he no longer enjoyed life and that he had lost all hope. The only thing I could do was to cry my eyes out. There was no one I could talk to. Finally, I decided to consult a psychoanalyst. This was a bit costly but my husband had not even touched the money I had earned and I decided to spend it this way. I went to consult with this doctor thrice and at the end I had had enough. She really was not at all interested in me. I could as well talk to the wall. All she was doing was to let me tell my story in detail and this did not help me solve my problems. Anyway it seemed that way to me, at the time.

Amidst all these complex and heart rending affairs, one day Zeyneb had brought home a tiny kitten. It was a kitten with a pedigree. It was a Siamese kitten. The saying is that such cats can either bring good or bad luck to their house. Zeyneb had named her "Menam." It was a wonderful cat. She could jump and hold onto door knobs and thereby open doors. Menam had not brought us good luck, but on the whole she had been friendly to me and would cuddle up to me when I was miserable and would cheer me up a little. I was miserable. Their father would not even agree to mention Ayşe and would not allow me to talk about her either. My father and some of our relatives had also started talking against my daughter. I could not stand to talk to anyone except my daughter Zeyneb and my son Ömer. They were the only people who appreciated my plight and still loved their elder sister. I had been almost geared to my meeting with my daughter once a week. I was in anticipation of that single hour.

Cenan and his wife Bibi came to help one day and asked if I would join them on a boat trip in the south of Turkey, the so called "Blue Voyage." They were chartering a boat and we could share the trip with them. Togrul said he had no time and besides that he could not afford to pay for such a trip. I had a vacation from my work and I had saved enough, so I took Zeyneb and Ömer with me and took off for Bodrum. Together with Cenan and his family we were soon on a sailing motorboat and started doing a tour of the bay of Halicarnassus. Never in my life had I joined a trip that revived me more. Every minute of this trip was full of beauty. At the same time, we were learning about the ancient civilizations that had prospered on these coasts. The boat was not luxurious, in fact it was pretty uncomfortable. We had a very capable captain. I guess we must have been ten people on the boat. Cenan's family consisted of husband and wife plus three girls, making five. We were three, plus that charming couple Jacqueline and Abdurrahman Hanci. The bunks were rather cramped and there was a single toilet for all of us. The kitchen was also rather small and there was no cook, only two captain's help, who were uneducated boys. Still we were enjoying ourselves tremendously. There really was no reason for me to stay in Ankara for those ten days. My husband hardly spoke when he was at home. Ayşe had mentioned that they were going on a trip. This boat trip was a godsend to both my children and to myself.

Cenan was a wealth of information concerning this area and had prepared maps showing the bays where we would spent our nights, being moored on lonely but beautiful bays. It was not just a relaxation and swimming program. We had many opportunities to climb steep hills and visit ancient sites, old agoras or historic theatres, etc. We had to purchase all our food requirements since there was little possibility of finding shops in lonely bays. All the food had to be stored. Then we had to get settled in our cabins. After that came the work program. Everyone was assigned to a certain duty. Some had to cook, some had to lay the table, etc. The children also had duties to perform. Before we started sailing, Cenan laid down another rule. Everyone was to take off their watches and we would live by the sun only. There would be no newspapers allowed on the boat even if we could find an unexpected vendor. I cannot recall every bay we stopped at. However, places like Sedir Island, Ingiliz Limani (the English Port) and finally the Knidos Bay were spots one could never forget. Everyone who had done this sort of a so-called "Blue Voyage" remembers these places. At Knidos we met Miss Love, who at the time was working on the ruins at Knidos. That peninsula, apart from its ancient treasures, is also a natural wonder.

In such a blue voyage, you start the day with the sun. First you jump into the blue and clean sea. Then follows a shower of sweet water and getting dressed and having some hot tea or coffee. By that time the captain and the crew go and withdraw the nets they had laid out the previous evening, full with all sorts of fish. Depending on the fish caught, the menu for the day is arranged. I must also mention that during that trip we had so much fish that someone made a crack about cooking some fishy dessert one day. We had fish stewed, boiled, broiled, etc. The only thing we did not do was cook fish with sugar.

After the morning swim, everyone has a chance to have a hearty breakfast. All sorts of butter, jam, white cheese, olives plus some warm tea and lots of talk. Sometimes when you spend the night in a settlement, the next morning there is the chore of going on land to do some more shopping. The boat then sails off during the day until we reach another safe harbor to our delight. Some days we would stop during the day to visit an ancient site. It meant climbing up small hills following the goats and returning after an exciting exploration to find the fish being cooked for lunch. When we found a sweet water fountain, it meant that everyone enjoyed a wash. Of course, either before or after a wash, one would still be jumping into the sea. During such times some people would go to sleep, some would sun tan on the deck. Sometimes the children would get involved in some sort of a parlor game. Above everything, there was no argument and everyone was friendly and loving. The peace and quiet was never lost. It was important that the boat should be moored safely before the night. So sometimes the children lingering in the sea would be admonished not to delay the trip but all was in good fun and friendship. All our children were most helpful. When the ship was securely moored the crew would go off to lay the nets for the night catch. During this time we had to sort of change for the evening meal and prepare the drinks to be served before dinner. Watching the sun go down and the changing of the colors both on the sea and over the land nearby was always great. It was all so beautiful.

The children had developed a wonderful sort of camaraderie among themselves. After the evening meal we had to clean the tables and do the dishes. After that it meant more conversation and pure enjoyment of the dark night. Some of us would take a last dip of the day before going to sleep. This wonderful trip lasted ten wonderful days. We were all very happy and satisfied. At the end everyone returned to where they came from. Cenan and others, back to İstanbul, I and my children back to Ankara. The children's school would soon be starting and I would be back at my secretarial desk.

XXX

A Sad Marriage Ceremony

Upon returning to Ankara my first call was to Ayşe. We again started meeting for lunches, once a week. She seemed healthy and looked like she was bearing herself well. However, from week to week I felt that she was getting more and more distracted. Weeks were going by. Then, at one of our lunches I found her very excited and happy. She gave me an unbelievable bit of news. M. had agreed to a marriage and that they wanted to have a baby. They had even picked out a name. It was going to be a boy and his name was going to be Y. However, he had all sorts of conditions for this marriage act. He would not be involved in any of the legal procedures of getting a license, furthermore no member of the family would attend the legal ceremony except me. Despite all these restrictions, Ayşe and I were very happy. I agreed to all these conditions and promised to carry out everything necessary. My own marriage ceremony had been so long ago and I had had nothing to do with the procedures at the time. It was not easy to find people who knew about these things. I had to take my daughter to a clinic for the required certificate of health. M. refused to comply with this regulation and refused to go to a clinic. Then I was able to obtain a certificate for him through the kindness of a friendly doctor who complied to my request. When all the paperwork was completed, I had a date set for the ceremony at the municipal building in Ankara. Then I informed my husband and also my father, who happened to be in Ankara. My father was happy and wanted me to arrange a family dinner, inviting M.'s mother and father plus my family at the hotel he was staying in, namely the Bulvar Palace. Her father showed no reaction and would do nothing about this affair. So I went through my family jewels and picked a ring for Ayşe that I had from Mother and also a gold plated lighter for M. as wedding gifts.

It was December 22, 1971. I was at the door of the town hall, waiting for the arrival of the couple. I was trembling in my excitement. They came in a taxi. Ayşe was dressed the best she could. She was radiant with her hair done. On the other hand, M. looked disheveled, without a shave and his hair uncombed. He would not even stay hello to me. He was looking at the door post. According to regulations they had to have witnesses. It seemed they were alone, they had nobody with them. I was to be hers. As we were going up the stairs toward the mayor's office, he was able to talk to one of the janitors to act as his witness. After a while the man in charge made a very perfunctory ceremony, reciting the legal sayings in a bored voice. We all signed various papers and that was it. They had been married. I felt a sigh of relief. My darling daughter was at least a married woman in the eye of the law and she was no longer an odalisque! I put the ring on Ayşe's finger and gave M. his gift. I kissed and hugged my daughter and wished her luck. In a hurry they jumped into a cab and they were gone. I was left on the doorstep of the ugly building. All by myself. What kind of a creature was this man?

I had taken leave from the office for that day. When I was back home I was crying profusely. To attend the wedding of her daughter is such a wonderful ideal of a mother. From the day your daughter is born you begin to imagine what a wonderful wedding you would do for her, just as your mother had done for you. You would dream about her being a mother and yourself a granny. Nothing is good enough for your daughter. She should have the best of dowries. She would be the most beautiful bride and on her side there would be a good-looking young man to be her husband and to take care of her. And look how my dainty daughter had married. She had looked almost afraid during the ceremony. She had to bury her feelings inside her. Lonesome and so forlorn.

As usual I had to pull myself together, so I washed my face and changed. I had to be ready before Zeyneb and Ömer came home from school. I had not told them about the ceremony. As soon as they came in I gave them the good news. We hugged and congratulated each other, laughed and danced. I was lucky to have my two children to share my happiness. They had some homework to do before changing for their grandfather's dinner at the hotel. It was Zeyneb's last year at high school. Ömer was attending the Lycée that year. He had grown into a rather silent and mature young boy. Their father came a little later and we all went to the hotel where father had arranged the family dinner. Father had a special table laid out for us and we all took our seats. A little later M. and Ayşe, together with M.'s father and mother all arrived. I was glad that even M. had shaved and put on decent attire. After some talk we were served a very nice dinner at the end of which Father made a nice speech congratulating the newlyweds and wishing them good luck for the future. That night I was able to sleep peacefully like I had not been able to sleep for a long time.

The next morning by 10:00 A.M. I was at my desk at the embassy. By 11:00 A.M. my door opened and Ayşe walked in. My God! My poor daughter was a sight to see. One of her eyes was so blue and swollen, she had to peer through her eyelids. Her lower lip was cut; she had bruises on her arms. Whatever could have happened? Was it a traffic accident? She was crying in my arms. Her head I was caressing had bumps! When I asked what had happened, she simply said, "M. beat me." Her lip was still bleeding. I almost lost my mind. Only the night before we had had their wedding dinner! My darling daughter was both crying and recounting what had happened. As soon as they had reached their home her husband had suddenly gone berserk. Broke everything he could lay his hands on. He tore down the curtains Ayşe had sown with her own hands. He called her names and when Ayşe tried to calm him down, he attacked her. All the way, fists, kicks, bare knuckles. My poor daughter was showing me her bruises. There was blood on her legs. After all this, he had shouted "You made me do something I hated. God damn you. I am going away." Then he had jumped into his car and took off, apparently for İstanbul.

Ayşe said, "Please Mummy, let us get in touch with Uncle Necip, the lawyer, I must get a divorce." I was crying over her condition and trying to calm her down at the same time. I was also thinking what would be the best way to act. I was frantic!

My reason said that we should first go to M.'s father and talk the situation over with them in a civilized manner. Ayşe was afraid to go to that house. I called up the lawyer and asked his opinion. He also suggested that we should first visit the boy's parents. He said if we do not do this they may later blame Ayşe for quitting their house without their knowledge. I had to take an hour's leave from the ambassador. We took a taxi to the boy's parents house. The lawyer joined us there as arranged. M.'s mother was home, his father was out. The mother knew what had happened the night before. When we asked why she had not intervened her answer was, "I was frightened. My son is not sane. I dare not sit for dinner with him. Sometimes, when he does not like the meal I cook, he turns the dining table upside down." The lawyer and I were more than surprised. The woman continued her saying by adding, "If Ayşe had any sense, she would never return to this house. He may do worse things." We left that house in a hurry and went to the lawyer's office. Ayşe went through a medical checkup and a report on her injuries was drawn up. Our lawyer promised he would start divorce procedures right away. Then we went home. The doctors had done various treatments that they had found necessary. I gave my daughter a hot bath and some clean things and put her to bed. By the time she woke I had prepared some things I knew she would enjoy. She ate a bit. Then she began to tell her story. She had to tell everything she had suffered. I was listening to her very sad story and wondering that one day she might want to go back to him. Of course, I was making some conciliatory remarks. However, my mind was not really there. What could I do? My dearest daughter kept crying and she was full of hate and disgust.

Our family was somehow under one roof once again but their father was coming home as late as possible and he would have minimum contact with his family. Zeyneb and Ömer were delighted to have Ayşe with us again. They had reached an age where they could understand what was happening and Ayşe had told them all her story. In a way, I was hoping that this might be an example to the younger ones. The divorce procedures had started but it turned out that since M. had gone to England, there were delays in getting an annulment. Summer came and

Zeyneb graduated from high school. Finally, both my daughters had completed their high school education. Ömer had passed his class as well. I was a happy mother. We had received a repeat invitation from Cenan for another boat tour on the Mediterranean. This time, to my surprise, Togrul said he would join us on the trip. There had been an earthquake in Gediz and there was a lot of reconstruction work in the area and Togrul had undertaken some work. He had not started, so he could get away. The wonderful times we had the last time was actually spoiled by Togrul, who had joined the trip as if he was purposefully making everyone miserable. He was bored all day long. He caused trouble incessantly and complained about everything. The trip lasted a week and when we returned home he said his contract was due to start and he took off for his worksite. This time it was for an extended period of time. There were no phone connections to his site. I was living with my children by my side and for a while at least I was content.

Togrul came back in two weeks' time. He had a great sun tan. I later learned that he had done a similar boat trip with the woman he was having an affair with. I also learned that his reason for leading me to work was so that he would be free from coming home for lunch and that he would be meeting the same woman in a hotel. I was really heartbroken. Somehow I kept on pretending I did not know and refused to face this issue with my husband. I was trying to keep my children out of this family dilemma. There was nothing I could do.

Ayşe was given her job at the office where she was working before her marriage. She was recovering her health. Zeyneb also wanted to start working and she had become the secretary to the ambassador of Argentina. Ömer was still in school. Every morning I and Zeyneb would take the bus toward Çankaya, and Ayşe and Ömer would take the bus going in the opposite direction toward midtown. Since their father would still be asleep at the time we left the house, the family car, the old Thunderbird would be parked on the curb waiting for his pleasure. He was the patriarch, he needed the car. My marriage was on the rocks. However, my priority was to save my children from worse things. Truly I had no idea how I was going to do this, but I was certainly going to do the best I could. For the time being keeping them in good health and providing them a quiet home, after all that had happened, was the best thing I could do. I could understand falling in love, furthermore, that one could eventually change one's mind. Love is a funny feeling. It could enslave a person. However, I just could not understand how a person of some quality could become a slave to someone who was not at one's own level. My husband was a personality with a position in Ankara circles, now he had become a slave to a woman half his age and he was making a fool of himself. Even if our marriage was to be broken eventually, I wanted to make sure that the children would still have some respect for their father. On the other hand, their father should not be together with a person that my children would be ashamed to be associated with. I must also add that never, not even once, did I blame the third person involved or the other women that came and were gone. The person responsible should have been my husband himself.

For the time being I had given up the idea of a divorce and I was pretending that his folly would one day end and that he would return to his family. At least for two or three years I would be able to give my children a peaceful life and at least the pretense of a family. Being patient, not delving into unfavorable subjects, we could keep on living as best we could. I should be protecting my children against all calamity in their difficult lives. Working on my own had brought back some of the confidence I used to have before I had gotten married. Many a prestigious lady had gone through such difficult times. It was impossible to go back to good times past, however, I should try and rebuild whatever I could, at least for the sake of my children.

Ankara was again going through difficult times. Politics of the day had gone sour. Government had declared a curfew once again. Ayşe seemed as if she had forgotten the experience she had had or at least she was no longer showing signs of it anymore. She had her friends, she had begun to laugh again and I was doing my best to provide her a warm and comfortable home. Working and earning their keep had given both Ayşe and Zeyneb a sort of economic independence and a sense of security. At least we had a roof over our heads and we were living together as best we could.

One evening we had invited two gentleman to dinner. Ziya Tepedelen was a bachelor at the time and Efdal Deringil's wife Zinnur was out of town and we had thought that giving the two gentlemen a dinner at home would be nice for them. Ziya was a classmate of Cenan from their old school, St. Joseph. He was a brilliant member of our foreign service. He was a bit of a dandy with the way he dressed but everyone loved him. Efdal was also in the foreign service but he had been unfortunate in the sense that when the old regime was overthrown by a military coup in 1960, Efdal, Hasan Işik and Semih Günver had all been blacklisted because of their close relationship to the deceased foreign secretary, Mr. Zorlu. All of them were having a difficult time in their jobs. In a way, having my house open to them whenever they required friendship was frankly making me happy. They had always been our friends and politics never intervened. We were having a lively conversation when the doorbell rang somewhat insistently. Our servant came and said there were two young men at the door who wanted to see Ayşe. I suddenly had a premonition. Ayşe was almost hiding behind Ziya. I went to the door. I was amazed with what I saw. There were two young men at the door. One was M. One of them had a gun in his hand. They wanted to push their way in. They said they wanted to see Ayşe. I was frightened and I called Togrul to come. He came and tried to talk to them in a civilized manner, saying that we had guests in the house and that there was no reason to create a scene. They would not even listen to what he was saying and they wanted to push him aside and force their way in. I was on the verge of collapsing. Luckily Ziya and Efdal came to our rescue. Both being well built men, they were able to push our assailants out of the door and slam the door behind them. After some discussion we decided to call on the military police. Next morning I took Ayşe with me and we called on the commander in charge of the curfew operations in Ankara. Unfortunately, although they took notes, they said they would intervene only if such an action was repeated. I told them that my daughter could be killed at a second time but somehow they could not be bothered with us. A few days later the incident reoccurred. M. went to Ayşe's office, forced her to come out with him to the corridor. Ayşe had balked and called for help. Then M. had said that what he had in his hand was a water pistol and that it was all a joke and had gone away. We were both frightened to death. But unfortunately we were powerless to do anything.

XXXI

Someone Is Running Away

People used to say misery never comes alone but in bundles and I never believed in this saying. How could I know that it was true? My husband had gone to İzmir. At the time he was doing the interior design of the Pan American office in Ankara. He had once taken me there, to take my opinion. The night Togrul had left for İzmir, at a rather late hour, the phone rang. I thought it would be my husband calling from İzmir, instead a male voice said, "I am calling to warn you that the architect has been coming to the site with another woman, lately. I heard they were going to İzmir tonight, together. I thought I should warn you." I had recognized his voice. He was one of the workers at the site. I told him, "You must have had some alcohol. My husband has gone with his assistants." He admitted that he had drunk some but he said, "Do not say that I did not warn you" and he hung up. My God! Why did I have to go through such things? We were belittling ourselves. What was Togrul doing?

For a long time Togrul had not mentioned anything about migrating to Australia. However, before he left for İzmir he did mention that he was thinking of going to America soon and perhaps to Australia as well. He had said that he was going to look for new job possibilities and since the cost was prohibitive he was going to do this trip by himself. It was Saturday following the telephone call. Since I would be at home, I had called my usual daily dressmaker to help me with some repairs and alterations. We were working together and I was helping her in deciding what to do. We were also chatting. She suddenly asked when my husband was going to America. I was very surprised. He had mentioned such a thing only the day before. I could not help myself and asked her where she had heard such a thing. She was very frank with me. It turned out that the mother of the person my husband was going around with had come as a visitor to a house where my dressmaker was working. There, the mother explained (mentioning my husband by name) that my husband was planning to settle in America with her daughter and that they were going there for this purpose. She meant to continue further but by that point my stomach had turned and I found myself in the bathroom vomitting. After having washed all over, when I came out of the bathroom I told the lady that I did not feel well and that we should continue the work at another day and I paid her daily fee and sent her away. This news had come as a shock. What was the meaning of this? On one side he was complaining that he had no money and on the other he was going to America with another woman? Our daughter had been forced to return home after a marriage that lasted just one day. She needed her father's help more than ever. Our two other children were also directly in need of their father's direction and advice. How could they go into the world with no backing from their father? These were the thousand and one questions I had to find answers to.

We had recently celebrated 1972. When my husband returned from İzmir I started by listening to his account of his travel plans. It was February 22, his birthday. I and the children had prepared little gifts. The children were happy to see their father home on his birthday and gave him the gifts. He showed no reaction. He was not impressed and he did not seem to care. When we were alone he brought out a fistful of money from his pocket and leaving it on the table, he said he was leaving the next day. The money did not look like a big bundle. He told me he was not sure when he would be back. He said now that I was earning my living I should be able to keep myself afloat. He told me that the rent was paid for two months and by that time I should find a smaller and cheaper apartment and move and that it should be something that we could afford. This meant that he would not be back for at least two months. He was rather fidgety and nervous. It was as if he knew he was doing something wrong and was rather ashamed of himself. He was like a spoilt child trying to hide his guilt by crying and shouting.

267

I was losing my patience. Trying to keep myself as calm as possible I told him that I had heard that he was not going on this trip all by himself and asked him if this was true. He stood up, walked around the room, lit a cigarette then came near me and said, "Since you have heard about it I might as well come clean. Yes, I am going with that woman. Now, what would you like to do?" I countered his question with, "What do you mean?" He said, "Would you be thinking of a divorce?" This was like a slap in my face. I had thought of this many times and even mentioned it to him, however, he had always begged me not to do such a thing and had promised to behave differently in the future. For four years I had been trying to keep this fragile relationship going. Whatever had happened to this man who had just turned fifty. I had to think fast. It was so strange! At some such critical moments a person can think thousands of things at a moment. He was waiting for my answer. I had to reply.

My reply turned out to be very simple. I said, "No." It seems he was hoping my answer would be positive. So he asked me why I had said no. Then I had a chance to explain to him my thoughts in detail. As far as I was thinking I believed he was going through a period of change, through an illness. Dalliances of a passing nature had happened before. Since I had been bearing this for four years, I should be able to stand it for some time to come, since I was hoping that a time would come that he would realize the mistake he was making and come back to his senses and return to the home he had helped build. On the other hand, he should also realize that if I became a divorcee now and since I was still considered good looking, I would naturally draw attention to other men and with my almost grown up children I would loath to get them into situations that would embarrass them. A father figure, even in absentia, would be better for my children than nothing. He countered this with "Can't you see? I do not love you anymore." He was really hurting me and knew it. So I forced myself to say, "Yes, I know and see this clearly. You are a great robber. You have stolen twenty-one years of my life. However, I shall not give you a divorce, no matter what you say." He was so incensed that he went on to explain to me that he had asked me to get a job so that he could be free to make love during lunch hours. My feelings were numbed by then. I told him I was glad that he had forced me to work to earn my living and that I had in this manner learned how to stand on my two feet. I stood up and left the room. For sometime now we were using separate bedrooms anyway. I told the children that I suddenly felt sick and that their father was leaving for the States in the morning and they should help him and tell him their farewells and I went to my room. The children had, of course, understood that something uncomfortable was going on but they did not press the point further. My husband left Turkey the next morning.

Our life continued with my children. I told my children that we had to move to a smaller apartment and that their father would not be able to support us much more and that my worries had been due to this sudden change. They did not dwell on the subject. During the following days I had already started looking for a new flat. Shortly after, we received an invitation from Pan American Airways. They informed us that they were opening a new route for their new plane, a 747, and that my husband and I were given a free ticket for their maiden voyage to Beirut for a few days. I called them up and told them that my husband was unavailable but could I use this invitation with my elder daughter. They said they would be glad to have us with them. I had thought such a change of environment would be good for Ayşe who had so much difficulty recently. I then consulted with Zeyneb and Ömer and they were both delighted and gave their approval to our traveling together. Ayşe was also very happy. Like her sister and brother, she too, had never been abroad. I had been very sorry that I had not been able to give the chance that my parents had given me but luck had now brought this our way. I was able to complete the procedures for passports very quickly. So the two of us, I guess it must have been March 22, left Ankara in a giant 747 for Beirut. We were placed at the Hotel Commodore. Apart from our extra requirements, we did not pay for anything. This was a three-day fun trip for free. I had been to Beirut previously. We had stayed at various good hotels and had always had a good time with their father. I can never forget that beautiful trip I made with my darling daughter. She was so excited and happy all the while. The Pan American people were taking us around but we had time for ourselves

269

as well. I knew that Fevzi and Leyla Gandur were still living in Beirut. On my return from America I had met these young people and we had also met in Turkey afterward on several occasions. I tried to contact Fevzi. He told me that his family was away for the holidays but he said he would be delighted to meet us and show us the town. He was very friendly and we made a date. He came to take us from our hotel and drove us out to his private horse farm. He owned the loveliest mares. Ayşe was very happy. She was allowed to feed the horses with carrots and sugar. Ayşe had fallen in love with these beautiful creatures. Fevzi had daughters about Ayşe's age. He was a loving father and he showed his affection for Ayşe also. He would not let us go. He said he would like us to have a taste of their food. So he took us to a very nice restaurant where continental as well as Arabic food was being served. Everything served was delicious. After lunch we thanked him and let him go back to his office.

In those days Beirut was still a very beautiful city. They called it the Paris of the Middle East. All the best shops of Europe were represented there together with everything Occidental. People from all parts of the world were there. We were having a very good time, the two of us. We would stroll along the clean boulevards, stop at a nice tea house and drink something hot or cold, return to our hotel room and take a rest before dinner. Naturally, half of my mind was back in Ankara with Zeyneb and Ömer. I wished that I could give them a similar vacation. I did not have enough funds but I could not help buy Ayşe a beautiful yellow dress that she had liked very much. I still keep this dress with love. It was so becoming on her.

One day in the lobby of our hotel we were having tea. A well-built, tallish man with a moustache was coming toward us with a smile on his face. Ayşe suddenly shouted, "Hey it is Uncle İsmet." Yes, the gentleman that joined us was İsmet Özbek. He was a genuine family friend, both Togrul and I liked him. He was also a friend of all my children. Whenever he came to Ankara he would be sure to call on us. Many times we would have him stay for dinner. Unfortunately, neither İsmet nor his dear wife are with us anymore. Not only was he charming but he was also a genuine friend. He was always full of fun and lively. For all those years I had not once seen him complaining or whining about life. He was surprised to see Ayşe and me on our own. Immediately he asked where Togrul was. We told him that he was in the States and explained how we had come to Beirut. He said, "Wonderful. You are both going to be my guests tonight. I had already arranged to go out with two Lebanese men I know, with the two of you joining us it will be great fun and Ayşe will see the nightlife of Beirut." Ayşe was delighted to be so invited. We were sure to be taken to some fancy place. Frankly, since I did not know Beirut well enough, I had not dared to take my daughter out at night until that day. Each gentleman at our table asked to dance with Ayşe and she really enjoyed her evening out. I was happy that at long last she had some fun and enjoyed her youth. On the other hand, I could hardly forget the recent sad episodes we both had gone through.

After this long weekend we were back in Ankara. I was delighted to find Zeyneb and Ömer safe and sound. As we had agreed, they had spent the weekend at home. This was a concession on their part but they wanted us to have a good time and not to worry about them. They were so mature and understanding.

By the beginning of the week we had all returned to our routine. However, after my working hours, I had started hunting for a suitable flat. This time I wanted to find a place where people would have difficulty in dropping in at all hours. I wanted to be left alone with my children as much as possible. We were walking with Ayşe on a street called Karyağdı opening unto Vali Reşit Caddesi and we saw a sign that said for rent and we walked in. This was a relatively quiet side street and the flat for rent was at the top of a five-story apartment building. The tenants were due to move out in June but they did let us see the flat. Ayşe and I had to climb five stories since there was no elevator. It was quite a climb but we got there. As I remember now, after a small entrance hall there was a living room that had a bay window overlooking Yenisehir. The dining room was sort of an extension of the living room and it also had a window overlooking Karyagdi Sokak. Next to the entrance hall there was a kitchen-pantry and on the other side there were three bedrooms and a sizeable bathroom. It had central heating and the living-dining room had parquet floors. The doorman would do small chores like delivering milk and the paper in the mornings. The rent seemed reasonable. We both liked the flat, however, it would hardly take in all the furniture that we had in our present flat. Ayşe had a good idea for design so she promised to draw some layouts to calculate how we would fit into this new flat. We called the owners and made an appointment to sign the contract the next morning. I wanted to talk over the arrangement with Zeyneb and Ömer in the evening. I wanted to get them to see the place and confirm that they had agreed to the move. The next day was a Sunday, so we had nothing to do. Well, we went to visit the flat again, I must say that the children were not very impressed but they were kind enough not to voice their dissent. Ayşe had already drawn some plans for settling. We talked to the doorkeeper of the apartment we were about to evacuate and he told us that there was an empty room in the basement and that we could store some of our extra furniture there. His wife used to come to us to do the daily chores and they liked us. Some of the furniture we had, like the crib in which my children had grown and which I used as a flower pot container, was of no use to us anymore. Still, there were many things we could not take to our new apartment. The question of what to do with my piano became a problem. It would be impossible to take it up all those stairs. Let us say that we had to lift it up from the outside and have it enter the flat through the window (I had witnessed such an operation in Holland) but then there was not enough space in the living room. Finally, I decided to sell my piano.

It was certainly a difficult decision for me. Ever since my childhood I always had this piano. Later on it was named Niniska's piano. I had played on this piano for so many years! Well, it had not done me much good after all. It was during our sort of honeymoon months. My husband had begged me to play something for him. I had consented and played one of Chopin's nocturnes. By the time I had ended the piece he was blissfully asleep on the couch. Although I did play piano when I was alone in the house by myself. I had never touched it when my husband was around since that experience. Later on I had tried to get my children interested in playing, but they had not shown any inclination and gradually my interest had dwindled. I should give up my piano. It also meant that I would be getting some fresh funds for our future. I was gradually getting myself around to run my own life. Although we had some more time to move, I started my preparations, getting cardboard boxes, putting similar things together, etc. I would try and do these things after the children had gone to bed.

I have quite a nice recollection concerning those days. In the past, when my children were still young, I had taken them together with Uschi, to the vegetable bazaar. It was to show them that interesting kind of shopping. This bazaar or other open market was organized one day a week. All the village people would bring in their fresh fruits, vegetables, eggs, butter, etc. One walks around, chooses the best or the cheapest stuff and buys. The first time I had gone there, a very young and miserable-looking young boy appeared beside me. He had a basket on his back. He offered to carry out stuff. Although my car was not too far away, trying to help this poor but honest child with a few pennies, I had consented. In the future, each time I went there this boy appeared and helped me. A long time had gone by. What used to be fun for me now had become a necessity. During one of my shopping days a well-dressed young man, with a clean shirt and necktie, approached me and offered to carry my stuff. I thanked him and said I did not need his help. I must also have seemed a bit disturbed and angry. I had not enjoyed that offer. When I gave him a dirty look, he said, "Didn't you recognize me? I used to carry your packages when I was a child." He was smiling. Suddenly I remembered him. I asked him how he was, congratulated him on his attire and enquired about his work. His answer made me very happy. Years ago he had found a way and had gone to Germany as a worker. Had found a job at a car factory and was now earning well. He had recently returned to Turkey and had gotten married. Before going back, he had wanted to visit the place where he used to work and had come across his old benefactor. I couldn't be happier. It proved that if a person wants to accomplish a goal, he can find the means.

After a long period of no news I received a note from Togrul. He said that he had found a job in Washington, D.C., and that he would not be returning back to Turkey for some time. He had also transferred some money for us. There was no return address on the envelope. A day after this strange letter arrived two policemen came to our door. They told me they were there to confiscate our belongings since my husband had not paid some bills and that there was a court order for confiscation. Even today I am amazed how I survived that shock. Never in my life had I heard of such a thing as confiscation. I promised the policeman that I would pay the required amount the next morning. Went to the bank to get money he had sent to pay the bill. Thank God I had some savings to keep my sanity and to be able to survive. There was no way I could communicate with him.

Meanwhile Ayşe was spending some time with a nice young man who had left behind a rather difficult engagement and whose parents were our old friends. He used to come to our house and they would talk or they would listen to records, etc. Their friendship was blooming within their family circle. However, since she had filed for a divorce, Ayşe also had to be careful. There was a holiday at the end of April. Curfew was still on in Ankara. One of my friends had told us that they, as a family, would be going south for the holidays. Zeyneb wanted to join them and get some sun tan and relaxation. Ömer also wished to go but they had space for only one person in their car. Zeyneb had been working at the embassy of Argentina and really needed a vacation. So I agreed to her going. I knew I would be worrying but I owed it to her. The night they left there was a reception at the Italian Embassy. My ambassador and his wife, being aware of the difficult life I was leading, insisted that I should join them at this reception. They had secured a personal invitation in my name also. In a way it was part of my duties to be with them. At that time we had only one woman for the daily work in the house. The doorkeeper's wife also came in once a week. I was doing the cooking for the family. As a matter of fact, one afternoon when Zeyneb found me in the kitchen, she had said, "Mommy, now you look like a real mother, for the first time." She was probably right in making this observation, not realizing that their father would never have agreed for me to work in the kitchen. Our children must have considered us as socialites.

Most of their friends had different modes of life. In most houses they visited, either the mother or the grandmother was the cook. I prepared the food for my children, put on my party dress. Jumped into my little Fiat car and went to the party.

Before he had gone to America, Togrul had sold the Thunderbird I had, saying that he could no longer afford it. Apparently it was registered in my name and he had taken me to an office where I had signed various papers. They had hoodwinked me at that office, as I later had to learn, with no redress. The Fiat 124 cars were relatively cheap and they were marketed on an installment basis. So, by using the money I had received from the sale of my piano, I was able to buy this new car. Since my husband was no longer with us I had thought having a car would make my life easier.

I came back from the reception at 23:00 hours. I found my children together with Ayşe's friend, playing dominos. I went into my room to change into something comfortable. Ayşe and Ömer came to my room and they both said, "Come on, Mommy, let us go to where Zeyneb went." I tried to forstall this adventure by saying, "Let us think about it in the morning." However, it was no go, they were both laughing and begging at the same time. They were kissing my cheeks. My objections that there was a curfew and that it was illegal to drive in Ankara after midnight was also of no avail. The curfew applied only in Ankara as the capital. If we had gone out of the city limits the curfew regulations would no longer apply. I just could not refuse them. So we all got into action. In no time bags were prepared. Actually children had already thought about this and had made preparations while I was at the reception. Ayşe was saying that the young man could also help driving. After all, I was giving my children so little for such a long time. They deserved a vacation and doing what they wished me to do, I would be giving them a moment of happiness. I looked at my watch, it was 11:30 P.M. We could get out of the city limits in half an hour. We rushed to pack the car with our things. I got the young man to sit by me. I was quite a good driver. I had received my first driver's license in Boston. It was a dark night and we were able to go off in a jiffy. We were out of the city limits before midnight and

275

then it meant that we had to drive for some six or seven hours crossing the Taurus Mountains. I still wonder how I was able to drive in pitch darkness, on roads I had never seen before. There was no obstacles in love. I only knew the name of the motel where our friends were going to stay and that it was in Silifke. By the time we reached that small town the sun was up and blazing. I called up the motel from a gas station and reserved two rooms. We had driven all night, singing songs and cracking jokes. It was easy to find the motel. They were just getting up by the time we had registered. Ayşe and I shared a room. The two males settled in the other. Zeyneb and our friends were delighted by our surprise visit. We had been feeding ourselves with homemade sandwiches all night long. We had a healthy breakfast and we jumped into the blue sea. It was a delightful vacation for all of us. We were able to forget our worries at least for those two days.

On our return a bad surprise was waiting for me. There was another bill that had to be paid. I rushed to the bank. We had made deposit accounts in the name of the children. I wanted to use them to meet this new bill. However, the clerk at the bank told me that Togrul had closed those accounts and took the money. Whatever was I to do? I was forced to ask for a loan from my ambassador. I would pay back in installments. Somehow a new check arrived from the States again with no return address. At least I was able to pay the outstanding loan.

Despite everything, I was having a reasonably happy life with my children. Every morning I would drive Ayşe and Ömer to Kızılay and on the way back drop Zeyneb off at her embassy and return home. I would take care of the house chores and get to my work place by 10:00 A.M. When I got out of the embassy I would do the daily shopping, come home and prepare dinner for the night. The children arrived at various hours, when all of us were united we would talk over the day's happenings and have dinner. When the time came for bed, we would all put on our pyjamas and meet on one of the beds, joking and sometimes having a snack and having fun in general. Then everyone would turn in for the night. We were almost like children in a college boarding house. Recognizing the fact that I was working hard for all of us, one day Ayşe, the eldest child of the family, came up with a list. She had named it "The Ten Commandments." This was a sort of division of labor. She had enumerated various chores, like doing the dishes or hanging up the washed linen, and had assigned a member of the family to do that work. Ömer was the first to quibble. He said he did not wish to do his bed each morning before going to school since he could not wake up so early. Anyway we were able to participate in the house chores, especially my daughters were a great help to me.

Saturday and Sunday brunches were always sources of great happiness. We would continue having tea, cup after cup, talk about everything and never wanted to leave the table. Ömer and Zeyneb were rather late sleepers. I and Ayşe, however, were early risers. One Sunday Ayşe was the last to come to the breakfast table. She looked rather sullen, without a smile. When I asked her what was wrong, she very solemnly answered, "Mother, I am going to die soon." I was really turned off. She continued, "I saw Grandmother in my dream last night." I cried out, "But my darling, seeing a dead person in a dream is a sign of longevity for the dreamer." She continued to recount the rest of her dream. "Grandmother had a long white tunic on. She was standing at a crossroad. She extended her arms and called to me saying, 'Please come with me.'" and Ayşe started crying. I could not resist this. I was crying and at the same time trying to console her that this was only a dream. Nevertheless, for a very long time we were all under the influence of that bad dream she had had.

Ayşe's divorce application was subject to many delays. That man was not eligible to become anyone's husband, let alone my darling daughter's. He was very elusive. The court ruling had not been delivered to him. When and how should we be free from this monster? My daughter, though, was trying to lead a normal life, as best she could. She never fully recovered from the ordeal she had suffered. Now he was making life difficult by not appearing in court. I was praying to God for my daughter, since I had no one else to turn to.

On May 27 there was a national holiday. Friends living in İzmir had been asking Ayşe to go and visit with them. This sort of an outing could give my daughter a chance to relax under a new atmosphere. We were all for Ayşe to go. We discussed many things, we prepared the clothes she would take along for a three day's trip. I am not quite certain, it must have been May 26. I had asked the manicurist Eleni to come to the house that afternoon. All of us girls would have our hands and feet done in one session. We were all to meet at home at 5:30 P.M. That night Ayşe was to take the bus to İzmir. When I arrived at about 15:00 P.M. I saw Ayşe's bag had been packed and placed by the entrance door. I thought she must have come in some time earlier to do her bag. In one of the envelopes I had found in our mailbox there was another bill that Togrul had not paid and which had to be paid that day. So I rushed out to finish that business. However, the procedures at the bank took a long time. When I finally arrived home, as soon as I had entered the flat I called for my children. Ayşe appeared and rushed to me. She whispered, "Mother, M. is here. He is highly agitated. Please do not start an argument." I went into Ayşe's bedroom and was taken aback. That horrible man was sitting there on the floor looking at me as if he would attack at any moment. I said, "This is my house. Get up right away." No reaction. He kept on sitting. He said, "I am taking Ayşe with me." Ayşe quickly pulled me by my arm and I was somehow forced to go with her. We went into the kitchen. Ayşe started whimpering. "Mother, darling, please do not make things more difficult. I just have to go with him. I will somehow get away later." I was almost frozen. Where was everybody? Where was Eleni? My other children, where had they all gone? I asked Ayşe, "What about your trip to İzmir?" She too was crying but she insisted that she had to go with him. We were crying in each other's arms. I had lost all hope. How could I let my beautiful daughter go with this awful man? What was this world coming to? Ayşe was crying and kept repeating, "Please let me go." I asked, "Has he been threatening you? Shall I call the police?" Ayşe was constantly saying, "Let me go Mommy, I have to go" and she left me in the kitchen. I was in a haze and utterly numbed. A little later I heard the front door slam. By the time I had run to the door they had gone. The whole house was empty. I ran to the window, only to see a car start to go. Ayşe's bag was also gone. I almost crumbled where I was. My beautiful daughter had been taken away. I did not recall anything else for quite some time. When did my other

278

children come home? Had Eleni come that afternoon or not? Much later I had two very brief phone calls from Ayşe, each time she said she was well and would get in touch with us, but never gave a phone number or an address.

June came and we moved to our new apartment. My darling Ayşe, who had done so much planning for our new home, was no longer with us. I had sold some of the furniture and stored some things in the janitor's room. So we had brought with us only the minimum that was required. It was a much smaller flat but we had enough room and if ever Ayşe came back we had a room for her too. All my feelings were geared to her return to me. On her phone calls to my office she would only say that she was well and that I should not worry. She would talk quickly and hung up as if she was under some strain or was afraid of being caught. My poor darling was in danger and I could do nothing.

Near the end of June a letter from the children's father instructed me to have his office closed and get a mechanic to open his safe box and deliver everything to his old accountant. That was it. He did not even ask about our health. It was a gruesome job. His so-called files were scattered and we had to put them into cardboard boxes. When the safe box was opened all that came out were some private and upsetting photographs and letters. At last we had to deliver them to the old accountant's house. Ömer, Zeyneb and Sertac, Zeyneb's boyfriend, who had become part of our daily life, were all there to help me. At first I had balked at Sertaç's presence, however, as things developed I recognized that he was a well-meaning chap, who was always polite and clean. At least he was not a dangerous lunatic like the man Ayşe had gotten entangled with. It was pouring rain and we had all gotten soaked going to Togrul's accountant. It was a miserable evening. We were all very tired. I do not remember why but I had to be at the embassy the next morning at 8:00 A.M. So I had begged my children to wake me up at 7:00 A.M. sharp. I put the food back into the icebox. Then I sat and lit a cigarette. All the grueling activities of the day and of the previous days were going around in my mind. There was no other

279

feeling except weariness left in me. I had had no good feelings from the past. For the first time in my life I failed to clean up the dining table. I went to bed and passed out.

XXXII

Disaster Strikes

When I woke up on the morning of July 5, the first thing that came to my mind was Ayşe. This was her birthday. How could I ever reach her? At that same moment Ömer rushed into my room saying "Mommy, the alarm did not go off. You have to rush, it is 7:30." I jumped from my bed into the shower. I did not have the time to prepare their breakfast. While I was under the shower I heard the doorbell ring. It must have been the doorman bringing our milk, bread and newspaper, I thought. Shortly after, Ömer was at the door of the bathroom. He was whining, "Mother, you are dead tired, please do not go to the office this morning and stay in bed." He kept repeating the same thing while I was dressing in a hurry. I told him, "I have to go, you and Zeyneb should have breakfast together." I kissed them goodbye and rushed out.

By the time I had reached the embassy the time was a bit after 8:00 A.M. My mind was still full of Ayşe. How would I be able to reach my child. At the same time I was busily handling the business that was urgent (whatever they may have been), suddenly the door opened and Ömer was there. My immediate reaction was, "You lazy boy, did you not prepare breakfast for yourself? Let me get you something to eat." Ömer on the other hand was saying things like, "Mother dear, please sit yourself down." Then he started staying something like, "Mommy— Ayşe." I immediately jumped and encountered him, "Of course I know it is her birthday and I do not know how to reach out to her." Ömer by now was shouting, "Mommy, please sit down and listen." I had to stop on my tracks. He again mumbled, "But Ayşe." I suddenly woke up to the fact that my son had kept on repeating his sister's name. He was holding a newspaper in his hand and kept repeating "Ayşe, Ayşe." Somehow I became alert to his condition. I remember asking him, "What happened, Ömer, was there an accident?" He literally pushed me to my seat and showed me the morning paper. There, in the front page was the picture of a crumbled motor vehicle. Underneath I could just read my daughter's name "AYŞE" and I saw the word "DEAD." I recall nothing else. Such a thing could not be true. My darling daughter could not be dead. I must have lost my mind. I realized I was in the car, racing. I had to brake heavily when I thought I saw Ayşe in front of me on the boulevard. But it was not Ayşe, it was Zeyneb. I had stopped thinking. Ayşe was back. Then I was at home. Father was there, some others were there. I want to go to Bodrum. There must be a mistake. The papers had the wrong name. I must find my daughter. I want to hug her strongly. They won't let go of me. They hold me down. Somebody said, "Ayşe is at the morgue." How could she be there? I had just seen her. Where is this place called the morgue? What is she doing there? I have to find her. Where shall I go? Then, I saw her. She was so beautiful. Why does she not talk to me? She can't get up. They tell me her knee is broken. She is cold. Her body is like ice. Why don't they cover her up? I kiss her, I hug her but I cannot warm her up. Why don't they get a blanket? My Ayşe is so cold. They said, "Ayşe is dead." No. This cannot be true. It is a lie. All of it is lies. What happened to my daughter?

On July 2, the year 2000, it is going to be the 28th anniversary of that awful day. It is still as if it is the same day. Every day of my life since.

Later on they told me that my first reaction was to get in the car and drive to Bodrum. Ömer had phoned Zeyneb to try and stop me. The guards at the embassy had also tried to stop me but I was able to push them out of my way and get into my car. Near the apartment I had stopped when I saw Zeyneb, thinking that the girl I saw was Ayşe. Father happened to be in town that day. Our good friends, the San family, had heard of the incident. Ayşe and M. were going from Bodrum to İzmir on July 2. M. was driving a Fiat with the top open. In a straight asphalt road their car had collided with a passenger bus coming from the other direction. According to witnesses of the accident M. was driving the car with just one hand on the wheel and with his free hand he kept slapping my daughter. As soon as the accident happened he was able to get out of the car's wreck alive and was able to get away from the scene of the crime. The driver of the bus, after a long try, was able to pull my beautiful daughter out, as she was squeezed between the front seat and the bent up car. After they had taken her out of the wreck, the driver left his passengers on the side of the road, had his helper hold my daughter in his arms and rushed her to the nearest hospital. My beautiful daughter died during the trip, on the way to the hospital, due to a concussion.

I still have the report prepared at the hospital. The report does not even show the name of my darling child. The report only shows the date and general descriptions, such as age, complexion, et al. That irresponsible man had left my bleeding, half dead daughter, had gone back to Bodrum and collected some money from his friends. By the time he had reached the hospital my daughter had died. He took her body, put her in a taxi and drove back to Ankara. When his parents had balked at having my child's dead body in their house, he calmly took Ayşe's body to the morgue. This disaster had happened three days ago and no one had even thought of letting me know. Can anyone understand such behaviour? How can people be so cruel or callous? We had to learn what happened through newspaper reports. We did not even know where her body was. I must have been wildly insistent. Finally Ayşe's body was found at the morgue of the Numune Hospital. These people (if one can call such horrible people humans) gave me none of her things, not even a memento. Not even an old sock. I knew she had a diary. I was able to send word and ask for it. Although at first they had promised to give me her diary, they later changed their minds. Probably they read and found some incriminating things in it. I was completely beside myself. I could do nothing. Nothing that I could do would bring me back my beautiful daughter anyway. The state however started a law suit against him, for disorderly driving and causing bodily injury and death. M. was sentenced on all those counts and put into prison. However, luck was on his side. Our famous politician Mr. Ecevit became the prime minster and declared an amnesty and M. was released from prison after a short while. I wonder though if his conscience was ever at peace? They later told me that in those first days I had even gone to visit M. at the hospital and wished him good health since his arm was broken. What foolishness. To make matters worse, we found out that Ayşe's divorce suit had terminated and that they had been legally divorced. The court's decision reached us after my darling daughter had been buried. What can one do against destiny?

My days after the loss of my daughter were horrible. I remember so little of those days. The flat was crowded. Yet I only noticed Zeyneb's and Ömer's presence. One thing I never forgot was that I had hugged my daughter's still body. Another thing I never forgot was that a very eminent and loveable lady, who at her age, had not balked to climb five flights of stairs to come to visit and allowed me to cry my sorrow on her shoulders. This special person was Mrs. İnönü, the wife of our ex-President. She was a wonderful person and a mother. May she rest in peace.

Later I found myself living in Cenan and Bibi's house on the island. My remaining children were also with us. In those days I also learned that sometime later Togrul Devres had returned from America and attended the funeral of his daughter. After the formalities, my daughter's body had been brought to İstanbul and had been buried in our family crypt at Erenköy. They told me that by the time we had driven to the cemetery, flying from Ankara, it was almost dusk and the people working at the cemetery had all gone. It was that real friend, İsmet Özbek, who had the energy to round up enough workers to be able to bury my darling to her final resting place.

Bibi was very kind. She took care of me and my two children for days and days. I am forever indebted to her. One day they told me that the children's father was on the phone and that he wanted to talk to me. I was very surprised. I had thought he was still in the States. It turned out that he had attended his daughter's funeral and had gone to Ankara for a while. He was now in İstanbul and was staying in my father's house. The voice on the phone said he would like to see me. Bibi was standing by my side and she reacted. "If you want you can see him but he is not welcome to my house." Apparently Bibi and my brother were very angry that he had left us to go to the States. On the other hand I had never mentioned what was going on in my life so that they would not turn against the children's father. My father also knew very little of what I had suffered. On Bibi's warning I told him to come to the house in a carriage and pick me up from there. Human beings are not easy to understand. Long periods of my life during that time are still hidden behind a haze, through which I can see nothing, although I remember certain things.

He came in a carriage as we had agreed. I was already out of the garden door. We went to the place called "Lover's Garden" and found a table to sit by. He was sitting on the opposite side of the table from me. I do not recall too many things about our conversation. However, when I had asked, "When are you going to return to the United States?" he had answered, "How can I leave you in this state." I was very angry to become the subject of his pity. I felt disgusted. It was true that I simply existed with the aid of injections and various medication. However, I had to get the truth out of him. So I simply said, "I am no longer the woman I was. I have died with my darling daughter Ayşe. You told me that you no longer loved me and that you did not want me. If you like, we may as well divorce." I had no idea what his answer would be but what he said as an answer to my question cleared everything. He said, "I don't have enough money to pay you alimony." My answer was curt. "I am not interested in alimony. I just want my remaining children. In the future, when you have the chance, I am sure you will help our children as best you can." His answer was, "Of course I will when I can." I told him he could take whatever he wanted from the house in Ankara. I also said that I would have the divorce procedures start as soon as possible and I told him that I did not want to see him in my house when I returned to Ankara. I then asked him to take me back to my brother's house. On my return to the house I told Bibi and Cenan what had transpired and asked them to let Father know and that his lawyers should proceed as directed. I had no more strength. I must have been appalled by the fact that he had nothing to say about our dead child and about our marriage that had lasted 21 years and at the same time he had not even inquired about the health of his two children who were still alive. How can people be so callous and indifferent. So this was the end. That night, despite being numb with all the sedatives I was taking, I decided that I should talk things over with my children and obtain their opinion. When I had finished talking Zeyneb and Ömer both said, "You were too late in reaching this decision."

I do not remember how long we stayed on the island. Ömer's school was due to start. I had to earn my living. Both Zeyneb and I should start to work. Together with my beloved children we took the night train to Ankara. I suppose he must have learned the time of our arrival. We found their father in the house. When I asked him why he was there, he said, "I brought some food for the children." I must have gone beserk. I told him to take whatever he had brought and leave the house at once. Where had he been all this while? Since he professed that he could not afford to pay any money for his children, I did not even want to see his face anymore. The children told me he was crying as he went down the steps.

It was the beginning of September. We had some sort of a message from the court. Father was also in Ankara and he had invited both of us, without having informed me of his presence, to his suite at the Bulvar Palace Hotel. He was trying to see if we could change our minds. On my absolute refusal and insistence, on September 13, 1972 we were officially divorced. I too had to attend the court and as soon as I had the divorce papers in my hand, I rushed to the registrar's office and changed my birth certificate to my maiden name. Only then did I feel like having an identity once again. This was my decision and it had been carried out as I wanted it to. From now on I was going to be on my own. No one would be there to protect or lord over me. So in a very short period of time I had lost a child, had terminated a marriage that had lasted for twenty-one years and was left almost a pauper. I have later wondered if I should not have been more insistent for an amount of alimony settlement on behalf of my children. However, in the years to come, I never felt the loss of such financial income earned in such a manner. Anyway, my children turned out to be such wonderful people that they never even once complained to me on that score. I am truly indebted to both of them.

Time was passing but the pain of the loss I had suffered never ceased. Actually it was going deeper in my heart. I was doing everything I was supposed to do or that was required of me, but I could not stop crying. Every morning I woke up crying. I was even crying in my sleep. This pain was unbearable. Life was going on but my pain never stopped. One day my son Ömer gave me an ultimatum. He said, "Mother, you may continue to cry until such a date, however, if you do not stop crying after that date. I will not stay in this house anymore." I had heard what he was saying but it appears that it had not registered. I simply could not stop myself from crying. One night Ömer did not appear for dinner. Zeyneb saw how agitated I was and she said, "Mother, don't you remember? Ömer had given you a date for you to stop crying. You did not keep to it and Ömer won't come anymore." Then what he had been saying really sunk in. Ayşe was gone never to return. However, I still had two children who were alive. I should be of use to them, to say the least. It was like a slap in the face. I had suddenly awakened to life's realities. I washed my face, dried my eyes and begged Zeyneb to find out where Ömer was. However severe my pain may be I should no longer show it to others from that time on. I used to cry my eyes out, beat the doors or the windows, only when I was alone in the house by myself. As soon as the children came in, my cries would be over. I had stopped talking about Ayşe with other people as well. I had one friend only, Leyla Pekdeğer. She was like a sister to me and much more than a friend. She was the only one to whom I could unburden my soul. Actually, I did not have all that spare time to continue with my mourning. I was still back in my old job. The money I earned was just enough to keep us afloat. My old working girl, Elif, was coming once a week. I could not afford more than that. Shopping, cooking, washing, etc. were all the chores I had to do, apart from attending the embassy. Furthermore, since our table was no longer fancy and since we were no longer a happy family, fewer and fewer people called on us. Nobody would climb five flights of stairs for nothing in return. So my evenings were mostly free. During the weekends my children would go out with their friends. During those times Leyla was my life-saver. We used to get together either in her house or in mine and share our misery.

There were two other friends with whom I was able to continue our relationship. One was Deniz Adanalı and the other was Erel Can (Bleda). My friendship with Erel had started through the intervention of my daughter Ayşe. This was a twist of fate. I had induced Ayşe to take French lessons and she had registered at the courses at the French Cultural Center. She had enough knowledge of German and English and I wanted her to learn French as well. One evening, when she returned from her French course, Ayşe was rather excited and had told me that she had met a young woman called Erel and had enjoyed her company as well as her husband's very much. She was sure I also would love this couple. They were older than Ayşe and younger than I. However, since Ayşe had liked them so much I suggested that she invite them for dinner one night. They came. I found that my daughter was right in her preference. They were young, beautiful and well-educated. Furthermore, they were friends of Mehmet and Deniz Adanalı and also of Dündar and Leyla Elbruz. Dündar was originally a friend of my brother Nur from years back (their high school days). I used to enjoy his company in the old days. So we became good friends with this young couple. Ayşe and Zeyneb being the go-between.

Fate would show its implacable ways in this relationship also. First it was Dündar who was killed in an auto accident. He was followed by Tulgar (Erel's husband) and Ayşe in that order. These disasters had come so soon after one another that we, those who were left behind, had no choice but to come to each other's aid. We used to come together and cry our eyes out at the same time we were trying to find ways of continuing this life. Sharing our misery probably helped all of us and in a way showed us the road to salvation.

We still get together whenever we can. Zeyneb was also a friend of Erel and she still is. Our friendship was built on pain and became lasting for life. We still share the good and the misery of this world.

Many years later, Erel married Ambassador Tanşuğ Bleda and we met many times in New York or Paris where Tanşuğ was stationed as the ambassador of Turkey. Now he too is retired and once in a while we try to get together, now in our country. In the same manner, I still see my friends the Adanalı couple on and off.

The various sedatives and injections were beginning to take their toll on my body. My mind was getting fuzzy. When I consulted my doctor about my condition he said, "I will agree to have you stop these sedatives on the condition that you promise to have a glass of wine or some whisky every evening." So I started following his advice and found that a bit of alcohol before going to bed really did help me to go to sleep. However, one night I was at Leyla's house and we must have had too much to drink. I was able to come home and find my way to my bed, but in the morning, I had to look for my car for a long time. I had parked the car a long ways off. That was a good lesson for me and since then I restrict myself to one drink, or at most two, a night.

XXXIII

Zeyneb Puts on Her Wings

My brother Nur was in Turkey with his new wife. They decided
to settle in the States. One day Zeyneb told me that she had
talked with her uncle and that he had offered to take her with
them to the States. Nur also confirmed this and said, "She can
share our house. She can find a part-time job and register at a
university. This way she can be safe and in a year or two she
will get her degree." It sounded very plausible but somehow I
had doubts about such a plan. Frankly, I was of two minds about
his present wife. She did not seem to be someone dependable.
At least for me. Furthermore, I was not sure how far they could
afford to help Zeyneb, making my daughter their dependant actually bothered me. I had no means to help Zeyneb financially
if she went to the States. However, Zeyneb had made up her
mind. Lately I was pressing her to cut down her relationship
with Sertaç. I was in no good mood myself and my manners
must have irritated her. After high school Zeyneb had wished
to enter the School of Fine Arts. She had an affinity for drawing.
I had backed this project fully. She had to enter the exams in
İstanbul. She was a very close friend of Elif, whose mother Mrs.
Ayiter had invited Zeyneb to stay in their house in İstanbul as
Elif's friend and sit for the entrance exams.

Unfortunately she had no backing and she had failed to earn
an acceptance. This had been a further blow to her. I could just
not get her to listen to reason. Finally she made a deal with her
uncle, without my consent, carried out all the necessary preparations on her own, without consulting me or asking for my help,
and left for the States. Zeyneb had always been headstrong and
she had shown her character once again. So I was to cry for the
loss of two daughters, for different reasons. I can never forget

the day we had seen Zeyneb off. On our return to the house Ömer had kissed my hand and said, "You are a wonderful mother. You let Zeyneb go on her own because she wanted to do so. You gave her her freedom." I still cannot understand why youngsters refuse to listen to sound advice coming from their elders. They just refuse to benefit from the experience of their parents. I was a child once, I was also a teenager, and I had always listened to my parent's advice. Maybe their advice did not give the required results sometimes, still I do not regret having done so. At least I had always tried to understand their motives. I have to accept the fact that the sort of family pressures experienced by my generation is no longer applicable for the new generation. Now, as I watch my grandchildren grow up, I am amazed at the change of their development.

There is also the innate differences of character between one child and another. Zeyneb was always a freewheeling child. Even in her crib, she would be extending her small hands out to touch people nearby and send them kisses to get their attention. When she was just a little older, she would always try to take her shoes or socks from my hand, saying, "By myself, by myself." The day she had graduated from high school, Zeyneb and her friend had built a bonfire with all their textbooks on the lawn of the golf club. Her independence would bring punishment many a times, however, Zeyneb has always been on her own no matter how difficult the conditions have been. Furthermore, she would never complain of the hardships her independence had brought her. She has been a model daughter, a wonderful sister and a perfect mother. She was lucky to have been able to bring up two wonderful daughters herself. Zeyneb has always been good-natured and full of help for all and sundry around her.

Very early in her stay in America, Zeyneb was to face very hard and difficult situations and in the meantime, as her mother, I was in continuous pain. I was not able to get much information but my pain was based on my intuitions and premo-nitions, as well as on our infrequent telephone conversations, which unfortunately proved to be correct in time.

My daughter had flown from Ankara directly to Denver, Colorado. Her uncle and his wife, at the time, met her at the airport and took her to their home. In a short while Zeyneb had found a job as a telephone operator at a hotel. One evening when she was back from work, the lady of the house asked her to do things she had not expected to be doing. What she was required to do was a little out of the ordinary and far beyond things that a niece staying in her uncle's house would be expected to do. So Zeyneb refused to do these and the scheme that the aunt had in her mind came to the fore. She had expected Zeyneb to work as their maid and when Zeyneb refused to do as ordered, the woman kicked Zeyneb out of the house. My poor girl was left stranded in the middle of the night in a strange town. Luckily she remembered the telephone number of another girl who was also working at the same hotel and she was able to get shelter with her. She had no money. She had refused my giving her what little I could have given her in Ankara. Unfortunately, my brother, since he too was frightened of his wife, was not able to help Zeyneb either. My poor girl was really in a very bad position but I do not want to go into further details here since these are her private experiences. I was feeling horrible knowing that I could not be of any help and that I had not been able to obtain enough information. I called up her father and asked if he could help our daughter. He unfortunately showed no interest in the matter. His curt reply was that she was old enough to take care of herself. With Zeyneb gone we started sharing life with Ömer. Despite his youth he was doing his best to help me survive. He was in his last year in high school and he was a good student. We used to have long discussions with my son. He wanted to study economics and wanted to go to England to get a university degree. Since his father refused to give any alimony or any other form of financial aid, I was at the end of my rope.

My father was a well-to-do gentleman but since the death of my mother his attitude toward his children had changed. My elder brother Cenan was also well off, but he had three daughters of his own and believing that I was well off, had never asked me how I was doing. And I don't mean this only as financial aid. I had to do the best I could and raise my son against all odds. There is no doubt that a boy of 16 or 17 will have a tough time growing as the son of a divorced mother. Still neither my father nor my brother ever showed any interest in my affairs. Once, when my father had come to Ankara, I had forced myself to ask him if he could help me to send my son to England for his university degree. He was very direct. He said, "I have seven grandchildren, I would like to treat them the same and my finances will not permit such a thing." The seven grandchildren my father was talking about were these: Cenan had three girls, the youngest being Zeyneb aged 10, then came Fatos aged 13 and the eldest Emine aged 16. Then Nur had two sons but both were in America. I had lost my Ayşe and my second daughter Zeyneb was also in America trying to survive on her own. In other words, only Emine could possibly be interested in a university education a year hence. So Ömer was the only one eligible. When I mentioned this, his answer was, "There are many universities in Turkey."

So it was again up to me. My salary at the Indonesian Embassy had been raised to TL. 2.500 a month. So I started saving some of this each month. I had started making calculations, trying to find out if I could do anything. My good friend Leyla came to my help once again. I also got in touch with Margeret Kapani, who knew some people at the British Council. We learned that Ömer could apply for a G.C.E., find a boarding house where he could also have his meals, and the amount of such a venture would cost me TL. 500 a month. So I immediately stated these negotiations and since Ömer had graduated with flying colors from his high school in June, I was able to send my only son, aged 17, to England in the fall of 1973.

Now I was left all by myself. No one can imagine how difficult it was for a single mother to go through the formalities involved, with no backing from anybody. The way the clerks at the ministry of education would make things as hard as possible and difficult for no reason at all. The way they would say, "Come back tomorrow" or "Bring some other document" or simply say "I do not have the time, now," etc. Nobody, nobody ever asked me whether they could give me a hand. I had to dash off from the embassy to catch the clerks at the ministry who were ready to go off duty and would delay everything as best they could. They would be having their afternoon tea and would not be bothered with signing the document I was waiting for. So I had to go to them the next afternoon. In the meantime I had to shop, I had to cook. My darling son was always working for his classes

293

with no help from me. How could a mother sleep under these circumstances! I had to dream of Ayşe, who was no longer alive, I had to think of Zeyneb who was far away and I had Ömer to think about. Their father had married as soon as he got his divorce. I was still the optimist. I always had said maybe he would help his son if he had the means. Anyway, I was able to send my son to England finally. My son had turned out to be a real gentleman. He was only 17 but he never complained, not once. He always kept his word. He was now far away but writes me a letter every week. He is proud and will never ask for anything, under any circumstance. He had made up his mind to work hard and obtain his university degree.

Before he had gone to England, my darling son used to do the best he could to make life easier for me. He would set the table, he would pick wild flowers (at no cost) and put them in a vase for our dinner table. He would cut the bread and so forth. His eyes were always shining whenever they met my eyes. He wanted to give me whatever happiness he could. He was also carrying the burden of having lost an elder sister and of course he was missing his other sister, who was away. He would like to have more pocket money than I could ever afford to give him but he would never ask for anything. He never mentioned how hard it must have been for him not to have a father and the fact that his father had never even called him once. He was probably trying not to hurt me by mentioning his father. No complaints. He was determined to handle his problems by his own means. Ömer had grown up rather early. No wonder, with all the things he was forced to observe at such a tender age.

I was really left all by myself after Ömer left Ankara. In a relatively short time a family of five had dwindled to one person. After I had lost Ayşe I had lost a lot of weight. I was weighing 40 kilos. I was really hopeless in every manner. I really felt lost. I knew my duties and tried very hard to carry my duties out to the letter. What really worried me was the fear of being penniless. Yes, I was working but what would happen if my funds would not be enough to finance the education of my son?

I spent a weekend in my apartment trying to evaluate the things that I could sell that were in the house and tried to guess how much each would bring in. My only relation with money was to try and figure out what came in and try to make it with what was going on. I really had started this calculation only since my husband had left me stranded. I had no idea about money until that time. As a young girl my allowance would be placed on top of my piano in an envelope. I had never asked for more. Even when I was registered as a college student in America and my student stipend began to come from Turkey, I used to collect the money from the bank and give it to Mother, never asking to keep some. As soon as I had gotten married all questions concerning money were taken over (for twenty-one years) by my husband. He bought the material for my dresses, as well as my underwear, even my shoes! Knowing my likes he would order everything for me and I was in a way his baby doll. For so many years, first it had been Mother who had made up my mind for me, then it was my husband who decided everything. I hardly ever demurred, let alone do something against their wishes and I had lost all my powers of decision making, trying to please them, for years and years. I had heard my mother telling me, "When you are married, you must do what your husband wants you to do." She had hammered this into my subconscience. Later it had become a means for not having a fight.

The things that could fetch some money were as follows. First there were the Meissen plates. They were a set of plates for 24 people. A number of gold plated frames Mother had given me when the mansion at Erenkoy had been sold. I had received a number of valuable gifts for my wedding. There was a Baccarat crystal set, all the silver and some of my jewelry. Some of these would fetch good prices if and when sold.

My loneliness did not actually mean that I was not seeing people. Actually, I was not interested to see anybody except the people at the embassy. My loneliness really stemmed from the fact that my family had deserted me. There was no shoulder that I could cry on. This was why I felt so lonely. There was no one I could turn to and expect some help or advice.

Later on in my life I began to appreciate being alone. I came to realize that one can be more lonely in a crowd that would not communicate. I found out that there is a big difference in English of the term "being alone" and to be "lonely." It can be lovely to be by one's self, if one knows how to deal with it. Whereas there

295

were days when I was feeling lonely. On one such day Zeyneb's old beau, Sertac, called. He said he wanted to talk to me. Frankly, I had never considered him to be worthy of my daughter. However, there was no reason for me to refuse to see him. As soon as he was seated in my apartment he came to the point. He said, "I know you do not consider me a good match for your daughter. However, I do love Zeyneb and I want to go to the States and marry your daughter. Can you please help me?" I was quite surprised. His request seemed genuine. He had no reason to call on me. He could have made his own arrangements and gone to America without consulting me. He knew I had no financial means to help him. He also told me that Zeyneb was having a tough time in Denver and that they had been exchanging letters. He simply was asking me to help him obtain a visa to enter the U.S. I saw no reason to refuse him. His intentions were very honorable. Their marriage would probably give my daughter a better deal. So I accepted the idea and started pulling strings and sure enough pretty soon we were able to get him a visa to enter the U.S. After all, my daughter would now be facing life with a man by her side who loved her and whom she also seemed to be in love with.

XXXIV
Return to Father's Home

It was during this time that Father had come to Ankara and came to visit me. Among the things he mentioned was that he did not approve of the fact that I was living all alone, now that I had none of my children with me. Since he too was living by himself as a widower, he said the best thing for both of us would be for me to go to İstanbul and live with him. He added that I really did not have to work for my living and that I could be the lady of my father's house. I was rather baffled and did not know what to say. One thing that made sense were his words about him needing me. That was a sensitive feeling in me. Since Mother died I had never spent any time in my father's house. Old habits die hard. Mother would never allow me to stay at someone else's house overnight. She would gladly receive my friends to stay overnight in our house but never vice versa. Once when we were just back from the United States, our mutual friend Cemile had invited us, together with Cenan, to a ball in the island and Cenan and I had spent an hour or so in their house before the sun rose and we caught the first ferry out of the island. We had also reached an agreement with my husband and we never stayed in anyone else's house, even our parents'. We always booked into a hotel. When we were engaged I had spent a night at the Devres house together with Mother and Cenan. Then the only time I had spent some time at Cenan's house was when I had lost my daughter, Ayşe. With all these considerations in mind, I asked Father to let me have some time to consider his offer.

After he was gone, I tried to think about my situation. The one important question in my mind was the problem of financing my son Ömer's university education. Father had said that he would meet my financial requirements. There were still a few things that I could sell for cash and I had some savings. Perhaps after a while I could find another job in İstanbul. Running Father's house would also keep me busy and I would be near Bibi and Cenan. I had also had a number of friends in İstanbul. Then there was the question of what to do with the furniture I had. After all there were many things that I should like to keep for my children, they were a sign of our life together. They would not bring much anyway, if I sold them. My father's house was already full of old furniture. I could not possibly take anything there. When I mentioned this to father, he said, "There is a moving company called Tuzcuoglu that can put them into storage for a nominal fee." One evening I took an empty page, drew a line from top to bottom. On one side I wrote the pros and on the other I wrote the negatives. It did not seem to make much difference how I lived, however, being of use to father in his old age seemed to be the important question. Those were days I felt like an autumn leaf moving with the blowing wind, whichever side it blew from. There was nothing that I could hold on to. Finally I made my mind to move to İstanbul. First I explained my situation to Ambassador Moersid and told him that I would be going to İstanbul in two months time and that I would do my best to help him get a replacement in the meantime. He was a very special person. He and his wife had been especially wonderful to me at the time I had lost Ayşe. Even when I had sent them to a black tie dinner at the wrong date! He had called me to his office the next morning, asked me to take a seat and then he explained what an exceptional night they had had. The rest of the story was horrible for me.

When they rang the bell of the residence, the door was opened by a doorkeeper in his daily outfit and the ambassador, who was to have been their host, appeared in his night attire. They had been asked to join the ambassador and his wife for a night cap anyway and in the end they had lots of fun. I was squirming in my seat the whole time. Ambassador Moersid still kept saying, "Don't worry Mrs. Sılan, we still had a very jolly good time." That wonderful gentleman had cautioned me in an elegant manner. How could I have made that frightful mistake? I was terribly ashamed of myself. Later on, the ambassador had received the news of my departure for İstanbul with the same understanding.

While getting ready for my move to İstanbul, I had heard that İsmet İnönü was not feeling well. I went to call on them at once. During our conversation with Mrs. İnönü I asked her opinion about my moving to İstanbul. She was very nice. She encouraged me to go. Her opinion was very important for me because as far as I could tell she had always done the right thing all her life. I was very indebted to her and I respected her greatly. When I started crying she pulled me close and hugging me looked at me with tears in her eyes. She had been almost like a mother to me when I had lost Ayşe.

I first had to discuss my situation with the Tuzcuoglu Transportation Company. They agreed to take my things into storage. Then I had to deal with all sorts of contractual obligations like cancelling the phone and having the electricity turned off, etc. Doing those things had really worn me out. I was at the end of my patience.

Then one day Cenan was on the phone. He said he was in Ankara for a short while and could not come to the house, but if I had the time he would be delighted to see me for half an hour at the Ankara Hotel. I jumped into my car and rushed to his hotel. I had just been back from the Electricity Company and was very upset. When we were together Cenan gave me his lovely smile and asked how I was doing, getting ready to go to İstanbul? I guess I must have been really rattled by the day's chores. I suddenly burst out, "What kind of people are you? You have hundreds of people working under your command and you never thought of asking me if I needed any help in Ankara?" Meanwhile tears were running down my cheeks. I really was sick of this life. Yet I did not have the right to die either, since I still had responsibilities towards my children. Poor Cenan was quite sad. He said, "I always thought that you were able to take care of yourself. Never thought you needed help. Please forgive me little sister." He finally asked me if there was anything he could do at present and my answer was simply, "Thank you, I need nothing." We were both shaken. Our half an hour had ended. He had other appointments. After all, his reasoning was right. We had started getting to know each other only in 1945.

Cenan had been sent to Germany for his university education as early as 1937. From there he had gone to France. The Second World War had started and we had been separated for many years. In those years he was my eldest brother and I was his "little sister." After 1945 and all the way until 1973 we had been good friends but I had always been on my own. Somehow none of my elders ever considered me as the youngest member of the family and as a person to whom the worst things had happened. I am not trying here to criticize members of my family, trying to obtain condescension, but rather to show what the facts were and also remind my children of what the future may hold for everyone. There is a saying in Turkey, they asked a mother which of her children she liked most. Her answer was as follows, "I love the youngest until he grows up, I love the sick child until she gains her health, and I love the one who is far away until he returns home." It is possible that my children may have felt jealousy against one another at one time or another. However, there is no question in my mind that I loved each one equally. My heart has always been beating for the sake of my children. How can a mother differentiate between her children? At the same time I was always ready to be on the side of my children whenever and wherever anyone of them needed me.

I must add further that I am not trying to find guilt in any of my relations nor am I angry at anyone of them. I have always loved all the members of my family. However, as I am now writing my memoirs, I felt that I had to write everything as it happened. No regrets, no accusations. The maturity I have reached at this stage and age makes me accept anything and everything. I am finally at peace with myself. It is easy to forgive but difficult to forget.

Shortly after this meeting with Cenan, the people from Tuzcuoglu came to the house. They were packing everything. For one wild moment I visualized that all these boxes which were the remains of my twenty-one years of marriage could just as well be thrown out of the window. I wished I had had nothing except Zeyneb's cat "Menam" and the dress I had on, nothing else, going to İstanbul.

When we were living at Güniz Sokak, a counsellor of the French Embassy had the flat above us and I had become good friends with his wife. The lady used to write poetry and always read interesting books. She was intelligent, sensitive and very well read. One day when she had come for tea, she found me on the floor trying to put together the pieces of a valuable Chinese vase which my son Omer had accidentally broken. I was very sorry for our vase. I had scolded my young son rather severely and caused him to cry his eyes out. When the French lady saw me in that strange condition, she told me that I should not feel so bad. She then went on to explain that they used to live in Algiers. When the troubles had started she was glad to have come out alive and all her belongings had been ransacked by the revolutionaries. "So," she said, "since that time, belongings are no longer important for me. They really have no value." What she had said was so true!

Before leaving for İstanbul I had to face one more calamity. Our beloved statesman, Mr. İnönü, had passed away. I had a chance to visit that honorable lady, Mrs. İnönü, and we shed tears together.

XXXV

Migration

On December 30, 1973 I left Ankara for İstanbul in my small car together with Menam, the cat. On the mountains of Bolu a snow storm started. A little further away the traffic police had cut the highway. They said it may prove to be dangerous to proceed any further. I was glad that I had left Ankara behind. I had nowhere to return to. I did not want to return anyway. There were a few cars on the side of the road, waiting to see what would happen, so I decided to follow their example and wait. I was lucky. After a few hours of waiting we were advised that the road was now safe to travel. Despite this mishap I was not sorry that I had driven. The new İstanbul bridge that had joined the two sides of the Bosphorus had been operational for some time but this was the first time that I would be driving over it. I can never forget. As I was driving over the bridge I was shouting with joy, "Look Menam, we are on the bridge of civilization." As if she understood what I was saying the poor kitten meowed back to me. It was certainly a dazzling view, looking over the bridge to the Bosphorus. Night was falling and the lights on the bridge had all been turned on. On the left I could see the Topkapi Palace and the grand minarets of the Ottoman mosques. On my right and below were the old Ottoman palaces and further up one could have a glimpse of the Rumeli Towers that Fiath Sultan Mehmet, the conquerer, had built. I had some good expectations, naturally—the possibility of sharing life with father, and Bibi and Cenan with their darling daughters. No more paper work to do. I was certainly looking forward to a future of peace and quiet.

I was able to reach my father's apartment at Acisu Sokak No. 12 just in time for dinner. He hugged and kissed me and took me to the room they had prepared for me. The room was also full of memories. The very elegant looking bed that Mother had bought for me just before my marriage was there waiting for me. The dressing table that Mother used was also prepared for my use. An armchair which had been part of my room in the past. That armchair had a special value for me since I had nursed all my children on it. I made myself comfortable in the room, fed the cat, washed my hands and face and then I joined Father for dinner. This was going to be a new chapter in my life. After having been the mistress of my own house I was once again going to be the daughter of my father. The "little Miss" of the house help! This meant a transition. Furthermore, in this new father's house, my dearest mother was no longer present. We chatted a bit after dinner, I had a shower and went to bed. I was exhausted.

My new life next morning started with loud noises outside my door and with a knock. It was the housemaid who was knocking on my door. I had just opened my eyes, rudely awakened. I looked at my watch. It was 6:00 A.M. It was still dark outside. I had to put on the light to be able to see my watch. I called her to come in. I said, "what is going on?" She calmly said "The master is up and waiting at the breakfast table for you to join him." This was a premonition of my coming days. It frightened me. I asked the woman to make me a cup of coffee, got up, washed my face, put on my robe and went to the dining room. When I got to the dining table my father met me very kindly and told me that this was his lifestyle and that he had breakfast early. I tried to tell him that I was not such an early riser, that I only had a cup of coffee and a cigarette in the mornings. I don't think Father was listening to what I was saying. Yes, my regulated life at my father's house was beginning to take shape. There were set times for breakfast, lunch and dinner. Breakfast was at 6:00 A.M. At 11:00 A.M. Father had a small glass of warmed milk and a cookie. I could have a cup of coffee with him. At 1:00 P.M. was lunch, at 5:00 P.M. was the afternoon tea and at 8:00 P.M. we had dinner. At 10:00 P.M. father would have his second cup of warmed milk and a cookie. At 11:00 P.M. we turned in for sleeping.

December 31, 1973 was my first day in İstanbul. We spent that evening at Cenan's house and celebrated the New Year, 1974. Naturally it was 1:00 A.M. when we went to bed. Again there was a knock on my door in the darkness of the new year. I was tired. I was sleepy and I was a sad, sad woman. That morning I sent word that I was not feeling well and did not join Father for breakfast. I just could not face it.

The next morning I had my alarm clock set to 5:00 A.M. I got up, dashed to the kitchen before anyone was up. Had my cup of morning coffee and my first cigarette of the day and returned to my room. I was back at Father's breakfast table at his usual hour and I explained my dilemma and begged to be excused from the ritual of having breakfast with him in the mornings. From that day on, as we agreed, I would ring for my morning coffee whenever I woke up and the maid would bring it to my room. I was always ready for the rest of the meals.

Ever since I was born, my mother's house was full of various animals and birds. Fish in ponds, birds in cages and cats and dogs running around. In her late years Mother had cut down the number of her pets somewhat but I remember she had kept the cat that shared Zeyneb's lamb chops always at her house. After her death, Tekir had been taken care of by my father until she died of natural causes. Despite this, within the week of my arrival Father started complaining about my cat Menam. "The cat is dirty and makes a nuisance, etc." So I started keeping my cat in my room and did not let it roam around the house.

Also Mother used to smoke a lot. In fact, that was one of the reasons why they used to have separate bedrooms. Shortly after my arrival Father had started complaining about my smoking. "It smelled bad and the house was full of cigarette smoke, etc." That meant I had started to stay in my room as much as possible. The funny thing was that when he had suggested that we should share a home together, I had the presence of mind to repeatedly tell him these two points—I smoked and I had a cat. He had somewhat ignored my warnings. I began to feel that I should make use of myself in the house. I told Father that I should start doing the shopping for the house. "That would not be the right thing to do," he said. Our cook Raşit Efendi was doing the shopping for all these years, if I took this privilege away from him he might feel offended. What could I say? Whatever I suggested that I could do in the house, I was met with a flat refusal. In one instance I had said that the doormat was too old and I meant to go and buy a new one. My father's answer was, "Ayşe (Cenan's wife) has a very good taste for such things, she will buy a new one for us." I thought I would go out of my mind. Even my going out had begun to give negative results. Especially if I was late in coming home in the evening. Once in a while I would be asked to stay for dinner in my brother's house. When I returned late that night I would find Father up and waiting for my return and felt bad about it. When I asked for a key to the house his answer was, "No. You might lose it." I really did not know what to say. He must have thought that I was an undisciplined ignoramus who could not tie her shoe laces.

In this regard of returning home late, I also have a "divorcée's night out" story to tell. Cenan and his wife had insisted that I should join them at a party at a friend's house. It was quite a crowded affair. My brother and my sister-in-law had developed a habit of introducing me as their sister and never mentioned my name. This meant that people to whom I was being introduced for the first time did not know whether I was single or divorced or what. I was a woman without a name as far as they were concerned. As women who have had similar experiences will understand my feelings instantly, a single woman without an escort is never well received especially among women who are not sure of their husbands. We had had a rather nice evening. However, since I did not want to keep Father waiting for me all night, I excused myself early. The hosts were taken a little aback that I was leaving so early. Also there was the question who was to escort me home. I told them that there was no question of any one bothering about me and that "Murat" was waiting for me. At first they had thought I had someone called "Murat" (which is a Turkish name for a male person) actually waiting for me to take me home. When I was at the curb entering my car called "Murat" by its manufacturers, I remember looking back to see some of the ladies in the party leaning over the balcony to see who Murat was! I was laughing bitterly when I had my Murat in first gear and waved them good-bye.

XXXVI

Vaniköy on the Bosphorus

Months were going by, I was still trying to adjust myself. Ömer informed me that he was going to have his summer recess. I was going to get him to İstanbul. When I mentioned this, Father simply said, "Of course he can come, he can sleep on the couch in the living room." In a way he was right. All the rooms in the house were occupied. Father had his bedroom and I had mine. My bedroom was too small to fit in a second bed. The rest was Father's library, then there was a living room and a dining room. By the kitchen there was the maid's chamber and there were two separate bathrooms. Suddenly I remembered that Father owned a yalı (a house on the water in Bosphorus) at Vaniköy. It was on Vaniköy Street No. 26. We had gone there once or twice. It was a beautiful wooden building and had three stories. The building was empty and no one was living there. So I suggested that we take out the furniture I had put into storage with the Tuzcuoglu firm and rehabilitate the building. I also told him that since I had my car, I could be of help to him, whenever he wanted to go to the city. "This way we could all enjoy the sea, you can sit and enjoy the panaroma. Omer and I can enjoy swimming in the Bosphorus and perhaps fish a little." In the beginning he did not like the idea and stalled but I was persistent and finally he gave in. Of course we had to go and see if this was a feasible idea. One entered the garden from the street and went down a stairway to reach a sort of spacious garden. Then one had to walk a bit, since the house was closer to the seas. One went in through some steps and on this first floor there was a living and dining area plus the kitchen and a bedroom and a bathroom. Then one climbed some stairs and reached the second floor. There were two bedrooms and a bathroom on this second floor. Then came the attic, where there was a huge room with the ceiling somewhat going down in a slope. Almost all the windows were either facing the sea or the garden. Near the entrance door of the garden and partially on the street there was a garage. Next to this garage there were also rooms where the servants could reside. When my furniture would be placed, the house would look heavenly. Father finally realized that my idea was achievable. My furniture fit in beautifully. Even my curtains fit the windows. All we had to bring from the city apartment was our clothes.

This yalı had a special position. There was almost a bay within a bay, which made our landing almost like a private pool. In any case, in those years the pollution in the Bosphorus had not reached the impossible limits that it has reached today. Anything that had been dumped into the sea would bypass with the current. I had almost forgotten the horrible months I had lived through. I was now able to provide a private bedroom for my son. He would have a wonderful vacation. I made sure to prepare this attic room for us so that we could sit there for hours and chat and enjoy each other's company. We moved to Vaniköy a bit earlier than Ömer arrived. Naturally, Ömer would feel a little uncomfortable in his grandfather's house. It was the first time that he would not be in his own house in Turkey. When the French windows of the living room were opened it seemed as if we were sitting in the sea. The sun sets slowly on the European side of the Bosphorus, and then the scenery becomes unbelievably beautiful. My father looked very happy. He had not even moved a finger and had found himself in this beautiful setting. We had neighbours on both sides and they too had turned out to be very respectable people.

Father chose the bedroom on the first floor for himself. I had prepared the two bedrooms on the second floor for my son and myself. The attic room was going to be our conversation corner. The view from there was really great. We would watch the Bosphorus from there, or we could relax with our books.

After what seemed like centuries to me I was finally able to hug my darling son once again. He was almost eighteen. He had again grown taller and he was incredibly thin. Of course he had missed his mother. He had missed the kind of meals we used to have and also his country. He loved the house on the water but he wanted to have the attic room despite the fact that he had to bend his head slightly, especially nearer the corners of the room. He certainly loved it. Probably it was fitting for him, under the circumstances.

Despite some unfortunate incidents, on the whole we had a wonderful time. Ömer and I would take a dip in the sea early and then join Father for breakfast. My son had a yearning for the white cheese we had and the black olives. After breakfast I would go shopping to the Çengelköy bazaar, together with my son. Some days I would drive Father to İstanbul and on other days he would be content to take the ferry. Omer would fish or read a book while we were gone. After making sure that everything in the house, like cleaning and cooking, were in order, I would join him. Gradually his cheeks began to fill and his color began to glow. Big oil tankers began to pass through and their waves would create havoc on the shore. Once or twice we lost some sun glasses, a portable radio, etc. to these waves. However, we were able to swim for hours and forget everything. My son turned out to be a model grandson. He was always ready to help his grandfather. He was also willing to help with the house chores. However, Father had the leaning to capture all our time. I even wondered if he was jealous of my son since my attention naturally had turned more to him than to Father. For example, just as Ömer found something he would like to watch on the television, Father would suddenly say, "Turn that thing off. It is not good for your eyes." When he was trying to catch a late evening fish, Father would say, "It is getting cold. You must get in." Even when Ömer and I would retire to my son's attic room, he would soon call from his room and complain about the fact that our noise disrupted his sleep and that we too should go to sleep. Both Ömer and I had become attuned to do whatever we wanted to do with the idea of not disturbing father. Ömer was so attentive. He had even prepared his grandfather's food when the cook was on leave one night. Still he was continuously causing a strain. One day when he was discussing the day's purchases, I heard him complain to the cook that olives and white cheese were being consumed too much! It had certainly hurt me. So I had started buying things on my own and I had tiny excuses like, "I saw it by chance and thought it was too good to miss," in order to eliminate the expenses.

In order to cut this uncomfortable summer holiday short and also to make sure that my son would be saved from an embarrassing situation that might develop any day, I suggested to Ömer that I should drive him back to England. I said, "This way we can be by ourselves for a longer period and also I will be able to visit your school." Ömer was delighted with the idea. How was I to broach this idea to Father? I was so reticent. I gathered my courage, waited for an opportune moment when Father was relaxed and I explained my program. Autumn was approaching and we had to move back to the apartment. We could leave the furniture in the summer house. I explained to Father that I was using this motor trip to be able to take my son to his school and actually get to see how he was getting along in England. Furthermore, the cost of driving for both of us would even be less than his airface. At the same time there were places I could visit in Europe. Our ex-nanny, Uschi, had been writing and inviting me to Germany. There were a number of my friends who were residing in Europe at various embassies, so I could stay with them on the way back. Much to my delight Father raised no objections, in fact he might have been some- what relieved to get us out of his hair earlier then he expected. Ömer and I were in "Seventh Heaven." As it had become a habit- ual thing for me to do, I sold some of my jewelry, got tickets on the car ferry that would take us to Venice. I took the car for a complete check to make sure that it would stand a long journey.

Some of the best experiences we had during that summer were when we had gone out with my dear friend Leyla. She was working as a translator at the German embassy and at that phase she was accompanying the German ambassador, who had come to the old German embassy building (their summer place) on the Bosphorus. It was a veritable palace. After her work hours she would rent a motor boat and come to our house. Sometimes we would eat at home. At other times we would go out to a restaurant and I would drive her back. One evening we were having dinner at a fish restaurant and Leyla asked Ömer if he had ever drank rakı (a local drink, like absinthe) and when his answer was negative, Leyla said he was old enough and should join us drinking. So at that fish restaurant that evening I was able to toast with my son having his first rakı. He had enjoyed this new experience, and Leyla and I enjoyed it even more. Such nice memories!

XXXVII

England, Here We Come

When the day came, we moved to the flat at Maçka. That night Ömer slept on the couch. I once again realized what a clever decision I had made by moving to the house on the Bosphorus. It would have been a disaster otherwise. In the morning we both kissed Father good-bye and left the flat. My car had just been retooled and was in perfect working condition. We stopped at a pastry shop and bought things to munch on the road. We were off to Kartal and we were as free as birds. Then there was the ferry across to Yalova. We rode all the way to İzmir where my old friend Bançi (Hümeyra Özbas) managed a hotel called Kismet. We enjoyed the evening stroll on the seaside and had some fresh fish. There were so many memories that came up. Their father used to take all of us to the Ephesus Hotel every summer. The children used to enjoy the big swimming pool. Also, after our blue voyage trips, on the way back, we would take a rest in this luxurious hotel.

In the morning we drove our car into the ferry and locked it. We had a nice cabin for two. We came across some old friends on the ferry. For example, there was the former Ambassador Taha Carim, the journalist Izzet Sedes and his wife. It was fun being with them and the trip was quite enjoyable. We landed in Venice and we started our trip on the highways of Italy. My little Murat was going quite well. After a while I realized that something was bothering Ömer. I stopped on the sideway for a rest and asked Ömer what was bothering him. His answer was somewhat annoying. He said, "Mommy, don't you see all those Ferraris or Maserattis that pass by us like lightning. How fast can your Murat go, do you think?" Well, we only had this little Murat! Yes, it was a small car but it was behaving perfectly and doing what it could. We were in no hurry to reach a destination either. Even at the speed we were doing we should reach Geneva that evening. Well, we did, but it was almost 10:00 P.M. and naturally there was hardly anyone on the streets. This was my first visit to Geneva. I had no idea where we could find a hotel to spend the evening. Apparently I also had no idea how organized the Swiss were! As I was driving in the center of the city I saw a sign that said Tourist Office. Thinking that probably the place would be closed at that hour, I almost passed it. On second thought I said to myself why not give it a try. Sure enough there were people in the place. I stopped the car and went in. They were very courteous. When I asked about a moderate place where I could spend the night with my son, they gave me a map and directed us to a place on the other side of the lake.

It was a small but inviting-looking hotel. Ömer was still looking a little sulky. They met us very cordially as the tourist office had informed them of our arrival. After the registration formalities were over, they took us to a very nice room. When our luggage was brought in, I had a chance to look around. The room had an adjoining bathroom. Suddenly I realized that there was something missing. Namely there were no beds. There was a locker, a table, some seats but no bed! We were both very surprised. Suddenly my brilliant son pushed a button on the wall and a sliding bed suddenly emerged, then a second one. Mother and son we were laughing like children. The beds were very nicely fitted with goose feather pillows, etc. We were very tired. We debated about going to bed but then changed our minds. We had a quick shower and went down to the reception. When we explained that we were hungry the gentleman at the reception told us that there was a restaurant nearby that would be serving until midnight. This was a bit of news that made us very happy. We went to this restaurant around the corner. It was very small but it was a pleasant, romantic looking place, with white table cloths, candles, flowers and crystal wine glasses. The prices were also very reasonable. We asked for a glass of red wine for each of us and then I started looking at the menu. Lovely! They had steak au poivre! Ömer never tasted this meat dish. I had to tell him that he could order something else if he did not like it. However, he liked his pepper steak and at once his mood changed. Despite the fact that he had a crazy mother who would drive on the Italian highways in a tiny Murat car, actually a small Fiat assembled in Turkey, he still loved his mother and could also trust her. Finally, we had become a loving mother and son, sharing our friendship, once more.

In the morning we got up rather relaxed. We were in no hurry. We had a delicious breakfast in our room. Gradually we were on the road again. We were enjoying the scenery and commenting on everything we came across. We were especially excited when we went through a small village called Omar. It was strange to see my son's name being given to a small village in Europe! The route we had taken would take us through Paris. I knew that city from previous visits and I loved it. I asked my son if he would like to spend some time there. The answer I got surprised me. Ömer said, "Mother, let us not stop in Paris. It would be too expensive and we could easily be sidetracked." Many a times when we were going abroad I had asked my husband to take our kids along and he had always refused. It was such a pity that I had not been able to take my kids abroad when we had the means to do so. How sorry I felt for the times lost and the things I could not do for my children. My son's answer had once again proved to me what a mature person he had become. He did not want to be heartbroken. Well, we went by Paris and reached Calais, safe and sound.

Since I had never driven on the left side of the motorway, I decided not to take my car across. So we parked the good Murat into a long-term parking lot near the wharf and took the boat across the Channel. It was not a long voyage. The sea was very calm. To be with my son was the biggest source of my happiness. From Dover we took the train and we found ourselves in the middle of London. Again we searched for and found a reasonable hotel. It was called Penta. It was situated in a big building block and the hotel had five floors only. One nice thing was that rather than having a common breakfast room, they had put in a small fridge plus there was a water heater and some coffee and tea bags as well as cups, plates, cutlery and a small oven. We could do our own breakfast in our room. The fridge contained milk, fruit juice, some croissants, butter and jam. So there would be no formalities in the morning about having breakfast in a dining room or calling the room service. I had been to London previously and had some idea about this big, sprawling city. Naturally, our conditions were very different than what they had been before. As long as I had my son with me, nothing could bother me much. We had to be careful about our funds. However, Ömer had some experience on how to live frugally. For lunch we had fish and chips, which costs almost nothing compared to a meal at a restaurant. We had our lunch in a beautiful park. We walked around this city full of flowers and parks. We raced around the city riding the Underground for long distances. Ömer had asked if we could visit a night club. However, I was somewhat frightened. I had seen many signs saying BEWARE OF PICKPOCKETS and since we could not afford to use taxis I refused to walk around the city at night. I still feel sorry that I had not been able to take my son to a place he wanted to go.

The next morning we took the train to Brighton. It was a tiny summer resort where the big waves of the Atlantic could be seen from every corner. I suppose during the summer this place would be livened up a lot. Ömer's school would start in two days' time. We went to the house where he was staying as a boarder. We left his luggage and I met the family. Then we strolled along the coast. I realized once more what a difficult life my son was leading and how lonely he must be feeling in this dismal town, especially in the winter months. I had wanted to give the whole world to my children. However, destiny does not follow one's wishes. And one cannot escape destiny. I had never considered money as an important item in my life, maybe because it was there all the time or maybe it was the way I had been educated. Money was something decent people would not even mention. But if I had it now, I could give my children the kind of life they deserved. Nevertheless, I had to be grateful. At least, difficult as it may be, my son was getting a good education. This was the most important thing that I could give him. Both of us were rather quiet on our return to London. This was to be our last night together, for some time to come. We did not know when we would be able to get together again. I was going to take something called the hovercraft from Dover to Calais. Omer insisted on seeing me off to the hovercraft. He had the time, so I let him do this extra trip. At least we would be together for a few hours more. We kept hugging each other and we were both crying. The hovercraft was something like an airplane, one had to buckle up. It was half way touching the sea and still was flying! In any case, I could not stop my tears to be able to see much of anything.

By the time I reached Calais, it was dusk and street lights were already on. My car was waiting for me safely at the parking lot. My original plan was to go to Uschi, who was living in Stuttgart. However, I was not at all sure which highway would take me there. I somehow had forgotten to plan this part of my trip. Getting out of the city I took the highway that looked like the best to me, at least its lights were the brightest. I saw BRUSSELS written on a plate. I had not thought of going there but now that I was on the highway to that city, I suddenly remembered that one of my best friends, Jale, was the Ambassador's wife in that city. Her husband, Orhan Eralp, was our Ambassador to NATO. Furthermore, Cemile's daughter and her husband M. A. Birand were also residents in Brussels. Unfortuantely, as I had not planned to go there, I did not have their phone numbers with me. I thought maybe I could reach the Turkish Embassy and obtain the numbers from them. I parked in front of a small but decent looking bistro just before getting into the main city. It was quite dark now. The bistro was a crowded place with lots of people talking all at once. I edged to the bar and tried to reach the phone. Most of the customers turned out to be male workers who were having a drink before going home. Their French was almost impossible to understand. They saw that I was a stranger and they were wondering what I was doing there. I was able to understand the barman's French and asked for a directory. I was able to reach the Ambassador's residence. One of the footmen answered the phone. I asked him who was our Ambassador, knowing that Turkey had more than one Ambassador in Brussels. I was surprised to hear a name I recognized. The Ambassador mentioned was a friend of my brother Nur and during their years at the St. Joseph he had visited our house many times. In view of our old relationship I saw no reason why not to explain my situation and ask for some guidance.

His reaction was not what I expected. He said he was hardly in the tourist business and would not know of any hotel that I could stay in and that he was sorry not to be of any help. I simply thanked him and hung up. How people can change with circumstances. At one time he had thought it was an honor to dine at our house! Now he was cold and shouldering me. This was not such a surprise for me because since my divorce I had come across such attitudes more than once. Even my own family members were looking at me with pity in their eyes and did nothing about it.

I rang the same number again, being sure that it would be the same footman who would answer the phone. This time I asked him to give me the phone numbers of my other friends. He was able to give me Ambassador Eralp's home phone. So I rang up that number. I was not quite sure, I thought Jale would still be in İstanbul, but at least Orhan could give me the name of a decent hotel. Unfortunately, I had not been able to find a tourist office like the one in Geneva. Orhan was on the phone. He said "Jale just arrived last night. You must come and stay with us." I was delighted, however, I was driving round and round and I could not find the address he had given me. Most of the streets were empty. Finally, in desperation I stopped in front of a single-story house where I saw the lights were on and rang the door bell. A little later a giant of a half-naked man appeared. My God! What had I done. I told him I was lost, showed him my friend's telephone number and asked him if he could help me find the place they were located. He spoke back in Flemish but he could understand my French. He told me I could come in if I wanted to, but when he saw that I was hesitant he did not bother, turned around and went to the phone. A little later he came back. He had put on a sweater. He said he would drive me to a point where the Ambassador would come and pick me up. He was very kind. I followed his car and by the time we entered a big gas station Orhan was already there. We both thanked the gentleman profusely. I then followed Orhan's vehicle and soon we were in their house.

Jale as usual was very warm and welcoming. All my troubles were over for that night. I was safely placed in the home of very good friends. We had two delightful days together and in the meantime I was able to phone Zehra and Vahit Halefoğlu, the Turkish Ambassador in Bonn and was invited to stay with them on the way to Stuttgart. The Autobahns in Germany were wonderful. All the highways were spick and span with lots of parking areas full of trees and places for resting. I did not have much difficulty in finding the residence where I was expected for lunch. Old friendships can last over many years and under any circumstances. The warmth and kindness these old friends displayed toward me had given me a new strength in my life. Then I was on the road once more. Now, Stuttgart was on my agenda. I was to meet Uschi, the governess we had for the children for many years. In the meantime, I had the chance of talking to my son on the phone and life looked rosy. After driving for some time I saw what looked like a nice park and decided to rest a bit. I had a bottle of Coca-Cola in the car and I was sipping my drink in peace. A car came to a stop a little further than where I was parked. A young man stepped out of the car. I was just resting with my door open. He looked like a decent fellow. Suddenly I saw that he had stood toward me and he was unbuttoning his trousers! In this beautiful park. In broad daylight. How could this be possible? I must have gone crazy. My drink was spilled all over the place. I still do not remember how I closed my door, started the motor and rushed out of that parking lot. After a while I stopped at a gas station and tried to dry my shirt and put my car into order once again. One can never guess what is to come, next!

I was on the road once again and it started raining. A little later it was pouring and it began to get dark quicker then I had anticipated. When I put the headlights on, I noticed that I was running low on gas. The wipers were hardly able to push the water away from the windshield. I was desperately searching for a gas station. What would I do if I ran out of gas? I was supposed to find Schwabstrasse 191. I had to fight with street names and worry about the dark, I really was frightened. The streets were all deserted. I could hardly see the houses around. The rain made it impossible to read the street names. Then I saw the sign of a gas station. I went in to the side road with hopes rising. There was another car getting fuel. There was nobody else in the gas station. I had gotten out of my car and using my broken German asked the elderly couple how would I get gas. They simply said, "Self service." I had never done that. This time I asked them how to do it. The mean-looking man told me to put in some change and fill the gas. I then remembered that I had no German marks but only dollars with me. With my sweetest voice I asked them kindly to change my dollars. They shook their heads negatively and just drove away. My God! What should I do, now? The rain was pouring and it was getting darker every minute. I was at a gas station but was unable to get any for my car. I was simply walking around my car hoping that some other driver would come and this time the newcomer would be more helpful. Suddenly a miracle happened. The window of a small house on the other side of the petrol station was slit open and I heard a voice calling, "Mrs. Sılan, Frau Sılan." Can anyone believe this? It turned out that Uschi's house was just across the street. I had come to the corner spot without realizing it. In a moment a gentleman (Uschi's husband) with a huge umbrella appeared. He took my keys and told me to go to the house and he would take care of the car. I was really crying with appreciation when I was hugging Uschi. The joy of getting together was mixed with the joy of having myself saved from a dilemma. It was a story that few people would believe. Luck was with me. It certainly was a miracle.

I believe that young woman and I never slept a wink that night. We had so many memories of our times together, so much pain to be shared, so many fun stories to repeat to each other. She had two daughters, Daniela and Jenny. I was hugging them with love as if they were mine. For three days they would not let me go and they treated me regally in their modest house, filled with love. Her husband Jons had not only filled up my car but he also helped me to change some of my dollars to German marks. The rain had stopped and we had enjoyed Stuttgart in fine weather. Uschi's mother, who was alive at the time, also joined some of our outings. They spoiled me to no end.

I was not at all sure where I was heading when I took leave of Uschi and her family. Once again it was with tears that we parted. It was time for me to go. The one thing I knew was that I should catch the Turkish Motor Ferry at Brindisi to be able to return to İzmir. I do not recall the details of my drive from Stuttgart onward but I do know that I stopped in Florence and in Pisa on the way but restrained myself from getting into Rome (a city I adored but could not afford at this time) and instead went into a place called Polignana a Mare, a very small fishing village near Bari. I have never visited such a lovely place again to this day. In the fishing village all the women wore black. They were all Catholics and were very strained. None of them showed the least bit of a festive spirit.

I asked about it and I learned that most of the families had lost a male in the family to the sea—a father, a brother, a son or a husband, and that most of the women would be in mourning most of the time. I remember that someone, in the hope it would bring me solace, had told me this story. There was a dervish who was hungry and he consulted his leader on how to go about it. His master said he could knock on doors and ask for food. However, he admonished by saying, "But you must ask if someone in the house had died recently and you must not accept anything from them if their answer is positive." The poor dervish called on many doors and each time the answer was "yes" and he had to go hungry for days. Finally he went back to his leader and told him his story. The leader then said, "You must share the pain of the people and then you can share their meals." It is true that every family has experienced death one way or another, in this world.

The little village looked superb and most of the houses looked very old. There was a small tourist office and they directed me to a hotel called Grotto Palazzesa. According to local legend the hotel was based on some caves where in the past the corsairs (the pirates) used to hide their treasures. Even where my room was, it looked as if there were hidden places and I was mildly scared. Soon I was in love with the place. It really was a fascinating place and I wondered how the tourist agencies were able to turn even the ugliest places into a wonder. Recently in İstanbul they turned an old prison into a hotel called the Four Seasons. Of course in the morning it was the church bells that awakened me. It was still dark. I was curious, so I got dressed and went out. It was a bustling city. All the women were going to church and the fishermen were boarding their boats. Soon everyone had disappeared. And the boats had left the coast. Nature was the only beauty around.

I stayed there for two nights before getting on the ferry to İstanbul. I had covered more than two thousand kilometers in Europe by myself in my small car. This trip had come as a panacea to me. I had a lot of time to consider my position in life, wonder about who I was and what was I supposed to do with my life. I was really coming nearer to finding my personality. I was becoming a human being once again. A person who could think and who had goals for the future. Last but not least, I must add that my lovely car had done this whole trip without causing me any trouble in all Europe. Then suddenly I had a flat tire, after I had landed at Kartal, İstanbul. It was a big nail and a final trick that my country had played on me.

XXXVIII
Back in İstanbul to Find a Surprise

When I arrived to my father's flat in Maçka a surprise was waiting for me. My lovely daughter Zeyneb in her last letter had written that she was expecting a baby! Father and life in his flat had not changed at all but I no longer cared. It was I who was suddenly changed. Soon I was going to be a grandmother.

A month later Father this time gave me good news. Since many years he had made a habit of going for a physical checkup at the Lahey Clinic in Boston. It was now the time to go and he suggested that I accompany him on this visit and be of use with my knowledge of languages. He had one condition though. He asked me to promise him that I would not desert him half way and that if I gave my solemn word never to leave him alone, he would then take me along to Denver, as well, to visit my daughter. My daughter was expecting her first baby. How could I just go and visit with her and return before she had given birth? But this was a condition that Father insisted upon. If I refused, then he would go by himself. After thinking it over for a while, I decided to accept his offer and promised not to leave him alone during the whole trip. I had not seen my daughter for more than two years. She had gone through difficult times and was now married and was expecting her first child. I had been unable to help her in any way and also had not been able to give her a proper dowry. My beautiful daughter had never complained and had never asked for anything. She had only now informed me that she was expecting, in the seventh month of her pregnancy.

Father had people to make all preparations for passports, visas and tickets and we flew to Boston. Father went into the hospital and I was settled in a boarding house near the hospital. Every morning I would join him at the hospital and take care of his needs. Naturally, the only thing in my mind was to be able to see my daughter as soon as possible. I do not recall anything about father's checkup procedures, most probably it was not fun or easy for me. But that was alright, I had my mind on my child.

Finally we were in Denver. I was able to hug my darling Zeyneb. Sertaç and Zeyneb took us to their home, which consisted of two rooms and a living room. They were living on the first floor of a two-storied house. The building was surrounded by gardens full of flowers and trees. In this very small abode they were able to receive us as guests and my daughter was able to prepare Father's perpetual diet meals without a whisper of protest. They had suffered in the hands of my brother's awful wife. I was to understand that she was making life miserable for Nur and his hands were virtually tied. For a while, she was even able to grasp the money Zeyneb was earning to cover her plane ticket to the States. Because of her, my son-in-law and daughter had to change their house to get away from her insults. My dear daughter was taking care of toddlers in her house until noon and in the afternoon she was knocking on doors as a salesperson marketing Avon products. Sertaç was working as the caretaker for the club belonging to the compound in which they had found this apartment, taking care of the lawn, etc. They seemed to be surviving and people living in the compound seemed to like this young family very much. Despite the fact that they were as poor as mice, they were very generous to us as our hosts. During our visit to Denver we met many of the people who had befriended Zeyneb and Sertaç. Some of them told me about the possibilities of finding jobs in America. This had given me ideas. Especially Boris, who used to work at 47 Restaurant in Ankara and who had cooked for us the New Year's dinner for our first New Year's celebration at our first home. At one point, later on, Boris had suddenly disappeared. It now turned out that Boris had a chance to migrate to America and purely by luck he had met Zeyneb in Denver. As luck would have it, my daughter had met another friend that she knew from Ankara also in Denver, Colorado.

It was time for us to return. Leaving my daughter who was about to give birth by herself in a foreign land was breaking my heart. I tried to reason with Father but he was adamant. He simply said, "Do not forget your promise, I need you as much as your daughter." I had no other choice. I had to adhere to his demands. However, I was beginning to realize that I would not be able to keep on living with him under these conditions. How I wished Mother had been alive, things would have been so different.

Father had planned our return trip long before. We were to fly Denver–Amsterdam–Paris–İstanbul. My old friend Jim Drabbe had already booked us rooms at the Amstel Hotel. While we were there, he and his wife took very good care of us. In Paris we were booked at the hotel called Royale Menceau. Cenan had made a reservation there. I caused quite a commotion at this very expensive hotel. They had given us sumptuous rooms and in the very elegant bathroom I found that they had no shower. I made quite a fuss, since I liked to have a shower after my bath. When I called the manager of the hotel about this problem, he was very concerned and said that another part of the hotel had just gone under renovation and that he would change our suite with another on that part of the building. Sure enough they had showers. I am not sure but I guess we must have spent some three days or so in Paris. Then we flew to İstanbul.

During our long trip coming back I had kept my habit of asking myself the question of what I was to do with my life. As a result, even before our plane touched ground in İstanbul, I had made up my mind. I was going back to the United States of America. With this decision taken, I had relaxed quite a bit. I had made my plans and fixed my way. I might even be there in time for my daughter's delivery!

XXXIX

Rebellion and Escape

A few days after our return from America, at dinner where
Cenan and Bibi were also present, I brought up the subject that
I had decided to go to the States. At first there was a moment
of silence. Then they all started asking questions. First my father asked in a quizzical manner where I would find the money
to go and he added that he certainly was not intending to finance
such a venture. I said I would find a way. Then came the question, "How do you propose to earn your living there?" My answer
was ready. I would apply to my old college, Simmons. I was sure
that their alumnae office would help me find a job. There were
millions of questions and there were many promises for my future if I stayed. I would keep arguing but nothing that anyone
said would make me change my mind. I was going. Frankly,
I had had enough of being handled by others as if I was an
incapacitated person. I believe I would be able to survive. The
important thing was that I believed that I was going to achieve.
I believed in myself.

The very next day I was offering everything I had for sale,
including my car and had applied for a visa to America. I literally
had very little cash in hand. I suddenly realized that I had no
winter clothes to speak of and that Boston would be bitterly cold.
When some of my things were sold, I took out the fur coat my
mother had given me just before she had died and took it to a
furrier that Bibi had introduced to me and had it redone for my
size. I also bought a black skirt and a black sweater. Since the
death of my Ayşe I was wearing only black. In the meantime, I
was trying to do everything Father asked to keep him quiet. He
suddenly sprang something on me. He wanted me to evacuate
the summer house we had used the previous summer. That

meant taking out my belongings from there. Thank God, the Tuzcuoglu firm agreed to take them back into storage. I had my Meissen service plates and some other valuable things, which I did not want to sell, to be packed separately. At the end I was forced to spend hours of work making packages good enough to last for a long time and had everything put into storage. My time was running low and I wanted to go as soon as possible. Finely I was able to empty the house in Vaniköy as Father had asked. I also had some things in my father's house that I had brought from Ankara. I was allowed to leave them where they were. Naturally, this meant a lot of running around and I was in a hurry to reach my daughter.

Cenan and Bibi had finally given up and had accepted the fact that I was going. Father, however, was still trying to cripple my decision. I was adamant. Nothing could stop me. I was very thin and weak, I had no money, but I was going no matter what.

On January 8, 1975 I received the most wonderful news that my first grandchild Seze was born. Both the mother and the baby were safe and in good health. It was Sertaç who gave me the news and I could hear him crying in happiness. This birth had brought me luck. My car was finally sold. I could not be with my daughter during her childbirth but now I would be able to go. I rushed to buy my airline ticket. After some calculation I realized that I could only afford a one-way ticket. Naturally, I had to have some cash on me. If things did not go right and if I could not get a job, how would I be able to return? This question I refered to be answered later on. I mentioned this situation at another family dinner. Nobody gave any reaction. I knew Father was well off and my elder brother had means but it looked as if they were not interested in my affairs. Maybe they did not have enough, I thought. Well, I had made up my mind to go and a one-way ticket would get me to my destination. Whether I would be coming back or not, time would tell. I had planned to finish all formalities and bought an airplane ticket that would take me from İstanbul to London and then to New York–Boston–Denver–Boston. I phoned and told Zeyneb my travel plans and gave her the dates. I also phoned Ömer but I only told him that I would first stop in London and spend two days with him. I did not give Omer any information about my plans of staying in America. After talking things over with him face to face, I would fly to Boston and then to Denver. The date of my departure from İstanbul was to be January 25, 1975.

A few days before I was due to fly the sad news of Leyla Şaman's death came from Ankara, I had neither the time nor the necessary finances to attend her funeral. All I could do was to cry a lot for my dear friend who had passed away rather young. Just a few months ago she was in İstanbul and we were getting together every other day. She was no longer with us. It was certainly a blow for me. Cenan and Bibi had arranged a big farewell party for me and invited all our mutual friends. All the people I liked, living in İstanbul, had been invited. At a rather late hour, as the party was still going strong, I found one of my very old friends in a room all by herself, crying! I knew she had some personal troubles and I was hoping to calm her down by saying something like all things pass, etc. She suddenly said "I am crying because I am jealous that you can take it upon yourself to go off, independent from your family." I certainly was more than shocked! What was there in my position that anyone could envy? I had buried a daughter, lost my marriage, was penniless, without a family and home and now I was going away on a one-way ticket. My friend was saying, "I know all that but you still have the courage to go!" What could I say to her?

After whatever I was able to sell, I had boarded the airplane with a small overnight bag that held all my belongings. I had two pairs of underwear, two pairs of stockings, a black sweater, a black skirt, a second pair of shoes, my night gown, toothbrush and comb, one linen table service, a single set of silver table wear, namely one knife, one fork and one spoon. There were three small silver frames for my children's pictures and one book. I had on another black sweater and skirt, long leather black boots, my mother's revised fur coat and a silk scarf that I had covered my hair with. In my purse I had 200 U.S. dollars, some Turkish lira, my jewelry that I had inherited from my mother and those that were given to me as bridal gifts, an address book, my passport and my one-way ticket. I was certainly going, but how I would return was an unknown factor.

As I had asked him to do, I found my son waiting for me at the Penta Hotel where we had stayed before. He did not even know why I was coming to London. After the excitement of getting to meet my son and hugging him over and over, I started explaining to him what my plans were. I wanted to get his approval for what I was about to do. If he would not accept my conduct, I could possibly turn back. On the contrary, he was very excited. He hugged me again and again and told me that I was doing the right thing and that he would back me all the way and he was certain I would find a job in the United States. Now, I was feeling even more confident that I was doing the right thing. I spent two lovely days with my son in London. I really had no idea when I would be able to see him again. I had paid in advance one year's expenses for him. After that I had no idea what I would be able to do. I put my son on the train to Brighton and went on to Heathrow. After the usual formalities I found myself on the plane flying over London. Many times sadness and happiness can go in hand. I was very sorry to have left my son all by himself and at the same time, the prospect of meeting my daughter soon, was something I was very much looking forward to. I really had no idea what I would be able to do. I was quite confused and also all alone in a great adventure. I had written to Pat, Nur's first wife, who was living in Boston at the time. She was living a little out of town and was working in a real estate office. I had given her my flight details and had asked her to find a decent but cheap room and also to meet me at the airport, if possible. Of course, I had added that if she could not do any of those things I would understand and that I would phone her after landing.

When I got off the plane, my ex-sister-in-law was waiting for me. This was another miracle, after all those years! We were instantly in each other's arms. We had not seen each other for many years. The last time she was in Ankara with her son, John, it was the year 1957 and they had spent only a few days with us. When they had their divorce John was just about one year old. Now I was to learn that John had started his college education! In accordance with what I had written, Pat had found me a room at a motel near where she was living, so we were able to spend that night together and she was to see me off to Denver the next morning. I don't think we had any sleep that night. Before going away I talked to the manager of the motel and

327

realizing that this was both cheap and clean, I made arrangements to return to the same motel in ten day's time. Darling Pat was able to drive me to the airport and see me off. My excitement was growing by the minute. I would soon be hugging my darling daughter and my first grandchild.

XL

My First Grandchild
and a New Kind of Life

Sertaç met me at Denver Airport and took me to their home. When I felt Zeyneb in my arms I could no longer keep my tears. My grandchild Seze was a delightful baby. It was an unbelievable kind of happiness to hug one's grandchild. So lovely, to inhale her baby perfume, to be able to kiss her tiny hands and feet. Instantly I had fallen in love with her.

I had made up my mind to come to America during my first visit to my daughter's house. However, this decision had not included the idea of living with my daughter. I did not want to become a burden to her and her husband. I could probably stay with them and make myself useful by taking care of my grandchild and helping with their house chores. On the other hand, the feelings I had inside me led me to think that it was better for me to be independent and start a career of my own and then be able to be of use to my children. At the time I was very thin, I was afraid that I might fall sick and become a burden to them. I also thought that it was always better to leave a husband and wife by themselves.

At the same time I was quite sure that when I applied to my old college they would be sure to get me a job and that way I would be able to help my children with some financial backing. When I looked at it from a geographical point of view, Boston seemed to be in between Denver and London, thereby I would feel in equal distances to both of my children.

After spending a most enjoyable ten days in Denver, I went back to Boston. My heart was still in Denver but I had made up my mind to start a new life in Boston. I landed at Logan Airport and went straight to my motel. It took 45 minutes to reach the center of the town from there. One had to take the bus first and then the subway. The place was called The Terrace Motel and the address was 1650 Commonwealth Avenue. That is the name of a beautiful avenue that starts in central Boston and goes all the way out and cuts into intersection No. 18 on the Massachusetts Turnpike. The motel was quite a flimsy place but I realized that I could hardly afford any other place. I had spent one night here ten days ago but this was the first time I was really seeing the room I was to stay in. Everything that one expected in a motel room was there. Bed, two armchairs, a table, two chairs and a locker. There was a tiny shower and an even tinier kitchenette. In the kitchenette there was a hot plate, a few glasses and some knives and forks. The room was warm. On the windows there were plastic curtains. The room had wall-to-wall carpeting of a very cheap kind. I put my bag on the side and sat on one of the armchairs. What now? My heart and mind was full of my dear ones who were miles away and here I was on my own and where?

I had to make up my mind and had to act with assurance and fast. I was once again in Boston after 30 years and under very different conditions. This time I was meaning to start a new life for myself. What different kinds of experiences I had had during those last 30 years! Actually, it could be said that I should end my life here, but this was something I could not afford to do, since I was determined to struggle and still be of some use to my children. The pain of my first born would never leave me. However, I had to bury that pain in my heart and look for the future.

Since they had given passengers some sort of an airline meal on the plane I was not hungry. I went to the reception and asked how I would get some coffee. They showed me a coffee machine. You dropped in a coin and something like coffee would pour out. It was more like dishwater. Still, that was what they had. I took a shower, put on my nightgown, while sipping the bad coffee, started thinking and planning for the morning. After a while I had made up my mind. My first destination would be Simmons College.

The first day of my new life! I got up early and got ready to go. I had taken with me my C.V. plus the letter of reference that

330

my Ambassador H. E. Moercid had written. While waiting at the bus stop I had my first shock. There was a big billboard sign that warned residents not to linger alone on the streets about 5:00 P.M. since it would not be safe! Citizens should be careful where they were going, etc. It was something I could not imagine to be true. This was Boston. One of the important cities of the U.S.A. and they were saying that the streets were not safe! I had to take the bus first, then the subway. To get to Fenway I was forced to take another bus. Fenway Park was beautiful under the snow, with the large pond and lots of trees. This place is situated very near Kenmore Square and Commonwealth Avenue. Around there are many college buildings. Some churches and the Boston Conservatory of Music, Emanuel College, Simmons College, Harvard Medical School, Hebrew College, the Museum of Fine Arts, the Isabella Stewart Gardner Museum and so forth are all in this district.

I walked to my old college, as I had done many years ago. I was both remembering things of the past and was in anticipation of the things to come. Everything looked like it was before, nothing had changed much in the past years. I went straight to the Alumnae Office. Many colleges had decided to go co-ed in the past twenty years or so, but Simmons was still a girls' college! In the room I entered there was an elderly matron with glasses. She asked me how she could be of help. I explained my venture, she looked through the files of the graduates and found my name in the class list of 1949. Then she asked me if I had a green card. A green card? This was the first time I had heard of such a thing. Was this a card issued by the school? On the other hand, the matronly lady was as surprised as I was. Who was this Turkish woman who had never heard of green cards? I am sure she thought I must have landed from the moon! She was patient enough to explain to me that according the laws of the land, anyone who wanted to find employment in the United States had to obtain a green card, otherwise they would be prohibited from being employed. Well, how could I obtain this green card? She told me that either a company who would be willing to hire me would have to get one for me, or maybe if I started some sort of a business in America I could get such a card. Lastly, I could employ a lawyer to get a card for me but that of course would take time and cost a lot. The lady said that she was very sorry but there was nothing that she could do for me. So that was the end of our conversation., All my hopes were lost! I did not know what to do!

Since there was nothing I could do there, I went out and decided to visit the Isabella Stewart Gardner Museum, to sort of refresh my memory and in a way compose myself. Since I was no longer a student, they even asked me for a charge, which I had to pay. I sat on a bench near the flower beds. I was saying to myself, there must be something I could do. I was crying at the same time. These were tears of hopelessness.

Despite everything, it was lovely to be there once again. After resting for a while, I got up and began walking toward the center of the city. My first idea was to have the pictures I had taken in Denver (of my daughter and granddaughter) developed. So I went into the first photo shop that I came across. The owner was a short and stocky fellow with a dark moustache. He had to fill in a card and therefore asked for my name. When my answer was Sılan, something he could not recognize. He asked me about my nationality. When I said Turkish I thought all hell had broken loose. He was livid. He was waiving his arms in the air, shouting, "You are a murderer! You have killed my father, my mother, etc." I was totally taken aback. I was shouting back, "I killed no one" but at the same time I was able to grasp my negatives and ran out of that shop. He was still shouting after me, "Murderers, you Turks you are all murderers. You have killed all the Armenians," and I was running!

All my life I had never made any differentiation according to creed or nationality. In our house no one bothered with such discrimination. We had lots of friends of different nationalities or origins or religions. As far as we were concerned they were Turkish nationals of Armenian and/or Greek descent, and that was all there was to it! Why was this man so full of hatred? What kind of luck had taken me to his shop? I felt very sad. I felt awful. I went into the first drugstore I came across and asked for some hot coffee. I was trying to pull myself together and also get my feet away from the snow. Walking on snow-covered sidewalks had looked like fun in the beginning but gradually my feet were getting wet all the way. On my way back, I bought some coffee, bread, cheese and milk, then realizing that I would need hot water to make coffee, I also bought a water heater. I walked to the subway station, after all, I knew my whereabouts in Boston. I had lived here in the past.

By the time I reached my warm room in the motel my teeth were chattering. My morale was even worse, sub zero. I warmed some water and made myself a cup of coffee. After resting a while I thought of Pat. I called her and asked her if she could make enquiries about how I could get a green card. She too was surprised. For many years she had had no dealings with non-Americans and had no idea about green cards, either.

I had bought a paper on the way back. I sat and read through the wanted ads. *The Boston Globe* had many pages. Perhaps I could find some place that would not bother with a green card. I called one or two places but each time they recognized that I had an accent (they all thought I was French) and immediately asked if I had a green card. Towards dusk Pat came in. From the way she looked I could understand that she did not have good news for me. She started by saying that getting a green card was a very difficult thing. While talking with her, the word Kiefer popped up into my mind. Dr. Kiefer was the head physician at Lahey Clinic where Father used to go for his checkups every year. He was retired now, however, a few months ago Dr. and Mrs. Kiefer had invited us to their home for the weekend. They both liked Father and over long years of patient-doctor relations they had developed a good friendship. Mrs. Kiefer was a very warm-hearted woman. Perhaps they could be of help. I called them. Someone else answered the phone and I was told that they were out of town and would return to Boston at the end of February. Pat tried to calm me down a bit and suggested that I should visit the specialty shops in the richer parts of the city, to look for a vacancy, and left.

That night I wrote a letter to Nezih and Fazilet Manyas. They were friends of the family. I wrote them about my condition and asked if they could help me in any way or give me some ideas about getting a green card. The next morning I went back to Boston. First I mailed the letter I had written the night before. Then I went toward Berkeley Street where most of the elegant stores were situated. First I went into Rodier. The sales girls were happy to see a customer with an accent. When I explained why I was there, they all showed pity. Two of them were of French origin but they had obtained their green cards by marrying Americans. No one could find a job without it in a proper store. That was a bit of news. So one could get a card through marriage! I had finished the shops on Berkeley Street with no luck at all. I was beginning to lose my nerve. How had I come all the way here with no knowledge of the conditions I would have to face. What was I to do? I returned to my dismal motel before 5:00 P.M. I was wet and cold. I got a hot shower to get my circulation going and jumped into my bed to get warm. When it became dark and I began to feel hungry, I got up and had some bread with cheese and some warm milk. I went through the daily papers once again. Maybe I should be lucky the next time? Perhaps!

Now my schedule was made up. In the morning it was Newburry Street this time. In the window of a small restaurant I saw an ad, they were looking for a woman to do the dishes. They were quite surprised that this tiny woman in a fur coat was asking for a position as dishwasher. I told them I did not mind as long as I had a job. They were skeptical about it but in any case a green card was again a must! I was really getting desperate. That night at the motel I wrote a letter to my children. One in Brighton, the other in Denver. I told them that I was doing fine and wished them well. Was not life a game, anyway!

When I woke up the next morning, I had no other choice. I would try as much as I could. I decided to wander a bit on the parts of Boston that I had enjoyed in the past. I went to the public gardens at the beginning of Commonwealth Avenue. I shared my slice of bread with the squirrels. Seeing and enjoying some beauty had given me some strength. Anyway, these things were free, as the well known Turkish poet used to say. Weather was free, beauty was free, etc.

Every day I walked along the streets. Boylston Street, Federal Street, Beacon Hill and even Cambridge. I was doggedly looking for a job. Some days I would stroll by Charles River and remember my happy youth with my mother and my brothers in this city. The apartment building where we had stayed with

Mother was now taken over by M.I.T. and turned into a dormitory. Despite the winter and the snow on the ground, ducks were swimming in the river and Harvard students were roving. What was missing on account of the weather were the canoes. February was coming to its end. For me, the days had become a repetition of the same thing, day after day. I would spend the whole day looking for a job and return to my motel room frozen and more hopeless then the day before. I would read the wanted ads and write down the addresses that looked promising, would eat a boiled egg or a slice of bread and go to bed exhausted. Unfortunately, I could never sleep a good night's sleep either. After the loss of my Ayşe my sleeping habits had become very topsy-turvy. I was having nightmares and would wake up in the middle of the night, usually in tears. I still am prone to these hallucinations now and then.

One night going through the ads in the paper I saw something that looked interesting. They were looking for "Elegant, well-dressed ladies, possibly of foreign extraction, who could speak several languages." As soon as I was up, I started to get dressed and was ready to go. However, I had to force myself to wait until 10 A.M. When I told the man on the phone that I did not have a green card, he simply said, "No need for it." I started for the address given. The man on the phone had said he would like to see me before he would give particulars on the job. It took almost an hour on the bus but I finally was there. From the outside the building did not look at all appealing! I opened the door and was faced with a long and steep stairway. I was almost breathless when I rang the bell. A rather heavy man opened the door for me. The shirt he had worn over his trousers was only halfway buttoned. His furry and suntanned chest was there for all to see. He had a golden necklace around his neck. There was a big office table and a few chairs in the room I had entered. On the table were a number of phones and lots of clips with notes scribbled all over. Neither the man nor the details of the room looked at all "elegant." He told me to sit. Asked about my nationality and why I did not have a green card. Finally he said, "I guess you can fit the sort of job we have." Naturally, I asked what the job involved. He sort of leered and said, "You will escort our out-of-town friends at dinner." I suddenly understood that

335

the job offered was to act as an escort. In other words, this was an "escort service" that I had come across advertised in some magazines. I was horrified. I suddenly jumped up and said, "I must have dropped my purse on the way" and before he could even get up from his seat, I dashed out of the room. I was running like mad. As if he might come after me. I found myself at the bus station. I was shaking like a leaf. What had I done? Where was I? I was lucky, a bus came at that moment and I jumped in. No one was coming after me! Yet tears were running down my cheeks. I hated everything. I wished I were dead. I could not stop my tears. What kind of a life was I destined to lead? How lucky I had not given that awful man my address and phone number.

It took me some days to get over this experience. When I felt a little better I again called on the Keifers. This time I was lucky. They had returned to Boston. I asked them to join me at my hotel room for dinner the next night. They accepted to come. I went and bought some chicken pieces, rice, some iceberg lettuce and a cooking pan. I spent most of the day working with the hot plate and made some sort of a chicken and rice meal. Since there were not enough chairs or a table to sit around we would be forced to eat from our plates, on our knees. I placed all the plates, etc. on the single table and waited for my guests. They arrived, as agreed, at 5:00 P.M. with a pot of flower in their hands. I guess they must have thought that I was staying at a posh place, as we used to do when we came with Father. That daughter of an ex-member of parliament that they used to know was now living in extremely different conditions. I could see from their expression how surprised they were. Naturally, they were forced to come in and say hello, etc. Then I told them my miserable story. I told them that I was especially trying to go on my own and not bother Father. I had received a good education and that should be enough. Now, I had to work and earn my living. They were very contrite and sorry to realize the condition I was in. Then we discussed other topics and nibbled our meal. They had become a little more sociable again. Then I approached the subject of finding a job. For example, I could do some typing for someone and charge less then the regular typists. Their answer was simple.

They had both retired. Most of their friends had also retired and hardly had any writing job.

I came up with another suggestion. I could accompany someone who was bedridden and needed constant attention, such a job would not necessarily require a green card. I could also work as a nanny. Well, their grandchildren were living in faraway cities. In America lonely and old people usually went into a "home" where they were taken care of by professionals. So, they could not be of any help. They must have realized my predicament. In my old days I would be inviting them to a restaurant and would not be offering such a miserable dinner in a rundown motel room. I had prepared coffee for them. As we were having coffee, Mrs. Kiefer started telling me about an incident that had taken place some years ago. "A few years ago, I had met a lady called Samia. She was from Egypt. Some difficult conditions similar to yours had forced her to immigrate and she was running a shop on Newberry Street. Maybe that lady could steer you to some position. Maybe you could look her up." The old lady could not even remember what the shop was called. Good old Mrs. Kiefer! After they had gone I remembered my mother's childhood friend from Ecole Francais at Ortaköy, Aunt Anahit! She was very happy to hear my voice. She had a house on Roxberry. Her tale of woe was almost as bad as mine. Poor woman had first lost her husband and then her daughter. We shared memories of old times on the phone and I did not have the courage to ask for her help.

XLI

A Ray of Hope

My first thought when I woke up was that I should look up this lady called Samia. It was a miserably cold winter morning. My shoes were getting worn out from constant treading on the pavements. On top of this, these were the only boots I could use on the snow-covered streets. I really ought to have bought myself a pair of woolen socks. I wish I had thought about that in Turkey. It would have been so much cheaper. I started from one end of Newburry Street, knocking on doors and asking if this was the shop owned or managed by a lady called Samia. Every once in a while, when the cold was too much to bear, I would go into a coffee shop, to warm myself a bit with some hot coffee and also continue to make enquiries. Usually the coffee served would be very weak, almost undrinkable. It was getting dark and I was freezing. I had covered the full street on both sides. I went into the last shop. An elderly gentleman suddenly said, "Oh! I remember Samia. I believe she sold her shop some time ago. She was a good woman." Then, when he saw how miserable I looked when I had heard that she was gone, he felt pity and added, "If it is so important for you, she now lives a little further away, on number such and such. She is now married and her name has become Samia Fisher." I thanked the old gentleman and started walking toward this address. I found the place! I walked up to the second floor. The door of the apartment was open and a man who had climbed on a ladder was nailing something on the wall. When he saw me coming he climbed down and said something like "Is there anything I can do for you?" My teeth were chattering and my strength was almost at end. I was barely able to ask, "Does Samia live here?" and I was shivering. The gentleman said, "Yes, this is her house, but first you must come in and have

338

something hot to drink." I was just about to collapse. He took me in, made me sit on a couch and gave me a glass of cognac. Just as I was beginning to pick myself up a bit, a small, dark-skinned woman came into the room where I was sitting. As I was trying to get up to meet her, she pushed me down from my shoulders and said, "Don't get up, you may not be up to it. Why were you looking for me? Yes, I am Samia." I could not stop the tears flowing from my eyes. Finally I had found Samia! Next, I found a very hot cup of tea in my hands. My leaking boots had made a little pool where I sat. The man, I later learned to be Samia's husband, leaned down and pulled them off my feet and he left the room. We were left by ourselves. I started telling my story. Samia was very patient. She listened to the end. Then she began to tell me her story. Years ago she had been married to a man in Egypt. Her husband had started to beat her and be mean to her. Whenever she threatened to divorce him, he would say that she would never be able to see her son again. So the poor woman had run away from Egypt to Boston. Her mind was always on her son. She naturally did not have a green card either. One day in the subway, she was crying by herself when an elderly and well-dressed gentleman showed interest in her plight. He turned out to be the dean of Brandeis University. After listening to her tale of woe he had asked her if she could help classify the books in Arabic at the University Library and Samia became an assistant librarian. While she was working there she met her present husband. They were able to start the shop on Newberry Street on their own and Samia was finally able to bring her son to America. Now they had both retired and sold their shop.

I begged her to help me find a job. She sadly said, "Since we have retired we are not really seeing anyone." However, she promised to call me if she would hear of anything and took my address and telephone number. I had caused them enough trouble for one afternoon. I thanked them for their kindness and left. Was this a ray of hope? That night I spent the whole night half awake. Despite my utter exhaustion it was impossible to sleep. The people who were staying in the motel were rather questionable types. There were disquieting noises all night through. I really should get out of this hell hole. What kind of life had I been forced into?

I must have finally fallen asleep since I woke up with Pat's telephone call, in the morning. She told me that she had found a room for me. We agreed to meet. She took me to a house on Commonwealth Avenue. I used to like that avenue very much in the past. The building was No. 26 on that beautiful avenue. It was an old mansion that had been turned into a number of apartments. These were the residences of old families which had been converted into flats or rooms for rent. We went up to the second floor. It was actually a big and comfortable room. The whole room had wood paneling and a huge fireplace. In front there was a sort of three-window frontage (a bay window) overlooking the avenue. In the old days it was probably the main bedroom of the master of the mansion. They had added a tiny bathroom and toilet, there was also a small kitchenette. It certainly had a beautiful view of the avenue. Apparently they had started as a rooming house and later changed these rooms into single flats. Pat was involved in the real estate business and had found this place for me to rent. The rent was $225 a month and they wanted me to sign a lease for two years! I had fallen in love with the place. However, even the money I had had was already dwindled. I thought of selling some of my jewelry. Then I remembered that I had some gold coins that would bring in some cash. I wanted to save my jewelry for my children. Well, where and how could I sell my gold coins? Pat said there was a diamond center in New York where one could sell them. I was also asking about the conditions of the lease. Pat explained that I had to pay cash for the first month and also a deposit that would be equal to a month's rent. I was not sure if my gold coins would fetch $450. Pat said she might delay the payment of the deposit for some weeks and that I should not miss this change. She was right. This was a Godsend as far as I was concerned. On the other hand, suppose I could find no job and I could not pay the rent in the coming months? What would happen? Would they force me to evacuate and perhaps kick me out of the country! Was there anything I could do to prevent such things? I had nothing more to lose anyway! I had to do something and I had

340

to get out of that miserable motel. I decided to take the apartment. I thanked Pat and took the first bus to New York, right away. I was able to sell my gold coins and return to Boston by the night train. I was back in my motel room for the last time. I phoned Pat and told her I had the first month's rent in cash, as she wanted. She too was glad on my score and told me to meet her at the flat the next morning. So the next morning, I packed my overnight bag, settled my account at the motel and made a beeline for my new apartment.

XLII

A New Abode—A New Beginning

It must have been the beginning of March. That day I signed the two years' lease and paid the first month's rent. I entered the room. The room (or the flat) was now mine! I cannot say that I had moved in, since all I had was what I had in my overnight bag. However, renting houses or flats in America has a very good side to it, since all places for rent automatically include things like kitchen ovens, refrigerators, some sort of shades (at least venetian blinds) and central heating, plus running hot and cold water. As a matter of fact it would be difficult to find a place without central heating (even if you wanted to). The other wonderful thing was the facility with which one could get a phone installed. You rang the company up and in a few hours they would come and connect you. Electricity would be connected anyway. All I needed was a bed and some pillows. Before night fell, Pat was able to bring me a mattress, sheets, a blanket and some pillows and towels. My phone was already attached. That night Pat and I shared a bottle of cheap wine and ended up by having a party of wine and cheese on my mattress. What a wonderful thing it was "to have a room of one's own." No wonder the famous English writer, Virginia Woolf, went on about this subject for so long.

The first thing I did the next morning was to look out at the avenue from my second floor windows. It was a wonderful scene. Almost like in a movie. There were high trees full of leaves and lots of squirrels running up and down. A little to my right I could see the Public Gardens and the bridge across the pond. I could not believe that this was my view now! I really was in a beautiful situation. For the first time in my life I had settled in a place of my own and it was wonderful. Yes, I had only rented it but it

342

was mine anyhow. Mine and no one else! I wonder how many people would know of that feeling. I made my coffee and I pulled the phone toward my mattress and first of all I called Samia. I wanted to inform her of my change of address and give her my new phone number. As soon as I spoke she recognized my voice and said, "I have been trying to reach you for two days now, where have you been?" After I explained everything she gave me a phone number to call for a possible job opening. My God! Was my luck changing at last. I called the number at once and asked for Mr. Ray Baldwin. A secretary told me to wait a little, probably talked to her boss and told me to be at Mr. Baldwin's office at 11:50 A.M. and that Mr. Baldwin would only have ten minutes for me. The address she gave me was on Federal Street, which was the business section of the town and somewhat far from my apartment. So I quickly got dressed and got out of the house. I reached Mr. Baldwin's office at exactly 11:45 A.M. Five minutes later the secretary took me to Mr. Baldwin's office and left me there. He was quite a handsome man, impeccably dressed. He shook my hand. His face was rather difficult to assess. One could see no movement or any kind of lines anywhere, his cheeks, his eyebrows, etc. All seemed as if they were frozen. Just the brilliant blue eyes that seemed to pierce you. His thin lips hardly moving, he asked me to sit. I had given him my C.V. and other documents. He looked through them and asked me questions.

After a few minutes, he got his secretary on the intercom and asked her to cancel his luncheon appointment. He then asked me to take off my coat and settle for a long conversation. He said he wanted to know all about me. And by his leading questions I found I was telling him my full life story from my earliest childhood to the day. After a while he also talked about himself and his family. He was of British extraction and his family had landed in Plymouth in the legendary *Mayflower* in 1620. He was a Republican and apart from his business interests he was also working for the Republican Party. His elder brother was a general who had been at the head of the NATO in Turkey. Their mother had visited the general in Izmir and she had liked the Turks very much. He himself had a great esteem for Atatürk and Turkey. He had met Samia and her husband through the connection of his friend, the dean of Brandeis University. He had heard of me from them. He said the Taiwanese ambassador had been looking for a private secretary and since everyone knew the Taiwanese were no longer represented at the United Nations, the Ambassador at present was ranked as a consul general. "Now that I have met you and learned of your capacities, I shall inform his excellency and refer you to him. If he is still looking for someone, I am sure you will be invited for an interview." This had turned out to be a wonderful meeting I was very happy. Mr. Baldwin also promised to ring me if some other possibility occurred. Thanking him, I left his office.

I was somewhat excited by this interview so I walked all the way to Boston Commons. The air was cold but dry. This walk was not enough. I went through the Public Gardens as well. I realized that I was now facing the Ritz-Carlton Hotel. A few houses away was my new mansion! Remembering my better days I decided to go into the hotel lobby. I walked around and went into their bookstore and bought myself the daily paper. Then I walked a few meters further, went up three steps and opened the huge wooden door of the building where I was now residing. I had not really looked around until this time. The entrance hall was huge and covered with wall-to-wall carpeting. In this hall there was a big, long, antique-looking table. The mail for the tenants was placed on this table and people picked their own. There was a wide staircase, also carpeted. I went up these stairs. Some of the steps gave small whispering sounds as old wooden stairs are bound to do. I put my key in the lock and opened the big door. Finally I was in my home. This was my room. I had lived in so many different and so much more elegant houses in the past but never before in a flat that I could call my own! This was my own. This one-room flat with very high ceilings had given me a degree of satisfaction that I had never had before. I had always lived in someone else's place, belonging to someone. But this place was mine. And it belonged only to me.

First I went over the day's happenings in my mind. Then I called Samia and Pat in that order, repeated my good news and thanked them once again for their help. I then went out again and returned after doing some shopping for food and deposited all that I had bought in the fridge. Now it was time to write letters. I wrote about my new apartment and about my hopes for a job, etc. I was naturally showing a rosy picture of my life in Boston. I did not want to cause anxiety on my behalf. Both my children had enough worries of their own. Then I was placing the pictures of my children over the fireplace. Suddenly my eye caught the ornate full mirror over the fireplace. Who was this strange looking woman that was staring at me in the mirror? Was this really me, so thin and blank!

The next day I was job hunting once again. However, I was no longer going too far and kept returning to my flat, afraid that I might miss a possible phone call. My house was in the hub of the town. Newberry, Boylston, Berkeley Streets were all around Commonwealth Avenue at this juncture. This avenue is probably the best looking one in town. It starts from Arlington Street next to the park called the Public Gardens and goes into Massachusetts Avenue by the Harvard Bridge that crosses over the Charles River. This is a well-recognized area in Boston, commonly referred to as the Back Bay Area.

During one of these days I received a letter from Nezih Manyas. He was answering the letter I had written. He was neither kind nor pleasurable. Fazilet (his wife) and he had been very sorry to learn about my misfortunes. However, they did not think I had done the right thing by coming to the States in this manner. All the qualities I claimed to have had would hardly be of use to me. Everybody in the States spoke English and many had second languages. Similarly, almost everyone had a college degree. As to typing, even high school kids wrote their reports on a typewriter in America. At the end, his advice was that I should pack up and return to Turkey. I thought a lot about what he had written. In many ways he was right. This got my already low morale lower. On the other hand I knew I was taking a chance and I wanted to see what I could do, come what may! I had nothing to lose.

The day this letter came (it was addressed to Pat and she had added my new address on the envelope) I decided that I should do something to boost my morale. I decided to go to a movie. I would take a bus on Boylston Street, travel a bit on the bus in order to get to a movie house that would cost less than the others. The weather was bright. The John Hancock Building

345

that the Japanese architect. I. M. Pei had designed and the Christian Science Church were all on this street. As I was walking around I saw a sign that said "Café Florian." I had a lot of time for the movie I had chosen to see. So I went into this elegant café and asked for a "café au lait" and a croissant. The young girl who was serving was interested in my accent and asked me if I was French. We automatically started to speak in French. When I told her I was Turkish, her interest doubled. She said she had never met a Turk before and went on to explain that she was herself an American of Swedish descent and her boy friend was of Greek extraction. She kept saying, "You look so French!" Then she asked me where I was staying and when I gave her my address she was very excited, she said, "I live only a few doors away from your building. I like you a lot. If you will agree, I would like to visit you one of these days." I too had suddenly warmed up to this nice person. She was much younger than I, beautiful, intelligent and civilized. A little later a gentleman who was sitting a few tables away from me, paid his bill and got up to go. When he took a few steps I realized that he could not see and was following the specially trained dog that he had with him. He looked quite normal and the way he had carried on a conversation with his friends, sharing the same table, one could hardly understand that he was blind. He had paid his bill very naturally. I felt pity for him but at the same time I appreciated the way he was able to act so normally.

Sometime later I also paid my bill and left the restaurant and boarded a bus that arrived shortly. I sat on the first available seat. Suddenly I realized that the blind man I had seen in the café had the seat next to me. I supposed he must have walked a bit and then had taken the bus one stop before me. The man must have felt that I was caressing his dog. He said, "He is my seeing dog. Isn't he a charming animal?" I concurred that his dog was lovely and asked, "Were you born this way or did you lose your eyesight later in life?" The young gentleman suddenly started to tell his story. He had been diabetic and some years ago he had been in an auto accident. He had lost both his wife and young son in that accident. His pain coupled with his sickness had caused him the loss of his eyesight. After a long while he was now getting accustomed to lead a normal life with the aid of his Seeing Eye dog. His story gave me such pain that I was ashamed of myself for thinking my troubles were great! He asked where I was from. Without recounting my plight I only gave him my nationality. The young man was somehow able to reach out, grabbed my hand and kissed it. He said, "I do not know how to thank you. Most people shy away when they realize I am blind. You asked me directly and gave me the chance to unburden myself." I could no longer hold my tears. He wanted to get off a few more stations before my movie house. He asked me to help him to get off the bus. Of course I did as I was asked. When the bus started I looked back, he was waving toward me. I remembered a saying in Turkish, "I listened to the woe of others and preferred my own." This chance encounter had affected me very much. I think I did see the movie I had chosen but I cannot recall what it was about. Actually, I left halfway. My mind was elsewhere. I was back in my room and in my loneliness.

I just could not find a job! It did not look like I would find something either. One night, sitting by myself, I wrote a letter of farewell to my children asking them to forgive me for what I was about to do. I also asked them to have me cremated and to send my ashes to İstanbul to be buried in Ayşe's tomb. Thus they would be saved from expenses. I had bought a bottle of aspirin and a small bottle of whisky during the day. So I started to swallow the pills with the whisky. I was beginning to get somewhat drowsy then there came a knocking on my door. At first I did not care. However, the knocking became louder and more insistent. Then a woman started calling, "Mrs. Sılan, please open the door, this is Barbara." Somewhat drowsily I obeyed, stood up and opened the door. It was the lovely young woman I had met at the café the other day. She had a package in her hand. She left it on the floor and forced me to go into the bathroom. She washed my face. I was beginning to come to my senses. The poor girl had understood what I was doing but had said nothing but made sure to make me vomit what I had swallowed. By chance she had bought some wine and some cheese and thought she would drop in for a chat. She was an angel sent to save me! What a great sin it was! How I could even think of doing such a thing! From that day on Barbara (Karras) became a great friend of mine. Furthermore, she was the first person to suggest that I should write my memoirs. This failed attempt of suicide was the one and only thing that I could hardly forgive myself for even having attempted. How could a mother of two children even contemplate such a horrible thing? Even as I am writing these lines, I feel ashamed of myself.

On March 30 I was awakened by the ringing of my phone. Again I had not been able to sleep that night. A woman's voice on the phone said, "Mr. Baldwin would like to speak with you," and Mr. Baldwin was on the phone. He told me that he had been in touch with the Taiwanese Consul General and that he wanted to see me. Could I please call on the consul general (ambassador) that morning at 11:00 A.M. Their office was at 934 Statler Office Building. I thanked him and told him that I would be there at the appointed hour. I was very excited and got ready to go. It was not far away from where I was staying, so I had walked there. I was able to reach my destination at 10:55 A.M. The Consul General's office was on the fifth floor. A young Chinese gentleman opened the door for me and took me to the Ambassador's office. His Excellency Shih-ying Woo was a stocky but tall man. Standing in his office with his hair half receding, he showed me a seat. He was extremely well-dressed and looked like a perfect gentleman with naturally slanted eyes. After I was seated, he took his seat. He told me about Mr. Baldwin's letter to him and asked a few questions about my past which he considered important. After answering these questions I gave him my letter of recommendation that Ambassador Moersid had written and my C.V. He read both documents very carefully. Then he started to say something like "I am sorry Mrs. Sılan—" when I thought I would die. I was about to lose my last chance! But still, come what may, I was waiting for him to finish his words with a rueful smile, he was going to say something like "you do not fit." However, the Ambassador finished his sentence by saying, "Under the circumstances, we can only afford to pay you 500 dollars a month. If you can accept our offer we shall be delighted. Naturally, we will handle the question of your work permit for you." I encountered this by saying, "Your Excellency, I am honored that you are offering me a chance to work for you. I am very honored to have been accepted," and I tried to reach for his hand, in order to kiss it. Being the perfect gentleman, he quickly took my hand in his and said, "I hope you can start work on April 1." I said, "Your Excellency, if you will excuse my premonitions I would rather start a day early, on March 31, so that this may not turn into an April Fool's Day affair. Naturally, I would not ask for any extra compensation for the extra day." The elderly gentleman smiled benevolently and said, "In this case we shall be expecting you at 9:00 A.M. tomorrow. My councellor will now take you around the office and explain the work that will be expected of you as my executive secretary." I spent some minutes with the counsellor and went out. Once in the street I literally sat on the pavement. I do not know whether I was laughing or crying. I had almost spent my last dollars. I had signed a lease for two years and I had no idea what was going to happen to me and now I had a job and a salary! Suddenly there was a bright future ahead of me. It looked like things would be different from now on. The predictions of Nezih Manyas would no longer be applicable. Despite the fact that everyone could type and everyone spoke English, I had finally found a job! Yes, this mature, correct Turkish woman, after so many hardships, thanks to her perseverance seemed to have found herself a job. Since the job I found was in a foreign representation, the question of having a green card no longer made a difference. What I have never been able to understand was why a friend of my family and generally a decent man, Mr. Manyas, had given me such a negative answer? For example, he could have very easily suggested that I should apply to foreign representations where work permits would not be a problem. Well, he had not thought of that, I guess. The help had come via an Egyptian lady and a Republican gentleman!

As soon as I returned home I started making plans and calculations. My salary would be paid at the end of April. I had in hand only 270 dollars left from the sale of the gold coins. If I paid the deposit expected from me, I would have only 45 dollars left until I got my first paycheck. This sounded rather slim but I was sure to handle it. Once I had my 500 dollar paycheck, I would be able to settle my rent and meet other expenses. I was no longer hopeless! Electricity and phone bills would not be excessive. In short, I was safe. In a short while I would be able to help my children, as well.

Thinking over these things brought to my mind an incident that had taken place only a while ago. I was still hopeless and looking for a job. Pat had called and asked me to go out with her. Her boss had an out-of-town business friend and they wanted to have dinner. It was a simple dinner invitation. Naturally, I said "No." I was in no mood to go out and make polite conversation. However, Pat was very insistent. She said this was important for her and she was depending on my help. Naturally, I had to agree. She had been helping me so much for such a long time that it would not do to refuse her one request. So that evening at 19:00 hours they picked me up from my apartment. They were in a luxurious car. In it, apart from Pat's boss, there was also a Jewish gentleman. We went to one of those famous steak houses. I had not been eating proper dinners for years now and did not feel at all hungry. The restaurant was a very big place, situated on several floors and it was packed.

We were seated at their previously reserved table. Soon they had placed huge plates in front of us. The others had really gone to work on their steaks with relish. I had been able to cut a few chunks which I could hardly chew. Realizing that I was not eating, they were concerned and they asked if I wanted something else. I said I was not hungry and they said, "That is all right you can have a doggy bag." My immediate reaction was, "But I do not have a dog." They all laughed and Pat's boss said "It will be for the cat then." I was still insisting that I did not have a cat either. In the meantime they were all making jokes about my prim behaviour. Anyway, the meal over they drove me back to my house. Pat gave me a brown paper bag and they said good-bye. I had thought Pat had brought me some towels that she knew I needed. However, once in the flat I saw that it was really the remains (or almost all) of my steak. I felt ashamed, but I put it in the icebox anyway. I called Pat up to let her know about the piece of meat and how ashamed I was. She was really laughing and telling me that this was something very much done these days. How many customs had changed during the thirty years I was away! It was only the next day that I had realized what a wonderful gift it was. I made sandwiches by cutting slices of the good steak and it lasted almost a week.

When I finished my calculations, I made phone calls to Samia, Pat and Mr. Baldwin to share my appreciation and reiterate my thanks. I also called on Mrs. Kiefer, who by remembering the name of the Egyptian lady, had accidentally saved my life. The Kiefers were very excited about the whole story and asked me to dinner to hear all about it. They took me to a nice restaurant and wanted me to tell the whole story in every detail. They probably had felt that I had pestered them for help and now they were relieved.

Then came the time for phone calls to Zeyneb and Ömer. We all cried with joy and shrieked with happiness. None of us could believe in this miracle. They were congratulating me for my courage. Now I was so much sure of myself. From now on I should be looking forward and not to the past.

Naturally, that was the decision of that day. Presently I am neither looking back nor to the future. The important thing for me now, is to live the day. Being constructive and creative is the only wish I have. I enjoy loving the people around me. This is happiness for me. How I wish to get over the frights of my past days.

Before I went to work the next morning I met Pat and gave her the advance rent I owed her. I also called Barbara and gave her the good news. I had hardly slept that night. I was too happy. At 9:00 A.M. in the morning I reported to work. Apart from the Ambassador, there were twelve Taiwanese men and one woman working in the office. So with me added, we were two females, totaling 14 employees. Everyone in the consulate was very kind and tolerant. I must add that I never heard an unkind word in that office during all the time I worked there.

From the first day of my employment they made a point of taking me out for lunch. One of them would be sure to ask me in the morning. Of course they used to take me to Chinese restaurants, but they never allowed me to pay for the meal. Not even to go Dutch, in the American sense of the word. The ambassador and Mrs. Woo also made a point of inviting me to their home for dinner, at least twice a month. Mrs. Woo was a wonderful hostess and a very refined and beautiful lady. She, like all others in the office, was fluent in English. The kind of Chinese food she served was out of this world.

351

I shared a big room with the lady counsellor, Jacky (Jacqueline Hu Yen), the other female in the office. There was one other counsellor, Dr. Yih Min Lin, who it turned out had done his doctorate in Ankara and had worked with Prof. Bahattin Ögel for his Ph.D. on Middle Eastern languages. His Turkish turned out to be perfect. Now and then he would come to our room and spoke Turkish with me. I enjoyed my work very much. Since I was working as the private secretary of the Ambassador, I had to report only to him and I was proud to have this responsibility.

On my first weekend I decided to take a walk. My boots were leaking and I was putting on woolen socks and once in the office, I would change into one single pair of shoes that I had. It was spring now, but showers came always unexpectedly. As I was walking along I was also looking if I could spot a cheap pair of shoes. I must have walked quite a while. Suddenly I saw three red painted chairs with their seats torn. They were just thrown to the street! I checked to see if there was anything wrong with them. Then, one by one, I carried them home. I was pretty tired but I could not help it. Then I went out again, first I went to a chemist and bought some Lysol and some cotton. Then I went to a hardware store and bought some sandpaper. I had completely forgotten my need for shoes. I was happily sandpapering my new chairs when Pat called on the phone. When I told her what I was doing she could not help saying, "By God, Şen, you were the last person I would have thought that would collect used furniture from the street and do such work!" I told her I was very happy doing what I was doing and that my chairs would look great very soon. I also added that I was learning a new profession.

Sunday morning I walked into the Ritz-Carlton, bought the Sunday paper and came back. In America Sunday papers have lots of additions therefore are quite heavy to carry, but I did not mind carrying it. Now I was quite relaxed. No more worries about a green card. I also knew when my next paycheck would be coming. This was my first Sunday morning in a long time, when I could relax and feel content. There was no one to wake me up. I did not have to account for my actions to anyone. I did not have to look over the "Wanted" ads anymore or walk the pavements knocking on doors. I was enjoying my first Sunday.

It was raining outside and I was going to write letters to my children and tell them about my new life. I would enjoy my freedom.

During the week I had visited the Boston Public Library, registered myself as a member and taken out some books. That night I was reading one of them when I heard sirens on the street. It was 10:00 P.M. at night. The noises began to rise. When I looked out from my window, the fire engines were almost in front of our house! Soon someone banged on my door and shouted, "Everyone must evacuate the building." I was undressed. So quickly I put on my fur coat, took my passport and my bag that contained my jewels and rushed out. Frankly, I was glad that the fire was in the house two doors away from our building and only a part of that house's chimney was ablaze. It was wonderful to notice how calm everyone was. The fire fighters were busy with their work and we were quietly looking on. The rain started and I realized that I had come out in my slippers. Everyone was quite calm. In less then two hours the fire had stopped and we were allowed to return to our flats. As soon as I returned to my flat I rang up Barbara, since she was a neighbour also. Thank God. She was safe and her house was not involved in the fire that had taken place on our street.

Before going to U.S. I had called on my childhood friend Erol Simavi who was now the owner and boss of one of the biggest newspapers of Turkey. I told him where I was going and asked him if he could let me have some sort of a representation as a news woman and that I would be glad to write articles about Boston whenever I could and that I was willing to do this free, without compensation. He was very kind. He got his secretary to prepare for me a sort of an identity card showing that I was in the employment of his paper. That night, following this incident, I wrote a report about how the American people had behaved in the face of danger. I later wrote some more articles, but none was published in Turkey. I still have some copies of my articles about life in Boston.

I had been living in my new apartment when one day I read in the *Boston Globe* that the well-known pantomime artist, Marcel Marceau, had come to Boston for a few performances. I had watched his Turkish student in Ankara and had been very impressed. I right away went and bought a ticket for one of his performances. Following that I learned that the artist was staying at the Ritz-Carlton Hotel. When I called up, he personally answered the phone. Introducing myself, I asked him for an interview for the newspaper I was working for. He was most kind when he excused himself on account of some previous appointments and offered to send me a ticket. When I told him that I already had one, he asked me my ticket number and, thanking me for my interest, ended the call.

The day of the performance I was just settling in my seat when an usher approached and told me that Monsieur Marceau was waiting for me and would I kindly follow him. We went backstage. The artist greeted me in his usual painted face and costume, ready to perform. He thanked me for my phone call, as well as for my interest in coming to his performance and asking my name he signed his program for me. He wrote, "A Şen Sahir Sılan, avec le coeur ami de Bip. Marcel Marceau '75" (to Şen Sahir Sılan with Bip's friendly heart) and gave it to me together with his Paris address. It was time for the show. I left after thanking him for his kindness. I had been stunned by his modesty and delicacy. When the performance started I was terribly in awe. How could one person make people laugh, cry and think all at the same time without uttering a single word? This must have been real art.

I was anticipating the arrival of May. My cash was almost wholly gone. That I had a home and a job were my blessings. I was happy at my job. The people I was working with were showing me respect and understanding. Especially Jacky had become a real friend. On April 22, which is my birthday, Jacky gave me a present. I was so excited that I hugged and kissed her. At first she was very much taken aback! She explained that kissing was not a habit in China. However, since she had enjoyed the act, we had started kissing one another on festive occasions. She had a very good-looking young husband and a two-year-old daughter. They would invite me for Sunday lunches and I would enjoy hugging that little girl as if she were my granddaughter who was so far away. The Ambassador, Mr. Woo, was also very kind and gentle. Whenever he called me to his office I would find him standing up and he would only sit after I was seated. He was a real gentleman.

The magnolia trees on the avenue in front of my windows had started blooming. The whole area smelled divinely. Boston's beautiful spring had started. On the first day of May I received my salary in a white envelope. It is difficult to explain my relief and happiness. I had to pay all my bills. That was the first thing to do. Then I had to save some for future expenses. I then went out and bought myself a proper bed and mattress and black paint and a brush. On the weekend I painted my chairs. They looked so nice, newly painted. Then I took the cotton material that I had brought over from Turkey, thinking I could later make a dress, cut it into pieces to cover the chairs. I had to visit the hardware store where they agreed to let me hire out a puncher. I came home and was able to fix the covers I had cut on the chairs. Now I had three very presentable chairs in my room! I placed my mattress on the left side of the room, making sure that it was in the middle of the wall. Two of the chairs I placed by the window overlooking the park and the remaining chair went to one side of the fancy fireplace. My room almost looked dressed.

I also had a very enjoyable experience. Now that I could afford it, I was looking for a shoe repairman who could repair my leaking boots. By luck, the repairman I found again getting interested in my accent understood that I was Turkish and explained to me that he was an Armenian from İstanbul. Contrary to my first experience, Mr. Aram turned out to be the son of our baker in Kadıköy! His father, Arto, was the best baker in the area and we used to buy our bread from him. He remembered all my family, including my grandfather, who used to take me along on his shopping trips. I spent some time with him reminiscing the past. So there were Armenians who still liked Turks! He was the kind of Armenian that I was used to know and that I liked.

My good angels were at work again. This time they had thrown away a small, worn-out writing table and a slightly dirty coffee table. I went around them and checked. They could become useful if I worked on them. However, it was impossible for me to carry them by myself. From the phone booth nearby I called Pat. No answer. She was out. In desperation I hailed a cab. The taxi driver turned out to be a nice guy. He even gave me a hand to carry my newly found furniture up to my room! despite the fact that he was looking askance to these broken down things. Anyway, they were now mine. First I had to give them a good scrubbing. Then I had to reinforce and fix the nails. I polished them from top to bottom. I placed the writing table in a suitable corner. I took the chair standing by the fireplace and put it in front of the table. I no longer would be writing my letters on my lap. Then I placed the coffee table in front of my bed. Unfortunately the chairs were high so I could not sit at the table but I could eat on the table sitting on some pillows on the floor. My house was gradually becoming a home.

My Taiwanese friends who took me out to lunch never used cash, they were all using a plastic card instead. One day I asked Jacky what that card was and how it operated. She said, "That is a credit card. If you like you can send in an application for it and they will issue one for you." Since I knew nothing about it Jacky got me a form a few days later to fill out my application and mail it. I answered all the questions on the form and mailed it as directed. I had almost forgotten about it but one day I found a letter from that company. I opened the letter with anticipation but was soon disappointed. They said they could not issue a card to someone who earned only 500 dollars a month. They were sorry, etc. So I tore up the letter and dropped it in the trash bin. I laughed, saying to myself, "Who did you think you were, asking for a credit card!" The next day when I told Jacky what had happened she was very sorry. She had had no idea about my salary.

A few days later I found another envelope from the same company on the big table where our mail was being placed. I thought they must be crazy. Why would they write to someone they had just turned down a few days ago? I was almost dropping the envelope into the trash bin when something made me stop and open it. I was astounded. There was a credit card in the envelope. In their covering letter they were asking me to forgive their mistake. They were addressing me as "Dear Şen. Sılan" and they said they had issued a Gold Card in my name and hoped that I would forgive them for the mistake they had made.

I did not know whether to laugh or to cry! Some secretary must have thought my first name Sen, written without a cedilla, was really short for Senator. I had to thank my lucky stars for that mistake. The world was suddenly my oyster. Now, not only did I have a credit card but I had a Gold Card. That weekend I went off on a shopping spree. Some pillows, a nice bed cover, etc. and I was paying everything with my card. Of course I had to be careful! I should not go overboard. They could always cancel my card! I was informed that I had to pay at least 74 dollars each month.

One Saturday I read in the paper that Lauren Bacall would help sell some signed prints of Juan Miro at a gallery. I had always admired the works of Miro and I knew that gallery. I had nothing to do, so I went to the exhibit. It would be interesting to see a movie star and the works of Miro at the same time. When I had arrived there were only a few people. I was able to look at the prints to my heart's desire. I also exchanged a few words with Ms. Bacall. One of the prints I liked was for sale for 200 dollars. On it Miro had written "Amnesty International." I was circulating around it in admiration. My heart was saying "Buy it" my reason was saying "Don't." I really did not have the means. I would have to be very tight once again. My heart was the winner, as a result I bought it. It was probably the first time in my life that I was doing something crazy! When one had been used to beauty and fine things around, it is only up to a point that one can resist. I ran all the way back home with my print. This time the problem of how to hang it arose! I took the print to a frame store. The glass, the frame, etc. were really going to cost a lot. When the kind salesperson saw how I was debating and calculating, he made a suggestion. He told me to get some two-way tape, which would not spoil the print or the wall. Put up the print with those on the wall now, and go back to him for framing when I could afford it. I did as I was advised. I pasted my print above my writing table. Now my room was completed. Incidentally, the Miro print, now properly framed still has a place of honor on my wall.

XLIII

New Friends

I had noticed in the telephone directory that there was an honorary Turkish Council resident in Boston. I thought I should call on him on a nice morning in May. I took the address from the directory and went to visit him. He was called Orhan and he owned a small gift shop. He was a rather heavy man with friendly eyes. I asked him if he was the Honorary Council of Turkey and when his answer was positive, I introduced myself. In the beginning I think he was afraid I was there to ask for a job or something like that. He looked a bit jittery. When I told him that this was just a courtesy call and now that I was a resident of Boston I had thought that it was a duty to call on him. This changed his attitude. His full name was Orhan Gündúz. I gave him my name and my phone number and asked him to let me know if ever there would be an activity of any sort, like a painting exhibit, conference, etc. concerning my country. He offered me some tea, but noticing that he had a guest in an inner office I declined his offer. Just as I was leaving I remembered and asked Orhan Bey if he knew about the whereabouts of a well-known photographer called Alex Costi. Orhan Bey was suddenly all smiles and the man who was sitting quietly inside suddenly jumped up and said, "That is me! And who could you be?" He had grown a slight belly and his hair had thinned but it was him. I said, "Alex, don't you recognize me?" Naturally, I too had changed over the years but his photographer's eye was suddenly alerted and we found ourselves hugging each other.

He was asking information about my mother, brothers Cenan and Nur and I was asking similar questions about his mother and his sister Marianti. This was surely another miracle. Orhan Bey was happily pouring hot tea for all of us. Alex suddenly said he would take me to his house right away, but I had to change this to the next day. I did not want to go to their house empty handed. Furthermore, this was enough excitement for one day. Orhan Bey also insisted to have me visit their house and meet his wife. A new family friend had been found. My luck was certainly turning around.

When I returned home I phoned both my daughter in Denver and my son in Brighton and told them about this happy encounter. On Sunday morning Alex came to pick me up from my apartment. I had bought a bunch of flowers for them. We went to their house in Wellesley, at 22 Attwood Street. It was a nostalgic scene of getting together after so many years. We were all crying and laughing at the same time. Mme. Costi had prepared several Turkish dishes. Marianti, as usual spick and span, asked endless questions. After all, we had been with each other some thirty years ago. I do not think there could be anyone in this world, apart from my mother, who was so glad to see me again. I spent the whole day in this warm family atmosphere.

About the same time I met Dr. Mary Miller, by chance on the street one day. She was the assistant of Dr. Nugent who was the head physician at Lahey Clinic where my father used to come for his checkups. She was very warm and acted as if we were old friends. She told me she had a summer house in Rockport and that she would be delighted to have me visit her there. We exchanged phone numbers. My circle of friends was growing. Then I called Aunt Anahit and visited her at her home in Roxbury. We shared memories that really belonged to many, many years ago, to her childhood years together with Mother.

One day Prof. Shapiro called. He was Cenan's good friend and also his professor at M.I.T. many years ago. He had visited İstanbul recently and Cenan had given him my phone number. I knew him and had met him during our visit with Father but had not thought it advisable to look him up in my miserable days. He invited me to a show. I had not been to a theatre for many years. I enjoyed that occasion very much. Slowly I was returning to become civilized, leaving my seclusion behind. It goes to show that humans can endure a lot and still retain their humanity.

One of the things that I liked best to do was to visit book stores and wander around the stacks of books. Nobody bothered you and nobody asked you what you were doing there. Browsing through the books I came across something that interested me. Since I could now enjoy the luxury, I bought it. It was about the excavations in Sardes, Turkey, and it was written by Prof. George Hanfmann and his wife. Both were teaching at Harvard. After reading the book I wrote them a letter and thanked them for the valuable work they had done in my country. A few days later they were on the phone. They said they would like to meet me. I invited them and Prof. Shapiro to my flat for tea one Saturday afternoon. My flat was now looking respectable enough to invite people. I had learned many things about my country through their writings. For example, I learned from them that the earliest minora was found in Anatolia, the cradle of civilization. These elderly and refined people did not find my simple home wanting.

Frankly, before I had dared to invite people home, I had done some more shopping. I had bought (secondhand) two standing lamps and two small end tables. What I lacked most was some kind of music in the house. So I finally had bought a table watch that included a radio and an alarm clock. I had set it up so that I would be awakened to the sound of music. As I kept it on, I would be returning home to the sound of music as well. They usually played classical music. According to my mood I could also find jazz music as well on my radio.

One day Ray Baldwin called and said that he and his wife would like to invite me for dinner. This meant that I was being accepted into their circle of friends. I was delighted that his wife was just as delightful a person as he was. They received me as someone they had known for years. That day I was able to learn about the incident that had caused Mr. Baldwin's strange face. During the war an exploding bomb had taken most of his face off. After years of plastic surgery they had made almost a new face for him. That was why his face showed almost no expression. She also showed me his picture taken prior to this accident. He was a remarkably good-looking man. She said she had loved him just as well. After dinner their children came and joined us. I was honored to be sharing their family life, filled with respect and love. I feel honored to this day. Anyway, I owed my life, in a certain way, to this honorable family man for having appreciated me. What the members of my own family were not able to do, those foreign people had done for me.

While I am writing these lines I do not feel any pain or anger. It has been a long time since I have come to accept people as they are. Neither am I blaming anyone. On the contrary, I am rather grateful for everything that was done and not done, for or to me! I think of my life as a sort of a wall put up. One stone more or less could not hold it together and it would all come tumbling down. One the other hand, it would be quite difficult to write my memoirs without being objective or without reckoning. In a way, this reckoning is with myself. No doubt that all the sufferings, difficulties, trials brought out this person that I am today. And I am at peace with this human being. All the past experiences have caused me to regain my personality, which I had lost. No doubt that I too must have erred in the past, as well. As Jesus Christ said when people were mad at Maria Magdelena, "Let him who has never sinned, throw the first stone." Is there anyone who has never done wrong before? Nevertheless, I know that I have never done anything in order to be mean! Especially toward my family.

Dr. Mary Miller drove me to her summer home in Rockport one weekend. This little hamlet north of Boston had reminded me somewhat of my country. Naturally, living conditions in this village were quite different. A lot of artists, pottery makers, etc. had become residents there and lived year round in this little town. During the summer they would have a sort of open house to market their wares or art work. This was originally a fishing village and there were still a lot of fisherman. The sea could be seen almost from every corner. A clinic, a resident doctor, a chemist shop and of course a post office, namely anything one would need was there, in this tiny village. Thus people did not need to move to the city. There was hardly any traffic since people left their cars outside the town and either walked or cycled in the village. Their winters were harsh but they had built accordingly. There were strict zoning regulations, no new houses could be built. They had not changed their small village for 200 years and still did not miss any of the modern conveniences.

Even the old cobblestones had been saved and repaired as the original.

Mary was a villowy, intelligent and active young woman. She had inherited this house from her family. She had a studio flat in Boston where she stayed while she was on duty in Boston and on every opportunity she would drive off to this lovely place. Even cooking had now been made easy in the United States. One could even buy spinach, washed and cleaned and ready to be cooked! One steak on the grill and a tossed salad was enough for anyone. They ate healthy food. That day we had bought, together with Mary, fresh fish and some greens plus a bottle of wine. That was a real banquet. Then we went out for a nice walk. When it was time to retire, having taken our showers, we went to our rooms with a book. We woke up to a lovely morning. Mary was already watering her flowers. We then went out to get some fresh bread and buns from the baker, butter and jam from the market place. We consumed all these delicious things together with coffee and milk. Following breakfast Mary wanted to go to church and I accompanied her. I said my own prayer and then went into the bookstore. Mary joined me there after the service and we visited the art shops. We took off for Boston in the afternoon. I had spent a peaceful weekend with an intelligent friend.

XLIV

Happiness of Welcoming Zeyneb and Her Family and Then Ömer

Summer was close at hand. Zeyneb was in Denver with her child and husband. Ömer on the other hand did not know what to do for the summer recess. He had nowhere to go in Turkey. It looked like the only thing he could do was to come and spend the summer with me in Boston. I checked various possibilities and looked for cut rate flights and finally found out that by using my credit card I could finance his trip. I wrote him a letter explaining my thoughts. The reply I got was enthusiastic. I could get another mattress and we could share our meals, etc. So I made arrangements with the airline. We were going to be together beginning of July.

It must have been early June when Zeyneb was on the phone. Unfortunately, that horrible wife that my brother had married had gone to the extreme cruelty and reported to the Immigration Office that my daughter and her husband were illegal immigrants. Zeyneb, on the advice of her friends, had been able to visit a Senator of Colorado, explained that she was expecting and would not be able to travel in her condition and was able to ask for a period of adjustment before deportation procedures would be put into effect. That kind man had provided Zeyneb a six months' stay under the circumstances. All this had happened some time ago. I had to arrange everything in a hurry. I was both happy to be able to see them and at the same time very worried as to their future. I made the necessary arrangements to receive them and in a week they were in Boston. After all the hugging and kissing, we had to sit down and reach a decision as to their plans for the future. We all agreed that they should not be deported from the United States since such a thing would prohibit them from ever returning to the U.S.A. My darling grandchild Seze was now six months old. She was such a lovely child. She took everything with a smile and was very intelligent. While I am writing these lines she has already proven her intelligence and perseverance by her accomplishments. Wherever they were, Zeyneb sat Seze down on a blanket and she would amuse herself by herself. No trouble to anyone. Zeyneb was always wise and would argue every point before reaching a decision. She was also a loving, dedicated and reasonable mother. They had sold everything they had acquired during their stay in Denver, so they had a bit of money for their travel. We discussed the option of their travel to Canada for a while and return from there with a visa. I further discussed the situation with our Honorary Council Orhan Gündüz. He kindly suggested a job for Zeyneb in his office. However, this could cause them trouble in the future. So they decided to return to Turkey as the immigration people wanted them to do. I thought my father or my brother Cenan could receive them as guests for a week or two, until they found some job. Then when they had a place to live, they could take my furniture still in storage at Tuzcuoglu.

I was forced to ask Ambassador Woo for an advance on my salary. That wonderful person did not even ask me why and gave me the advance I had asked for. So I was able to finance their voyage back to İstanbul. In this manner they would be able to return if they wanted to do so in the future. My real worry was that I could not really know how their grandfather would receive them. They had no one else to go to. Finally word came that my brother Cenan had accepted them as guests at his house in Büyükada. That was welcome news. However, I was very surprised when it turned out that they had not been able to find a job in İstanbul. I really could not understand what was going on. Cenan was an influential manager who ran more than one company. All right, he may not want to employ a relative but could he not find employment in one of his friend's firms? Well, I really could not complain since they had taken Zeyneb and her family as their guests in their summer house. Naturally this could only last for the summer period. In town, Cenan had an apartment just enough for his family. Of course, they had no funds, even getting their meals free for the summer was something. Finally word came that Cenan had found employment for Zeyneb but the job was in İzmir. So Zeyneb, with her six-month-old child and her husband would be moving to İzmir. Since Zeyneb was going to work as a secretary they would be living on her salary and Sertaç would stay home and take care of their baby. It certainly was a different sort of a relationship. The husband would be doing the housework and the wife would become the bread earner. It took me some time to learn that my father had been afraid that if they had settled in İstanbul they would make a nuisance of themselves and he had arranged to have them settle down away from İstanbul. This had made me realize once again that not everyone could deserve such a beautiful word as "father!" Still I could not get myself to blame him and I tried to understand him. Most probably Mother's death caused him loneliness as well as making him forget the meaning of family.

Zeyneb and her family had settled in Karşıyaka, İzmir and they were able to get the furniture that was in storage into their new home. Zeyneb nursed her daughter early in the morning, then they got extra milk into a bottle, and she went to work. At noon she would rush to her home, feed the baby once again and then off to work. Sertaç was taking care of all house duties and their daughter's demands. In the evening Zeyneb would cook and wash the diapers by hand since they did not have a washing machine and go to sleep exhausted. This scenario was repeated day after day. The only help they had came from the fact that Sertaç's parents and an aunt also resided in İzmir. However, these people were elderly and not financially well-off. Still, despite everything, they could comfort the young couple by giving them a free meal once in a while. Later on, when this question of Zeyneb's and her family's being forced to settle in İzmir, Father would defend his actions by saying, "After all, we helped them to settle where they had their elders."

I was in a real quandary. What had I done that was wrong? Should I have not divorced my husband? Would my children be more comfortable or happy. Should I have forced him to pay alimony? How could I exist in a house knowing that he was in love with another woman and did not care at all for his own beautiful children! He had hardly suffered for his own daughter!

He had hurried off to marry his beloved without delay, in the city where his child had died!

I really should not be considering these things. Especially now. I was in a new country. After fighting tooth and nail I had found myself a job and had made myself a home of my own. Although I was poor, I could at least help my children morally if not financially. No, I never felt any regret. I had done the right thing by divorcing my husband. The future would certainly bring us better things. All my life I had been playing "Pollyanna." No, I must not look back.

In the meantime my son Ömer had come from London. I found that he had developed for the better. He had matured even more and developed into a real young man. On the other hand, he had reached a stage where he was interrogating everything and trying to find answers. I also realized that he was not always prone to give voice to his questions. He was a very sensitive boy becoming a man. Somehow he did not seem happy. Questions like "Why do I exist? Or what am I doing on this planet?" seemed to be hovering in his beautiful brain all the time. I was at a loss since I had no way of finding answers to all his questions. He seemed not only sensitive but also very introspective in his feelings. How could I tell him that life was a game worth playing no matter what and that we should never lose hope. In the past I had lived in a world of pink clouds, thinking that I would be able to give my children the whole world. And look at me now! All I had to give was my silent love. I was also trying my best to give him a proper education, a chance to ensure his future. On the other hand, I had sent a boy of 17 who had no father or mother into an unknown world and asked him to educate himself. I was unable to give him enough pocket money so that he could feed himself properly. He had no one to talk to. Of course he would be asking questions, a million questions. One of them must have been "What kind of a person is my father?" Since aged 12 he was not able to enjoy a father's affection or interest! Since he was 15 he had not actually seen his father! Since he had gone to England, Ömer had received not a single letter or phone call from his father. More than that, absolutely no material aid was coming from him. At the time I had divorced their father I was still under sedatives. I had no mind to ask for alimony. Neither had my inadequate lawyer thought about it. However, the good judge had protected my interest and had put in a clause on my divorce document saying, "She has the right of asking alimony in the future."

Before my departure for the United States I had brought this subject up to my father and we had decided that he would proceed through his lawyer. Unfortunately, during my fight for survival in Boston I had no way of following it any further. On the other hand, at the time he was leaving for England, Ömer had been able to say good-bye to his father and he had given his address and telephone number in Brighton. When I asked my son, he told me that he had written to his father from England but had received no answers. What a pity. A father that had attended the funeral of one of his daughters, had lost all interest in his surviving daughter and his only son! Whenever my children asked me about their father, all I could say was that he was a brilliant architect and that we had lived happily for 17 years. My children knew the rest of the story anyway. I had not known the man that I had divorced either! As to my own feelings, in order for them to at least have respect for their father, I had kept my sorrow to myself. Love exists only where there is respect. Maybe one day they could love him. Zeyneb's relations with her father were on the same line. As the French proverb says, "ni vue, ni connue (not seen, not known)."

I can never forget. Ayşe had died and following the custom of Moslem religious ceremony, on the fortieth day of her death I had called in some religious men to the house and they had performed a ceremony for the soul of the deceased. That evening Togrul was on the phone, he was asking for some papers and I had mentioned that we had just concluded the prayer ceremony for our daughter. He was utterly cynical, all he said was, "I see that you are turning to religion now." He had completely lost interest in his children, dead or alive! No interest at all. Nothing!

To get Ömer's interest on other things I gave my son a map of Boston and asked him to wander along this interesting and historical city during my working hours and when I came out of the office we would be doing other sights together. On weekends we would go to different beaches and swim together. There are some lovely spots around Boston and we were seeing them one by one. Swimming in the Atlantic was nowhere as good as what we were accustomed to in the Marmara Sea but it was fun anyway. At least I was able to give my son a chance to relax and enjoy the sun and the fresh air. I was both his mother and father for the time being and he, with his unreserved love, was making me the happiest person alive. He was about to enter the University of Sussex. I was proud of my children. Not once had they complained of their difficulties let alone ask me why all this had happened. They were enjoying being alive without any reservation. Finally, summer came to an end and I had to hug my son for the last time and said good-bye to him at the airport. I had been able to give both my children a sort of home that was full of love and now they were both gone. My flat, however, was the richer now with their memories and photographs taken during their stay in their mom's home.

My good friends started to invite me to their homes and gradually I began to enjoy such visits. On the whole, however, I was happy to be on my own. In my quiet times I was reading, listening to music, taking long walks and I was always thinking about things. My memory, especially toward the time I had lost my darling daughter, seemed to be a long period of blankness. My memory had been split into two. I remembered everything before Ayşe and I remembered the present. Something in between had been lost. Maybe it was some sort of a self-defense for me to forget those horrible days. I would remember many things concerning my children when they were young and happy, but somehow I could not remember how Ayşe looked at the time she had left home, not to return anymore.

I especially wanted to remember things about Ayşe, her words, her looks, the way she walked her voice, etc. I failed no matter how hard I tried. Then I would cry out my eyes, quietly but without stopping. Every night before going to sleep I would pray to God to let me see my daughter in my dream, but she never appeared. My pain was very deep and colored everything that I did.

It must have been around October when the Honorary Council Orhan Gündüz phoned. A group of doctors had planned a trip to İstanbul. For one reason or another, one member of the group was forced to cancel her reservation. Now they wanted someone to fill that space and since this was a last minute arrangement they would let that person join them for a payment of 100 dollars only. The tour operator was a friend of his and he was making me an offer. Orhan Bey, knowing that my daughter was in Turkey, thought I would enjoy such an offer. The trip would start on a Saturday and they would fly back on the following Sunday. They would be staying at the İstanbul Hilton. I had been working almost a year now and I had had no holiday during that time. So I consulted with the Ambassador. This was too good a chance for me to miss. He was very kind as usual and allowed me to take a week off. I rushed to the tour operator's office on Newbury Street. There were two men managing the tour. One of them was Turkish, married to a lovely American girl. I used my credit card to pay for the trip. The 100 dollar payment covered everything.

I packed a small overnight bag and was on the plane two days later. The plane was not very full so I was very sorry for the tour operator but delighted that I could make this trip. I had the opportunity to share this flight with interesting people and I was going to embrace my children. Once at the Hilton I rushed to the THY office and I got a ticket for İzmir with the return trip arranged to catch the tour flight back. I was still using my credit card. After this was done, I called Father and Bibi and also Zeyneb in İzmir giving them the surprise information. That night I met father at Cenan's house. Our reunion was quite festive. I had reported about my finding a job and my new house, etc. and they seemed to have accepted my new life. Anyway, I was in no way a burden on any of them. I tried to sleep a little when I returned to my room at the Hilton, however I was too excited to be able to sleep much. I had already informed the group that I would not be joining in the activities organized for the group. I was still able to keep my hotel room.

I do not remember anything about my flight to İzmir. I was too excited. Finding Seze and Sertaç at the airport was wonderful. Seze had began to walk on her own. When I hugged her, she was able to hug me back with her thin arms. I cannot explain how happy I was at that moment. I could only see Zeyneb when she came home for lunch. Their life was not at all easy. I was very sorry to see Zeyneb was working so hard and poor Sertaç was doing the housework and acting as a mother to Seze, who did not even have her own bed. I was sorry to see the life they were leading. I suddenly thought I should give up my job in the States, start a new career in İzmir and help them in their fight for survival. Finally, I decided that I could probably help them better from the United States. Days passed swiftly, I had to return to İstanbul and join the group for the flight back.

We had formed good relations with some couples on the tour. We naturally exchanged cards and addresses. One couple, Dr. and Mrs. Sears were older than I. Dr. Sears had retired from his work at the Massachusetts General Hospital. There was another couple that I had liked. Prof. Charles and Edna Schotland. There was still another couple whose name was something like Smith. This younger couple gave me the impression that they belonged to a wilder set of Bostonian society. This last couple, whose name I vaguely remember as Smith, did invite me to a party at their home, once we were back in Boston, and that was the end of my association with the younger Bostonian set. The dinner was very good. The conversation was lively. They were all condemning me for smoking, however, at the end of the meal we were offered cocaine! I was shocked. These people, all young, all highly educated and quite rich, would condemn smoking and would see nothing wrong with offering cocaine to their guests after a great dinner. I excused myself before the party or the smoke got thicker. They never asked me again. Anyway, I would have refused if they had done so.

I was satisfied with my job. I was earning enough to keep my body and soul together and even continue to finance my son's education. Still I had the urge to do something more with my free time, to be somehow productive. I was at the Museum of Fine Arts one weekend. I saw that a very refined and elegant, elderly lady was acting as guide to a group of visitors. From the way she was dressed I saw that she could not be an employee of the museum. My curiosity had arisen. I asked one of the guards who she was. He told me that she was not an employee but that she was a voluntary guide who came in once or twice a month. The idea seemed to be interesting. So I called the management of the Museum and asked if I could also act in such a capacity and what would I be required to do for such a position. The person to whom I was addressing these questions showed great interest, explained that I would have to go through a course for getting acquainted and then go through a test before the curators. I did apply and got through their courses and after two months I received a letter advising me that I would start my duties from the New Year on. This "job" would only take a few hours of my time on weekends. Naturally, there was no question of any pay. I was donating my time. However, my work as a voluntary guide in the Museum opened the way of getting introduced to a very select society of Boston. Some of the elderly guides owned mansions on Beacon Hill or Chestnut Hill. It turned out that I was the youngest among them and I soon had met most of the people. As an example I could cite Mrs. Bea Stone, wife of Harold Stone, Ruth, wife of Bob Morse, and Mimi, wife of Gerry Berlin. They would call me on the phone, send their drivers to pick me up and have me at their dinner table. This went off to such an extent that some of them even suggested marrying me off. My answer was a flat refusal. I had my children to think of. I had a mission to rehabilitate my family. I had developed a pat answer to such suggestions. I was saying that if ever I was to marry again, I had to find a man who would be very bright, very sentimental and responsible. Since it was almost impossible to find a man who had all these qualities combined, I was going to stay by myself. Many years later I was able to meet such a man after all.

XLV

The Year 1976

I celebrated the new year at Pat's home. Nur and Pat's only son John and a few of their friends were there. It had snowed that week and pine trees with lots of snow on them had reminded me of my happy times at Erenköy. The left over candles from Christmas plus the snow covered streets had created a festive spirit. As a matter of fact I had difficulty in accepting Pat's invitation. An experience that I had a few weeks ago had made me change my mind. It was Thanksgiving Day. Since this is a festive occasion I thought I should go to the restaurant of the Ritz-Carlton Hotel. However, I was very disappointed. First I had to be careful with my money, but more important than that, I found out that there were only a few tables occupied and they were all groups of families. I was the only one who had no company. I ordered a clam chowder to start. This is a local soup I had always enjoyed. The soup may have been excellent but being all by myself in a half empty restaurant made me feel lonely and very miserable. So I had quickly asked for my check and dashed out to the comfort of my home. I had therefore decided not to go out on such festive occasions. This sad experience had made me accept Pat's kind invitation.

It also was not a very festive occasion but at least Pat was someone I had always liked and being with her and her son John, my nephew, had made me happy. Of course how could I forget my children! Especially Ömer, who was all by himself in a foreign country. At least Zeyneb had her daughter and her husband with her, but poor Ömer was utterly by himself. That night I realized that until I could get my family together I would never feel completely happy.

Now and then I used to stop by Mr. Gündüz's shop. It was called Topkapi and it was in Central Square, Cambridge. They also would invite me to their house every once in a while. In the beginning of March, Orhan Bey was on the phone. He told me that on March 14 they were going to celebrate the Medical Day with the Turkish doctors in town and that he wanted me to attend. He would not listen to any excuse and insisted so much that I had to accept. It turned out to be quite a big party and I was able to meet many people that I enjoyed, especially Dr. Müjgan Coates, who turned out to a special friend. She had lost her American husband and she was living by herself in an apartment on 100 Memorial Drive, No. 11-14a. She was involved in cancer research. The place she was living was very near to where Mother and I had stayed years ago. Visiting her was a nostalgic experience of my past life. At the same party I had met Dr. İlhan and Elçin Birkan, who turned out to become great friends whose company I had enjoyed immensely. I had received a letter from Father informing me that he would be coming to Boston for his usual checkup. Usually he would spend a week or ten days in the hospital and then return home or spend a few days at a hotel before returning to Turkey. This time he was suggesting that he would enjoy a few days at his daughter's home. This would be a great opportunity for me to show him the small but valuable world that I had created for myself. I had done it without his help or family support, without any money or titles. I had done it all by myself. I would also be able to introduce him to my beautiful circle of friends. In a way I would also be returning the hospitality extended to me so graciously and so often by them. I should arrange a party! But how, where and with what budget? Well, isn't there a saying, "Where there is a will, there is a way?"

One afternoon I was visiting Dr. Müjgan Coates and she wanted me to see the facilities of her building. There was a big room on the roof of the apartment building surrounded by a terrace. Apparently people living in the apartment used this place for sun tanning in the summer. I saw it was big enough for a reception and shared my idea with Müjan. "Would it cost a lot to rent the place for 3 or 4 hours?" I asked. Her answer was sweet to my ears. She said there was no question of paying a fee. Most dwellers used this place for such occasions and she had the option as well. She said, "Give me the date and I will arrange it for you." This was a favorable omen and an important first step. The room was big enough to hold maybe a hundred people. The idea of throwing a big party in honor of my visiting father and show him how his daughter he had discarded and almost deserted had finally made it and was able to entertain her new circle of friends and introduce them to her father, who had come to Boston for his checkup, sounded very tempting. That night I made my list of guests.

My Taiwanese friends at the embassy, including wives and husbands, totaled 25. Prof. and Mrs. George Haufmann. Prof. Asher Shapiro and his girl friend. Orhan Gündüz and his wife. About five doctors including the professor in charge of the hospital. Pat and her boy friend (I was instrumental later in their getting married). Eddie Schuman, who had given me my first "doggy bag" and his two daughters. The travel agents Deniz and Vangie Gürak. My father's old friends, Dr. and Mrs. Kiefer. Samia and Bob Fisher and the gentleman who was instrumental in my finding employment, Ray and Jay Baldwin. Auntie Anahit (Bashian), Barbara, Dr. İlhan and Elçin Birkan and finally, Dr. Müjgan Coates. Last but not least, Father and me. I believe the list contained 65 names. I remember laughing out loud. How was I able to make friends with so many fine people in a year? I was only able to offer these valued friends my love and respects until this date. Maybe I was able to ask a few of them to my house for a cup of tea or coffee, that was all I could do. I was living in a single room with furniture that was collected mainly from the street and a few reproductions pasted on the walls. Life was always full of unexpected things. I was much better off even in my last flat at Karyagdi Sokak in Ankara. But then only two or three friends would visit me there. Funny world.

Now came the question of what could I offer without going out of my budget? I consulted the Woo's cook to see if he could help me buy things cheaper. Would it be cheaper if I bought wholesale? The kind man was very helpful. He got me two dozen relatively cheap but good wines. In addition, I would be offering things like soda or Coke and fruit juice. Now, what could I offer to eat? I knew that Pat had a good-sized oven, so I could ask her to let me use her oven and I could make some borek (Turkish pastry filled with cheese, etc.). These could be cut into small portions, prepare some deviled eggs. I could also buy some cheeses. I could get some fresh fruit, red and green grapes. I would be using paper napkins. I needed to offer some places to sit and Eddie came to my help there. It turned out that his daughter had a fully furnished flat and since she was away, the place was not being used. So Eddie offered to have some of her chairs and armchairs and small tables removed from her apartment to my party for the day. Mrs. Woo promised to lend me a cover for the buffet table and also bring one of her male servants to act as a waiter at the party. I rang up everyone to invite them and to give them the address. Everybody promised to come. A day before I prepared all the food and stacked them in Müjgan's fridge. Father arrived and the day after we had the party.

This unexpected occasion went off very smoothly. Father was amazed and enjoyed himself immensely. Everyone complimented me for the party. I also had done it without putting my budget out of order! I still have pictures taken at the party showing Father chatting with everyone. My good daddy never asked how I was able to finance such a party! He went to sleep on my bed when I was using the mattress I had given my son during his stay in Boston.

I placed Father in his hospital bed in the morning. Many years ago, I think it was a psychologist who had told me that there were two breeds of men. Those who knew how to take and those who knew only how to give. I always belonged to the second breed from the day I was born. This did not bother me. In fact, I had always looked at the other kind with pity and misgivings. Father, who was a born grabber, had always tried to make a slave of me. He could be so demanding. During his stay in Boston I fainted more than once trying to make ends meet and at the same time do the chores he demanded, finding time in between for my office hours. He would ask me to do such outlandish things that I could only go to my house about midnight. I was also wondering what he had been doing when he came here on his own. Now that I was around and willing, he enjoyed making me serve him to no end. I remember some mothers talking about their children as if they owed it to their mothers. It is quite common to hear, "But I brought her (him) into this world, of course he (she) must serve me." I always wanted to ask these people, "Were you interested to ask the child before he (she) was born?" or "Does the baby have the chance to choose his (her) parents?" Do babies come to this world because of their own desire? Instead, the poor darlings are brought into this world to make their parents happy.

As he kindly observed how hard I was trying to please my father and do my duties as well as my work at the office, Mr. Woo asked Father and me to dinner many times, especially after Father had left the hospital. I am not going over these observations with a sense of grievance. I have always tried to be a dutiful daughter and do the best I could for him. I was doing these things because I was brought up in this manner and never complained about such duties. My conscience is perfectly clear on that score and I did not force myself to take these notes down. Remembering comes naturally. However, since I promised myself not to cheat or write something untrue, I am jotting down everything as it happened. I now realize that I was taken in by most of the people who should have known better and feel assured that others in my position would have reacted much more aggressively. Well, what can one say? People are made differently, is it not so?

I had two weeks' holiday in June. Apart from getting together with my daughter, I had other thoughts for making a trip to Turkey. I was determined to look for some of the things that were in storage in İstanbul and if possible bring some of my valuables with me on my return to the States. There were some valuable kilims, my great grandmother's prayer mat and a few silver antiques. As much as I would like to have them around me, I was sure that these would fetch better prices in America in case I needed to sell them. Another thought I had was finally to start a law case for alimony to cover the expenses of my son's education. Their father had absolutely forgotten his children.

On the other hand, Zeyneb and Sertaç had moved to Ankara and both had a job. Seze was somewhat older and was placed at a kindergarten. Since they had settled in Ankara, so Zeyneb had written to me, she had phoned her father and on the phone had heard his wife shouting loudly that she would never allow them to set foot in her house! Zeyneb simply said, "Do not fret Daddy, maybe we can meet somewhere else and you can see your grandchild," and terminated her call. It was about time that I reminded him of his duties to his children. During the winter I had spent in Father's apartment I had brought some of my things there, in my room, and also left many things in the summer house at Vanikoy. Then when I had left for the States, all the things in the summer house had gone to Tuzcuoglu but what I had in the city flat had stayed there.

This time when I visited Father's apartment I was sorry to notice that many things that belonged to me had disappeared. Possibly the persons working for Father had appropriated them for their own benefit. For example, my portable typewriter and my sewing machine were no longer there. My beloved armchair was nowhere to be found. I picked whatever I could find and that I could carry with me, signed a power of attorney to a lawyer Father had picked up and went on to Ankara to visit my daughter.

Zeyneb and Sertaç had rented a small apartment on the slopes of Çankaya. Sertac was working as a receptionist at the Bulvar Palace Hotel. My daughter was a secretary at a commercial office. Seze had been registered at a kindergarten nearby. They felt better in Ankara despite all their hardships, at least they had many friends in that city from old days. They were certainly better off in Ankara then they were in İzmir.

My daughter had fallen ill, with jaundice, during their stay in Izmir. Since she was new at her job she was denied any health benefits and had to stay at a cheap hospital. The conditions in that hospital were so bad that they had found out that the patient in the next bed had died only a few days after the woman's death! They had failed to report these things to me. The hospital had informed her grandfather and her uncle of her condition hoping to get help but nothing was heard from either of them! However, some manager in the firm she was working at had heard of Zeyneb's situation and had agreed to finance all the hospital bills and practically saved my daughter's life. Learning these things even a year after, had certainly hurt me. However, what could I do. Whatever happened had happened. You may forgive but it is impossible to forget. It does really hurt somewhere deep in one's heart.

Being together with my loved ones and really feeling their warmth and genuine love I had returned to Boston with a new appreciation of life. I was now doubly sure that far away from the family I was better off working on my own. I could help my children better in Boston than returning to the slavery of my father. Now, at last, slowly but surely I was learning how to say no. I was no longer going to be a slave to my kindness, obediences or to any people.

XLVI
With Ömer in Boston

As soon as I returned to Boston I sold some of the things I had brought with me and was able to finance Ömer's trip to Boston. My tourism friends had told me about a weekend trip to New York that was fairly cheap, covering the bus fare to and from and also the hotel for two nights. So, we went to New York with my son. This was one of those long weekends that Americans enjoy for short holidays. I had not felt good for a long time. Being with my son and having nothing to do, a trip seemed appropriate. We were not rich by any means, we were staying at a second rate hotel but we were free and without any constraint. I did not know New York too well but I had an idea about what we could do. I had been there a number of times in the past but had never spent much time. From my old experience, I decided that we should enjoy Central Park first.

So we walked to the Fifth Avenue entrance of the park where we haggled with a horse and carriage driver for a drive in the park and finally brought his fare down to what we could afford. This was a very enjoyable experience. However, after a while my son suddenly found out that there were bicycles for rent! Ömer asked me, "Mom, do you think you can still cycle?" It was a most wonderful idea. It was also a challenge as well. It had been a very long time since I had been on a bicycle but with Ömer beside me I would dare almost anything! We rented two bikes by the hour and we really enjoyed cycling. We started going downtown on Fifth Avenue and stopped at Rockefeller Center. Soon we were all the way down south. We even took the ferry to the Statue of Liberty. Whenever we felt hungry, we would eat something in a corner shop or buy something from a street vendor. It was an incredibly happy day for me. We took

Madison Avenue on the way back. We had spent so little and seen so much, all in one day. Next day we were walking. We visited museums, churches and a big bookstore where one can browse a long time without spending a penny. We were back in Boston on the third day.

They have Pops concerts by the Charles River during summer, as I have already mentioned while writing my college days. People go to listen to the music together with their picnic boxes, books, blankets, etc. Most families go much earlier, lay out their picnic blankets, eat and let the children fall asleep, being exhausted from running around. The great thing about this outing is that despite all the crowd, one hardly hears a disturbing noise. Somehow even the children seem to behave! The elders make sure that the lawn on which everyone is sitting is not disturbed or that their leftovers are properly packed. By next morning you could not imagine that such a crowd had been there the night before. I had been to these concerts maybe thirty years ago! On the other hand, I had been to such open-air concerts during my years in İstanbul and Ankara. However, the noise and the commotion was quite unbearable. Especially when the day was over. The lawn would turn into a garbage dump. One thing I could never stand was the children shouting after their mothers. Usually the women would gather and either play games or gossip among themselves and the children would be let loose on the lawn. Very soon the child would be bored and would try to get the attention of his (her) mother and the continuous whining of these abandoned children would drive me crazy. In Boston, however, since the children were generally approached as grown-ups, one did not hear such whining and crying. Unless someone is really hurt. I am not trying to belittle my countrymen but this is a fact. Possibly it is a question of education. Anyway, we enjoyed those concerts with my son. We would take our picnic basket, lie on the lawn and enjoy both the scenery and the music for hours on end. It was most satisfying for both of us. Ömer also made himself a few friends this time. Eddie's daughter and her friends took Ömer around for swimming or other activities.

Happy hours go by quickly. Ömer had to return to England to continue his education at Sussex University. I will never forget the day he was leaving. I had rented a car, hoping to take him around for the last time and drive him to the airport. His flight was due for late afternoon. About noon Ömer said he wanted to see a movie called *Star Wars* before he left. I said, "Why not?" and we rushed out. We put his baggage in the trunk and parked the car at a huge car park and ran to catch the early showing of the film Ömer wanted to see. On our return to the car park we were aghast! Neither of us had noted the number of the parking lot and would not find our car where we thought it was. Time for the plane was getting short and we were frantically running among the lines of cars. We finally found our rented car on the very top of the car park. We were hugging each other with relief while laughing and crying at the same time. This was a good lesson for me also. From that day on, I learned how to make a note of where I had parked the car. Another good lesson to learn.

With my new friends I was able to travel first to Montreal and later to Maine for weekends. I had fallen in love with Maine. It was probably because I liked nature so much. Despite the cold weather we were able to take long walks by the seaside and devour famous Maine lobsters. The best thing about this was that the lobsters were so cheap in Maine.

During October our office had to move. Our new address was 545 Boylston Street, Apartment 800, namely we had the eighth floor of the building. From the window of my new office I could see the beautiful Hancock Building and right next to us was a very old and lovely church. It made quite a nice contrast, a very modern edifice next to an old one. All the windows of the Hancock Building, due to some calculation error, had come down and they had to redo all the window frames. This completely glass covered building was designed by the Chinese-born architect I. M. Pei. Another interesting thing that this architect designed is the little glass pyramid he did at the entrance of the Louvre Museum in Paris. Apart from having a better view in my new office, I was also lucky since this building was even closer to my home.

XLVII

Is It a New Horizon?

I spent the New Year's party at the home of Mr. and Mrs. Woo. These delightful Taiwanese people were doing everything possible to make my life beautiful. I had been working for them for almost two years now and I had become a part of their group. Mr. Woo had become a father figure for me. It seemed that my father was only my biological parent while Mr. Woo had been instrumental in giving me a new life and personality and furthermore, he was always ready to help me in any contingency.

I was also carrying on my work at the museum and getting to meet many interesting people. The reception that I had organized to introduce my father to them had given them cause to appreciate me even better. Naturally, they had enjoyed meeting Father, after all he was a man of the world who had enjoyed a long political career. He could be a very amiable man when he wished to be so. But he had never understood me! On the other hand, I understood him very well but I just could not accept slavery.

The winter of 1977 was rather uneventful. My very trusted Dutchman, Jim Drabbe, had reached me as soon as he had heard the loss of Ayşe. Soon afterwards, when he had heard that I had divorced Togrul, he again wrote and offered to help with financial aid if need be. When we had gone through Amsterdam with Father, he and his wife had gone out of their way to host for us during our stay in that lovely town. I had also advised them of my then recent new decision to move to America. Once in a while we had continued exchanging letters. This very good friend had always given me courage. Once he had written, "You have the courage to do anything for your children." During 1977 he was on the phone one day. He told me he was coming to Boston for

382

one day and would like to have lunch with me. I was still in my bad days and had not been able to eat the food on my plate. The place we had gone to was probably the best restaurant in Boston and the meals they served were famous. So he had asked, somewhat bewildered, if I had not liked the food they served. When I tried to explain that I had no appetite, he admonished me and told me about his experiences during the Second World War, when his country was under German occupation. It seems they went hungry many times and had even cooked the tulip bulbs and ate even the candles. They must have had a terrible time. His tales had made me realize what excellent diplomacy İsmet İnönü had exercised in Turkey, keeping the country out of that terrible war.

Spring was almost with us when our Honorary Council, Mr. Orhan Gündüz, called me up and invited me to dinner. During dinner that night Orhan Bey told me that Ambassador İlter Türkmen and his deputy, Mr. Altemur Kılıç would be coming to Boston to attend a conference and that our Ambassador was going to speak. I was both surprised and happy. The funny thing was that in my misery I had never realized that Turkey had a Permanent Mission at the U.N. Ambassador Türkmen's wife, Mina, was an old friend of mine. Furthermore, Deputy Permanent Representative Mr. Kılıç was also an old friend. I had written Nezih Manyas but had failed to learn about other Turks living in New York! I was somewhat at a loss. Meeting them in entirely new circumstances could prove to be difficult. We even had had a rather funny experience in Ankara. I was still married and living in Ankara. One day retired Ambassador Feridun Cemal Erkin had phoned and said he was very sorry that I was not inviting him to my parties anymore. He was a very good friend of my father and had always been very kind to me. I felt sorry and promised to call him at the earliest opportunity. He had been our foreign secretary before his retirement and he was a very likeable gentleman. I was wondering what kind of a party I could organize for him. Mr. Kılıç was at the time the general manager of the National Press Bureau. His wife Guzide was a charming hostess. So I planned a party for Ambassador Erkin and invited among other presentable people, the Kılıç family. Since all of them were kind enough to accept to come, I called

Ambassador Erkin and set the date. I had invited fourteen people and with us (the host and hostess) we were going to be sixteen, seated in four separate tables. Everyone had arrived on time but Altemur and Güzide. Ambassador Erkin became fidgety. It was time for dinner. He did not like waiting for others. So I was forced to ring Altemur. He was notoriously forgetful and it turned out that he had indeed forgotten the dinner party and he said that they could only join us for dessert. So I had my other dinner guests seated without them.

I was delighted to learn about the arrival of Permanent Representative Mr. Türkmen and my friend Mr. Kılıç. I therefore arranged through Mr. Gündüz to have them all for a drink at my place after the conference.

When we were all together and drinks were being served, the first question they directed to me was, "Why did you not think working at the Permanent Mission in New York?" During our talks I had explained under what conditions my daughter and son were trying to carry out their lives. I had told them that I was finally settled in Boston and was working with people I enjoyed very much and that they were very helpful to me in every way. I also told them that I was thinking that living in New York would be very expensive. They, however, told me that if I was settled in New York, it would be easier for me to find a university for my son and also employment for my daughter. They said I should reconsider these possibilities in earnest. For the first time I realized that since I was now properly installed in Boston, I probably could bring my son over to complete his education in America. Perhaps I could get my daughter to Boston as well. The last time she had gone through Boston, Mr. Gündüz had offered her a job but somehow they had wanted to go back and try their luck in Turkey. Now they were in Ankara but I knew that Zeyneb was not satisfied with her life there.

A short while after this get together I received a letter from Ömer that caused me consternation. He was saying that he was fed up by living on his own and that he wanted a home and a family. I spent the whole of the next day trying to find ways of answering him. Finally I wrote back and said that I was thinking of going back to Turkey and asked him whether he would like to continue his education there. I was trying to sound him

384

out and see if he just wanted to come to the U.S. His reply was very encouraging. My good boy was saying that he did not care what country it would be, he just wanted to have a home and a loving mother near him. He was just tired of having to live with strangers. I was almost at the end of my wits. I knew I had to decide, but I did not know which way to go.

Father, in his last letter, asked me to arrange his appointments at the Lahey Clinic for April. The Clinic had recently moved to their new building. I knew the secretary to the director of the clinic, Dr. Nugent. She was a very competent person called Pamela. I gave her all the information and Pamela made all the arrangements. Pam also agreed to help me further. We would drive out to Burlington the Sunday Father arrived. He would be placed in his room for the night and his procedures would start from Monday morning on. This way I was able to forstall his overtaking my home. With my children it was alright. They had respect for me, however, Father would not accept to be a visitor but would dominate my whole life. After all, I had been my own master for too long and without any help from anyone. I was now a grandmother and would not enjoy parental hegemony. I do believe, now more then ever, that the most important thing for a woman is to be financially independent.

I had met a nice man named Paul Farris at a museum party and we had started going to concerts and openings now and then. He was a delightful friend. He always teased me about my obstinate ways of thinking. He also was surprised to find me so outspoken.

I was still carrying on a correspondence with Wendy Harris. We were on the phone a couple of times. She had recently lost her husband and was staying at a mansion at Goldsboro district of Pennsylvania beside a big lake called Bear Lake. Her only daughter was at college. Unfortunately, in the coming years Wendy would also lose her daughter in a motorcar accident. After having met her as the ambassador's daughter, we had come together once more in Ankara when Wendy had come a second time as the wife of Mr. Walter Harris. At that time we both had had children and our children had also enjoyed one another. The third party to this friendship was Mina Türkmen, the wife of the Permanent Representative, Ilter Türkmen.

385

While Father was in the hospital Wendy called and asked me to bring Father to her house in the country, as soon as he was out of the clinic. Father enjoyed this idea also. Wendy had a two-storied wooden house in a great piece of property and her own lake. The property included a forest as well. Gazelles and deer wondered around. Wendy was running everything by herself. She was the perfect American pioneering woman. Since Father enjoyed his siestas, I was trying to give Wendy a hand. We were also having long talks and sharing our problems. Meanwhile, I had told her about the offer from New York as well as Ömer's letter. That intelligent friend, upon hearing of the invitation from New York, immediately told me that I should accept the position offered and bring Ömer to New York. When the weekend was over I took Father to his hotel and from there he went back to Turkey. As soon as I was on my own again, I started making plans. Meanwhile, Father had mentioned that my lawsuit for alimony, or rather the financial help for Ömer's education, had started. I contacted Sotheby's, the famous auctioneers in New York for the sale of an old statue of a horse that I had brought from Turkey. I had to send photos, descriptions, etc. beforehand. Then I delivered the statue to them. As I was progressing with my programs, I received a check for four hundred dollars from Sotheby's. This was wonderful.

I then called Ambassador Türkmen and asked what I had to do to start working for him. It turned out that they had some exams I had to sit through and I should go to New York. I naturally would. At the same time I sent Ömer an air ticket from London to Ankara. I was hoping to go there myself and see my family together after so many years. I consulted Pat about my lease. It turned out that since I had been a tenant for more than two years I could cancel the contract against payment of two months rent. I asked Eddie if I could store my furniture in his garage for a month or so. He said, "Naturally." I had also made some investigations about a new building a while ago. It was going to be available for rent in September. I had already made an application. All my days were spent planning and making arrangements. Luckily I had three weeks' leave this year. I bought an airline ticket. New York to İstanbul. I went to New

York by bus two days earlier and went through the various exams at the Mission, like translations and compositions in English, French and Turkish. I slept in a sleazy but cheap hotel and was glad to get away from New York. I was told that I would be able to learn whether I had been accepted as secretary to the ambassador from the foreign office when I was in Ankara.

I remember taking off from Kennedy Airport late one afternoon, most probably in July 1977. I, however, do not remember the day. As we were flying over Manhattan, that beautifully lit city suddenly was pitch dark under us! It turned out that the famous power cut incident that made history in the States had taken place.

The next morning I was in İstanbul. I went directly to see Father. This time I was adamant. I asked him to give me a loan and that he would be able to get my alimony to set it off or that I would pay him back in installments. At first he tried to evade the issue by saying that my position in Boston seemed to pretty set, etc. I was really persistent this time. At long last he said he would let me have a loan. We had not set the amount but at least he had agreed.

Right after I left him I bought my plane ticket to Ankara and I called Zeyneb and informed her about my flight. Ömer was already in Ankara. When I came out of the plane in Ankara none of my children were there to greet me. Better still, I should say that I could not recognize my own children who were there to meet me. I had to force myself not to faint. My children looked like they were just out of a concentration camp. My God, were they my own children? This time the tears that flowed from my eyes were not just for joy but out of misery as well. What had I done? We then all started to cry. All my children had had to go through so much hardships. The first thought that came to my mind was whether the money I had would be enough to take my loved ones on a short vacation.

I had written in my last letter to Ömer to bring with him all his credentials from Sussex University short of telling him that he might be due for a change of school. I asked my son-in-law and my daughter if they could take some time off. They both said they could. The next day I called on the foreign office and I was told that my employment had been approved and that I should report to the New York office in September. Although I was very happy that I had gone through this trial, I was also afraid of the future. Up to that point all the plans I had made had worked out. But what about the next ones? These were not yet completed. During those days I had come to realize another reality concerning myself. All the decisions I had made alone, by myself, had resulted positively. All my life long others had decided for me and most of them ended in disaster! Now I was walking on the line that I had drawn myself. I still had a long way to go. Meanwhile I had said nothing to the children about my plans.

As soon as I learned about my position in New York, Zeyneb and I went through all the ads and selected a holiday resort that we could afford. In Marmaris we could rent two rooms where five of us could stay for a reasonable price and we took the first available bus. Zeyneb, Sertaç and Seze had one room and Ömer and I had the other room. Fresh air, an azure sea to swim in with lots of good food and peace of mind, almost on the second day of our stay my children began to get their coloring back. Even the twinkle in their eyes had began to return. Of course, we did many things together but mostly I was trying to leave them by themselves and not to intrude in their private lives too much. I would take my book and go to a secluded spot for a suntan and begin to read. They often came after me to see what I was doing. I had a long talk with Ömer and asked him if there was a good university in New York he would like to attend, if he had the chance to transfer to New York. He told me that NYU was known to be very good in economics and he would love to get his degree there. He was studying the same subject at Sussex University. As a matter of fact, even in high school he had said he would like to study economics. When I broke the news that he might be able to do what he wanted, he almost jumped with joy. Later on that day, I mentioned this possibility to Zeyneb and suggested that she should come to İstanbul with me for a few days. She also looked like she was overjoyed.

By chance on the beach I had come across two of our diplomats that I knew from my days in Ankara. One of the couples was Mr. Tevfik Ünaydın who is at the present an ex-ambassador and his wife Solmaz Ünaydin, who also happened to be a career diplomat. They told me that they had both been appointed to New York. He was appointed as our Consul General and his wife would be working as counsellor at the Permanent Mission of Turkey. I refrained from pressing the point but during our talks they both said that they lacked good secretaries in both offices. This seemed promising anyway.

When our ten days in Marmaris was reaching its end I called up Bibi and Cenan to ask if they would put us up for a few days at their house on the island, as they had done in the past. They invited us with their usual hospitality. My time was running short. Sertaç had returned to Ankara to continue his work. The rest of us went to the island. Now, a few more hurdles had to be taken. I asked for Cenan's help. My dear brother was very kind. He helped me to get a visa for Ömer from the American Consulate General. Now remained the last hurdle to jump.

I took Zeyneb and Seze with me and called on Ambassador Türkmen and Mina. Naturally I was asking about what would be required of me, once I was in New York, but in the mean time, I had a chance to ask if it would be possible to get a job for Zeyneb as well. Ambassador Türkmen advised that Zeyneb should first apply to the Foreign Office in Ankara and Zeyneb agreed to do that as soon as she went back. So, with at least some parts of my overall plan having been accomplished, I sent Zeyneb and Seze to Ankara. Then Ömer and I took our plane back to the U.S.A. We went directly to Boston and got settled temporarily at a boarding house I had already selected before starting my trip. Ömer was rather late for applying to American universities but he needed a rest anyway. He had ample time to prepare the necessary forms for New York University for the next semester.

The first day I was at work, I immediately informed Ambassador Woo about the developments that had taken place in my life and told him that I was asking his permission to move to New York. As usual he was very kind. He listened to my story patiently and agreed that I was doing the best thing for my family. He also said he would be very sorry to let me go and asked me if I could try and find a replacement, preferably another Turkish lady to take over my duties.

During my years of duty at the Taiwanese Consulate General, I had been twice awarded a certificate of performance and in both cases the certificate came with a bonus (equal to two months' pay). Both my attitude to my work and my attention to my duties had earned me these. I was proud of this. I would never belittle their confidence in me. I was very lucky. I had met a Turkish family during my last year in Boston. Nuri and Lale Kılıç were a very nice couple. They had a daughter who had just graduated and was looking for a job. I had met their daughter as well. So without any hesitation I was able to introduce her to Ambassador Woo and after an interview he engaged her to replace me. So I had done one more good deed.

I must also add that during that time I had to live through a terrible incident. An Armenian maniac had assassinated Consul General Mr. Gündüz for no reason at all. Or rather for something that had allegedly happened years and years ago and in another country! I cried and cried for days after him. In fact anybody who had known this wonderful person shed tears after him. He was one of those rare, good, helping and accomplished people. He was a real gentleman.

My last days in Boston were spent with farewell meetings with my best friends, namely Pat, Eddie and Paul and all the others. Most of my belongings, such as pictures and books, which had filled a number of cardboxes, was left in Eddie's garage. He promised to send them on to me as soon as I had settled there. My Taiwanese friends also gave a number of farewell dinners in my honor. They all gave me many gifts and Ambassador Woo was again very generous and gave me a good-bye bonus as well. It was time to go to New York. It was such sweet sorrow to part with friends who had helped me so much to direct and change my life from one of misery to one of at least new hope. I was once again on an unknown mission, but this time I had my son with me. Furthermore, I had the hope of getting my daughter to move to New York and to be able to have all my family together in one city. I was praying for the best.

XLVIII
And Finally, New York

Friends in New York had booked a room for us in Manhattan. It was a relatively cheap hotel, situated on 38th Street and Madison Avenue. Our room was tiny and since the small building was surrounded by skyscrapers our room was perpetually in the dark. The one good thing about the room was that we had a television. Both Ömer and I were turned off when we saw the room reserved for us. The room we had stayed in Boston for a while was so much more roomy and full of light. In this tiny room we tried to get settled as best we could. After hanging our few clothes we dashed out of this claustrophobic room and looked for some place to eat. The place we found was not very appetizing but we had to eat something. This was not at all like New York we had visited as tourists some time ago. I had to start work the next morning. I gave Ömer some pocket money and suggested that he should look around a bit. We would have to do something about finding a place to settle in. I was not even sure if I could come for lunch or not. It was a nice day in September. I had to walk something like five large avenues and eight blocks before I could reach 1st Avenue and 46th Street, where the Türkevi was! Our Permanent Mission occupied the 10th and the 11th floors of the building. Good friends that they were, Ambassador Türkmen and Mr. Kılıç were kind enough to introduce me to the people assigned to this office. I was appointed as the private secretary to the ambassador. However, I found that a very kind and gentle lady called Ferda was doing that job. So they put me into another room. All the employees were in a constant flux, people were rushing about. I was told that the General Assembly was in session. Up to that date I had always worked as an executive secretary. Now I was being asked to do things

I had never done before. In fact, I was asked to do things without knowing what I was doing. Someone came in, gave me a slip of paper on which a name was scribbled and said, "Please invite this person" and left the room before I could ask to what sort of a meeting I was going to invite this person. Someone else would pop in, thrust a handwritten document to me ask me to type it. Realizing that I could do nothing properly under these conditions, I went back to Ferda to ask her help. I was actually exhausted without having done anything. I had not even had any lunch. Anyway, nobody had told me our office hours. It was already getting dark and everyone was leaving the office. I tried to get some information about transportation and the only answer I got was something like "Use the bus, it is better." However, no one would tell me which bus went what way! Of course Manhattan bus service is excellent but it was going to take me some time to learn about it.

This time, walking back all those streets to the hotel, I had lots of time to reconsider many things. Until that date I had always been employed by foreigners. This was the first time I was being introduced to our national manner of working. By the time I had reached our hotel I had also developed some decisions. On the other hand, a very good bit of news was waiting for me. As soon as I arrived Ömer was delighted to tell me that he had applied to NYU and since his transcripts from Sussex were highly satisfactory, he was advised that he would be able to start his education at mid-term. NYU would accept students only if their grades were above average. In fact, since Ömer had taken many courses at Sussex University, the administrator had suggested that he should skip the first year and start taking courses for the third semester. Luckily Ömer had the wisdom to consider the differences between the curriculum and had suggested that he should begin from scratch since he wanted to get a good and sound education and was not in a hurry to graduate. At first I was a little perturbed that he would be losing valuable years but later I had to agree that he was doing the right thing. He was set to doing a double major in economics and finance. He believed this would be enough education to start a career. When he told me about school fees I was again frightened. It was true that Father had agreed to help finance Ömer's education and

Ömer had also suggested that he was willing to work and earn his keep. This last was a very refreshing idea for me. My son was beginning to take responsibility. There were a few months ahead of us. The second good news was that Ömer had scouted around and had found a small Japanese hotel, which also had a small restaurant close to our hotel. He had actually gone in and had liked it. So after I was able to refresh myself, Ömer and I went to this restaurant. It was a small place and all the clientele were of Japanese descent. We were the only "strangers" in the place. They did not have tables, one had to sit on the floor. All these were new experiences for us. I had eaten Japanese food once or twice in Boston and had enjoyed it. I even asked for some saki, which they serve slightly warmed in very small cups. Sushi, sashimi, etc. whatever we ate was very tasty, so we enjoyed our meal and returned to our tiny room to go to sleep.

I left the hotel in the morning earlier than I should. Once more I had not been able to tell my son at what hour he should expect me back. I was, however, determined to learn everything that day. While walking I bought a large map of Manhattan. It contained all the information I needed. The bus system as well as the subway maps were there. There were also addresses of the museums, parks and even theatres. I realized that I could work out the answers to many questions by the aid of this booklet. After all I was an intelligent and determined woman. I would be able to go over this hurdle as well.

Manhattan was a highly well-organized city. Avenues went north and south and the streets crossed them from east to west. Busses went from south to north on First, Third, Madison, Sixth, Eighth, etc. Avenues from north to south on Second, Lexington, Fifth, Seventh, etc. There were many bus stops and there were crosstown busses on certain streets. They were all marked on the map.

By the time I had reached Türkevi (Turkish House) it was still early and there were not many people around. So I took this chance to go up to the 11th floor and called on the Counsellor. I had understood that he was a patient and kindly man. Luckily he too was early at his desk and answered all my questions, like what was the General Assembly. Why there was a reception for which invitations had to be sent, what were my duties and my

393

working hours, etc. With most of my questions answered I was able to return to my desk and carry on the work I had to do. That morning I learned that there was another deputy representative to the ambassador apart from Mr. Kılıç. Mr. Nazmi Akıman was a very elegant, art loving, refined gentleman. *Sotte voce* music would be heard coming from his room. Actually, when I entered his room to receive his orders I heard "The Four Seasons" playing and could not help myself to remark, "How nice, you are enjoying Vivaldi." His reaction was "I am delighted that you recognized the music." Our mutual understanding and respect was to last all the while he was in New York. I also enjoyed the company of his charming wife.

At noon, while I was going out for lunch, I came across a couple of secretary ladies from the 11th floor, whom I had met the previous day. They were good-looking, intelligent and hard working young women. As soon as I had finished my lunch I returned to my desk rather early. I was anticipating the return of these ladies. As we started talking I asked them where and under what conditions and with what sort of a rent they were living. And then I mentioned my troubles with the hotel room and asked if they could be of any help to me. I was enchanted to find that they would gladly give me a hand. Our working hours had been set as 10:00 A.M. to 13:00 P.M. and then from 15:00 P.M. to 19:00 P.M. Once a week one of us had to stay in the office during lunch hour when everybody would be going out. Our holidays were adjusted according to the holiday schedule of the United Nations. As I have mentioned before, Americans had developed a nice habit of adding a Monday to the weekend and have a three-day holiday on certain celebration days. Since we had to be in continuous contact with the world, on such American holidays some of us had to stay in the office on duty. Another duty everyone dreaded was the telex duty! One person had to control the telex machine even after office hours. Sometimes this could continue on to the early hours of the following morning! Such work became more frantic when the General Assembly convened. The terrible thing was that sometimes the telex machine would show a default and it could last for hours and the person on telex duty would just have to wait for hours with nothing to do. Since that meant that we had irregular work schedules during such times, everyone was given a five-day leave after the General Assembly was over. Our summer leave was three weeks, this naturally concerned the secretaries.

On my second day in the office I was able to return to the hotel by bus. It broke my heart to find my son lying on his bed in the dark watching television. The light in the room was so bad that he could not read a book and we were paying a lot of money for a third class hotel room by the day. My monthly salary would become payable only at the end of the month and I did not have much cash left. This was another time when I had to thank my lucky stars for my credit card. After feeding ourselves in one of those dreary coffee shops we went back to our room and we had a chat. When I asked Ömer if he would be willing to get some sort of a job, he was quite interested. I had met a young man who was working as a bodyguard at Türkevi. I suggested to Ömer that he should talk to him about the possibilities, at least until his classes would start. This young man was the son of a retired ambassador and his mother had also worked at the mission as a secretary for a while.

Ömer applied and was accepted as a bodyguard at the Türkevi. Coming down from my office on our fourth day in New York I saw my handsome son in a uniform. In a way, I was very hurt but at the same time I was proud of my son. He was taking everything in his stride and helping me enormously. He had never worked for compensation in all his life, on the contrary he had led a life of almost luxury and now he looked perfectly at ease and willing to work. Most of the time our working hours were the same, so we started commuting together.

A week later the two young secretaries gave me a wonderful bit of news. They each had a flat in an apartment building on 54th Street and Second Avenue. They had found out that there was a furnished, one-bedroom apartment to let. During the lunch recess we all went to see the place. The flat consisted of one bedroom, one sitting room plus a kitchen and a bath. The most important side of this place was that it was relatively close to the office. The furniture provided was not up to my standards but it would have to do for the time being. We asked about the rent. They wanted 450 dollars a month plus a two-month deposit. The place would be free in October. I could barely meet this payment with my credit card but it looked like I would not be able to use my card for a while. I had to think twice, but I could find no other way. I used my card to make the payment and signed the lease. I thanked my new friends for their kind help. Then we bought some frankfurters and returned to the office. I had not been able to take Ömer with me since he was on duty. I gave him the good news as soon as I entered the building and informed him that he would be able to see the flat that evening. His reaction was, "Dear mother, whatever flat you may have found is bound to be better than that awful hotel room." We were becoming New Yorkers.

XLIX

Many Things Can Happen
Before Daybreak

On the first of the month we paid our last bill to the hotel, and taking what baggage we had, we moved happily to our new apartment. I prepared the bedroom for my son, I was going to use the couch in the living room. We hanged our few items, made a list of what we lacked and went to work. Food, etc. would have to be bought after office hours. There were many things lacking, in this so-called furnished flat—sheets and towels, some kitchen ware, etc. For those things we had to wait for the weekend. The kitchen had a stove and a few pots but there was not much else. That sort of shopping had to be delayed.

Our first night in our new house, since the sheets provided did not look clean enough, we slept with our clothes on. We were happy still. We now had a home. Our dinner consisted of some bread, salami and water. The situation of the apartment was not too bad. Both the kitchen and the living room had windows opening to 54th Street. There was a little corridor leading to the bathroom and the bedroom. This meant that we would not be in each other's way, too much. There was a small entrance hall, which would save us from the incessant noise of the elevators.

In the evening I rang both Pat and Eddie and asked them to kindly send the things they were keeping for us to our new address. I had realized that I had put a number of towels and sheets that I had acquired in Boston into a cardboard box, though I could not remember where it was placed. If they arrived early it would save me some shopping.

It was wonderful to be able to receive part of my salary on the second day of the month. I had asked for a small loan the day before and the Counsellor had kindly given me an advance.

397

We had a lot of shopping to do. From light bulbs to brooms and brushes. The next day our cardboard boxes reached the apartment and we were able to at least partially settle down.

I was naturally keeping contact with Zeyneb all the time. She had been successful in the exam she had to take at the Foreign Office in Ankara and was waiting for her appointment to be announced. She had been using the furniture I had put in storage while they were living in Turkey. I advised her that apart from a few things that I would like to keep (like the porcelain table by the well-known artist F. Koral) she should sell everything and buy dollars, since they would need the money when they came to the States.

Toward the end of October, Ambassador Türkmen gave me the good news that Zeyneb's appointment had been approved. He added, however, that there was a bad catch. He said, "Under a new regulation, two persons belonging to the same family cannot be employed in the same office." There was a big lump in my throat. How could that be? I knew of two brothers who were working in the office. When I reminded him of this, he answered that their appointments were made prior to this regulation. Well, what was I to do? After all the exams, etc. would my hopes be dashed suddenly?

The General Assembly was on and our Foreign Secretary, Mr. İ. S. Çağlayangil, had come to New York and he would be speaking at the General Assembly. I had not met him before. He turned out to be a very nice gentleman. He was kind, well-mannered and always had a good word for everyone. Everybody in the office enjoyed his presence. The news that Mr. Çağlayangil had been appointed as the Foreign Secretary had at first caused consternation among the Foreign Office diplomats in Ankara (he was not a career diplomat). His background was from the Ministry of Interior. He had been a governor and the chief of police in the past. So the diplomats were a little leery. Years ago, when I was still married, we had heard about his appointment, the first time, at the reception given to celebrate the Shah's birthday at the Iranian Embassy. However, he was to prove that one should not judge anyone by his previous appointments but by what he could achieve in a new environment.

I was very concerned with the difficulty of getting my daughter to New York. One morning, Mr. Çağlayangil must have noticed my constraint and asked me why I was so worried. I could not help myself and I explained my daughter's situation. He laughed heartily and said, "Do not worry on that score. Her exam in Ankara was exemplary and she will be appointed to the Consul General's office as executive secretary." When I started thanking him profusely he encountered this with, "No need to thank me, you should thank you daughter for such a brilliant exam."

When talking with friends in the office I had mentioned that I had had to pay a deposit for two months' rent, they told me I should talk to the City Council's office at the U.N. since the legal deposit was only for one month's rent and that I should be able to get my money back. I was at a loss, since I liked the apartment, I did not want to cause unnecessary trouble.

Toward the end of October Zeyneb's call, advising me of their arrival, had made me very happy. After five long years, I was going to be able to collect all my children under one roof and would be able to give them a home. Together with Ömer we went to meet them at the airport. Seze, Sertaç and Zeyneb all arrived in good health. Seze was only two and a half years old. While driving from the airport I was giving her some advice and she kept answering "Oldu. Oldu." Meaning O.K. in Turkish. She was a clever and well-behaved child.

We went into the apartment, baggage and everything. It was a great jubilation. After years of wandering half around the globe, we had at last come together. Ömer had a double bed and I had hoped the three females could sleep on it, with Sertaç and Ömer using the couches in the sitting room. Naturally, five people in a two room apartment was going to be pretty crowded but this was the best I could manage for the moment. Anyway, everyone was both excited and tired, so we all went to sleep early.

Zeyneb was to start work early next morning. So Zeyneb, Ömer and I, we three went together to the Türkevi and Sertaç stayed at home with Seze. We left Ömer at the entrance, Zeyneb went out of the elevator on the fifth floor and I went to my office on the tenth floor. We were quite early and there was no one about. Suddenly I had this idea. The fact that they had charged me two months deposit could be used to my advantage. I rang up the City Council's office and arranged to have a consultation with them during my lunch hour. Zeyneb went home for lunch and I went to the City Council. A gentleman called Stegman received me. He was an elderly and portly gentleman who was quite amiable. I explained my situation and showed him the contract I had signed. As he read through the contract his anger began to show. He rang the phone number of the agent who had devised the contract. He gave them a long lecture and hung up. He then told me, "Mrs. Sılan, the agent is willing to return to you the full deposit he has collected from you against the law, provided that you vacate the premises before the end of the month. There are only two days to go, can you find another apartment in such a short period?" I was rather taken aback. Such short notice. However, in the meantime we might be able to find a much larger apartment where we could feel more comfortable. I thanked him and asked him to let me see what I could do. I had to do something.

L
Looking for a Roof over My Family

There was time before I had to report to the office, so I ran home. Zeyneb had come in for lunch. When I explained the situation, we decided to make two pairs. Sertaç would take Seze along and start hunting for a new flat. Zeyneb and I would start looking, as we were going back to the office. We had also split our areas. Zeyneb and I would start searching around 1st Avenue and the connecting streets and Sertaç and Seze would concentrate on 2nd and 3rd avenues. As we were walking by 49th Street we saw a sign "For Rent" at a newly painted and renovated apartment building. I took down the phone number written on the board and we had to rush to our respective offices. We were on time and I told Ömer what had transpired since he was on duty at the entrance. I called the number I had taken and made an appointment for early next morning. On the way back we looked over the situation of the apartment and it looked satisfactory from the outside. Sertaç had found nothing suitable. Seze was quickly tired of walking and they had returned home after a short search.

The excitement of getting together once more and with whatever food we mustered to arrange plus the stress of searching for a new apartment had tired us all and we were sound asleep pretty early. Still, we were all deliriously happy. We had come together again after being scattered around the whole world. We each had suffered in our own way but such trials had strengthened our willingness to succeed in life. Family ties meant so much for a person. I was surprised that I had survived to stay alive for five years without my children. Yes, I was very tired, but the excitement of having my children around me once again would not let me sleep that night.

Early in the morning Zeyneb and I rushed to our appointment. The man in charge was waiting for us. He took us up in an elevator to a triplex apartment on the fourth floor. In other words, on each floor there was one room and the rooms were arranged one on top of the other. One entered a small hall plus a small kitchen and up three steps there was a room. Then there were steps going into a vestibule. On this floor there was a room that included a tiny bath and a toilet. Then one went some more steps and there was a bigger room with its own bathroom and toilet. There was another vestibule on this floor and through a balcony door one could go out onto a terrace. This last room was the largest one in the apartment. Three separate whitewashed rooms! Very spick and span. No previous tenants and nothing dirty. The rent was 450 dollars per month and they were asking for one month's deposit. It looked like this would serve our needs. The first room would be made into a living room where I could sleep. The small room in the second floor, we could let Ömer have for himself and the sunny and big room on the third floor would be the bedroom for Zeyneb and her family. I asked the man showing us around to keep the apartment for me until the afternoon so I could get the family to see it. It was totally empty! Where could we sit, eat or sleep? The next day was the last day of the month! I did not have much cash. We talked the situation over with Zeyneb. She did not have much cash left, either. She had been through bad times and was more practical about things. She said, "Don't worry Mommy, we can buy three mattresses to sleep on. For the rest we shall use paper plates for our food and eat sitting on the stairs. We can change the stairs into a dining room, with one person per step! It could be fun. In the future, one by one, we can buy the necessary furniture. At the moment this place will be our salvation! During our lunch break I took Sertaç and Ömer to see the place. Since both approved, I signed a new contract and rented the place. I called Mr. Stegman and told him what had transpired and he promised me to get back my deposit and cancel the contract I had signed for the apartment we were going to vacate. In the excitement I had clearly forgotten, this meant I would be getting 900 dollars cash.

402

On the last day of the month Zeyneb and I went to a furniture store and bought two beds and a settee that had folding sides that could be used for a bed as well and had them delivered to our new flat. After work "the boys" searched around and found that one could rent something called "U-haul." This was a two-wheeled contraption that can be attached to an automobile and carry a lot of bags, etc. Well, since no taxi would agree to attach this to their car, the boys had to haul it themselves! So whatever we had as our belongings or furniture, which consisted mostly of bags and card boxes, were hauled in this manner. I remember that we had to wait a while until the rush hour traffic abated and 1st Avenue got somewhat deserted. Ömer and Sertaç were hauling and we girls were showing them the way. As the boys had to take the contraption back, Zeyneb and I made up our new beds. As is usual in America, the flat had an icebox and a gas oven already installed and there were venetian blinds in all the windows. When we had placed the bed into Ömer's room we found out that there was hardly any place to walk around the bed. He practically had to jump into his bed and out! Zeyneb's room was a little more comfortable. We had already bought the cheapest paper plates and glasses that we could find. By the time food was ready the gentlemen had returned. We had a lovely meal sitting on the stairs and laughing all the while. At long last I had been able to get my family together under one roof. Nothing could make me happier.

403

LI
What the Devil Is This?

The first day of October I was forced to run to Mr. Stegman's office. The news was terrible. The people who had agreed to return my down payment for two months not only had refused to return it but had now started a lawsuit against me. I was stunned. What was going on? Mr. Stegman told me that I had to wait until I would be given notice by the court and advised me to find myself a lawyer. How long would this procedure last? Where can I get a lawyer? How much would I have to pay as lawyer's fees? All sorts of questions were whirling in my mind. Mr. Stegman gave me the name and address of a lawyer and told me I had to be patient. What else could I have done, anyway? Had I not been forced to be patient all my life?

Luckily I had been paid my full salary on the first day of the month. I had to pay some installment plus interest to my credit card account. There was also bills to be paid, like electricity, phone, et al. Also I had to buy food, however little we ate. Someone in the office had told me that there was an Arabic financed bank that gave small loans. I applied to them for a loan. Ömer was now able to bring in some of his earnings. I had reached the conclusion that life is never calm and one should not expect complete peace of mind. On the other hand, I was determined to do the best I could. My biggest luck was to have my children and their positive reactions in face of our mutual calamities. They were willing to fight for their lives and they were willing to back me up. We had become a well knitted family ready to back each other up in everything we did. There was no one we could turn to, anyway.

The same evening I rang the lawyer whose name Mr. Stegman had given me and made an appointment for the next day.

His office was downtown, namely on the southern tip of Manhattan. Taking a taxi would cost a fortune and the cheapest way was to take the subway. However, everyone had warned me about the subways, especially it was dangerous traveling at night. I had no other choice. I took the plunge and went on the subway. It was pretty dreary and this was the first time I was riding on the New York Subway. The lawyer was a middle aged snobbish Jewish man. I must confess at this point that Jews are a race that I very much admire. Especially in New York, they usually occupy the best positions in every profession, doctors, writers, you name it. Usually they are the tops. Having been brought up in a late Ottoman family I never had any prejudice for races.

I do not remember the lawyer's name. After I explained why I was there he first asked for an exorbitant fee. When I told him my financial situation was not good and that I would prefer to pay his fee from what we would obtain from the claimants, he began to change his manner. He started trying to make a pass, saying that there would be other ways that he could be compensated. I was aghast. I quickly jumped up and before he could do anything picked up my file and dashed out of his office. I was so fed up that once I got out of that dirty office building, it took me some time to find the subway station for my return trip. I cursed my luck all the way to midtown. I did not tell the children what had happened. I just said he had asked for a large fee and I had not trusted him. They could be drastic and I did not want any trouble.

So next morning I was at Mr. Stegman's Office, once again. I told him the full story and asked for his help. He was very sympathetic. He really was a fatherly figure. He promised to help me and showed me the way I could start a court case against them. However, I still had to wait until papers from the court would be served. I did as he advised and started a court case against that company. Meanwhile I received a notice from the court. The date at this point is obscure. I had to go to the court. The judge took me in, I told him all my story, when he asked why I had no lawyer I explained that I could not afford one but I had been advised by the City Commission to do what I was doing. The judge was kind and when he said "You may go now"

405

I left and went back to work. After a week papers from the claimants were served to me. I had to appear before another judge on such and such a date.

Days were passing by, we were as poor as church mice. Despite anything being together with my children was my biggest consolation. Especially the times I was able to spend with my darling granddaughter were the best times of my life. On weekends we would try to do our house chores. Our apartment was still almost empty but there was cleaning to do even in an empty house. Preparing dinner for my children was never a bother for me. We had to learn about Manhattan and explore the many treasures available. I still had to work along my ideal program, like furniture for the house. Even more important, we had to find a job for Sertaç and a kindergarten for Seze. These were some of the basic things we should be accomplishing in the near future.

A few days before my court case was due I visited Mr. Stegman once again and reminded him of my case and asked for his help. Unfortunately, he had had surgery on his foot and so he said he could not possibly attend my case. When he saw that tears had began to cascade down my cheeks and when I promised to hire a cab both ways to downtown and back, he relented and promised to come to the court. He really had difficulty in walking and was using a cane for support. He too was Jewish but he was so different from the lawyer. What sorts of difficulties I had to go through! Many times, I would wish that I had dropped dead. I knew, however, that such a thing would only end my misery, but my children would be worse off in this utterly foreign city.

On the required day, I bundled Mr. Stegman, as I had promised, into a yellow cab and rushed to the court. This was a different courtroom and it turned out that my counter charges had also been transferred to this court to be heard together. I was very frightened when we went into the courtroom. The rich company that was suing me was a Jewish firm. They had three uncompassionate looking Jewish lawyers ready to cut me to pieces. This was such a society. Everything had to be done according to set rules and no one could go against them. What was I to do? They called out for us to stand up when the judge came into the courtroom and we were told to sit down when the judge took his place. The clerk read the various documents, then the judge asked the lawyers to restate their case against me. Each of the three lawyers spoke one after another belittling me and accusing me of all sorts of things. Here was a Turkish woman, etc. Finally, it was my turn. The judge asked me if I had a lawyer. I told him I could not afford one and that I would present my case personally. I explained everything that had happened and finally said that I had a witness to all the things I had said and presented Mr. Stegman. He also looked up his notes and read them to the judge, explaining what had happened. It took an interminable time but finally the judge began to read his verdict. His decision was in my favor. Not only were they forced to return my deposits but they were also forced to pay interest on it as well as all court charges. People in the room started congratulating me. Mr. Stegman was also very happy. I had won a case against three experienced lawyers at their own game. I was quickly given a check in front of the judge. This was worth the world to me. Not only was I proud of myself but I also felt like a millionaire! I put Mr. Stegman into a yellow cab and took him back to his office. Now I had the money and had gained confidence. His being a witness had turned the tables in my favor. American justice had worked for me. When I gave them the news my children were also delighted that evening. I was surprised to find that they had had very little hope of my success. On the other hand, I had always been confident that since I was right I would have to win in the end. I never give up hope.

In the coming years, I was to learn how to get what I wanted from poor Jewish lady shoppers in New York. Both on getting into a bus or reaching for an item that was on sale, they were always the first to reach. I having been brought up the way I was, used to talk to the salesperson, saying things like "Please, can I have a look at that" and by that time someone would have grabbed it and it was gone.

I do not know why but for many years I had fancied myself as an "harlequin," laughing on the outside and crying in the inside. I guess my name also influenced this funny feeling. Being named "Joy" which is "Şen" in Turkish, I could not be a sullen person. I had to smile. However, the real "me" hidden behind the smiling face could be crying! Perhaps deep down under the feeling that comes uppermost in me is love. I am using this word in a general sense. One can love a flower, or a picture, or a leaf, an animal or yet a person. If one finds love inside oneself, then one can love anything. Love makes a person shine, inside and out. Suffice it that one can find this love inside oneself. Once, a much younger person who was working in the same office with me had enquired, "How can I be happy?" I countered this question with the following. "How's your health?" and "Do you earn your living?" and since her answers to these questions were positive, I had told her that she had not to look anywhere else for being happy, that all these were happiness. She was somewhat taken aback and went away. However, some time later I saw her with her young daughter, they were laughing, she saw me and said, "Now I know what you were talking about and I thank you for your advice. Now I am happy."

When I had first come to New York I was somewhat disappointed. This was due to the fact that I had been so pleasantly installed in Boston. My apartment, although very small, overlooked the magnolia trees of Commonwealth Avenue. In New York, gradually I began to look at people who were passing by. Smiling faces, cunning people, thoughtful faces, dynamic people, etc. In Boston I was able to watch flowers and little chipmunks. More and more, people had become more interesting for me. I had began to try and find out the feelings of people who kept rushing by me. So I gradually began to forget the nature that I had enjoyed in Boston and began to get interested in the people of New York.

When I was a child, living in Kadıköy, whenever I was walking on the sidewalk, I would always try to look at the windows of the houses. I used to make a point of imagining what was going on inside and wondered, "Did they have nice furniture? Was their mother as beautiful as my mother was? Did they have nice toys like I had?" And I used to pray that they too should be happy as I was. So it seems that I had developed this kind of inner satisfaction at a very early age and would never lose it.

I lived in New York for eight years and regardless of the hardships, I enjoyed every minute of it. It was a fantastic city.

One could reach beauty without spending hardly a penny. On a bright weekend one could walk on the boulevards for say forty or fifty blocks. At many points one could encounter lovely flowers, listen to street bands performing, gaze at art work, at galleries. All for free. Just as the Turkish poet Orhan Veli had written, "The air is free and fresh water is free." If it was raining, I would go into one of those giant bookstores and read a book for hours without paying a cent. One could also listen to records for hours without being obliged to buy one. There were always free concerts and choirs and lectures at various churches. I would spend hours searching for old churches or sights.

Then I had found out about Central Park. I learned that in the year 1857 a fellow called Frederick Law Olmsted from Connecticut had the wild idea of building such a place and he was able to realize his dream. The gardens started from the corner of Fifth Avenue and 59th street and go up to 106th street and later in 1863 was extended until 110th Street on the East side going up-town, and then on the West side it covered the same area going up Eighth Avenue. I read somewhere the park covered 800 acres of land. Mr. Olmstead was a self-educated landscape architect and became the manager of the park he designed. Among the giant skyscrapers of Manhattan, Central Park is a paradise waiting to be discovered. You can sit under huge green trees surrounded with colorful flowers and read a book or a newspaper in peace and quiet. In another corner of the park there is a skating rink. If you are not young enough to skate you can enjoy the youngsters gliding on the ice for hours. There are many statues scattered around the park. All New Yorkers will find something that they will enjoy. Of course all of these things are free of charge. If you have the means you can ride a horse or you can enjoy a lovely meal in the many restaurants or cafés scattered around the park. The place is the breathing lungs of the city.

I eventually had picked a corner for myself in this immense garden. On Sunday mornings I would leave the house early and let the youngsters enjoy a late morning. I would haul the huge Sunday *Times* to my favorite place near 72nd street on the East Side. I would also carry my thermos of hot coffee with me. Sometimes the children would come and find me in my favorite site. This was a few peaceful hours spent listening to the birds.

The name plate we had devised for our apartment also caused some merriment among the children. We were forced to write SİLAN, BÜLBÜLOĞLU, DEVRES, one after the other. One mother and her two children and each had a different surname! This was the requirement of civilization.

Those years my sleeping habits had become quite erratic. Some nights, when I felt bad and not wanting to awaken the children, I would slip out of the house quietly, walk north along Third Avenue toward P. J. Clark's on the corner of 53rd Street. This is an Irish Bar which stays open 24 hours. The bar is almost always crowded with people chatting and enjoying themselves. After theatre crowds, including well-known actors and actresses would also appear at times. After a few visits, they get to know you. Especially the bartenders will recognize faces almost automatically and professionally. What is wonderful about the place is that you do not need an escort and single females are accepted cordially. What is more, once the bartenders know you, they sort of take you under their wings. Once, a rather drunk gentleman insisted on my having a drink with him and the elderly bartender quickly intervened and said, "The lady has her own drink, let her alone." That was it. No one dared to offer me a drink from then on. Being in a crowd, watching people talking and laughing somehow soothed my nerves and after an hour of this, I would return home and go to bed. What was wonderful was that one did not have to drink some hard liqueur. I could not afford whisky anyway but a Perrier with a twist of lemon would be quite enough.

I have a very sentimental recollection connected with P. J. Clark's. It was sometime later, when I had become a real New Yorker or that I was thinking of myself as such. I had invited a dear friend from Turkey to that unique place that I liked so much. While being shown a seat by one of the gentlemen, I told him that I was from the Turkish Mission. I guess Mr. Ennis had been with P. J. Clark's for some time. Hearing the Turkish Mission mentioned, he asked me whether I knew of Ambassador William Macomber. During those years that elegant ambassador and his delightful wife, my good friends from Ankara, were in New York. Mr. Macomber was heading the Metropolitan Museum. When I answered him positively Mr. Ennis told me that he and Mr. Macomber were school friends way back and he asked me if I could inform him of his whereabouts. I was happy to write a note to Bill and give him this news. Sometime later I received a letter telling me that he had gone to P. J. Clark's and met his old friend Mr. Ennis. A few weeks later when I saw Mr. Ennis, he was very grateful.

The following weekend, after I was able to get my deposit back, we realized there were many sales in town. We sorely needed a dining table and six chairs. So we went shopping from store to store. By the afternoon we had been able to purchase a dining table and six chairs. The legs were metal and the seats were straw. They were things we enjoyed and we could afford. We also bought a table lamp, since the dining table would have to be used as a writing table as well. These had given the house an air of being lived in. For the first time that night, the family was able to sit around a common family dining table and eat a proper meal. We had become civilized. Zeyneb had also received her paycheck and had contributed to the expenses of the house. The only one who had no paying job was Sertaç and he was helping in many ways. The new year was close by.

While I was busy running after lawyers and so on, Zeyneb had been able to locate a kindergarten that was called the Montessori School. This was an organization that was recognized all over the world and it was quite expensive. The school was next to a Catholic Church on 47th street between 1st and 2nd Avenues. They had a small but lovely garden and next to them was the Japanese Cultural Center. The school was only a block away from where we were living. This was an ideal situation. So Seze was comfortably placed in her school and soon Ömer was to start at NYU.

I had brought a few pieces from Turkey hoping that I could sell them for cash. So I decided it was time for me to try and sell those things. Since we had recouped my rental deposits our financial situation had turned from bleak to acceptable. However, I felt we had to have some further guarantee. One of the things I had brought from Turkey was a prayer rug. It belonged to my mother's grandmother. It was of red colored, heavy silk and embroidered with golden threads. I had found it in my wedding trousseau and Mother had said "it could come handy some day." Well, that day had come. It had family connotations also but I was in no condition to go into sentimentality. Our family needed cash desperately.

I had met a few well-to-do ladies in New York and when I showed this prayer rug to them they were charmed and said this must be priceless. There was one lady whose husband was a rabbi. They were very well off. I had met her at one of the receptions of our embassy. We had enjoyed each other's company and she had even sent her private car to pick me up from my apartment and had me driven to her country house. During one of these outings I had met another lady who was married to an Italian businessman and they had a flat at one of the very special places in New York, namely the UN Plaza apartments. She too was interested in me (maybe my being Turkish had been a source of interest) and she had invited me to her fabulous apartment more than a couple of times. I also had dared to invite these ladies to my house, which was a modest Turkish home and I had made sure to put some Turkish objects around the house. These were things like some silver and some kilims to make the place more livable. In one such visit I had shown the prayer rug to these ladies and they were very impressed. Finally, one of these ladies offered to pay a very handsome price for the prayer rug. I hated selling a family heirloom, dating more then a century, after all it was an heirloom! On the other hand, I could never use it functionally and I was in no position to put it on show.

I spent the New Year's Eve with my darling granddaughter, Seze. We had a family dinner. Then the youngsters went out to one of their friend's for a New Year's party. I was able to enjoy Seze and I put her to bed at midnight, wishing well for the world and for my family. I lit my cigarette and as I always did, started analyzing my life. I thought about the things the New Year might bring. I looked back, one by one, at the variety of things life had brought my way. I listened to the joyful noises coming from the street and finally I decided to forget about the past until the day I might want to write about it. I had made a home for my children. I felt very, very happy. The first day of 1978 had already started when I turned in.

LII

Unexpected Happenings

We were getting well accustomed to life in our apartment on 49th Street. Finally, Sertaç had also found a job. He had began to work at a store that sold records, called Sam Goody. Seze was attending kindergarten. Zeyneb was working as secretary to Council General Mr. Tevfik Ünaydın and I was secretary to the Ambassador. Ömer was enrolled at NYU and he also had kept his part-time job at the Türkevi. We were gradually making our house a livable place and purchasing things we sorely needed, one by one.

Gradually, we were also beginning to develop a circle of friends. My very old friends Mina Türkmen (Özdoğancı) and Sara Korle were very kind and friendly as always. Mr. Korle, her husband, had already retired from his post as chief of protocol at the United Nations. Altemur and Güzide Kılıç always invited me to their parties. Apart from these old friends, I began to make some new friends. Actually, one of them, the well-known painter Burhan Doğançay, was an old friend from Ankara and I had also met and enjoyed Erol Akyavaş, another Turkish painter who had made a name for himself in New York. I also enjoyed the friendship of the wives of both these painters. I had also found Attila Türkkan, who was a great friend of my brother Nur, and his charming wife. Deputy Permanent Representative Nazmi Akıman and his wife had been very cordial to me. I would also like to recall with regret (they have both passed away since), the two archeologists whose acquaintance had enriched my life. My childhood friend Cemile Garan had introduced me to Prof Kenan Erim. Our friendship with Prof. Erim over the years developed into a lasting one. I was naturally a part of his "Aphrodisias Lovers" group. Through him I met Ms. Theresa Goell. She was a great admirer of Turks and she had done several excavations at the famous Nemrud Mountain in Eastern Turkey. She was elderly and I thought she resembled Prof. Jale Inan, at least with her unending energy. Although they had reached a certain age, they could still compete with many of the young archeologists around them. Being together with such "doers" has always given me strength.

My circle of friends kept growing. Berna and Üner Kirdar, Esin and Engin Ansay, Seniha and Talat Halman were the couples I had met and enjoyed. Engin's uncle was a great friend of my father's and I had met the gentleman while I was at the university. They had asked girls attending the university to join the military for two months during the school recess. I had been assigned to work as a nurse at the military hospital at Haydarpaşa and for about two weeks. I had been assigned where Dr. Ansay was the chief physician. He was certainly a man to admire. Also Mr. Kirdar's father, who was for many years the governor of İstanbul, was a friend of my father.

Along with these social contacts I would like to mention another friend whose lifelong assistance to me and to mine can never be forgotten. I mean the good Doctor Muhtar Yıldız and his long-term assistant, Ms. Esther Post. Today he is still the only doctor in whom I have complete trust. Not only is he a good physician but above all he is human and understanding. He will always be at your bedside at the drop of a hat. He is truly priceless for me. One of the happenings of those days that gave me so much happiness was the wedding of Burhan and Angela Doğançay. Angela has always been an angel, as her name implies, and our friendship still flourishes.

They say "there is never a dull moment." Our life was a very good example. The flat we were living in was a triplex. There was an elevator but there was no regular doorman. To enter the building one either had a key or rang the bell of the apartment one was trying to reach. One day our door bell rang and thinking that one of my children had arrived I buzzed the main door without asking who was at the door. A little later when the elevator stopped at our flat I opened the door. However, instead of one of the children there was a very well-dressed gentleman. He took one look at me and into whatever he could see in the

414

apartment and he promptly turned around and rang the bell of the apartment next door. That evening I was explaining to the children about the gentleman caller. They all said that they also had come across well-dressed, elderly gentlemen in the elevator and that they all rang our neighbor's door. We were under the impression that an important dignitary must be residing there to have such visitors!

The next Sunday everybody was relaxed and the youngsters were browsing the *Village Voice*. Apart from Cue listings showing all theatres, etc. that paper has also many pages assigned to sex and related happenings. Well, quite by chance they found that the address of our apartment was given under the title of a house of indecency and things like being thrashed by experienced operators and things like that! We really were surprised and they were all laughing. It meant that the dignified looking gentlemen were coming to that flat for exotic fun! The technical term was "sado-masochist." Laughing about such things was something but when it was related to your next door neighbor, it was quite something else. At least the walls and heavy door did not permit us to hear what was going on.

After a while news seeped through the embassy that Ambassador Türkmen was going back to Turkey. I was very sorry. I was told that ambassadors usually enjoyed a term of four years at the seat they are assigned to. Mr. Türkmen had been assigned to the U.N. in 1975 but he was leaving New York in 1978. My sorrow to learn that Mr. Türkmen was leaving suddenly turned into joy since we heard that Mr. Orhan Eralp would be replacing Mr. Türkmen. Jale Eralp was a very old childhood friend. Sometime ago Ferda, who was also the Ambassador's secretary, had decided to get married and had gone to settle in Missouri. This meant that I would become the sole secretary for the new Ambassador. People always try to develop some sort of a direction for their lives but it is not possible to overcome the vagaries of fate.

When Mr. Türkmen had engaged me to his office, I had always done the best I could. But that I was going to work for people I had known well, or had been good friends with, was certainly unexpected. This was certainly a vagary of fate! On the other hand, Mr. Türkmen's wife, Mina, was a good friend

415

from my Ankara days. So I had to prove myself as a good secretary to the Ambassador. However, the newcomers were also old time bosom friends. Especially our friendship with Jale Eralp went back to our teenage days.

Our relations with both families went back to my married days in Ankara when I was comfortably well off and we socialized with most of the so-called Ankara society. However, my position in the Embassy now required a completely different approach. I had to arrange my relationship with the gentleman in the office in a totally different manner than outside it. I never asked for any special favors depending on our relationship of the past. I would never allow the other employees to feel that I was utilizing my special relationship with the Ambassador for my personal profit. This meant that I made sure to be in the office before the Ambassador arrived and never to leave the office before he went out. At a certain point I must have developed some sort of grievance. I remember complaining to the councillor that many people in the office had been coming later than the time they were supposed to be working. He laughed and said, "Not to worry, do just as they are doing." When I protested that my conscience would not allow me such laxity he had again laughed and said, "You see, you are not that sort of a person, so you should grin and bear it." I really had my lesson and never thought about it again.

Despite all my efforts, I know that there were many instances when I was criticized as the "privileged" employee. Just as the French proverb says, "Honni soit qui mal y pense." I am certain that I did the best I could.

My employment in New York had given me a chance to meet a different class of foreign office personnel. During my past as the child of an Ankara politician I had met all sorts of dignitaries. For example, I can never forget the charm of Mr. Numan Menemencioglu, whom I simply adored. There were many others, some I liked, some that I thought very good-looking and many were just friends.

However, I had met them in an utterly different social circle. I had never known anything about their working lives. I used to know how they danced, for example, but had no idea about how they worked. This time I was seeing them at work. I was a witness to the difficult conditions under which they were operating and for some, my appreciation had doubled. At the same time, as a private secretary I felt it was my duty to make their life as comfortable as possible. My working life, which had started by the time I was forty, was gradually changing my outlook toward life. I wanted to do everything I did perfectly but at the same time I would not let anyone boss me around. I would not allow anyone to belittle me in any way. During my working days in New York I experienced two such occasions both due to the bellicosity of junior elements who did not know how to behave. As I may have mentioned before, one of the secretaries would be on lunch hour duty, namely they had to stay at their desks when all others would go out for lunch. In a way this was to ensure that urgent messages would not be delayed. One day, when I was on duty, one junior executive called me to his room and asked me to go down and buy a sandwich for him. This was hardly my duty. However, I simply told him that I was sorry but I could not do that. He was rather angry and asked "Why not?" I said, "I happen to be on duty and cannot leave my desk." He then said, "I am ordering you to do something, are you not duty bound as well?" My answer was as follows: "I am sorry. I am a secretary and not an errand boy. Furthermore, I happen to be on duty. If you like I can phone for a sandwich and the receptionist who is also on duty will ring you when it arrives and you can go down to pick it up." He was too surprised to be able to manage an answer and I quietly left the room.

The second occasion involved a more senior person. I was working to finish up a document for the Ambassador. The gentleman reached me by phone and asked me to connect to him an airline. I tried to explain the situation I was in and I gently reminded him the receptionist could do this service for him. Before I could finish what I was saying, he banged the phone down. This was certainly an insult. I could not bear the idea of someone hanging up before I could finish my sentence. I was really pressed for time and had to continue writing the document I had to finish. However, at a later hour I went to that gentleman's office, told him that such an action was beyond any insult I had experienced and that if he did not apologize for his action, I was going to resign from my post. Luckily he proved to be a gentleman and he did apologize. The affair ended there.

At another time I was again angry for some untoward action someone had perpetuated and was almost puffing when that most amicable gentleman, Mr. Sinan Korle, walked into my office. He was always quick. He sensed that I was fuming and asked me about it. When I explained what had happened, he sort of laughed and reminded me of an old Turkish adage. They say that anyone who does not behave properly has never had lamb chops (lacking proper education). I could not help laughing.

I am not quite sure whether Father came to the States or not, on the other hand, I am sure I had not gone to Turkey for the summer of 1978. Frankly, there was little in Turkey that interested me. So during summer leave I agreed to join two other ladies and we rented a small cottage in East Hampton for ten days. It was sort of a rustic house by the sea. It was a short but nice vacation.

On my return from my short vacation, I found that some things had began to go wrong in our flat. In the first place, some people had called, said they had orders from the municipality and they came in and boarded one of the windows overlooking to the south. Apparently that window had been opened against the municipal regulations. So our dining area became dark even at noon time. Meanwhile one of the drain pipes in the kitchen had developed a leak and despite our frantic requests no one had bothered to have it fixed. As a result, we were all uncomfortable. Our lease was coming to an end and I suggested we should look for another place to live and move. I asked the children if they wanted to continue living as a single family unit or should we all look for separate quarters. Ömer said he would prefer living with me. Zeyneb and Sertaç naturally wanted their own home.

So we all started looking around. Finally, we found a studio apartment at 47th and 2nd Avenue that Zeyneb and Sertaç could move into with Seze. As soon as they could, they moved into their new apartment. I and Ömer were still looking for something we would like. There were three apartment blocks I had my eye on. All were very near the office, mainly between 46th and 47th Streets, between 1st and 2nd Avenues. At one of the buildings

418

an old friend, Nilüfer Reddy, had a flat and I had visited that building many times. The other one was on 2nd Avenue and finally the third one was the block of flats where Zeyneb had just moved in.

After a short interval I was able to find an apartment they designated as a one-bedroom flat. That meant that the flat had two rooms, a bedroom and a living room. It had a beautiful view and was very sunny. It was affordable and I paid the required down payment and signed a lease. I was really happy and was already dreaming about how I would decorate it when a letter arrived from the owner. I was being advised that they were returning my check since their son had decided to move into Manhattan and would be occupying that flat. Apparently they had the right! I was very heart broken but there was nothing I could do.

Labor Day in America is a recognized holiday that no one can ignore. Almost all the places, even the smallest diners, would be closed. That morning Sertaç, Zeyneb and Seze had gone off for an outing. Ömer was on duty at the Türkevi and I was in the flat trying to finish some delayed housework. After I was through with the cleaning, I was just having a cup of tea when Ömer called. Apparently no diner would answer his phone calls and he could not leave the building since he was on duty. He asked me if I could bring him a sandwich. I quickly prepared one and went joyfully to my son. It was a beautiful autumn day. We chatted a bit with Ömer and on the way back I was again looking for apartments to let. I was sure I must have been back home under one hour at most. When I came into the flat, I was shocked. The flat was upside down! We had been burgled. All the drawers were on the floor. Our dresses, etc. were all strewn about. Everything I had had been ransacked. When I had first moved into New York I had thought of renting a strong box at a bank. However, at the branch where my account was they did not have one for rent and later on I hardly had the money to rent one. Consequently, all my family heirlooms (the jewelry I had inherited from mother, et al) was bundled in a scarf in one of the drawers. Who would have thought a burglar would bother about such a poor apartment with hardly any furniture in it? I had not thought about the jewelry and I was picking up my underwear scattered about the room I suddenly jumped. Yes. They were gone. I went under the drawers and everywhere. Nothing! They were stolen. No. No. No. Yes. Yes. Yes. They were gone. Every valuable thing that Mother gave, that Father and that the children's father had given me, some gifts that were given to me at my wedding, some that were really valuable, some had sentimental value involving the people who had given them, etc. I was saving some for my children and some could be sold in a real emergency. In fact, these were almost like a diary for me. Like, Mommy gave this to me on my nineteenth birthday or this was given when I had my first child, etc. Tears were pouring down while I was calling the police department. I told the police that I had a diplomatic passport so detectives came to the flat. Together with the jewelry, our small radio, the tennis racket that I had recently bought for my son and every other thing that had any value were stolen. They searched the flat, looked for finger prints, and asked if I suspected anyone. None of the doors were broken. They decided that the thief had entered the flat through the roof. That meant the thief had to be someone who knew the layout of the flat. There was a sort of a doorman whose employment had been terminated by the owners a week ago on account of his being a thief. I asked them to go and search his place. Apparently under the law they could not enter a man's house without proper evidence and a court order. They promised to continue looking for them but nothing was ever returned.

I was lucky in a way because two rather valuable pieces had been saved. I was invited to a party the previous night. A broach Mother had given me decorated with sapphires and pearls that I had worn for the party was still in my handbag plus a "face-a-main" in gold that also belonged to my mother. The glasses I used most of the time. I had taken off the broach and placed it in my handbag in the taxi coming home and luckily had forgotten to take it out of my handbag. My aquamarine ring, given to me some years ago by my ex-husband, was also saved because I never took it off my finger. Years later I was to give that ring to Ömer's wife at their wedding. It was a piece remaining from his father anyway. For a few days I was grieving for my jewelry but gradually I came to decide that my most precious jewel, my beautiful daughter Ayşe had been lost, I was not to worry about the stolen jewelry. Now, we had to get out of this flat. Everything had gone wrong. God is always at the side of the poor they say, so a few days later, Norman, who was the doorman of the apartment where Zeyneb had found a studio flat told me there was a one-bedroom apartment that had just been vacated. He had taken pity on me since almost every day I was calling to ask if anything was available. I went in and took a look. It was lovely. One could even see a part of East River from its windows. It was also open to morning sun. I called up the management and was able to rent it as of 1 November 1978. So Ömer and I moved to our new flat. I then found out that by luck almost next door a lady I knew also had a flat. This neighborly relationship has lasted nearly a quarter of a century.

The day I had signed my lease and had gotten my keys, I gave the good news to Zeyneb, together with a key to our flat. I told her she could always share whatever I had and was free to go into her mother's house for whatever reason she had and that she could help herself to everything that was in the icebox. She too was delighted that we were in a way under one roof. Her studio was on the sixth floor and our one bedroom flat was on the fourteenth.

Before we had found this flat Ömer had made a suggestion. He said we could probably find a better house in the outskirts of Manhattan, if possible get a used car and commute to town. I was totally against the idea. I told him that I would be driven crazy every time he came home late. Also I wanted to be in town where one could do things. Suburbia life was not for me. After a while he saw my reasons and finally we were settled in our new flat.

I gave Ömer the bedroom and made a bed-sette in the big living room for myself. In the mornings I would change my bed into a couch. During weekends all the family would get together and have a joyful brunch on the fourteenth floor.

421

LIII
Father Again

It must have been about a month after we had moved to our new flat that word came from İstanbul that Father would be coming to New York. Of course, he was always to be welcomed but we had hardly moved in. Father arrived early in December. Ömer had to vacate the single bedroom and started sleep on the second couch in the living room. I had to travel with Father to place him at the Lahey Clinic and return, then go to pick him up again in ten days or so.

Father had a well-established life in İstanbul. He had a big apartment. He made a male cook plus a daily charwoman who worked in the house. Namely, there were two servants for one man. Father never thought about anyone but himself and expected me to give him similar service. He never considered that I was a fully employed secretary and furthermore that I was very poor indeed. Disregarding all this he was asking me to do the same service that his double personnel did for him. Even at the slightest delay or objection he was quickly angered.

My father was accustomed to eat six times a day. Furthermore, all the things he ate had to be especially prepared. This was on account that he had ulcers and also he was diabetic. As an example, his breakfast consisted of one glass of freshly squeezed orange juice, a glass of slightly warmed milk, freshly prepared tea, one three-minute egg, a cup of oatmeal, one slice of toast. In a separate plate he wanted white cheese that had been soaked in water to lessen its salt content, plus a cup of diet preserve. This was what he had to have for breakfast at 8:00 A.M. in the morning. All this had to be prepared before I went to work and the dishes would have to be handled as well.

At 11:00 A.M. he had to have a glass of warm milk plus the kind of cookies he liked. These had to be ready for him, as well.

422

For lunch at 13:00 hours, he wanted three kinds of boiled vegetables, for example one carrot, one zucchini and one potato, all of which had to be boiled separately. Plus a cup of soup and either a piece of chicken or fish, boiled, or cooked in the oven together with rice or spaghetti. Then some fruit compote. He would drink tea or linden tea after lunch. All this preparation meant that I had to get up at 5:00 A.M. in the morning. It also meant that I had to go and purchase all sorts of cups and pans to be able to prepare his meals. I would serve him breakfast, put the dishes away, prepare his eleven o'clock snack, get things ready for lunch and rush to the office. I had to rush back to prepare and serve him his lunch and again prepare his afternoon snack. This time tea and milk with cookies and go back to the mission. In the evening his food, as well as something for Ömer and me, had to be prepared, and all the dishes had to be done. After our evening meal Father dictated some letters for me to type the next morning in the office. Father always had a nap for some half hour and after that he had to be taken to walk in the park. Zeyneb or Sertaç tried to be with him at those times since I could not get away from the office. After he had his nightly warm milk and cookies he would go to bed and I had to start getting ready for the next day before I fell into bed exhausted.

This was truly a trying period. I had not even been able to read the daily papers. Father returned home after spending a full month with us. Not only was I physically exhausted but my finances had also been very much upset.

We spent New Year's Eve of 1979 together with my children at home. People generally make up resolutions for a new year and look forward for new and good things to happen. Hope is a wonderful feeling. In those years the Armenians had been demonstrating everywhere against the Turks. In one instance they had washed all the pavement in front of the Turkish House with red paint, signifying blood. Somehow they would not put their grievances aside. My son was working part-time at the Turkish House as a guard and he saw the people splashing red paint on the pavement. He even tried to send them away. After this incident reporters had come from NBC and other news organizations and they interviewed my son. As this had happened after office hours, we had not seen what went on. Of course I was worried. They had assassinated some of our Ambassadors. I was afraid for the safety of my children. Troubles never seemed to leave us alone.

We had bought a secondhand bicycle for Ömer to facilitate his transportation. On a Sunday morning in March he had gone out cycling and to shop for a few things that we needed. I was at home. Suddenly the intercom bell rang. It was Ömer. He was crying. He had had an accident. He said he might have broken his hand. I rushed down madly, hastily putting on a coat. When I saw my son with his hand hanging on his side I was almost losing my mind. We jumped into a cab and went to New York Hospital. My son was in terrible pain. That institution is on 33rd Street and 1st Avenue and it was the nearest. We went into the Emergency section. The man at the reception desk gave us a lot of papers to fill, which almost required our whole life history and also told us he would want a deposit of two thousand dollars. I was stunned. I did not have such money and even my credit card would not allow such a credit. Since it was a Sunday I could not ask for help from the office. When I told him this, he said, "You better get to Bellevue Hospital, they don't charge anything for their services." When I asked him where I could get a cab he said it would be easier to walk since 1st Avenue goes up and we would reach 27th Street better walking. So we started half walking half running toward that hospital. We were both crying. Ömer because of his pain and I because of my helplessness. We finally reached Bellevue. Although their services were free the persons working there turned out to be more humane. While they were taking Ömer to have X rays they gave me various forms to fill out.

A little while later a young doctor came and explained to me that most of the bones in his wrist were broken so he said the best way was to operate right away placing nails both on the wrist and to the elbow and put a cast over. I was slightly taken aback. First of all he seemed so young and inexperienced. He saw my hesitation, confessed that he was new at his job but he said if I trusted him he would do the best he could. Every minute was working against us. I could do nothing but accept his offer. I was not allowed into the operating room, but I could hear my son's cries through the doors of the operating room.

After a lengthy period of suffering, they came out of the operating room with good news but said Ömer would have to be kept in the hospital for a few days. We were lucky. They had an empty room. Ömer was put into bed, exhausted. I went back to the house, told what had happened to the rest of the family and took some necessary things like slippers, etc. and went back to the hospital. Naturally, there were some bills to be met, it was not completely free but comparatively the cost was affordable. I still pray for that young Mexican doctor for the way he worked on Ömer's wrist. It took some months but in the end both his arm and his wrist returned to normal. It was such a relief.

As I mentioned the costs were affordable and I was able to save and meet our bills but I have to mention that since Ömer was an employee of the embassy under the regulations he should have been entitled to get his medical expenses paid. However, the gentleman who was in charge of such dispensations was cross with me and stopped the payment. Since I was too proud to apply to the Ambassador (who was a good friend), I had to bear the cost. One can forgive such enmities but somehow one cannot forget.

There were some good things also happening at the time. At the Turkish House there was an African-American messenger called Jimmy. He must have been elderly since his hair was turning white. He was a very kindly gentleman. However, I had not talked to him much and had not heard him say anything more than "Yes, Madam" or "Yes, sir." Somehow I used to appreciate his dignity. He would hardly talk unnecessarily and seemed to be an independent sort of fellow. So I began to talk to him, mostly things like "What a good morning it is," "Is not the sunshine divine." One day when we were alone in the lobby we started talking about jazz, spirituals and gospel music, etc. I was very interested and told him so. Then one day Jimmy said to me, "If you like I can take you to my church on Sunday morning." I was delighted and accepted his invitation with alacrity.

That Sunday, since I knew how they went to church, I put my best clothes on and met Jimmy at the decided bus stop. He was also impeccably dressed. He was a well-built man and big. We went to his church in Harlem. I was the only white person in the congregation. Since they all knew Jimmy nobody looked puzzled by my presence. After the priest finished his sermon everybody started singing. They were clapping their hands and some were even dancing in their seats. I could not help joining the crowd. It was certainly a pagan ritual but I enjoyed the kind of prayer they performed where their God was benign and joyful. I also prayed to this God with tears in my eyes. It was an extraordinary experience for me.

Later on Jimmy gave me another chance to experience something very rare. He asked me if I would go to a concert with him at the U.N. When we went into the auditorium the usher gave us seats that usually are reserved for high dignitaries. Frankly, I was a bit apprehensive. A secretary and a messenger were being offered the best seats in the house. Jimmy had absolutely no qualms. Neither his color nor his employment would bother him in the least bit. He soon realized that I was a bit excited about the preferential treatment given to us and he explained, "I know the man who is performing, he is my old friend. He wanted us to have these seats." This was a xylophone concert and the artist was Lionel Hampton. Mr. Hampton greeted the audience and came toward us and taking Jimmy in his arms, he turned to the crowd and said, "This is my childhood friend, my buddy." Jimmy took his hand and brought it to mine and said, "And Mrs. Sılan is my friend, you must meet her." I had the honor of shaking hands with this great musician. I was treated to a wonderful concert.

That summer I was able to spend two weeks in Turkey for my vacation. Cenan and his wife Bibi had arranged for a yachting trip (the so called Blue Voyage in Turkey) on the Mediterranean. Also staying a few days in İstanbul I would be able to follow up my alimony proceedings, try to get some of my old things left in storage, etc. His father had to pay some of Ömer's expenses but the court case was still pending.

We had visited Antalya years ago when we were coming home from Haifa on the passenger vessel, *Güneysu*. The city had changed very much. The new well-known Hotel Talya had just opened. Since its architect/decorator Mr. Hancı and his wife had joined us for this voyage, we spent a day at this hotel before boarding the vessel that took us into the sea. It was certainly a fabulous trip with ancient cities like Batık Şehir and Phaselis scattered on the way. It took us ten days to do Kekova and we returned to Antalya. I spent a few days in İstanbul and returned to my children, whom I had missed all the way.

On my way back my niece Fatoş joined me. She had graduated from a Turkish high school and her parents wanted her to have her college education in America. They were able to register her to an English course for foreign students at Cornell University. Since I was residing in New York she would have her aunt within reach. We showed her around Manhattan, especially with the aid of Ömer. Then I took her up to her residence. After a short while her elder sister Emine also came to New York. So they were coming to visit us whenever they were free and this gave Ömer and Zeyneb a chance to get together with their cousins. I believe they decided to go to California the next year.

We spent the New Year's Eve of 1980 in the house of Mr. and Mrs. Arif Mardin. They were very gracious. They had invited me with all my children and we were able to meet a lot of friends at the same party.

I am not quite sure of the exact date, I believe it must have been the year 1980, just as I got out of the bus on the corner of our street. I heard an enormous noise, like a bomb exploding! It came from the direction of the Turkish House, which was on the other corner. Without even thinking about it, I had started running toward the Türkevi. Everybody was running. The sirens of the fire engines were heard close by. Just as I was turning the corner I saw Ömer coming toward me. His face was almost white. He had just come out of duty and turned the corner when the explosion occurred. The whole avenue was littered with broken pieces of glass. Thank God nobody was injured. It was a close call but my son was safe.

LIV
Şen, the Saleswoman

The bombing episode had really shocked my son Ömer badly. A few minutes difference and he could have been killed. He did not say anything but we both felt that he should not carry on his job as a bodyguard. Wanting to contribute to our mutual life, he had been willing to do this job 49 hours a week and attending school at NYU full time, attempting to get a double major. I still wonder how he was able to do all this. It was getting to be too risky and the pay he got was not much anyway. On the other hand, despite the fact that his pay was low, we did need that income. My position was such that I could not accept outside employment. I knew that some of the people in the office were forced to do what they call in America "moonlighting jobs." So I casually asked a few friends if I could not get a job for Saturdays only. Among the people I had asked was a lady called Ginette, she had a shop on Madison Avenue selling hand-embroidered pillows and things. She said, "How lucky, I know that at Porthault they are actually looking for someone like you." I told her that I did not have a green card and she said that should not cause any trouble. Porthault is a well-known European store that markets things like towels and sheets, etc. It is a rather expensive shop that caters mostly to royalty and the very rich. It is all silks and linens and embroideries. She gave me their number and I called their New York manager. They were glad to take me on. I was to work from 9:30 A.M. until 5:30 P.M. every Saturday with only 15 minutes for lunch break and no smoking was allowed on the premises. I was not to be paid a percentage on the sales I managed to finalize but instead I would be paid 50 dollars for every eight-hour day I worked. No taxes or anything. However, the question was would I be able to manage this job?

They called me one Sunday and trained me. That was enough. Next Saturday I started work.

Ginette had been a godsend, in a way. We had been seeing one another for some time. I had been invited to their home many times. I believe her husband Jerry had high blood pressure and I was the only guest that was allowed to smoke in their house. In my first dinner at their table the meal was cooked almost without salt and I saw that there were no saltshakers on the table either. When I enquired about it Ginette was rather annoyed. She said something like, "But Şen, every vegetable has its own taste and I used all kinds of peppers and spices so that you should not have salt." Whereas I like salt in my meals. Gradually we came to an understanding and I was allowed to bring my own saltshaker whenever I was invited to dinner.

The shop I had started working was on 57th Street between Fifth Avenue and Madison. This was a street full of very posh shops. For example, next door to Porthault's there was an art gallery that belonged to the son of the world-renowned painter, Henri Matisse. Now is the time when I must recount how I met the younger Matisse.

This happened before my adventure as a salesperson had started. I had been to the Matisse gallery to look at the marvelous paintings on show. In the gallery I saw a gentleman slightly balding and rather heavy. I said "Hello" and started looking at the artwork. As I was walking in front of the paintings he came to my side and said, "Have we met before?" My answer was rather curt. I said, "If you happen to be Monsieur Matisse, I am rather sorry to say that our paths has never crossed before." He mumbled a few words and went to his desk. In a few minutes the man was back. He took my hand into his hand and directed me toward a corner of the room and said, "I know where I have seen you before. Look. You look like Jeanette." Sure enough there was a sculpture of a woman's head on a pedestal signed Matisse and the lady did have a resemblance. I was very surprised. Somehow the way she had done her hair, etc. Yes, there was a resemblance. We chatted a few more minutes and when I asked my leave it was gratifying to hear him say, "Do come back again, Jeanette." It was lovely to hear those words. We were friends and I did visit the gallery many times.

On my first Saturday I went to the store dressed with extreme care. It was 9:30 A.M. and I punched a card by pushing it into the machine. There was a cashier plus three other salesladies in. The store had two floors. On the entrance level towels, handkerchiefs, specially designed porcelain pieces were on display. On the second floor bed sheets, embroidered bed covers, table cloths, etc. were arranged. All the women had brought with them (from the nearby coffee shop) muffins and hot drinks. After a makeshift breakfast and having a smoke on the sidewalk, they were all ready for duty by 10:00 A.M. Since this was my first day, I had joined them for a cigarette and tried to get some advice on how to go about this job. The whole day I had had a chance to sit for only 15 minutes! It certainly was a trying job. The worst part for me was, of course, not to be able to smoke. In those days I was smoking two packs a day. Another thing that surprised me was that the more professional sales persons would actually push me aside if they saw a client they liked. However, there were so many customers that even on my first day in the shop I was able to make a few sales. Of course, I was delighted to get paid in cash at the end of the day.

I had started working every Saturday. Since it was a posh store many famous people would come in. One Saturday a group of young men came into the shop, they looked like they were down and out street bums, the way they were dressed and I was very surprised when the other salesladies were kowtowing to them. When the time came for paying, I suddenly had recognized the leader of the group. He was Andy Warhol. He really looked like a bum in his half-torn jeans, very thin legs and a funny toupee. On the other hand in less than a half hour he had spent something like 20,000 U.S. dollars. No joke.

On another Saturday a mother and daughter came in. The daughter was very choosy and could not make up her mind on anything and was behaving like a very spoilt child. She was stunningly beautiful, lovely body, etc. She must have been 18. Well, she was called Brooke Shields. The mother was also a good-looking lady. Anyway, after all the running around they also paid a large amount of money and left the shop.

Ahmet Ertegün is a very well-known figure in the American music industry. His father, who was an Ambassador of Turkey,

430

was a friend of my father. So Ahmet and his wife Mica were very gracious and asked me to some of their parties. One day when I was on duty Mica walked into the store. There was no way I could hide myself. I quickly went to her and explained my situation. She took it very graciously. She said something like, "Do not worry, I won't say a word" and she kindly asked another salesperson to help her. Not only did she never remind me of that encounter but they continued to invite me to their parties on and off. I certainly appreciated her behavior.

I had another funny experience in that shop. We were all waiting for someone to come in. A rather elegant man, tall and middle-aged, came in. He was impeccably dressed. He certainly had an imposing personalilty. He walked toward me and in a well-modulated voice said, "I wish to give my wife a wedding anniversary gift. What would you suggest?" I asked what would her reaction be to some embroidered bed covers. He said, "Splendid." So we went up to the second floor and he was very gentle and took almost everything I suggested. By the time we had come down his bill had been pretty stiff. After he left all the ladies were agog. They were all saying, "How did you manage this?" Of course they had a percentage and had lost a nice sum. One of them said, "Did you not recognize the guy? He was David Rockefeller."

Strangely enough this story did not end there. A short while later, there was a reception at the Turkish House. My very good friends Ayşe and Salahattin Beyazıt happened to be in New York and naturally they were invited. As we were chatting, Mr. Beyazıt suddenly took me by the hand and said, "I would like to introduce you to a friend of mine." Suddenly I was taken aback. The man I was being introduced to was no one else but David Rockefeller. As we were being introduced Mr. Rockefeller said, "I seem to recall your face, where did our paths cross I wonder?" I could not help it. I asked him, "Did your wife enjoy the gifts you bought at Porthault?" He was quite surprised for a moment and then burst out laughing. My friend Salahattin who had no inkling what the joke was about let it go at that. These are sweet things to remember. But there were also bitter ones.

Father had come to New York once again, on his return from Boston, and he was expecting full treatment as always.

Luckily he was in good health and in good humor. On a Friday I told about the explosion in front of the mission and that I was now working full-time on Saturdays as a sales person. I told him I would prepare his meals as usual. When I was leaving the house that Saturday morning, he took my hand into his hands and said, "I am so sorry I can do nothing to help my dear daughter." I felt rather sad. Only the day before he had given me a long list of things that cost almost a fortune and had said they were gifts for his friends in İstanbul. I could not help thinking that if he had stayed in a hotel in New York how much more he would have to pay. He was not even considering how much I had to spend for his special meals let alone the cooking, etc. If he really thought about me he could at least suggest to give me fifty dollars and keep me away from the shop. I needed that income and if he had paid it, we could have gone for a walk or something. I really do not know, but in such a situation I should be ashamed to be spending thousands of dollars for unknown friends. These "gift" items would also surprise me. Here I was, living in New York for years, but Father's so called "lady friends" living in İstanbul knew the shops and the merchandise they wanted better then I. Father used to say, "The wife of so and so" or "the daughter of general somebody" and the list would go on and on.

I could never decide. Maybe Father was doing the right thing. The only things that he ever brought to us, coming from İstanbul, was either a box of Turkish Delight or some dried figs which I dumped into the trash bin when he was not around. My children used to make jokes about their grandfather's frugal gifts. Once Seze had difficulty biting into a dry biscuit he had brought and Father calmly advised that she should first dip it into her tea and then bite! However, on this trip Father had given me a very unexpected gift. After we had traveled to Boston and back, one evening he gave me a colored document. It was covered with many printed or typed things but I recognized my picture in the corner. When I asked him what it was he said, "Why don't you read it. It is a title deed." Well, I had never seen one before. I started reading some of the typed parts. It said I was the titular owner of a flat measured so and so. When I asked about this term "titular" Father explained that he was keeping the right of usufruct and the property would revert to me fully at the time of his death. My immediate reaction was to say I do not want anything subject to your passing away, God forbid. I really was not quite satisfied nor had I understood what it was but since he said so I took the document. He went on to explain that he had done a similar transfer to his eldest son Cenan for the elegant apartment he was using at Maçka, so he had done similar transfers to his younger son Nur and me these apartment flats near Taksim. These flats were opposite the Hilton Hotel and quite expensive also. There would be no immediate income since he was going to collect the rentals but we would inherit the flats at his death. I just put the document into the drawer. There was no immediate income and since it was dependant on the death of a party, who could tell who would die first.

It was in 1980 that we learned that Ambassador Orhan Eralp would be retiring that year. This was a double blow to me since not only was he a grand gentleman to work for but his wife Jale was my childhood friend. Orhan had been exemplary in the way he showed me the ropes on how an embassy should be run. He was a man to be missed. Well, times had given me the necessary experience. Life meant change and one had to survive under changing conditions. However, soon news arrived that he would be replaced by Coşkun Kırca. I was reminded of the song "Our hearts were young and gay." When Kırca was a junior executive in the foreign department we used to dance at the night club in Ankara to that song. We had both married some years apart and were socializing in Ankara as married couples. Many a night after long hours of dancing we would end up in the hills around Ankara having a morning drink at a bus stop café. Again, as the song says, "we were young and gay." Now of course conditions had changed.

I cannot forget the day Mr. Kırca arrived at the Turkish House as the newly appointed Ambassador. In accordance with protocol all the employees were present in the big reception room. The undersecretary was introducing everyone in the room one by one, announcing names and ranks. When it was my turn to be introduced, Mr. Kırca stopped the undersecretary by saying, "Do not bother to introduce her she is an old friend." He had been remarried in the meantime but his new wife also turned out to be a warmhearted person and she also treated me very properly all the time. Their two daughters were exemplary children.

One of the things that had impressed me about Ambassador Kırca was the way he arrived to the office in the morning. I had worked with a number of ambassadors to date but I had never seen one that came to his office humming a popular tune! On the other hand, Ambassador Kırca was a workaholic. He could come in very early in the morning and work through to all hours in the evening. The only trouble with this was that I could never plan my evenings (getting tickets for a concert of something similar). I could not very well leave the office when he was there working! After all, I was the executive secretary and had to be there at his beck and call.

This reminded me of a funny experience. I had read that Arthur Rubinstein would conduct a concert at Avery Fisher Hall. I would love to go but since I could not tell at what time the Ambassador would leave, I simply could not afford to pay a big price and miss the concert. I was sure if I had told him about this he would be sure to give me special permission but since we were old friends I could not bring myself to use this to my advantage. So I had said nothing. As it happened Mr. Kırca left the office at an hour which was early for him and I thought I had enough time to catch the concert. Only forty minutes to go but I was lucky, the bus on the corner made good time. The ticket office had been closed. I was told that touts would be selling tickets and I was desperately trying to find one. In my desperation and not quite thinking about it, I accosted a uniformed policeman and asked him about those people who sold tickets. He was a portly and kind man, he laughed heartily and then said, "Lady I am not supposed to know about those things but I think you were looking for the man behind my back." I almost gave him a hug and ran to catch the man who still had tickets. I asked the price and he said 40 dollars. My heart sank. I could not afford such a sum. I waited a bit debating in my mind what to do. There was only five minutes to go. So I approached the guy once again and said, "Look I am dying to listen to Rubinstein but I have only ten dollars, you will do me a good turn and you will lose only thirty dollars." He had also given up selling the ticket, so he accepted and I was delightedly dashing into the building in a mad hurry. The seat was great and it was a wonderful concert and I kept thanking my lucky stars for it ever since.

I also had some sort of an altercation with Ambassador Kırca. We, the secretaries, had to stay over for telex duty. It meant that one of the secretaries would be waiting to check if any telex messages came in or were to be sent out, all through the night. Especially when the U.N. had their General Sessions there would be a lot of last minute communications. Following such an evening I had reached my home something like 5:00 A.M. in the morning and by the time I was in bed it must have been something like 6:30 A.M. The insistent ringing of my phone woke me up from deep slumber. The assistant secretary was on the phone, quite agitated and she said, "The Ambassador is looking for you." I could actually hear Mr. Kırca's voice angrily demanding that I should be there. He was certainly fuming. I quickly got up, got dressed and ran to the office. Everyone who had heard his raised voice was telling me, "Quick, go to his office." When I got into his office he was still fuming. I tried to explain that when secretaries did night duty they were given the next day off, but he still would not even listen to me. Then I could not help blurting out, "Mr. Ambassador if you want to make sure that your secretary be in the office whenever you are there, then you should take her off night duty." Finally he realized the truth in what I was saying and ordered that I be taken off such night duties and that my service should be confined to him all the time. It was not easy to work as the personal secretary of ambassadors who were also chums of your past years. On the other hand, I really learned a lot from these important gentlemen and I am not at all sorry that I did the work I did.

I had become an experienced New Yorker. I knew most of the streets and had become quite accustomed to the quarters I visited. In New York the primary thing on the streets is that you cannot find anyone loitering, everyone moves about swiftly. Having been forced to find the best thing at the lowest price, I began to take Turkish friends on shopping expeditions.

I do not remember the exact year but Zeyneb had quit her job at the Turkish Consulate and had joined a local firm. Ömer was doing a double major at NYU. He was studying both finance and economics. One evening he said that he was thinking of returning to Turkey when he graduated. I had given up the idea of returning home. There was hardly anything left for me to return to! I had no home, no furniture, not a cent in Turkey! Well, Father came visiting almost every year for his checkups. Cenan and Bibi came every two or three years for a short visit. Nothing was left for me in Turkey. Both my children were with me in New York. Yes, only Ayşe had her burial place in Turkey, but I was certain that we would get together whenever I also died. So to the best of my ability I tried to explain to my son my position as far as returning to Turkey was concerned. However, he had other ideas. He told me, "Mother I am very indebted to you for all you have done, specially the kind of education you were able to provide for me. However, I am not an American. Yes, after graduation I am sure to get a job somewhere. On the other hand, who will be my friends? I have high school friends in Ankara. My native language is Turkish. Although we are not together I still carry the surname my father has given me. It is true that I have to start from scratch but the situation will not be too different here. After all my fatherland is there. There is the republic founded by Atatürk. I am sure to find people who will share their destinies with me. I also hope to be a good citizen and become of some use to my country."

Love of Atatürk and of our country was a feeling that had been cultivated in us from childhood, most probably by our parents. I am certain that everything that I have ever been able to accomplish was due to the freedom that Atatürk had given to us, to Turkish women. It was obvious that Father and Mother were the sole people who had brought me into this world. However, I am also certain that it was what Atatürk had done that made the woman I am now. I have always been proud to be a Turkish woman and an Atatürk woman! I owe everything to the reforms he was able to develop in Turkey.

In a way, although I was a bit apprehensive, I thought it would be best to give him a chance to go to İstanbul on his own and see the possibilities before he made up his mind. Therefore I decided to send Ömer there during his summer vacation.

That spring Father came again to Boston for his checkups and when they were over we came back to New York. I noticed he was a bit apprehensive. One evening he blurted out that he was in financial difficulty and that his pension was no longer enough for him. So he wanted me to return the flat he had donated me. He would sell it and use it for his expenses. I was really shocked. I could not help asking, "Did you talk this over with my elder brothers?" He had previously told me he donated real estate to them also. Father said he had approached both my brothers and both had refused. I said how could they refuse your request? My father said that Bibi and Cenan had proclaimed that they would refuse to give back the flat he was enjoying since if he sold it he would be forced to live in a smaller place that would not be fit for him. I asked what was Nur's reaction? Father explained that Nur had said that this was the only gift he had received and under no conditions would he consider returning it. So I could not help but say, "But Father why am I the only one?" He simply said, "Because you are my forever docile daughter and that is why I am asking you." So having satisfied my curiosity, I said, "Yes, Daddy, you may do as you like. That flat has never meant anything to me anyway. I hope when the time comes and you appreciate my need you will come to my aid that day. I will give it back." And I laughed.

What else could I have done? I was his only daughter. I had lost a daughter, my marriage had been shattered. I was toiling like a slave. I had been able to make a home for my children, had given my son an education that he deserved. Still I was the "docile daughter" and Father could do everything he wanted with her.

I was not thinking of ever going back to Turkey. He had the usufruct on the flat, so it would bring me no income while he was alive. What was the use. I accepted to give away the title to the flat. He kissed me on both cheeks and thanked me. I thought this was over. However, he told me that I had to give him an authority via a notary public. Later he relented and said those formalities could wait and that we would carry them out when I next went to İstanbul.

That summer Ömer went to İstanbul. He was very happy. He had not only enjoyed his country and friends but he was also offered a job. Under the conditions I could only give him my blessings despite my continued reservations. Everyone had to choose his own path. Ömer's father had also returned to Turkey. However, since many years, he had neither seen his son nor had done anything for him. Now he was still doing everything he could not pay his son the money the court would decide.

Around the same time Sertaç and Zeyneb decided to divorce. What could I say? They were old enough to decide for themselves. It was a very long time ago that they had put on their wings. The only thing that bothered me and made me apprehensive was the difficulties that my grandchild, Seze, might face. Luckily that did not happen. Both parents were civilized persons and thereby were able to protect their friendship. Thus they were able to give their daughter a balanced and peaceful life. Seze, on the other hand, was a very mature and sentimental child. She made no caprices. To this day she is the same, namely unique.

New York is a crazy city. One can find almost anything under the sun, if one tries hard enough. I never forget. A very old friend had come to stay with me. I had mentioned to her that Julio Iglesias would be singing. She was dying to see him live. I told her she could listen to him that evening at Radio City if she wanted, but she would have to go alone since I could not afford it. After some argument back and forth, she paid for both of us and we enjoyed the show very much. What I want to say is that when you begin to learn the ins and outs of New York there is hardly any end to it. You can get the best Chinese or the best Japanese food in Manhattan. For that matter, quite probably the best Turkish food as well.

LV

Ömer Goes to Turkey

As soon as he graduated from NYU in 1981, Ömer flew over to Turkey to start in his new job. I was content for the fact that he had made his own decision and did what he thought would be best for him. On the other hand, I had the fear he might not be able to find the peace of mind and the inner happiness over there. Since I had discussed the question previously. I had told Ömer that he could stay in his grandfather's apartment for some time before he could settle somewhere. However, soon after Ömer's arrival, Father suddenly announced that he was going abroad on a trip and he wished to close up his apartment and therefore Ömer should find himself other accommodations. My son, who was too proud to object or to ask for financial assistance, had consented to leave and moved out to a third rate hostel. He had not even mentioned that he did not have the financial means to rent a flat. After a few days Bibi (his aunt) had given him another address where he could stay within his means. Ömer quickly moved there, but again he was awakened by an awful smell early in the morning and when he looked out he saw that the sewage pipe was broken and flowing into the garden next to his window. So he had to move a third time. When I had learned about his experiences I did not say anything like "I told you so" but of course I was grieving for my son very deeply.

A week later I received the news that finally Ömer had found an apartment for himself in the basement of a building called Pamuk Apartment at Nişantas and I was somewhat relieved. Just about those days I had another interesting experience. When Mother had died, Father, who used to adore and admire her, wanted to do something that would be of a lasting nature. At first he had thought of building a school in her name. Then he was confronted with an interesting project. The entrance and a portion of the State Library of Beyazıt in İstanbul badly needed repairs and restoration. Father took over this project with a donation to cover the expenses. He was happy to be able to do this. In his own words, "Thus people will always remember an intellectual Turkish lady who was a supporter and admirer of Atatürk, as well as a perfect wife and a wonderful mother." Father certainly had a hard time dealing with bureaucratic wrangles. Shortly, he was morally and materially worn out. Soon after the completion of the construction, I received in New York an invitation asking me to attend the opening ceremony. At the date the invitation had reached me, the library had already been inaugurated. I would have so much liked to be there on that occasion. The place was named after my mother!

The State Library of Beyazıt published a book for the 100th year of its foundation and the following lines appear in that small booklet:

"Mr. Necmeddin Sahir Sılan, who had been a member of Parliament for Tunceli and Bingöl towns and who had been the Private Secretary of both the Prime Minister and of the Leader of the House of Parliament, has made it possible to add this pavilion through his personal donations where we can commemorate special occasions. The pavillion has been named after his deceased wife, Mrs. Cemile Sahir Sılan. This pavillion has been inaugurated to the public by our Minister of Culture, Mr. Cihat Baban on February 19, 1981. Mr. Sılan has also donated various books, collections of periodicals totaling some 5,000 volumes."

After reading this invitation over and over again, I could not help thinking that such a cavalier husband who had been willing to spend so much time and effort and means in memory of his wife, would then simply be content by giving my address to the library for them to mail me an invitation which arrived too late. How come he would not write a few lines, or call me up and more than that, why not send me a airline ticket so that I could attend the ceremony? Then he would also have been a true father. This had hurt me so very much. I could at least send some

440

flowers and share that unique occasion, if I had been advised in time.

I have a recent recollection in connection with this library. Right after I had started writing my memoirs (I had started writing them in 1998) and during a period when I was in İstanbul, I wanted to visit the library. I also had the desire to see the lovely space around the library with the huge plane trees and also look at the "relief" of my mother, which father had asked the well-known sculptor Mr. Sadi Çalık to design, and naturally to also visit the library. Mr. Çalık, to design the relief had used a photograph of my mother.

The relief stood right in the middle of the library and I saw it as soon as I walked in. I stood in front of it with tears in my eyes and looked at the beautifully carved face of my mother. Suddenly a young woman appeared, she was looking at me and then at the relief and she said, "You sort of look like the lady, who are you?" I introduced myself, thanked her for the compliment. I was once again proud to be her daughter.

Shortly after Ömer had settled down in İstanbul, in the summer of 1981, I had the occasion to visit my son at his own flat in Nişantaşı. No one could have been happier. Both my son and my daughter had their own flats and Ömer was able to receive me as his guest! This was a very special kind of feeling for a mother. Especially for this mother!

The first thing I did, as soon as I reached İstanbul, was to go to a notary public and sign a document returning what rights I had on that apartment which Father had given me and now wanted back. I felt sort of relieved. Now he could do whatever he wanted to do with it. I had never even seen the place. Again I went back to New York and my new routine started. I was actually enjoying my freedom and liberty. Naturally, things kept happening, sometimes good and sometimes bad, but that is what life is about is it not?

After a few months my son informed me that he wanted to do his military service. Of course this was again a source of delight for me. My son doing his military service. Being a mother I could not avoid being worried about the hardships involved at the same time. Unfortunately, I was too far away and could do nothing to relieve him in any way. There was a way of cutting down this service period but that involved money and I did not have such a sum in hand. So he would have to do his full service for one and a half years. First he was going to attend the cadet school at Tuzla. All I could do was to wish him luck from far away.

When Sertaç and Zeyneb had decided to divorce, I had offered Zeyneb to share a flat with me. However, with her ever practical mind she refused the offer and said such a move could develop complications later on. Of course she was right. There is a saying in Turkish, "Two houses do not add up." We belonged to different generations as well as cultures. So we decided to enjoy our separate houses. She had her daughter with her and now I was alone. The room that I had given Ömer now became my bedroom, so I had a spacious living room where I could welcome friends even for lengthy periods of time, relatives or friends coming to New York.

My youngest niece had been enrolled at a college in California and Bibi, who missed her daughter, wrote to advise that they would be coming first to New York together with her aunt. On my invitation she and her ever so lovely Aunt Mefkure Şerbetçi spent some time in my apartment. On their invitation I was able to attend a number of Broadway shows that I could never afford to see. Speaking of theatre tickets, I would like to refer to an occurrence that meant a lot to me and was very precious. Since I had been working at the Turkish House for some years I had developed what I called "telephone connections." This meant that I had developed friendships over the phone and was able to book tickets or plane seats at the last moment.

One day a very old friend whom I had not seen for many years called up. He told me he was staying as a house guest at a couple's house, whom I also knew and liked and said that they wanted to go to a musical and although he tried hard, he had not succeeded to find tickets. They had suggested that he would ring me up and ask for help. I told him that I would do my best and asked how many seats he wanted. He said, "I would like to get four seats, as you know we are three people in the apartment and if you happen to be free that night the fourth would be yours." I automatically told him that he did not have to do that and that this was something I did for everybody anyway. He

442

went on to insist, saying that the couple at whose house he was staying would also enjoy my company. This was a gesture I had never encountered in so many years at the mission. On the other hand, there were some people who had invited me to a show and when we were parting, I considerately had asked whether I owed anything and the reply was the price of the ticket! So naturally I was forced to pay. People are not made the same way!

In this city where I had been living for some years, I had the possibility of watching excellent plays. Naturally not the Broadway activities, those were too expensive for me. I used to go to off-Broadway or off-off Broadway theatres. Thus I had the opportunity and the pleasure of watching plays by David Mamet or Sam Shepard while they were not very famous.

Bibi, my sister-in-law, had gone to Los Angeles from New York. One day she called and gave me the great news that Fatoş, one of her daughters, was getting engaged to be married. The future groom was an American and the engagement party would be in İstanbul, next spring. Unfortunately, I was not able to go at the set date. However, I was able to scrape enough to get to İstanbul in the summer to attend the ceremony where my son graduated as a leftenant. I was delighted to see my son in uniform. I can never forgot his saying, "Mother, doing my military service for eighteen months has given me a personality build up and has also earned for me many personal friendships. I am very proud and happy." He had been so serious in his service that he had not even asked for leave for the engagement ceremony of his niece.

Ömer was then assigned to Ankara as an interpreter at the general staff. I was able to go to Ankara together with my son. This city was full of memories for me. I had gone there as a young girl and had left that town for good in 1973. All those years had left their mark on me. I spent three nights in Ankara trying to help Ömer in getting accommodated and left all my memories behind. I did not even visit some of the old places. The city had been changed anyway. I was very glad to return to New York, which was the city where my daughter and my grandchild were and where I now belonged.

In 1983 the wonderful news reached us that Fatoş was getting married in Los Angeles. Father was to come to New York

443

a little earlier and I would again be involved in his checkup program at the Lahey Clinic in Boston. He certainly had a full program ahead. After his health program he was going on a Carribean cruise with some of his newfound people who were after his money and for whom he was playing the benefactor. After that jaunt was over, he was going to Fatoş's wedding in Los Angeles. I was rather amazed at his energy and will power. He was 87 that year and he was going from one trip to another as if he was a young man. In the meantime he had given me and Zeyneb our plane tickets to and from Los Angeles. He also had booked a room for us at the hotel he was staying in. This was certainly a welcomed gift. It would give us the pleasure of seeing Fatoş as a bride and most of the family would be gathered together in one ceremony. We left Seze with her father and flew to Los Angeles. Fatoş was like a doll in her wedding gown. The groom, Spencer Segura, was a handsome lawyer and a tennis pro. The whole wedding was like a dream. We enjoyed every minute of it.

A new surprise was ahead for me. After the wedding was over Father said he had something special to discuss with me. He told me that he needed me and that he wanted me to go back to Turkey, etc. My answer was clear and direct. I said, "Darling Father, to make you happy would give me pleasure. It is also my duty to help you. But I have nothing, no income in Turkey. Also it is now very easy for me to live in New York as a common person. Whereas in my country I have always lived an elegant life. All my friends over there are living that sort of a life. I would be hurt seeing the social differences that I would have to live in. It would be difficult for me to be living within the conditions which were not like the ones in the past. Please daddy, do come here, to New York and live here with me. I would do all I could to make you comfortable. If you are not happy, you can always go back." Then I kissed my old father.

Now it was his turn to talk. "Look, my dearest daughter, I did not sell the place you had kindly returned to me. If you come I will give it to you without any conditions. You can either live in it, rent it and use the income or sell at your own pleasure. I will also buy you a car so as to make you comfortable among your friends. You can easily find a job with the qualities that you have. With all these possibilities you can have a decent life and also be able to help me." I thanked him and asked him to allow me a while to think and consider. Meanwhile, this was quite a difficult decision for me to make!

After the wedding, Zeyneb and I had planned to take a side trip on our own to San Francisco. Under the spell of my father's latest proposal I did not want to spend more time and money and returned to my Manhattan apartment directly. Zeyneb did the trip we had planned and returned later.

When I was by myself in my flat the first thing I did was something that I always did before reaching an important decision concerning my future. I took a clean sheet of white paper and wrote in black and white all the pros and cons of returning to İstanbul. After completing my list, I put it aside to let it simmer in my mind. That summer I would probably go to İstanbul for a visit and I would see how things were working out. It would be better to wait and see. During 1984 two things developed. The first was a very happy event. After finishing his military service as interpreter in Ankara, Ömer was now thinking of getting married to a young girl he had met. He phoned and asked my opinion. What could I say, I was so far away and furthermore I had no means to back him. I told him that I was sure that his choice would be right and that I believed in his judgment utterly. I said, "I wish you all the happiness together with my future daughter-in-law." I could not mention funds but Ömer and his fiancée saved me from any embarrassment by declaring that they did not want to have an elaborate wedding and that they would be content to develop their own household as they went along. This was such a relief to me. Of course, I wanted to give everything to my son and his bride, but I could not. My children were great people. Their frugal and stoic approach had not diminished my embarrassment but had at least had let me save face.

On August 17, 1984 Ömer and Asuman were married with a ceremony that covered only the closest family members. I had liked my daughter-in-law very much. She was a willowy, elegant and intelligent young lady. Better than all, she loved my son. All her qualities were proof that she had been very well educated by a medical doctor father and a school instructor mother. I was

445

assured that she would be a valuable companion to my son. Cenan and Bibi, knowing that I could afford almost nothing, were kind enough to let us use their house on the island and arranged for a garden party. They had thought of everything and the party was very successful. I was able to see the newly-weds well installed at the Pamuk Apartment basement flat and flew merrily back to New York.

Then came a phone call. Bibi informed me that Cenan had had surgery in Paris. They had removed a lump from his neck. This was a very bad blow. At first they reported that he was getting better, but the situation was serious and I was utterly worried.

I took my list of pros and cons once more from the drawer I had put it in and started going over them once again. My brother Cenan had always been very dear and close to me. He had been my advisor and councellor all my life. I had learned a lot of things from him. I not only loved him but he had my full respect as well. The fact that he was probably incurably sick and was in İstanbul suddenly had developed a very heavy influence on my decision to return to İstanbul. Father was saying that he needed my company. As for me, years were passing by very fast. Sixty percent, in order to share the good and the bad with Cenan, thirty percent to be of help to my father and ten percent to make a new life for myself. I had come quite close to the decision of going back to Turkey.

LVI

Can I Survive in İstanbul?

In 1985 Mr. Kırca was appointed ambassador to Canada. He was replaced by Mr. İlter Türkmen, who was my first ambassador at the mission. Soon we heard that the Armenians had attacked the Turkish Embassy in Canada. This attack was condemned by everyone. I personally was very sorry for that family that I genuinely liked.

Before taking my summer vacation, I mentioned to Ambassador Türkmen that Father wanted me to return to Turkey and that there was a possibility for me to move, in the future. I subleased my flat temporarily and, taking my grandchild Seze with me, flew to İstanbul. My son Ömer and Asuman would be hosting us. However, when they met us at the airport they informed us that we were expected in my brother's house on the island. We were also told Father was there already and that they would be coming for the weekend and the whole family would be united under one roof. So Seze and I took the ferry to the island.

When we reached the house on the island everybody welcomed us with cheers. We were enjoying our Turkish coffee when Father suddenly said, "My dear Şen, I made you a millionaire. I sold the flat you had graciously returned to me. I took half of the money myself and the other half I put into a bank account for you. I also rented a fully furnished flat for you on the Anatolian side of İstanbul. Now you can move to İstanbul." All this was said very quickly. I was very surprised and did not know what to say. Finally I blurted out, "But I have not yet decided to come." He continued, "When you see the house tomorrow, you will make your mind up." Bibi was saying, "The house is beautiful Şen, you will like it."

447

Saturday morning Ömer and Asuman joined us. Towards noon Father took all the girls, Bibi, Asuman, me and Seze and we crossed over to Bostancı by ferry. We walked a bit and reached an apartment house. Two flights up, Father used a key and we entered an apartment. I was totally crestfallen. It was a miserable place. Everything in the flat was third class. The floors were mostly covered by the cheapest tiles. There were two bedrooms both with the worst kind of used furniture. The kitchen had been painted in the worst possible manner. Even my single room flat in Boston was a palace compared to this dump. Father was looking toward my praise but I could not help saying, "Father it is a pity that you are paying rent for such a dismal flat. I am sorry I cannot possibly live in a place like this. You have seen the places I lived in Boston and in New York. Did they look anything like this?" Asuman was also in shock and could not say anything. My ten-year-old granddaughter was almost giggling, but thought better of it. Bibi, sensing that Father was rather shaken and quite furious, tried to find a middle way, but she knew me and she too was quite surprised. When I saw that Father was about to make a scene I said, "Maybe if one did some work on it the place could become livable." Father was very cross with my reaction and he simply said, "You can do what you like with the money I am giving you and that is that." We left the flat and returned to the island. No one was saying anything. My God! What was Father trying to do. He had seen both my houses in Boston and New York. Yes, they were small flats but they were reasonably furnished, despite my poorness. How could he expect me to live in such squalor? Did he think I was so desperate, or so pitiful?

On the other hand, I felt very bad for my brother. He did not look well. He was very tired and hardly said anything. His condition did not look at all well. Could one not do anything?

My time in İstanbul was limited. Before I came I had been inclined to return to İstanbul but my first shock had been when I saw the flat. After a while I was able to ask Father when I could I have the money (half the value of the flat he had given me) and he said he had put the money into bonds. They were in his safe and would be turned into cash in three months or rather each 10 million would be free in several months. So, there was no cash and nothing was available. In talking further it came out that Father had not rented the flat in Bostancı but he owned it. This was another shock. Why was he behaving in this manner? Why the lies and the pretense? The money supposed to be in the bank was not even deposited in my name. And the bonds were kept in his home!

I thought a long while, then I composed a long letter to Father, made a copy for Cenan and Bibi. I explained my position and said that under these conditions I was facing, such as the house and the cash, I saw no reason to return to İstanbul. I was hoping that they would understand my position. That I could not possibly return unless I was given certain guarantees for a decent life in İstanbul. That I had had enough experience to know better. I would continue to work in New York. Since I had sublet my apartment I would be living in a rooming house and would not be able to host them anymore either.

Seze and I spent a few days with Ömer and Asuman and returned to New York. I stayed a few weeks at Zeyneb's studio. Then a letter came from Father. He was saying that he had reconsidered everything and agreed that I was actually right and he added that he would do everything I wanted, if I returned. He also promised to buy me a car since travel to and from Bostancı would be difficult and he would see to it that I did all the repairs I saw fit. He further added that Cenan did not look at all well. It looked like I should be going back. However, I had to take every precaution possible. In those days there was a foreign exchange scarcity in the country and people who had been working abroad were allowed to bring home their furniture or cars, etc. This had given rise to a sort of half illicit business in the sense that I could market my rights to someone who had the money. Sure enough, I found somebody who paid me cash for the import license drawn in my name. I also had some income from the man who was occupying my flat for a term. However, foremost in my mind was the fact that Cenan was on the verge of dying and I should be at his bedside at this time.

I took my leave from the office, turned in my resignation, paid a visit to my ambassador, called my Taiwanese ambassador on the phone, kissed my daughter, grandchild and her father and I returned to İstanbul on September 26, 1985. Father met his promise partially and paid me ten millions in cash. He said the other two installments would come later. I was staying at my son's flat. I started work on the apartment in Bostancı. All the flat had to be repainted. I had wall-to-wall carpeting and I put in an independent heating system just for the flat. Then I had to send out all the existing furniture, they were either re-painted or repaired, etc. Gradually the place was becoming something like a flat I could stay in. Bibi had been very helpful in finding the furniture repairmen and giving practical ideas for handling various problems. Realizing that my life in İstanbul would entail almost daily trips between father's house at Maçka and mine in Bostancı (this entailed crossing the Bosphorus Bridge twice, back and forth) and I realized Father was rather reluctant to buy me a car as he had promised, I managed to buy myself a car with part of the cash I had gotten from the sale of my import license. Writing over these lines now, I realize how inflation has been rampant in Turkey. A car that costs billions in the year 2000, costed about 5 million in the year 1985. I had only two kinds of security in my own name. I was able to extend my American Blue Cross/Blue Shield health insurance policy and I still held on to my gold credit card.

Cenan's health was going from bad to worse. They had gone to Paris for an operation and they were following their doctor's advice in İstanbul. I felt that this was not the right approach. It took me some time but I finally was able to convince Father that Cenan too should be taken to the Lahey Clinic that he knew so well. He finally agreed and we did go to Boston, all four of us. I was acting as their guide. Under these conditions I had not been able to look for a job in Turkey. I did not care about myself anymore. The only thing that was important for me was Cenan. We flew directly to Boston. When all the checkups and consultations were over, we were getting ready for our return trip. Somehow I got some sort of a bug and fell sick in Boston. Father and Cenan and Bibi returned to İstanbul via New York but I was sick in bed in the hotel where we had stayed in Manhattan. Later I had to spend some time at my daughter's flat until such time that I could take the long flight to İstanbul.

It was almost a whole month that I was able to return to my home at Bostancı. My life had developed into this an unexpected routine. Almost every morning I would drive to my father's apartment, take him out for a drive and spend some time with him at his house. As soon as I could leave him, I would drive over to Cenan's house to see how his illness was progressing. If I had the time I would also call on my son before returning to Bostancı. However, there were days when Father would call and ask me to do some errands for him in the afternoons as well, so it would well be that I would cross the İstanbul bridge four times in the same day! Thus there was no way (or time) for me to look for a job.

A new ritual had come about. Father had started coming to my house on Sundays for lunch. Sometimes Cenan and Bibi, at other times my brother Nur and his wife Güzin, who had recently settled in İstanbul, leaving their residence in the States, would also come. Gradually I had made my flat a livable place where I could entertain my old friends. I had finally retired and was receiving a certain monthly income from the Turkish Social Security System. It was not much but it came in handy. Everybody liked the house that I had developed for myself. One of these Sundays two of my very old friends had come just as we had finished our brunch with Father. Father usually enjoyed their company too and he stayed over for tea as well. However, when one of the girls jokingly said to my father, 'Uncle, how nicely Şen has arranged this flat, I am sure you must have turned the title to her." He suddenly got very angry and suddenly came out saying, "Do not interfere with my life. This house is mine and it is going to stay mine! Mind your own business!" My two very good friends were very much hurt.

That year we celebrated New Year with Ömer and Asuman at Cenan's house. Bibi as usual had prepared a wonderful reception. On another day Bibi was kind enough to reiterate that if in case we lost Father unexpectedly, they would see to it that I should have the use of this flat for life. Funny enough but Nur's wife Güzin had said similar things in the following weeks. Father had donated flats to both my brothers but had given me nothing. Both my brothers knew this fact and were trying in a way to protect my rights. Come what may, it was comforting to know their feelings.

I had met Asuman's parents only for a few hours at their ceremony in Bibi's summer house. Since I loved my daughter-in-law very much, I wished to get to know the family better. So, during the summer we decided, with Ömer and Asuman, to go to Antalya, stay at a motel and meet my in-laws. Dr. Orhan and Sevim Yener had three wonderful children all grown up with proper university degrees.

When I was getting settled in my Bostancı apartment one day Father called up and said that we had been invited to Ankara. It turned out that Mrs. Özden Toker, the daughter of İsmet İnönü had phoned and asked Father to join a symposium she was arranging. It turned out that the family had set up an İsmet İnönü Foundation and that they had arranged a meeting to commemorate İsmet Pascha. Father was included among the list of speakers since he had been with the Pascha for many years. The idea that the family had remembered and invited him had pleased Father to no end. He felt honored and gave an intimate speech where most people attending cried and laughed at the same time. For me, this was a most precious occasion as well. To be actually in the famed "Pink Kiosk" where the Pascha had lived and where I had attended many festive occasions was important for me also. At such times, memories can be invaluable.

On the way back from the symposium we met Ömer İnönü, who was flying on the same plane with us. When he did something rather endearing I told him, "How very kind you have been." He laughed and said, "But Şen, don't you know, we happen to be the last of the Mohicans." How true it was. Those days were gone forever.

I could not quite fathom it out, but felt that Father, who was very annoyed with his eldest son being seriously sick, had decided to get out of town as much as possible. Since one reason why I had returned to İstanbul was to provide him the companionship he required, he would arrange all sorts of trips abroad without even consulting me, at least for the timing. As a matter of fact, when my good friends Ginette and her husband reported they were coming to İstanbul, Father was adamant and would not accept to cancel the trip he had arranged (of course without informing me about it) even for just two days. He had actually forced me to lose one of my good friends.

452

Something similar developed in a trip we made to Antalya. It turned out that Father had mentioned to my son's in-laws that he would be interested in buying some real estate in Antalya since that was a town newly developing. They had advised him about a plot that was available so we made a trip to that town. The negotiations were finished and as the title deed was about to be drawn, Mrs. Yener suddenly said, "Will you have the deed written in the name of your daughter?" Father was not at all taken aback and gave a negative answer. The poor woman was somewhat taken aback. So that night when we were having dinner by ourselves at the hotel I said to Father, "Daddy, you have given both my brothers some valuable real estate. Their position is much better than mine. Why have you not given me anything? You even took back the flat you had given me?" He was rather taken aback and he quickly changed the subject. Apparently, later on he told the Yener's (Ömer's in-laws) that he would be willing to buy a flat for me in Antalya if the price would be reasonable. Then came the news from the Yener's in Antalya. They had found a flat that would be suitable. However, Cenan's health had deteriorated rather badly and we said we could not come. Unfortunately, in the month of November 1986 Cenan passed away. That was a terrible blow. There is no way of stopping destiny. We were all very grieved. He had gone to another world leaving behind his lovely wife and three beautiful daughters.

They say that some good news will always follow the bad! Asuman announced that she was expecting a baby. This was wonderful news. I was going to have another grandchild. While I was basking in this wonderful feeling a phone call came to Father from Antalya. Someone wanted to purchase the plot he had bought a year ago and was willing to pay the price Father had asked. As usual, Father called and said, "We are going to Antalya tomorrow, prepare the car." So we went. By a coincidence Ömer and Asuman were also in Antalya giving the good news to his in-laws. The young couple who had bought Father's plot were very nice people and they kept wining and dining us. Somehow Father had mentioned to them that he was considering to buy a flat for me. The dealer they had introduced came and showed us a few places. Father even refused to get out of the car to take a look. Probably he had not liked the places that were shown. That evening my son Ömer told me that Father had said that he had changed his mind and that he was not interested in buying me a flat anymore. That morning at the hotel I had settled our bill and had gotten my car ready for the long haul back to İstanbul. Since I was the driver, I wanted to be safe. While we were having breakfast a phone call came. I took it, it was the dealer who had taken us to places the previous day. He was saying things like he had not appreciated who we were and that he had some very special places he wanted to show us. I replied curtly saying that we were no longer interested in looking at flats and that we were leaving town shortly. Father, in the meantime, had heard what I was saying and suddenly showed interest. He insisted that we should take a look at the new places the dealer wanted to show us. Whatever Father wanted had to be done. There was no other way.

So the dealer promptly came to the hotel and took us to a construction site where some of the buildings were still under construction. The site was wonderful. We could walk up to the second floor only since the construction was gradually rising. Father had liked the place as well. He suddenly said to me, "If you are willing to give up the 20 millions I was supposed to give you, I am willing to cover the difference and buy one flat for you and I will buy the adjacent flat for myself." What could I say? In the end I was paying most of the price but on the other hand he had not paid me that money anyway and most probably he never would! I simply thanked him and said I loved the site. In any case, finally the real estate would become mine in a year's time. This time it would be mine!

During 1987 I lived through two wonderful occasions. On May 15, Asuman gave birth to a son they named Murat. This was my second grandchild. He was a healthy baby, blond as his mother, he also had some lines of his father. The boy was not only very healthy but the way he looked, there was no question that he was a boy. With his birth, my life had a new meaning.

Then came the news that my daughter Zeyneb was getting married again. So Father and I went to attend their wedding on May 31 in New Jersey. My new son-in-law was an American, he was an architect working with an architectural firm in New

York. This young man not only loved my daughter but had been willing to accept Zeyneb's daughter as his own. He came from a very good American family. As a matter of fact, Guy's mother came from a family whose ancestors went back to the Mayflower people who had migrated to America way back. Calvin Ewald, the father of the bridegroom, was a retired insurance executive. They had two sons and one daughter and they had accepted my daughter as one of their own from the start. I was very happy. A man who would love and protect her had come to her life. Zeyneb was elegant and lovely. Her grandfather gave her to the groom feeling very proud. The wedding ceremony was performed in Guy Ewald's parent's house in New Jersey. It was a very nice house surrounded by a large yard filled with trees and beautiful flowers. Aside from the family, there were two couples, who were the Ewalds' best friends. Zeyneb had also invited my very dear friend Wendy Harris. My granddaughter Seze was the bride's maid. She was all around the place with her beautiful smiling face, taking care of everyone's needs. I had really liked and appreciated Guy's parents. Both Dallas and Calvin were very warmhearted, elegant people.

I was thoroughly thankful for all my blessings. Years ago I had come back to life, once again realizing my responsibilities. And now, fate was giving me a life filled with beautiful surprises.

LVII

A Great Shock

It must have been in the year 1988. Due to some religious holiday there was a long (five days) vacation. My good friend Cemile (Garan) phoned and told me that Bibi, Nuyan and herself had planned to drive south, stopping at Kuşadası they would go down to Bodrum. My first reaction was, "No I cannot go that way." That was the highway where my Ayşe had lost her life. However, Cemile kept insisting. She also told me that the old highway had been abandoned some time ago and that they had built another İzmir-Kuşadası-Bodrum highway, which also had cut the travel period by almost half. She was very insistent and told me that it would do me good. Finally, I agreed to travel with them. It was true. I should not live with ghosts. However, I first had to consult with Father. I was always on call and leaving İstanbul without his permission could be disastrous. He turned out to be lenient and told me I should go with my friends and have a holiday. It turned out to be a perfect holiday. Four of us, old friends, were really having a lovely time. I was careful to ring Father up daily, to make sure that he was alright during my absence. He kept assuring me that he was well and that I had nothing to worry about.

On my return home, I found some mail had been pushed through the door of my apartment. One of them looked like official mail. I opened that one first. It was a protest note issued by a notary public. And it was issued in the name of the owner of the flat I was living in. As far as I knew this flat belonged to my father. Some time ago Father had said he wanted to put a sign to one of the front windows that the flat was for sale. He told me he had no intention of selling but wanted to have an idea how much people would be willing to pay. "Anyway, I will put my own phone number on the sign and no one will bother you" he added. Since it was his flat I had simply said that he could do as he wanted. He had put up that sign. It was still there on the window where he had hung it. I was reading this document over and over again trying to digest what was written in it when the phone rang. Someone I did not know introduced himself as "I am Hasan Kucukagiz" then he went on to explain that he had bought this flat from my father and that in the usual fashion he had sent me a notice through a notary public and he would like to call on me to discuss the situation. We agreed to meet the next day. I had not even opened my bags. I jumped into my car and rushed to my father's flat. It was my father's lunchtime. He should be home. His maid opened the door and instead of her usual welcome she mumbled something like "What are you doing here?" From the entrance I could see into the dining room. Father's meal was placed on the table but he was not in his seat. I asked where he was and she said he was in the bathroom. When I walked into the room I saw that there was someone else. A gentleman who was one of my father's newly found acquaintances. He was a docile man, very courteous. We shook hands and started talking. When Father came into the room I went straight to him. I tried to kiss his hand in the old-fashioned way, but he pulled his hand away and said, "I have a running nose therefore we should not contact." He sat at his place at the table. After a few words, I took the papers I had received and showing them to him I said, "Father is there any truth in all this?" He would not even look at the papers and curtly answered, "Naturally it is true. That flat belongs to me and I sold it." I could not help asking, "Then what am I going to do?" He was cutting his meat and had the knife in his hand. He tapped the table with the end of the knife. "You will return to your father's home." This was an order. He was adamant. I tried to explain to him that I was no longer his little daughter, that I had grandchildren of my own. I had been working for many years and had been living alone and now I could not live with anyone. He was furious. He shouted, "I am not anyone." I said, "Of course. You are my father and I always have the respect for you. However, you must also realize that I have had my own place to live in for many years independently and I am too old to wait in line for

457

the bathroom." He suddenly lost his nerve and started shouting, "GET OUT, GET OUT OF MY SIGHT." I could not believe my ears. I asked him if he meant what he was saying. He not only repeated what he was saying but he was almost having a fit, his voice went all the way up. I was shaking from head to foot. Could this be true? What had I done to deserve this kind of a reaction? To a person like me, who gave up everything just to help him out! All this must have gone through my mind. It took me a few seconds to compose myself. I got up. I said, "Thank you Father, good day to you." I also said good-bye to a startled gentleman there. As I was walking out of the flat I saw that the maid was laughing behind my back. My father had the third flat in that apartment. Naturally there was an elevator but I could not even find the door for it since I had already started crying deliriously. I do not know how I got to my car. As I was opening the door of my car I saw that Father had come out to his balcony and was still shouting behind my back. I took one last look. He was waving his walking stick in the air and shouting "Go to Hell." A venerable gentleman who also owned a flat in the same building was just going into the apartment and naturally he showed his amazement. I told him Father had these seizures unfortunately on account of his diabetes and started my car. I went by the Swiss Hotel, a bit ahead and stopped the car. I was crying and trembling so much that I could not drive. Calming down a little later I started to think. A thousand things were at once on my mind. Ömer was no longer living at the Pamuk apartment. They had since moved to a condominium. I first thought I should go to them. Then I changed my mind and drove to my place in Bostancı. I wanted to have a shower and wash this dirt from my body. Of course I was still crying.

What sort of a fate had I? Was it not enough? The unexpected disasters that followed me all my life, when would this end? Was this why I had agreed to return to İstanbul, leaving my job, my daughter and my grandchild in New York. After all the hardships I had suffered and had been such a docile daughter to him, was this the way I was to be treated? I was ready to go out of my mind.

After a shower and a black coffee, I tried to calm down. I called up the construction company in Antalya. They told me that work on the building was in progress and that they would be ready to let me use the flat by the end of the year. Toward evening I went to Ömer's house. My daughter-in-law and Ömer were naturally aghast. Ömer rang a lawyer friend of his and gave me some advice, especially about how they could not evict me from my flat at short notice. Finally, I was back in the flat I no longer owned.

In the morning a young couple came to visit me with a bouquet of flowers. They were the new owners. I told them that I had a new flat under construction in Antalya and that I was advised that I could move in by the end of the year. I believe I had the right recourse against them and that no judge would evict me at short notice. If they agreed to give me some time, namely till the end of the year, I would give them a promise or a signed release and there would be no necessity to go to court and incur a lot of expenses. Furthermore, they would be getting most of the installation like the heating system, etc. intact. They turned out to be reasonable people. They agreed to my proposal and they never bothered me again.

The first objection to the idea of my moving to Antalya came from my daughter-in-law who had lived in that town for many years. She was saying, "But that is a dead town. You would simply suffocate there. There is no intellectual activity." My son tried other ways, could I sell the flat in Antalya and buy something else in İstanbul? The market was such that I would be selling a proper flat and then buy a one-room apartment in İstanbul. I really had no means. What little money I had would not last me more than a few months. However, Antalya would be a cheaper place to live in. I was not going to give up. I was adamant I would make a go of it. I was healthy and I had courage. If I had done it in America, I should be able to do it in my own country. I started getting cardboard boxes from the corner drug store and began packing. There was much to do and very little time to do it in.

When I had first settled in Bostancı, I had thought I should be able to do something to fill my empty and lonely evening hours. Since my youth I had always been interested in creating things with my hands. As a matter of fact, years ago in Ankara, I even had lessons for making ceramic objects, from a well-known

459

artist, Mr. Cemil Eren. Later I had asked my husband to buy me a furnace to make my ceramics at home, but he had baulked at the cost and would not let me further my studies. During the time I was trying to decide what to do, while I lived in Bostancı, my friend Hayriye Neyzi gave me her daughter's paints for glass. I had happily started painting small glass objects I had in the house. Whenever I was invited I used to give them to my hosts as gifts. They seemed to like them. Most probably out of the kindness of their hearts. Nevertheless, while painting on glass I used to find a certain peace of mind. When I was ready to move to Antalya, I bought myself some fresh paint and brushes.

LVIII
The Last Stop

Toward the end of December Asuman took her baby son to Antalya to visit her parents. This was primarily a move to help me
settle there. Ömer had arranged for a moving company and all
the furniture, the boxes, etc. that I could possibly carry away
from my apartment in Bostancı was hauled into a big truck.
After the truck started its journey toward Antalya, Ömer and I
started the same journey in my car, hoping to get there before
them.

It was winter and snow had started falling. Especially after
Bilecik, snow had precipitated and traveling was becoming more
and more difficult. We were not sure to make the whole trip in
one day. The truckers had told us that they would need two days
to reach Antalya. We also were forced to spend the night in
Afyon. The next day, on December 29, around noon we had
reached my new home. If it had not been for the help Ömer
provided, it would have proved impossible for me to move into
my flat. He and his dear wife both gave me help and encouragement all the time. Ömer even carried the butane gas tanks four
stories up. The carriers had climbed all those stairs but had left
all the trunks, etc. unopened. Theirs was not an easy job either.

The building had just been completed but the elevator was
not yet running. After having dinner with the Yener family I
had returned home. It was cold as ice in the apartment. Even
the walls were almost wet from recent painting or whitewash.
There was no central heating. I had some heaters. The moment
I put one heater on, flash! The electricity went off. I was left in
total darkness. Taking my flash light I had to walk all the way
down to the basement, change the fuse and trudge all the way
back. Again I turned the heater on and the same thing happened. Realizing this was impossible, I went down once more

461

and fixed the fuse. Going down 83 steps. Coming up another 83 steps. This time I had given up the idea of using my heater, and I turned the gas on and boiled some water and used a water heater between the sheets. That way I could heat my bed. Some warmth felt good.

I was up at sunrise. I put on some warm clothes and went on the balcony. The sun was very bright but still it was really cold! As I looked around I could see that only two of the buildings had been completed. But all the floors were empty. I was the only person living in this building. Consequently, the elevator would not be working and there were no lights on the stairways.

Ömer brought in a gas heater and we started using it. It at least broke the ice. He also found me a small hotel where I could stay a few nights. Meanwhile, I had the electricians change all the fuses so that the lights would not go off as soon as I put the electric heater on. Once that was done and both the electric and the gas heaters were going at full speed, the rooms began to thaw a bit. I had gradually begun to get settled in my new home thanks to the help of Ömer. One of the things I enjoyed most was to put on some winter clothes, make myself coffee and sit on the balcony enjoying the sunrise. The weather was unbelievably clean and there was always the fresh smell of trees. The famed Beydag Mountains and the sea made a very beautiful panaroma. Even the few constructions going around had not yet closed my view and I could see all around the flat. Unfortunately, man's unstoppable desire to make more money has now clogged most of the view in less than ten years.

We spent the New Year's Eve of 1989 at Ömer's in-laws, together with Ömer and Asuman. The holiday was over. So the children returned to their home in İstanbul. I had been installed willy-nilly. Now it was time that I should find some sort of a job to earn my living. My savings were almost gone. The children returned with misgivings about my future and kept asking me what I was proposing to do in Antalya. I promised them that I would try this as an experience and I would at least spend one year in Antalya. At the end of that time, if things did not prove to become positive, I would consider selling the flat and return to İstanbul. Only God knew what was to happen next.

My life was full of hardships during the coming days. In order to warm the house I was using the catalytic gas heater almost twenty-four hours of the day. That meant I had to have replacements. In those days there was no company serving the place where my apartment was located. So I had to go by car and purchase the gas tubes. The dealer had men to place the tubes in my car. On arrival to the apartment there was no way I could carry the tubes up four flights of stairs. So I would start loitering around until I found an itinerant laborer that I could trust, talk to him and pay him a price to carry the tubes up to my flat. Another problem was protecting myself from wayfarers. In my building there were ten apartments. Apart from mine, nine were empty and somehow their keys were on their doors. Some of the laborers who were working in the construction were using these to sleep in. Under these conditions no charwoman had agreed to come to my place even for daily cleaning. One night quite late someone knocked on my door. It sounded like a drunkard. When I asked what he wanted, he said that he would get me a charwoman. In the middle of the night! I told him to go away and would not open the door. Probably one of the laborers had heard that I was looking for a charwoman and wanted to use this as an excuse. Next morning I told what had happened to the contractor who was at the site very early every morning. He was sorry and I believe he discharged the man he suspected.

Mustafa Bey, the contractor, was a very hard working man. He would be almost the first person on the construction site every morning. I was also an early riser, so we used to talk over the balcony. Seeing him there always gave me a sense of security. I started going out for a walk very early in the mornings.

I realized I had to do something to earn my living. Then I thought about painting on glass. If I realized my thoughts, could I market them in town? So I started working. From 6:00 A.M. to 10:00 A.M. I could work. After that the sun was too bright anyway and my eyes would get tired. So I started calling on stores that could market my wares. A few shops showed interest and indeed, did sell some of my wares. However, I had soon realized that earning a living from this line alone would not be enough. One day I saw a sign that advertised for translations. So I went in. A young chap was sitting behind a big desk. I asked if I could get

463

some job as translator, either French or English. As we started chatting it turned out that he too was a graduate of the French School of Languages in Ankara, namely the Dil-Tarih-Cografya faculty, this created a friendship. He wanted to take my phone number and said he would call on me if something came up. However, I had not been able to install a phone to my new apartment. So I suggested I would knock on his door daily to see if something came up. Gradually I started getting some translation work. I had also started translating a book from French. However, that was done on a friendly basis, I was doing it with no charge for a friend.

Then one day at the corner store where I was buying my daily bread, milk, etc. the shopkeeper asked me if I knew English. When I said I did, he showed me a handwritten advertisement stuck on his window. I had not noticed it. So that brought in a couple of students. Soon I was working almost full time. In the morning following my half-hour walk and shower, I was painting on glass from 7:00 A.M. to 11:00 A.M., teaching English from 12:00 noon up to 4:00 P.M. Then I would take the glass work downtown, market them, take some translations. Shop on the way and come home. In the evenings I would translate and type them. Following all this I would have a bite, read a while and go to bed, quite exhausted. I gave lessons mostly at home. One of my students was a married woman and when she said she was pregnant but wanted to continue with her lessons I agreed to go to her house.

One morning the contractor of our compound said to me, "Mrs. Sılan, you are the only person who lives in this block. I am having qualms about your being all alone in this construction site. Could you not move somewhere else, at least until the lay workers are gone, or else can you not take in a tenant to get some company." I was both amazed and flattered. He was perfectly right. Most of the nights I was very afraid. Being alone, or waking in the middle of the night in a lonely spot can be terrifying. Especially if I came home after dark, walking up the dark staircases was a problem. I had a strong flashlight and a policeman's baton, one at each hand. I told him that he was coming to the site very early and if I had been annoyed that night I would tie a red scarf to my balcony and he would call on

464

me for help. Mustafa Bey suddenly started giggling and when I looked at him with amazement he stopped laughing and told me why he could not help giggling. It seems that years ago when he was a young man in his old town, Trabizond, he had fallen in love with a lady and that lady used a similar ruse to let him know that her parents were away and the coast was clear. This time we were both laughing.

After a few months spring arrived. It was gorgeous. The construction work in my building was over and a few of the flats had been sold. However, there were no tenants or owners living in the building, yet I was able to install a phone by that time. Gradually they would finish the installations and the elevator would start to function.

I had not seen Father since the day he had sent me away from his apartment. My son, who had turned out to be the perfect gentleman, had started helping him in his affairs. On one hand I was very frightened that one day he would be faced with a similar treatment, but I was also proud that he was doing something he felt was his duty. I did not wish to meet Father anymore. Nevertheless, I had not stopped my old courtesies, namely I would call him on his birthdays or other religious days, etc. He too must have felt sorry at what he had done, since he was always very kind to me on the phone and always mentioned that he wanted to do things for me, help me, etc. I always answered that I was praying for his good health and that I did not want anything from him. As far as I was concerned my pride came foremost in every case. Even more important than my dad.

My life was difficult. I was hardly trying to exist with my meager income. Life for me was "a loaf of bread and a coat," as the old Turkish proverb goes. With the arrival of spring my routine had slightly changed. I was doing what I had to do with less anxiety. I felt the relief of being away from the stress and the gossip of İstanbul and had found peace in this marvelous place. What did it matter that intellectual activity was lacking! For years, even between all the bustle, I had had it anyway.

One morning when I was having my morning coffee on my balcony, enjoying the bright sun, a taxi stopped near my apartment. A well-dressed lady came out of the car, walked toward my apartment and called out my name, "Şen." I could hardly believe my eyes. It was my very old and dear friend Ülker Ergin-soy. I ran down the stairs, opened the front door and we were in each others arms. I was very, very happy. She was returning from Fethiye, wondered what I was doing in Antalya and had decided to make a stop over. It was so gratifying to find that someone still cared for me. We spent two beautiful days mostly visiting ancient cities and sharing life. Our friendship goes a long way back. We had attended the same primary school. And then we were together again in Ankara as married young mothers. While our small children played at the park we took them to, we would be making future plans full of hope.

Talking about Antalya I have to admit that this town is full of ancient sites. Many a day I would drive out, taking a book with me and a thermos full of coffee, to Aspendos, Phaselis or Perge and spend beautiful hours in each site. The museum in Antalya was always a center and since has become internationally known. Taking Ülker around town had brought me so many memories of the past.

In the beginning of that summer, Sertaç and my granddaughter Seze came for a visit. My daughter in New York was pregnant and I was anxious about the newcomer. We, Seze, her father and I, spent many days, swimming, chatting, going around the sites, etc. Seze was on the way to becoming a lovely girl. She had developed a talent for painting and in fact during her high school days some of her paintings had been displayed at the UN Children's Show. I had realized that she would become an artist. After they were gone, I kept swimming and sun bathing. It was something like eight months that I had left İstanbul, it now looked like that my worst days in Antalya would be over. I had started to really like this city. I was considering to settle down here, if I had the elevator and the lights would function!

On August 9, 1989 the happy news arrived from New York. Zeyneb had delivered another baby girl. Both mother and child were in good health. We were both crying and laughing on the phone. I knew Zeyneb was expecting and I had been trying to find a way of going to New York to be with her in her time of need. Zeyneb had suggested that I should get to New York after the baby was born. So I was able to go to New York. The moment that I had the beautiful child in my arms I knew that I was the happiest grandmother in the world. They had named her Lara. Actually I had suggested the name and they had thought it appropriate. My third grandchild was also very beautiful, with large violet eyes. When I took her in my arms I enjoyed smelling her beautiful fresh baby perfume.

As it is, every good thing had to come to an end. It was time that I should go back to my own quarters. Visiting had to be short. Once back, I found I had to be more careful with my spending. I was hoping to increase the number of my students. On my return from America I had found that the elevator was working in my apartment. This showed that I could exist in Antalya, the worst was over. My son and daughter-in-law also agreed with this viewpoint. They were glad to see me happy.

My luck was turning. I had a call from the Falez Hotel, which was a new five-star hotel in Antalya. The general manager wanted me for an interview. A good friend, Mrs. Betul Mardin, had given him my name and advised him that he should talk to me. The general manager, Mr. Ünsal Şinik, told me about some openings at the hotel. I wanted a part-time job and running the new art gallery at the hotel suited me best. I had always been interested in art. I was to be at the gallery between the hours of 2:00 P.M. and 7:00 P.M. except Mondays. This meant that I could still carry on with my English students. The salary I would be getting at the hotel would give me a financial boost. The income from my students added to this, I could breathe better. I had exhausted all the money I had put aside for unexpected occurrances.

I certainly enjoyed working at the Falez Hotel. It was interesting, since it was rather a new experience both for me and for the Antalya public. In this connection I also made many good friends. I certainly appreciate the experience. I ran this gallery for something like a year. Finally I quit for personal reasons.

As I was getting settled in Antalya two couples helped me in many ways. If it was not for Mr. and Mrs. Aktaş and Mr. and Mrs. Kırkpantur, I do not know if my Antalya experience could be so successful. Both were very much younger than I but the kindness and help I received from them were immeasurable. This was certainly luck on my side.

467

In the year 1992 Father passed away. He had completed a long and venerable life and had died peacefully. It was my son (his grandson) Ali Ömer Devres who took care of his grandfather's funeral. Ömer had been helping his grandfather run his life during the last years. So at the end he gave us, the inheritors, Cenan's family, Nur and me, detailed accounts of all the expenditure. He had kept all receipts, etc. and paid us the amount due to each. He had shown his integrity and honesty once again. I was proud once more of Ömer.

As far as I was concerned, it was true that I was heartbroken but even so I cherish his memory together with all my loved ones that I have lost. We did not see eye to eye for many years but he was an honorable man, in love with his country, a follower of Atatürk's deeds and I feel honored for having been his daughter.

Many years ago Father had said, "I never got any inheritance from my father, so do not look for anything from me." True to his word he had spent most of his money during his lifetime. I was not interested in the contents of his flat, but asked the other inheritors to let me have his papers and his books. After consulting with my friends, I was able to make a donation of all his library (including letters from well-known people he had received) to a new foundation formed to collect and evaluate all historical documents. I believe that he would have appreciated this donation. As I was sifting through the various documents in Father's apartment, I found a piece of paper that excited me immensely. This was a letter he had written but never mailed.

My dearest daughter, Şen, last night at 2:30 A.M. I woke from a dream in which we were together. What a pity, you were not at my side. I must have missed you so much that I keep seeing you in my dreams. Thank God I am now 93 years old. My dear daughter, you must forgive the way I have behaved towards you at times. You are my one and only daughter. I wish you all the happiness possible forever. I kiss you many times. Your father.

What a pity he had not mailed this letter. It was still a blessing that I had taken the trouble of sifting his papers and had found this note. I was full of thanks. Without this I would have always doubted his intentions. Doubts are of no use in life. I have many times wondered how things would have developed if Mother was alive. And yet, the whys and ifs never help.

It is now more then ten years since I have settled in Antalya. I had my ups and downs, worked in a gallery, sold my painted glass and gave lessons in English and all that. All these are over now. I love my modest home that I can finally call my own and the city I live in. I can now call myself a citizen of Antalya. I think that finally I have deserved to stay home, read, write, listen to music and paint on glass.

Writing these memoirs was in a way some sort of an evaluation of myself. When I look at these pages and think about my life, with all its ups and downs, I have only one feeling. I DO NOT REGRET anything that I have done, have not done or have not been able to do.

Acknowledgments

First of all, I want to thank my dear American friend Barbara Karras for encouraging me to write my memoirs by bringing two large notebooks from London on July 8, 1979 with the inscription:

Enfin Sen, des pages vides!
Il ne faut plus nous priver.

Barbara

I am duty-bound to remember my dear friend, the Dutchman, the late Mr. Jim Drabbe, who had always wanted me to write my memoirs and had always supported me in my difficult days, even if only with letters from afar.

I would like to extend my gratitude to my dear companion for life, Mr. Ali H. Neyzi, for having supported and encouraged me all through the translation of my book with his knowledge, advice and patience, as well as his printing every single line I wrote by hand, into his word processor. I also thank him for listening to my endless complaints and worries with patience and sharing my life with all its complexities.

I would also like to express my thanks to Mr. Nihat Tuna of the İletişim Publication Group, first for publishing my memoirs in Turkish and then encouraging me to do this translation.